"Finland is a leading country in the academic adult learning. This excellent volume brings tc___ tributors on cutting-edge adult cognitive development and learning topics, and I'm certain it will be of great interest to the English-speaking research community."

Oliver Robinson, University of Greenwich, London, UK, President of the European Society for Research in Adult Development

"This book remains one of the benchmark introductions to adult cognitive development and learning. Dr. Kallio has done a remarkable job of editing this work, maintaining a philosophical tone throughout with connections to current wisdom research implicitly and explicitly. The authors offer fundamental information on the major theories and models, but also critical insights for pondering basic concepts further. I recommend this as an introductory book both for students and professionals. Well and fluently written and researched, it provides a multiperspective – and integrative – approach that ties together different traditions that illuminate the same phenomenon: adult change and transformation."

Judith Stevens-Long, Professor, Human Development, Fielding University, USA

"This book is a must-read for everyone working with adult development – as practitioners or as researchers! Presenting and discussing perspectives from psychology, education, and human resources, *Development of Adult Thinking* edited by Eeva K. Kallio, gives well worked out introductions to concepts, theories, and models of adult learning. The anthology will be pivotal not only to the field of adult psychology, but across higher education, including the vast field of teacher education."

Guro Hansen Helskog, Associate Professor, University of South-Eastern Norway

"Organisms, human and otherwise, are composed of multiple component systems. However, humans do not act as assemblies of independent parts – humans are integrated beings. Any slice of action necessarily involves some type of integration of all the psychological subsystems that make up the human organism. It is difficult, of course, to study the human action and experience as an integrated whole. The contributors to this volume show how human thinking operates as an integrated process and develops toward increasingly integrated outcomes. Over time, thinking that brings knowledge and practical problem-solving together with social and ethical understanding moves in the direction of wisdom. This book points to the types of thinking that we need to cultivate in order to address this lack."

Michael F. Mascolo, Professor, Academic Director, Merrimack College, USA

"In 1984, *Beyond Formal Operations*, the first book to focus on development beyond Piaget's formal operational period, was published. Since then, the field of Positive Adult Development has greatly expanded. From the original Society for Research in Adult Development (USA), there arose a European Society for Research in Adult Development. Eeva K. Kallio was one of the founders of that Society, and has been one of the most important contributors to both the ESRAD, and to research on a wide variety of aspects of Adult Development. This edited volume, whose contributions represent the work of a large number of Finnish researchers, is an example of the resulting expansion of ideas about adult development that has taken place. It shows well how many different aspects of adulthood can be studied from a developmental point of view."

Michael L. Commons, Assistant Professor, Harvard Medical School,
Department of Psychiatry, USA, founding member of the
Society for Research in Adult Development

DEVELOPMENT OF ADULT THINKING

Development of Adult Thinking is a timely synthesis and evaluation of the current knowledge and emerging issues relating to adult cognitive development and learning.

Focusing on psychological and educational cutting-edge research as well as giving an overview of the key theorists such as Piaget and Kohlberg, Kallio and the team of expert contributors offer a holistic view on the development of adult thinking, representing perspectives from developmental, moral, and social psychology, as well as education and philosophy. These topics are divided into three sections: Adult cognitive and moral development, Perspectives of adult learning, and Open questions and new approaches, offering introduction, analysis, and directions for future research.

This text is essential reading for students and researchers in developmental psychology and related courses as well as adult educators and teachers working in adult education.

Eeva K. Kallio, PhD, is Adjunct Professor at the University of Jyväskylä, Finland. She is the leader of the Wisdom and Learning research team and founding member and Honorary President of the European Society for Research in Adult Development (ESRAD).

DEVELOPMENT OF ADULT THINKING

Interdisciplinary Perspectives on Cognitive Development and Adult Learning

Edited by Eeva K. Kallio

Routledge
Taylor & Francis Group

LONDON AND NEW YORK

First published 2020
by Routledge
2 Park Square, Milton Park, Abingdon, Oxon OX14 4RN

and by Routledge
52 Vanderbilt Avenue, New York, NY 10017

Routledge is an imprint of the Taylor & Francis Group, an informa business

British Library Cataloguing-in-Publication Data
A catalogue record for this book is available from the British Library

Library of Congress Cataloging-in-Publication Data
A catalog record has been requested for this book

ISBN: 978-1-138-73350-3 (hbk)
ISBN: 978-1-138-73359-6 (pbk)
ISBN: 978-1-315-18746-4 (ebk)

Typeset in Bembo
by Swales & Willis, Exeter, Devon, UK

Printed in the United Kingdom
by Henry Ling Limited

In gratitude to all the persons I have met in deep discussions during my lifetime. To friends and family – and special thanks for the eternally blissful moments of *taiji* and *qigong*.

CONTENTS

FIGURES

TABLES

ACKNOWLEDGEMENTS

First of all, my sincere thanks to all the authors contributing to this edition with their articles – this was truly a joint effort!

There are several people to whom I would like to express my gratitude. With his sharp perception and advice, Professor Klaus Helkama from the University of Helsinki, Finland, turned my interest into the question of whether there is further cognitive development in adulthood beyond Piaget's stages. I followed his advice and thus so-called "postformal" thinking became a major field of interest to me for a few decades. He also led me into contact with Professor Michael Commons from Harvard University, USA, with whom we have had some very fruitful disagreements in discussion. Also, Professor Michael Mascolo from Merrimack College, USA, has been a brilliant partner to debate with about many philosophical questions in the field.

All of my colleagues in the established scientific society ESRAD (European Society for Research in Adult Development) have had an impact on my thinking and me. Thanks for your collaboration in all phases of creating the new scientific organisation, which is not always an easy thing to do.

This book wouldn't have been possible without many of my friends and – actually – without my whole life experience. I would like to thank all of my dearest friends for their love: especially Pirjo, Hannele, Virpi, Riitta, and Helena. I am afraid that I cannot list all of my friends who have always supported me so strongly and deeply. Owing to them, I have learned what true and lasting friendship is. Of course, I am grateful for all the friends I have had during my long 20-year period of taiji and qigong training: all other teachers and trainers of our club and other Finnish clubs – thanks especially to Harri who gave me so much support in the first years. I am also grateful to my other teachers of Chinese metaphysics – especially Päivi in Spain. Thanks also to my relatives, who often ask what I am doing, and I routinely say I am thinking and writing. I also greatly appreciate the contribution and support of all my colleagues at the Institute, especially Professor Päivi Tynjälä, whose dedication to research surpasses anybody I know, and Professor Hannu L. T. Heikkinen, another expert of wisdom. Of course this includes all my colleagues in the current Wisdom and Learning research team in my department – what refreshing discussions we have had!

This edition is partly based on my earlier book which was written in Finnish (2016), the title of which can be translated as *The Development of Thinking in Adulthood: Towards Multiperspective Thinking*. That book has already had seven reprints within a few years. The present book is not, however, just a translated version but an extensively modified new edition of its own. I want to thank once again the Finnish publication editor Anna-Maija, who did such a great job with the Finnish book – without it the present book would not have been possible. Furthermore, I want to thank all the specialists – especially secretary Minna Jokinen, proofreader Tuomo Suontausta, graphic designer Martti Minkkinen – who have done a vital job in getting this book published, and all those who have contributed to having this book published by Routledge, especially the publication editor.

Jyväskylä, Finland
October 10, 2019
Eeva K. Kallio

CONTRIBUTORS

Salla Ahola, PhD, is a postdoctoral researcher at Tampere University, Finland. She has previously worked at the University of Helsinki where she obtained her PhD in Social Psychology in 2016. Her research interests include personal epistemologies, stances towards expert knowledge, public understanding of science, values, and well-being at work.

Hannu L. T. Heikkinen is a Professor of Education in the Finnish Institute for Educational Research at the University of Jyväskylä, Finland. His recent work has involved collaborative philosophical studies on wisdom – often from the perspective of philosophy of praxis and theory of recognition. He has also done research recently within the framework of the ecosystems of learning in the context of higher education, learning in the world of work, mentoring, as well as professional learning and development.

Klaus Helkama is an Emeritus Professor of Social Psychology at the University of Helsinki, Finland. He has published books and articles on the social and developmental psychology of morality, on values, and on the history of social psychology. Helkama has taught in a number of universities, including Harvard, Moscow State University, and the Universities of Coimbra, Geneva, and Padua.

Jukka Husu is a Professor of Education and Vice Dean at the Faculty of Educational Sciences, University of Turku, Finland. His research focuses on teachers' pedagogical knowledge, reflection, and ethical judgment in teaching. He has published extensively in internationally refereed journals and edited books. Professor Husu is a member of the editorial board of *Teaching and Teacher Education*, and an Associate Editor in *Teachers and Teaching: Theory and practice*. Together with D. Jean Clandinin, he is the Editor of *The SAGE Handbook of Research on Teacher Education* (2017).

Heidi Hyytinen, PhD, works as a Senior Lecturer in University Pedagogy, at the University of Helsinki, Finland. Her research interests are students' conceptions of knowledge, critical thinking, and performance-based assessment in the context of higher education. She received the best educational dissertation award of the year 2015, granted by the Finnish Educational Research Association (FERA). She is leading and co-leading several international, multimethod research projects on higher education.

Tuike Iiskala, PhD, Education, is a Postdoctoral Researcher in the Department of Teacher Education and in the Turku Institute for Advanced Studies (TIAS) at the University of Turku, Finland. She has versatile experience of research and teaching in the field of learning research. Her research interests are related to learning interaction and skilful learning, particularly metacognition.

Soile Juujärvi, PhD, holds positions as a principal lecturer at Laurea University of Applied Sciences and an Adjunct Professor in social psychology at the University of Helsinki, Finland. Her research interests are focused on moral development and ethics education, especially pertaining to the ethics of care in professional practice. She is currently active in studying professional competences and developing new pedagogical models for higher education.

Eeva K. Kallio, PhD, works as an Adjunct Professor at the University of Jyväskylä and the University of Tampere, Finland, and as a senior researcher in the Finnish Institute for Educational Research (FIER) at the University of Jyväskylä. Her edited book on adult cognitive development (published in Finnish in 2016; the title can be translated as *The development of thinking in adulthood: Towards multiperspective thinking*) became a landmark book in Finland. She leads the Wisdom and Learning research team at FIER, and is a founding member and Honorary President of the European Society for Research in Adult Development (ESRAD). Her research interests have been mainly theoretical and focused especially on the development of adult thinking and wisdom. Her alternative publishing name is Eeva Kallio (without the middle initial).

Erno Lehtinen is a Professor of Education at the University of Turku, Finland. He has worked as a teacher and researcher in several universities in Finland, other European countries, and in the United States. He has published more than 350 scientific publications. His research has focused on the cognitive and motivational aspects of learning, development of mathematical thinking, educational technology, and new forms of expertise in the rapidly changing working life. He was awarded the Oeuvre Award of the European Association for Research on Learning and Instruction (2009) and was the Editor-in-Chief of *Frontline Learning Research*.

Sari Lindblom-Ylänne is a Vice-Rector and Professor of Higher Education at the University of Helsinki, Finland. She has been the Director of the Centre for University Teaching and Learning. Sari Lindblom-Ylänne is a licensed psychologist. She is a former President of EARLI (European Association for Research on Learning and Instruction) and WERA (World Education Research Association). Her research focuses on student learning at university, for example, on approaches to learning, procrastination, self-regulation, and self-efficacy beliefs.

Jaana-Piia Mäkiniemi, PhD, Doctor of Social Science (DSocSci) in Social Psychology, works as a postdoctoral researcher in Tampere University, Finland. She has studied moral decision making in the contexts of moral dilemmas at work as well as regarding ethical food choices. She is especially interested in how work-related moral questions are associated with occupational well-being.

Mirjamaija Mikkilä-Erdman is a Professor of Education at the University of Turku, Finland, in the Department of Teacher Education. She is an experienced scholar and university teacher. Her research profile is focused on learning and teaching research. She is currently leading a research project on internet reading among primary school children and also a large-scale further education project that deals with systematic in-service training for teachers. Furthermore, her multidisciplinary research projects have dealt with the development and testing of next generation digital texts, text comprehension, and online methodology for investigating comprehension processes, learning of complex scientific phenomena in science and medical education, and research-based teacher training, especially the role of research skills in developing teacher expertise.

Laura Mononen is a Doctoral Candidate in the Faculty of Information Technology, University of Jyväskylä, Finland. Her major is Cognitive Science. She is a Master of Economics and Business Administration (Entrepreneurship) and a Bachelor of Cultural Studies (Fashion Design and Marketing). In her PhD research she is investigating creativity from a systems perspective with the intent to profoundly understand the dynamics of emerging perceptions. Her research interests include mind, design, and the process of renewal in all its fascination. Through her work, she wishes to bend deeply-rooted mental models and bring new insights into the interfaces between scientific and practical fields.

Mari Murtonen is a Professor of Higher Education Pedagogy at the University of Tampere and the Research Director of the UNIPS project at the University of Turku, Finland. Her research focuses on the development of higher education teachers' pedagogical expertise in digital and traditional environments, and on university students' development in scientific and methodological thinking during university education. She has been the Editor-in-chief of the Finnish *Journal of University Pedagogy*, and works now on the editorial board of *Educational Research Review*. She is leading the national unips.fi project involving digital learning solutions for university teachers' and doctoral students' pedagogical support.

Anna-Maija Pirttilä-Backman is a Professor of Social Psychology in the Faculty of Social Sciences at the University of Helsinki, Finland, and a lifelong member of the Teachers' Academy of UH. Her current research interests include personal epistemologies, social representations, trust, global identity, human rights, and history teaching.

Liisa Postareff, PhD, is a Principal Research Scientist at Häme University of Applied Sciences. Her research areas cover student learning in higher education (e.g., approaches to learning, academic emotions), higher education teachers' teaching and pedagogical development, future work skills of teachers, students' and teachers' well-being, and assessment of student learning. She is involved in many national and international research projects and networks.

Inari Sakki is an associate professor of Social Psychology and a Finnish Academy Research Fellow at the University of Eastern Finland. In the years from 2004 to 2018 she worked in the Social Psychology Unit at the University of Helsinki where she received her PhD in 2010. Her research interests include social representations, collective memory, identity, discourse, social image, otherness, and social change.

Hannele Seppälä, PhD (Education), is a deputy director of the Finnish Education Evaluation Centre (FINEEC). Her specialisation areas include adult learning and thinking skills, post-experience higher education, and quality in higher education, as well as the development of evaluation and knowledge-based decision making in the education sector.

Pirjo Ståhle has been a Professor of Intangible Capital and Innovation Management at Aalto University School of Engineering, Finland, since 2014 and worked earlier as a Professor at the University of Turku, Finland Futures Research Centre (2004–2013). She has published several books and more than 100 articles in popular and scientific publications, and given numerous lectures on self-renewal in organisations, innovation ecosystems, and knowledge-intensive economy.

Auli Toom, Professor of Higher Education, is the Director of the Centre for University Teaching and Learning, University of Helsinki, Finland. She is also a Visiting Professor at the University of Tartu, Estonia. Her research focuses on knowing, competence, expertise, and agency among students and teachers in basic and higher education contexts. She is leading several research projects on higher education and teacher education.

Miira Tuominen, PhD, University of Helsinki, is a Professor of Philosophy at the University of Jyväskylä, Finland. She has published on a wide array of topics, mainly on ancient philosophy, including numerous articles and book chapters as well as two monographs; *Ancient Philosophers on Starting Points for Knowledge* (2007) and *Ancient Commentators on Plato and Aristotle* (2009). She is just about to complete her third monograph on Porphyry's ethics in *On abstinence*.

Päivi Tynjälä is a Professor at the Finnish Institute for Educational Research, University of Jyväskylä, Finland. Her main research field is teaching and learning in higher education, but she has also conducted studies in the field of vocational education and training. Her current research interests include learning at the interface between education and work, workplace learning, and teachers' professional development. Päivi Tynjälä has worked as the Editor-in-Chief of *Educational Research Review* (2010–2013) and has published widely, both nationally and internationally. Currently, she is a member of the editorial boards of *Educational Research Review* and of *Vocations and Learning*.

Annukka Vainio works as Associate Professor (Behavioural Change toward Sustainability) at Helsinki Institute of Sustainability Science (HELSUS), University of Helsinki, Finland. In her previous research, she focused on cultural aspects in the development of moral reasoning. Her current research focuses on individuals' ethical and normative reasoning related to the global environmental sustainability challenges.

1

INTRODUCTION

Eeva K. Kallio

The overarching idea of this book is to seek and offer an integrative view on the development of adult thinking and learning processes. Nevertheless, it is obvious that it is impossible to cover the whole range of these issues with any single theme. There is just such a large variety of different approaches that it is impossible to fit them all in a single edition. Thus, the basic aim of this book is to describe some fundamental models and theories, and their links and connections to relevant major rivalling or parallel approaches. Hence, this book looks at the various aspects and research domains from multiple perspectives in an attempt to provide an integrative view on the complex phenomena involved. The general motto of the book could be *"Nullius in verba"*, as borrowed from the Royal Society, who adopted the phrase as their motto in the midst of the (first) Scientific Revolution.

The authors represent not only various fields of psychological research such as developmental psychology and social psychology, but also education and philosophy. This book introduces fundamental issues of both everyday and scientific thinking, accounting also for different thinking patterns relative to various real-world objects, concepts, values, social relationships, and existential issues. Some of the most important adult cognitive psychological and adult learning theories and models are addressed. Developmental psychology and learning research are independent but very closely associated areas. They both focus on the change processes of human beings during their lifespan. However, in literature these two fields are rarely examined simultaneously or together, which actually became the main impetus to this book.

This introductory chapter seeks to give an overview of the main research trends and specify the domains discussed in the articles of this book. After this introductory chapter, the edition is divided into three thematic sections. The first one of these (Chapters 2–6) deals with the so-called major developmental stages, i.e., the models by Jean Piaget and Lawrence Kohlberg and related derivative models by William Perry and Carol Gilligan, which have had, and still have, implicitly or explicitly, a significant influence on the research of adult cognitive development. This section deals with the research and development of both everyday and scientific thinking. The second thematic section (Chapters 7–10) concentrates on adult learning and knowledge construction and presents major trends in this research area. The third section (Chapters 11–13) presents some new perspectives and attempts to define methods and terms in the field.

It will be demonstrated metatheoretically that the developmental psychological and learning approaches presented in this book are closely connected and have much in common. There seem to be a certain group of models with mutual commonalities, worth studying further, both empirically and theoretically. Across the thematic sections there are also references to wisdom research. Certain problematic philosophical questions will also be analysed and the results have implications, especially to the field of adult development research, but also to wisdom research as well as more generally in psychological epistemology research.

In Chapter 2 Eeva K. Kallio presents the views of modern developmental psychology on how thinking develops in adulthood and how it is linked to wisdom research. The focus is on the neo-Piagetian models of adult thinking, and thus the definition of thinking is restricted to such forms as relativistic-dialectical, postformal, or contextual integrative thinking – there are many terms in present usage. This chapter provides an overview illustrating the wide scope and multidimensionality of this field of research. The notion of universal, similar development is not new, as arguments of this kind have been presented since the days of Piaget regarding the nomothetic generality of cognitive development. Contextual integrative thinking is proposed as a term most appropriate to describe adult cognition, and this type of thinking can also justifiably be seen as part of the current psychological construct of wisdom, as a form of wise reasoning.

In Chapter 3 Hannele Seppälä, Sari Lindblom-Ylänne and Eeva K. Kallio start with Piaget's highly significant theory of developmental stages of logical thinking. In essence, Piaget's theory is focused on the development of causal thinking in childhood and youth, albeit that the attainment of the highest developmental stage has been studied also in adults. Seppälä and colleagues also proceed to describe epistemological development research by Karen Strohm Kitchener and Patricia M. King. Moreover, they analyse the results of a study in which both domains, logical and epistemological development, were studied together. The article also addresses the interesting question of how these two cognitive fields relate to each other and whether there is mutual dependency between logical-causal thinking and beliefs of knowledge.

In Chapter 4 Anna-Maija Pirttilä-Backman, Salla Ahola and Inari Sakki integrate social psychology with research on the development of knowledge conceptions. Human thinking is seen from two different perspectives: as personal epistemologies and as social representations. The article deals with individuals' assumptions and related justifications pertaining to the nature of knowledge: how Finnish people form everyday understandings of the human species within the frameworks of the evolution theory and creation story. The discussion is extended to the possibilities to integrate the respective perspectives of personal epistemologies and social representations in further research.

Chapter 5 by Soile Juujärvi and Klaus Helkama examines Kohlberg's and Gilligan's theories of the development of moral thinking from the perspectives of reasoning pertaining to rationality, on the one hand, and care, on the other. They trace the origins and history of these traditions and review some empirical results. They conclude that both these traditions of moral development share some similar interests, such as progress from self-concern towards concern for others.

Chapter 6 by Jaana-Piia Mäkiniemi and Annukka Vainio concludes this thematic section by taking a broader look at the field of moral thinking and development. The chapter presents three key models of morality: the Big Three model of morality (Richard A. Schweder), the Moral Foundations Theory (Jonathan Haidt), and the cultural-developmental model (Lene A. Jensen). Based on the theoretical evaluation of these multiple viewpoints, it is concluded that the definitions of morality have gone through profound changes and become broader and more varied. There is obvious diversity and multiplicity in the definitions and the phenomenon can be seen as multidimensional. The major critical concern, based on their theoretical evaluation, is that the models have not so far addressed the wider context-dependency of moral concerns.

The second thematic section deals with some models connected to adult learning. It offers first a general introduction of the field, followed by chapters on conceptual change, tacit knowledge, and expert knowledge.

In Chapter 7 Mari Murtonen and Erno Lehtinen give a preliminary introduction to some current adult learning theories. They argue that learning theories can be understood and viewed by a multiperspective approach. Learning can be studied and understood from individual, social, and cultural perspectives. On the individual level, learning is not only a cognitive phenomenon but a complex system where learning processes of different levels interact but are not reducible to each other. Some basic psychological functions, like memory, executive functions, deliberate practice, plus motivational, metacognitive, regulation, and conceptual aspects are regarded as components of learning. Learning can also be understood in larger, social and cultural contexts, as studies on situational and collaborative learning have shown.

Mirjamaija Mikkilä-Erdmann and Tuike Iiskala (Chapter 8) examine adult learning from the viewpoint of conceptual change and metacognition research. Their article is also focused on multiperspective and integrative thinking, but here specifically on the development of scientific knowledge as contrasted to non-scientific assumptions. Conceptual change refers to learning processes in which an individual intentionally changes his or her initial understanding concerning counterintuitive concepts. Metacognition can be seen as a cognitive mechanism which monitors and regulates these thinking processes. Existing concepts can be recognised, evaluated, reviewed, and restructured when the person becomes aware of his or her prior knowledge and possible alternative models (e.g., conflicts between these and scientific conceptions). Furthermore, the authors point out some pedagogical implications as regards developing such teaching and learning practices for adults that would support conceptual change.

Chapter 9 by Auli Toom and Jukka Husu explores an expert's or expert group's tacit knowledge in terms of a learning product and process. Tacit knowledge refers to practice-based knowledge which has become partly latent, yet functional knowledge. The characteristics and role of tacit knowledge and knowing in the construction of expertise are discussed – the concept of expert knowledge is closely linked with tacit knowledge. In this chapter tacit knowledge is addressed in relation to various components like skills and competences and by way of explication and argumentation as to the process and product aspects, plus individual and collective aspects of tacit knowledge. Based on these, the chapter also presents a tacit knowledge model with four different perspectives. As a complex and multidimensional phenomenon, tacit knowledge and knowing are difficult to explicate, and they are closely intertwined with various cognitive and emotional aspects in thinking and action. Toom and Husu's article points out the importance of taking into account non-logical cognition and its' fusion to other psychological processes, and secondly, the essential role of these in deep learning processes.

In Chapter 10 Päivi Tynjälä, Eeva K. Kallio and Hannu L. T. Heikkinen continue the discussion on expert knowledge in the light of adult cognitive development and research of *phronēsis*, i.e., practical wisdom. Learning cannot be reduced just into a change in thinking or knowledge structures: it involves a complex set of phenomena. Adult thinking is viewed from the perspective of professional (learning) expertise and *phronēsis*. It is argued that professional expertise requires holistic thinking involving the ability to integrate or reconcile various and even conflicting perspectives in order to find new solutions to problems. Also, the role of emotions and ethical reflection is emphasised. This leads the readers to the notions of practical wisdom, and a related model of the nature of wisdom in professional expertise. The development of expertise and practical wisdom calls for pedagogical approaches that promote the deep integration of different perspectives and forms of knowledge, and ethical action in complex problem-solving situations.

The third thematic section, Chapters 11 to 13, serves as a kind of critical evaluation and epilogue for this edition. The purpose of these three chapters is to open up further views and questions on the development of adult thinking and learning processes.

Chapter 11 by Heidi Hyytinen, Liisa Postareff and Sari Lindblom-Ylänne discusses methodological challenges in the study of knowledge conceptions and psychological epistemology. Similarly to the other chapters of this book, a multiperspective approach is adopted also in this methodological context. Various mixed-methods and other combined approaches have much to offer to current adult developmental and learning research and there is also a need for an enhanced dialogue between theoretical, methodological, and empirical perspectives. The authors argue that there is an urgent need to develop and elaborate authentic and mixed methods to be used in future research.

In Chapter 12 Pirjo Ståhle, Laura Mononen, Päivi Tynjälä and Eeva K. Kallio address the connections between systems approach, adult cognitive development and learning. Firstly, they offer an overview of the history of systems approach and describe the three main systems paradigms. They conclude that Jan Sinnott's model of adult thinking can be partly traced to the general systems theory and chaos and complexity theories, theory of self-organising systems, and the views on self-renewing systems. They question, however, the individual-centred approach of many adult cognitive models and call for more attention to systemic, social, situational, and collaborative levels in further research.

In Chapter 13 Miira Tuominen and Eeva K. Kallio present theoretical and philosophical criticism mainly with respect to current claims and assumptions regarding adult cognitive development. They begin with the notion that the concepts of relativism and dialectical thinking are often used with reference to the core features of adult cognition and absolutistic (dualistic) thinking associated with the cognition of youth, in particular. They draw a distinction between philosophical and psychological epistemological claims and discuss the logical difficulties implied in current psychological theorisation. Furthermore, they conclude that rather than in light of epistemological relativism and dialectical thinking, mature adult cognition should be neutrally described in terms of integration. Here, integration means understanding that people have a variety of views that may differ from those of ours or some others, but we still need mutual ethical understanding and respect for each other as people while also taking into account not only rational but also emotional aspects.

All authors of these articles are Finnish scholars. This edition is based on an earlier book in Finnish (Kallio, 2016), but is a modified and enlarged version of it. In recent decades there has been considerable interest and internationally acclaimed scholarly activity regarding adult cognitive development, social psychology, and adult learning processes in Finland (e.g., Helkama & Sortheix, 2015; Hyytinen, Nissinen, Ursin, Toom, & Lindblom-Ylänne, 2015; Lehtinen, McMullen, & Gruber, 2019; Mahon, Heikkinen, & Huttunen, 2018; Pirttilä-Backman & Kajanne, 2001; Toom, 2012; Tynjälä, 2008).

This book offers an introduction to the closely interconnected fields of adult cognitive development and adult learning. We hope that this book will bring about further discussion on these issues more generally. The main conclusion based on these articles is that there is a need for diverse approaches, multiple perspectives and different methods, including theoretical, conceptual, and philosophical ones. In this regard, the actual challenge for the future is, however, how these diverse approaches could be integrated in one way or another into a functional framework, which in itself will probably need, and be under, constant construction.

References

Helkama, K., & Sortheix, F. M. (2015). Moral development, cultural differences. In J. D. Wright (Ed.), *International encyclopaedia of the social and behavioral sciences* (2nd ed., Vol. 15, pp. 781–787). Amsterdam, the Netherlands: Elsevier.

Hyytinen, H., Nissinen, K., Ursin, J., Toom, A., & Lindblom-Ylänne, S. (2015). Problematising the equivalence of the test results of performance-based critical thinking tests for undergraduate students. *Studies in Educational Evaluation, 44*, 1–8. doi:10.1016/j.stueduc.2014.11.001

Kallio, E. (Ed.). (2016). *Ajattelun kehitys aikuisuudessa: Kohti moninäkökulmaisuutta.* [The development of thinking in adulthood: Towards multiperspective thinking] (Research in Educational Sciences No. 71). Helsinki, Finland: The Finnish Educational Research Association.

Lehtinen, E., McMullen, J., & Gruber, H. (2019). Expertise development and scientific thinking. In M. Murtonen & K. Balloo (Eds.), *Redefining scientific thinking for higher education: Higher-order thinking, evidence-based reasoning and research skills.* (pp. 179–202). London, England: Palgrave Macmillan.

Mahon, K., Heikkinen, H. L. T., & Huttunen, R. (2018). Critical educational praxis in university ecosystems: Enablers and constraints. *Pedagogy, Culture & Society, 27*(3), 463–480. doi:10.1080/14681366.2018.1522663

Pirttilä-Backman, A. M., & Kajanne, A. (2001). The development of implicit epistemologies during early and middle adulthood. *Journal of Adult Development, 8*(2), 81–97.

Toom, A. (2012). Considering the artistry and epistemology of tacit knowledge and knowing. *Educational Theory, 62*(6), 621–640.

Tynjälä, P. (2008). Perspectives into learning at the workplace. *Educational Research Review, 3*(2), 130–154.

PART I
Adult cognitive and moral development

2

FROM MULTIPERSPECTIVE TO CONTEXTUAL INTEGRATIVE THINKING IN ADULTHOOD

Considerations on theorisation of adult thinking and its place as a component of wisdom[1]

Eeva K. Kallio

Theoretical background: basic concepts

This chapter introduces the field of adult cognitive development by means of critical literature review. Major trends, schools, and traditions will be described and analysed to get a comprehensive, yet critically evaluative synthesis of the field.

Psychology as a discipline examines human action, behaviour, and experiences and the ways in which they change over time. In Anglo-American and "Western" cultures the root of many current terms can be traced back about 2000 years, to ancient civilizations of Near East and Southern Europe. Etymologically, the Greek term *"psykhē"* refers to "the soul, mind, spirit; life, one's life, the invisible animating principle or entity which occupies and directs the physical body; understanding, the mind (as the seat of thought), faculty of reason" (Psyche, 2019b). Oxford Lexico refers to the term "psyche" (Psyche, 2019a) as follows: "Mid-17th century via Latin from Greek psykhē 'breath, life, soul'." *Cognition* comes from the term *cognicioun* (Latin), "ability to comprehend, mental act or process of knowing" (Cognition, 2019b). Furthermore, the term "cognition" is defined as coming from "Late Middle English from Latin 'cognitio' (–), from 'cognoscere', 'get to know'" (Cognition, 2019a).

In modern scientific research, cognition refers to all phenomena that are related to acquiring, assimilating, and processing knowledge, such as perception, attention, learning, memory, logical thinking, decision-making, creative thinking, socio-cognitive skills, and intuition. In short, cognition refers to the mental functions that we use to acquire knowledge, or as Sternberg and Funke (2019) say, how people represent and process information. On the one hand, it is always intrapersonal but on the other hand, essentially also a social and collective phenomenon. In other words, cognition is about personal, internal, and experiential processing in an individual's brain and mind, but at the same time shared and collective (Resnick, 1991). It is worth noting, however, that the concept of cognition in our rapidly changing world can be extended beyond our physical bodies and to technological fields, as integrations of human being with artificial intelligence, for example. Thus, the whole concept of cognition may soon need to be revised in some way.

Interestingly, the nowadays widely used term *"development"* appears to be a relatively recent term in English vocabulary; according to Oxford Lexico (Develop, 2019) the term *"develop"* traces back to "Mid-18th century (in the sense 'unfold, unfurl'): from French 'développer', based on Latin dis- 'un-' + a second element of unknown origin". On a general level, development as a scientific concept can be defined as a change that is predictable by nature and that emerges sequentially and consecutively. *Adult development* refers to consistent, qualitative changes in the outer and inner behaviour of mature individuals as a result of both internal and external interaction with the environment. These changes are partly based on hereditary, endogenous, and exogenous effects, the ability to adapt, and individual factors, such as goal-setting, will-power, agency as well as goal-oriented decisions (Hoare, 2011). The highly general rubric "adult cognition" refers to information processing theories, i.e., progress and decline of intelligence or memory in general (Schaie & Zanjani, 2006). More importantly for the present context, *adult thinking* can also be studied from a developmental psychological perspective, which is predominantly based on Piagetian theorisation, but also on some other major psychological theories as well (Kallio, 2015). In further discussion, I will focus especially on the "postformal" and "relativistic-dialectical" thinking models, and at some instances, also on some notions associated with these, especially on learning and wisdom.

Development in adulthood is twofold: it can include both progress and regress, going forward and backward (Hoare, 2011). The most significant differences in theories of this field are related to how this change is described. Different terms are used, such as stage, level, substage, and related transitional periods between these. The models often refer to general developmental progress which is more or less stable and structured. Change is typically, but not always necessarily, understood as something progressively hierarchical; advancing towards higher and higher stages, assuming the trend to be toward the better. This was the dominant idea at the end of the 20th century, but rivalling perceptions have been emerging since then. After the introduction of biological evolutionary theory, these hierarchical models and theories had their heydays, but they do have influence still today (Kohlberg, 1984; Piaget & Inhelder, 1969) with various neo-Kohlbergian and neo-Piagetian approaches (see articles in Part I in this book). (Note that as an alternative for "neo-Piagetian", also the term "post-Piagetian" is used in this book; similarly to e.g., neo-Kohlbergian etc.). However, non-hierarchical development is also a possible assumption, i.e., non-normative consecutive periodicity as phases (Erikson, 1978; Freud, 1989).

There are several puzzling questions regarding the concept of development. The main antinomies in human development include, nature vs. nurture, mind vs. body, maturation vs. experience (or innate vs. acquired), continuity vs. discontinuity, stability vs. instability, constancy vs. change, quantitative vs. qualitative change, and individual vs. context (Lerner, 2018, p. 136). There are also several different assumptions regarding the direction and nature of development. For instance, we can ponder whether development is uni- or multilinear and whether it is proceeding along a particular route or various routes, and whether there is *telos* or not. In addition, what one person regards as development, may well be regression to another. Besides normative development, individual variation may be an important factor in producing unpredictable development. Universal development is a tempting model of explanation for many theorists. In summary, the concept of development is complex and the above-mentioned questions are constantly discussed by various scholars (Lerner, 2018; Lerner & Overton, 2008; Overton, 2006, 2010).

According to Lerner (2018), development is *not* an absolute observation-based concept. If it was, all researchers would agree when they observe the change of human behaviour over time, always defining it as development. The same phenomenon, however, can also be defined as learning or some other kind of change in the already existing structure without the emergence of something qualitatively new, depending on the conceptual background of the researcher who observes the phenomenon (Lerner, 2018). Any interpretative claims of reality should thus always be contextualised with our world-view and its mode of reasoning (Kincheloe & Steinberg, 1993). It is also worth reminding that our knowledge and implicit assumptions are Eurocentric and Anglo-American, based on the paradigmatic scientific shift which emerged first in the Scientific Revolution (Kuhn, 1962). According to Hans-George Gadamer (2008) and his idea of hermeneutical pre-understanding, an observer is ontologically tied in fundamental pre-existing conditions in perception – here "philosophical ontology" refers to "a branch of metaphysics concerned with the nature and relations of being" (Ontology, 2019). In their interpretations and meaning-making the observers are never free from their conditioned minds and they understand objects and things according to their pre-existing thinking patterns.

Learning as a concept also includes an idea that something new emerges. As a term it can be traced back to medieval times: "Old English leornung 'study, action of acquiring knowledge,' verbal noun from leornian ... Meaning 'knowledge acquired by systematic study, extensive literary and scientific culture' is from the mid-14th century" (Learning, 2019). According to Hoare (2011), adult learning refers to the change in behaviour and action, acquiring new knowledge or skills, as well as to change in earlier knowledge structures. Learning outcomes and results are usually ranked as a hierarchy from lower to higher levels according to socially predetermined criteria and values. This implies analogical developmental stages or levels, even if there are less strict claims of intrinsic structure of normative transformations. Learning is also expansive in the sense that something learned earlier can be transferred to new settings. On the other hand, the concept also includes the possibility of unlearning (Becker, 2005). Both learning and development have to do with the concept of change, which will be addressed later.

Illeris (2009) argues that there is no established, consistent definition for learning. On the contrary, new models of learning are constantly introduced – which applies to adult developmental models as well. Illeris states that the research of learning is no longer focused on skills and knowledge, while the research field has expanded to encompass the meaning of emotions as well as the social and societal dimensions. This means that learning is viewed in relation to the context. The definition of learning presented by Illeris (2009, p. 3), however, comes close to the one suggested by Hoare (2011): learning refers to any process where there is a permanent change in the skills (capacity) of a living organism; change that is not a result of biological factors or age. In developmental psychology, however, age with related physiological changes, especially in childhood, is regarded as an essential factor (Piaget & Inhelder, 1969).

Change as a core concept in development and learning

What is actually meant by *change* in general? The concept of change can be formally defined shortly as follows: "There is change if and only if there is a subject S that persists and retains its identity along from x1 to x2, and there is a difference that is exhibited by a property, state or part properly predicated of S, from x1 to x2" (Hussey, 2002, p. 105). S means here anything that can change (e.g. moral code, way of thinking, learning), and x1 and x2 are distinct locations or suitable dimensions (e.g., time) (Hussey, 2002; Kallio & Marchand, 2012). However, a mere change between two points in time as such does not necessarily mean the emergence of something new. Besides, change is not always for the better (e.g., aging with deteriorating health).

A philosophically important question in relation to change is whether the identity of the changing object remains logically the same in the process or not (Kallio & Marchand, 2012). The concept of change is paradoxical in its nature; it involves a qualitative shift during which the earlier form of a phenomenon stays structurally the same, but simultaneously changes to an extent and thus includes a new element. It is a philosophical issue: we can define the phenomenon either as remaining the same or as being different, either consistent or inconsistent at different points of time, depending on which perception is conceptualised (Kallio & Marchand, 2012; Mortensen, 2016).

Mortensen (2016) points out that Buddhism, for example, denies the permanence of identity over time, and assumes in general that nothing is permanent. Thus, our Western way of looking at identity as a sustained, even if changing property is just *one alternative approach* to the concept of change, and cross-cultural studies in various fields should study and explicate latent cultural, historical, and philosophical beliefs and other assumptions more closely (Gidley, 2016; Kincheloe, Hayes, Steinberg, & Tobin, 2011; Malott, 2011).

We usually suppose that developmental progress is linear in time, growing from lower to higher levels through constant change, or with certain *telos*. Linear progress in time is, however, only one possibility to understanding change. In some cultures change is seen as a cyclical, continuous spiral-like process without any specific beginning and end. Linear time can be defined in very simplistic terms as an interval from point A to point B on a timeline: moving from past to present and from present to future (a metaphor "time as an arrow" has often been used). Moreover, time is not dependent on the subject perceiving it. These two conceptions of time may, however, be complementary to each other, so that both linear and cyclical time and processes can be combined in understanding change within some time period, visualising it as a spiral-like change (see Chapter 3). The notion of spirality may originate from the rhythmic patterns of the natural world, like the cycles of day and night or annual seasons due to the Sun's apparent rotational motion in relation to the Earth. This cyclic-rhythmic perception of time can still be seen in our weekly, monthly, and yearly rhythms (Zerubavel, 1989).

When describing development and learning, important conceptions include the direction of change: change can be both *vertical* and *horizontal*. The first refers to an assumption that there is at least a partial hierarchy for the state of affairs. The term *hierarchy* comes from Pseudo-Dionysius (ca. late 5th to early 6th century), as "hierarchia", neologism from Greek "hieros", "sacred" and "arkhia", "rule" (Kleineberg, 2017): its roots are thus religious, with reference to "sacred rule" issued by a god. Historically, the idea of the hierarchical order of reality ("Great Chain of Being") is a long-standing one (Lovejoy, 1936). It can be traced back to Plato, Aristotle, and Plotinus and other neo-Platonists. Kleineberg (2017) also argues that similar ideas are included in Hinduism, Judaism, Buddhism, Taoism, and Islam, thus implying that this notion could be almost universal in cultures (cf. Wilber, 2001).

Hierarchy is defined as a chain of growing stages or phases where each new phase is linked to and built upon past or existing lower stages. Hierarchical development theories assume that there are developmental phases organised in a certain way, so that they cannot be crossed, and that the change in these chains has only one direction. This line of thinking, i.e., based on vertical developmental phases, always includes a normative, value-based assumption. Instead, in the horizontal change the developmental phases can be consecutive and they can exist without the assumption about an internal hierarchy. However, this does not exclude the possibility for successfully reviewing a previous phase so as to enable new development for the next one (Alexander & Langer, 1990).

One example of how world-view is implicitly rooted in our thinking of change comes from the history of sciences. Psychological, qualitative changes during the lifespan are not something only modern scholars have been interested in. For example, several classifications of the human lifespan were presented in Tetrabiblos, one of the major books in the Western world before the Scientific Revolution (Ptolemy, trans. 1940). Ptolemy considered four and seven phases of the lifespan, referred to as the "Ages of Man", each having their own qualitative psychological features. The lifespan was understood as analogical to the four seasons: childhood, adolescence, adulthood, and old age. The seven phases were connected to the ancient cosmological system, as the phases were "governed" by each of the known seven planets according to the microcosm – macrocosm analogy ("as above so below") (Burrow, 1986; Sears, 1986). The starting point was holism: the lifespan of an individual (microcosm) reflected a broader reality (macrocosm), which were analogically connected in terms of their rhythm. It was a dogma based on equivalence, sympathy and correspondence. According to this dogma, a part reflects the entity: life on Earth was a reflection of a larger unity, the highest environmental system, the cosmos (Burrow, 1986).

The beginning of *adulthood* can be defined in different ways. For example, it can be considered juridically as a formal shift to majority, i.e., attainment of full legal age (Robinson, 2013). Based on the age defined in years, adulthood can be divided in different ways into several stages, for instance, ranging from 20-year-olds (young adults) to adults, middle-aged, and late-middle-aged people, up to the final stages of old age (Cavanaugh & Blanchard-Fields, 2014). Another, more sociological classification divides the lifespan into the first, second, third, and fourth age (Laslett, 1994; cf. also Settersten, 2003). In this work, the discussion on adulthood is mainly targeted at the stages between early adulthood and the late middle age, or in Laslett's terms, the second age, but also with some references to the third age as well.

The development of adult thinking: starting points for modern research

Piaget, Perry; Kohlberg, Gilligan, and the development of thinking: logic, knowledge, and morals

Piaget's (1896–1980) theory concerning cognitive development in childhood and adolescence is still an important theory in developmental psychology. This theory has been expanded to the post-Piagetian direction with new openings and influencing several later research trends. Piaget (who was a biologist) defined his research interest as the highest form of biological adaptation, scientific thinking, and he called his project "genetic epistemology". It includes several different areas, such as the formation of sociological and psychological knowledge, the development of logic and moral thinking, and the emergence of visual thinking plus metacognition (Beilin, 1992; Piaget & Inhelder, 1969).

An essential part of Piaget's theory concerns scientific thinking, more specifically the development of *causal thinking*. Here, causality refers to the relationship between the cause (x) and effect (y), where $x \leq y$, in terms of time. The theory describes the basic features of scientific thinking: how we perceive the phenomena of physical object reality and the causal relationships between them. This also defines the best-known part of Piaget's theory, the developmental stage theory. Causal thinking can also be described with terms such as logical reasoning, or hypothetico-deductive thinking (Inhelder & Piaget, 1958; Piaget & Inhelder, 1969; see also Barrouillet & Gauffroy, 2013).

Piaget's entire theory is focused on studying how knowing is possible and how it reflects the (assumed) *general, universal development of humankind* (Piaget, Garcia, Garcia, & Lara, 1989). Thus, it does not only concern individual development but also depicts how it has become possible for the humans to realise scientific knowledge with different developmental stages; from magical thinking towards scientific-rational thinking (cf. also Dux, 2011).

According to Piaget, the development of logical thinking is about a constant change or process – causal knowledge is under continuous construction within an assimilation and accommodation process. His developmental theory includes four main stages. During childhood, interaction with the material environment is a prerequisite for later internalised reasoning. External action enables the creation of sensorimotor schemas as behavioural patterns. Schemas are internalised and later emerged at the stage of concrete thinking, logical operations based on direct observations appear approximately at the age of 7. Formal thinking is the highest form of causal understanding emerging at the beginning of puberty: based on hypothetico-deductive, abstract thinking but still open to experimental testing. It is possible to isolate, combine, and control the variables in well-defined problem-solving situations (see Table 2.1; see also Inhelder & Piaget, 1958; Kallio, 1998, pp. 16–20; Piaget & Inhelder, 1969).

As regards adult cognitive development, the assumptions of "Piagetian-like" universal fixed stages comply with the following criteria: 1) the unchangeable order of the stages, which means that their development always follows a certain order; 2) each stage consists of a qualitatively unique structure, the internal and mental structure; 3) the integration of lower developmental stages with a higher one, the later stages build on and incorporate the lower stages as part of new development; 4) the stages include different sub-stages, during which the change becomes stabilised; 5) the state of balance where the features of the stage are established (Brainerd, 1978; Marchand, 2001).

Piaget's theory was interpreted in its heyday in a way that it comprehends the development of thinking in all domains. In this form, causal thinking could be applied in any field, from physical object reality to processes of emotional and social life. Nevertheless, not all researchers, including later Piaget himself, accepted this claim at face value, which led to new developments in theory formation. The assumption that any object or topic could be studied with causal reasoning has been seen as one form of reductionism: any action could be interpreted with formal language (Kincheloe & Steinberg, 1993).

Regarding formal thinking, it is possible to formulate various hypotheses. At first, Piaget assumed that it is a general stage of thinking, and in terms of *scientific thinking* it can develop towards higher and higher levels (Inhelder & Piaget, 1958). Later, as the notion of generality was rejected, Piaget assumed in his work that formal thinking only emerges in the specific areas of work, hobbies

TABLE 2.1 Cognitive development stages and the development of logical thinking according to Piaget's theory. Printed with permission. Copyright The Finnish Educational Research Association

Cognitive development stages and chronological age	Abilities for logical thinking
Sensorimotor stage (0–2 years) Preoperational stage (2–7 years)	The sensorimotor stage covers the first phases of cognitive development in early childhood: understanding the connections between movements and consequences, a grasp of elementary causal relationships and object permanence. For cognitive development, also the initial stages of linguistic development are essential. In the preoperational stage the child starts to understand that words and concepts refer to certain objects (symbolic function). Thinking is egocentric. However, already at this stage the environment is very important for the child's cognitive development. In the sensorimotor and preoperational stages the child still lacks abilities for internalised logical operations.
Concrete operational stage (c. 7–11/12 years)	During the concrete operational stage, logicality in thinking increases and thus enables operations of logical thinking. However, thinking is still bound to concrete situations and abstract concepts are difficult, which for its part limits the child's thinking. For example, the sense of time and understanding of distances becomes easier. Thinking develops so that the child can at least partly see things also from the viewpoint of others instead of highlighting solely the perspective of one's own.
Formal operational stage (from c. 11/12 years onwards)	Abstract thinking is enabled so that thinking is no longer restricted to concrete things. Abilities for the mastery of logical mental operations (isolation and control of variables, creation and use of formal models and logical reasoning) are developing. The formal operational stage also includes abilities for comparing different hypotheses and for deductive reasoning. Theories can be used as cognitive tools.

etc., that the individual is specialised in and motivated for (Piaget, 1972). Still, in the light of empirical results it is obvious that formal operational thinking is not a universal developmental stage, not even in highly developed economies and cultures (see Chapter 3 for recent results regarding Finnish students; see also Kallio, 1998 for similar results; Barrouillet & Gauffroy, 2013). A third hypothesis, proposed by Lourenço (2016) presumes that it is possible to integrate formal thinking into a larger cognitive system. Furthermore, he also argues that formal thinking as such is not an obstacle for, neither incompatible with the development of some other areas of the psyche (for example, in association with emotional and socio-cognitive development). Lourenço's notions come surprisingly close to those of postformal thinking, though *without assuming a new stage* after formal thinking.

The critique on Piaget's views can be considered a turning point in the study of adult thinking. The observations that formal thinking is not a universal developmental stage (Barrouillet & Gauffroy, 2013), as well as Perry's (1913–1998) research on the development of university students' thinking and ethical reasoning were significant in this respect (Perry, 1999). Perry was the first one to study the development of adult cognition from different perspectives instead of that of logical reasoning only. In the Piagetian tradition, reasoning is always mechanical-logical and closed, based on dichotomic truth values: an answer is always either right or wrong. According to Wu and Chiou (2008), closed systems are based on a limited number of variables, while other contextual aspects of the problem are irrelevant to the solution. There is a single right answer and it can be applied to all similar circumstances.

In his research on the development of thinking Perry focused on *epistemic assumptions regarding knowledge* and *how these are justified*. He discovered that university students' perceptions of knowledge changed qualitatively as their studies progressed; from unquestioned thinking at the beginning of the studies towards relativity in the middle of the studies, and finally towards independent evaluation and formation of opinions. The research trend starting from Perry has been very strong throughout the past decades (see Chapters 3, 4, and 11 in this edition).

Perry's major innovation was the triangle of three thinking modes: dualism, relativism, and evaluative thinking. It includes the following notions: firstly, in epistemological dualism knowledge is perceived as consisted of either-or, absolute-like truths, without doubting the premises and argumentation. Secondly, epistemological relativism takes into account different viewpoints enabling differing but equally valid assumptions. And thirdly, evaluative thinking is characterised by independent and critical evaluation of different viewpoints, and forming a subjective conclusion or synthesis of them.

Development stage theories for moral thinking mainly stem from Lawrence Kohlberg's (1927–1987) and Carol Gilligan's (1936–) work. Kohlberg's theory was inspired by Piaget's studies. Hence, it includes a progression of universal and hierarchical moral-ethical reasoning stages. Gilligan's theory, in turn, can be seen as a counter-reaction to Kohlberg's notions. In addition to rational reasoning, her theory takes into account the expansion of social points of view in the development of moral thinking.

Kohlberg emphasises the rationality of moral reasoning and its relational independence from feelings. Altogether six stages pertaining to moral reasoning have been suggested based on socio-moral viewpoints and also what an individual considers right and correct as opposed to wrong and incorrect action. A higher development stage is guided by a comprehensive desire towards commonly and coherently abiding ethical principles. Kohlberg's theory has been challenged most significantly by Gilligan (1993). She points out that the ethics of justice based on rationality describes the way of handling moral dilemmas mainly from a male perspective. In moral thinking, her focus is on human relationships, care, and responsibility. At the lowest stage the moral of caring is self-centred, whereas at the highest stage it reflects the idea of individuals' mutual dependency, i.e., caring for oneself and others (see Chapter 5).

Postformal and relativistic-dialectical thinking in adulthood

We can distinguish between three major lines of research into adult cognitive development. So-called derivative models originate from Perry's (1999) model and focus on the study of *epistemological assumptions*; they do not link their theorisation to formal thinking as such (see Chapters 3 and 4; Moshman, 2013). Another school has evolved around *context-free complexity models*, which are designed as to be applicable to any domain. The third trend, which emerged in the 1980s and is perhaps most significantly present in this chapter as well, assumes a new stage called *postformal* or *relativistic-dialectical* or *dialectical thinking*.

Regarding the second tradition, some scholars, like Kurt Fischer (Wozniak & Fischer, 1993) and Michael Commons (Commons & Kjorlien, 2016), have created context-free and domain-independent constructs (as alternatives to Piaget). These models are described here only briefly. A unifying principle in the respective models by Commons and Fischer is that development to higher levels is indicated by increasing complexity of tasks and performance in them. The Mathematical model of Hierarchical Complexity (MHC) presented by Michael Commons is gaining ground in scientific research. Currently there are altogether 15, even 16, different stages in this model. It is a model where understanding of task complexity is used to define the individual developmental stage of the problem-solver (Commons & Kjorlien, 2016). Kurt Fischer's Dynamic Skill Theory (DST), in turn, assesses the increasing complexity of skills (Wozniak & Fischer, 1993). The model starts from the organisation of action towards higher stages, up to stage 13. Both models are intended to serve as a comprehensive model which could be used to define any action meeting certain criteria of a developmental stage. In lower stages, a child is only capable of coordinating certain factors, but in the more developed stages it is possible to connect different structures that already have internally linked components. Both models for complex actions are hierarchical: each developmental stage requires and is always built on top of the previous one.

As mentioned, the third school or trend is the most important one in our context. Despite the fact that empirical results on the mastery of formal thinking did not support Piaget's original idea of this being a universal stage attainable to everybody, researchers began to speculate whether there could be an entirely new developmental stage after it. Most of these scholars detached themselves from the research on pure causal thinking, and included notions of relativism and evaluative cognitive components in their models. Most importantly, they also included other cognitive factors into their models. Thus, cognitive development is integrated into the development of other contexts. Therefore, thinking cannot be studied distinct from other processes and domains, such as those comprising emotion (Labouvie-Vief, 2015), autonomy of self (Edelstein & Noam, 1982), socio-cultural (Kincheloe & Steinberg, 1993), system theory (Sinnott, 1998), or even religious and spiritual elements or higher states of consciousness (e.g., Alexander & Langer, 1990; Kamppinen & Jakonen, 2015; Perttula & Kallio, 1996; Wilber, 2001). By the same token, another important field of study deals with dialectical thinking, understood as the ability to reconcile contradictory viewpoints to reach a synthesis (Basseches, 1984).

Conceptually, the presented models of postformal or relativistic-dialectical thinking include similar characteristics as noted by various scholars (Gurba, 2005; Kallio, 1998; Kramer, 1983; Marchand, 2001). Postformal thinking is supposed to overcome the limitations of formal logic with multiple logics, and widen the boundaries of thinking to a more sophisticated and nuanced direction. Marchand (2001) distinguishes between "hard logic" vs. "flexible logic", the first referring to dualistic true/false logic, and the latter to subjective, open, arbitrary, and contextual logic. Thus, flexible logic includes affective, systemic, and holistic understanding, instead of just linear-causal knowledge. For example, Labouvie-Vief (2015) traces her model back to Carl Jung (1991) and his idea of the integration of rational vs. irrational spheres of psyche, as in the individuation process in adulthood.

According to Kramer (1983), these models follow more or less the progression from absolutism to relativism and dialectical thinking (even if the models have more than three stages or levels). The first of these is considered a stage of development taking place in youth, and the latter ones in adulthood. The lowest level, *absolutistic* thinking is understood as parallel to formal thinking. Thus, absolutistic thinking ends up with true-untrue statements in closed systems. In contrast, the following notions about knowledge are typical of *relativistic-dialectical* thinking: realising the non-absolute nature of knowledge (relativism); accepting that there are contradictions in knowledge; and integrating contradiction into a totality (dialectical thinking). However, mature thinkers also recognise that any resolution or established conception will be challenged by new data, results, and theoretical analyses; i.e., knowing is an open and constant process (Kramer, 1983). Thinking becomes thus flexible, complex, contextualised, and integrated in adulthood. The diverse, relative reality calls for an autonomous pluralistic synthesis (Kallio, 2001).

Contextual integrative thinking as a form of adult thinking and a component of wisdom

Ontological pre-understanding and adult thinking

The theorisation around postformal or relativistic-dialectical thinking encompasses implicit beliefs, which so far have not been properly analysed theoretically (with the possible exception of Kramer, 1983; Kincheloe & Steinberg, 1993). According to the post-Piagetian scholars, the context of thinking must always be taken into account, like problem identification, i.e., the type of problem or situation in question. Thus, focusing solely on logical thinking is inappropriate, as it is obvious that not everything can be solved by logical inferencing. As for the capacity of formal thinking, it would suggest that adults are capable of implicit *hermeneutical preunderstanding* regarding the *domain* in which their thinking processes are applied. However, this point is rarely, if ever, stated explicitly in theoretical discussion.

Hermeneutics (from Latin *"hermeneutica"*, Palmer, 1969) refers here generally to theories of interpretation and understanding. We are hermeneutically situated: our understanding and knowledge formation occurs within a particular horizon, but at the same time, it is under constant and ongoing construction (Gadamer, 2008; Malpas, 2018; Peters, 2007). Adult thinking does not take place in a cultural or contextual vacuum but rather within a diverse community of paradigms and values. It is based on historically, economically, and ideologically conditioned phenomena. Tradition serves as a base and condition to any knowledge formation, and is present and underlying both scientific inquiry and everyday thinking. These hermeneutical conceptions are mostly tacit, hidden and not openly discussed, if even recognised (Kincheloe & Steinberg, 1993).

Neo-Piagetian scholars seem to criticise basically a philosophical ontological problem behind Piaget's notions. Causal scientific thinking focuses ontologically on *physical object reality*, but generalisation beyond this domain is questionable. It might be absurd to use hypothetico-deductive logic so as to understand, for instance, an emotional conflict between partners, where both of them are involved in a complicated situation. Which features of the situation/object need to be taken into account and prioritised, and which not? Is the chosen approach, way of thinking and action, appropriate and relevant regarding the situation? All this refers to increasing sensitivity to situational properties, i.e., denoting context-sensitive and content-wise thinking.

Another important issue with regard to Piaget's theory has been raised in current scientific discussion. Formal and postformal thinking also include so-called well- and ill-defined problems (Schraw, Dunkle, & Bendixen, 1995). In studying formal thinking in the light of Piaget's Pendulum problem, we are dealing with a well-defined problem (see Chapter 3). The subjects are provided with choices where it is clear in advance which factors they need to use when solving the problem, and there is only one correct solution. By contrast, if the problem is defined in a way that the conditions are not clear enough, the outcome cannot be straightforward either: problems of this kind are called ill-defined problems (e.g., Chi, Glaser, & Farr, 2014, for more about this kind of problems, see e.g., Chapter 4).

Georg Henrik von Wright (2004) has argued that there is a definitive ontological difference in the way knowledge is constructed in the respective domains of natural and human sciences: natural sciences seek to explain *why and how things happen* in the natural world, whereas human sciences seek for practical *understanding* of human actions and behaviour. Von Wright argues against a causal theory of human action: behaviour can be understood only by referring to the intentionality of humans; "Things move, persons act" (Kenneth Burke, according to Henderson & Williams, 2001, p. 164). Any social action is tied in the persons' hermeneutical understanding of implicit social rules and situation-specific characteristics. In conclusion, it seems that the Piagetian and neo-Piagetian scholars have different ontological premises and hermeneutical preunderstandings of how human action should be understood. Causality cannot exhaustively explain human action (see also Mascolo & Kallio, 2019, 2020). Moreover, human action cannot be understood in terms of the machine paradigm, since human mind is constantly creating new internal and external meanings of reality based on one's experiences, agency, and plasticity (Kohler, 2010; Teo, 2010).

I have already re-labelled adult thinking as integrative thinking (Kallio, 2011), arguing that the terms "postformal" and "relativistic-dialectical" thinking should be replaced with integrative thinking. The position of postformal thinking as a new developmental stage has not been confirmed, and there is always a risk of confusion when using philosophical terms in psychological research (see Chapter 13). Absolutism can be understood as single-perspective thinking and relativism as multiperspective thinking (Figure 2.1). Moreover, the term "postformal" may be misleading if it is understood as a developmental stage in the original Piagetian sense: the same criterion for "stage" is not applicable to both formal and postformal thinking (Kallio, 2011). Hence, I suggest here that *"contextual integrative thinking"* or just *"integrative thinking"* (Kallio, 2011) could replace the terms postformal and relativistic-dialectical thinking in the theorisation of adult cognitive development.

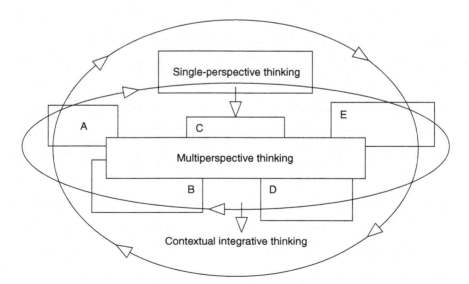

FIGURE 2.1 Development of contextual integrative thinking: three stages or different modes of thinking. (Markings A through D refer to different perspectives). Printed with permission. Copyright by The Finnish Educational Research Association.

Contextual understanding seems to be one of the necessary conditions in adult knowledge formation. This understanding is about tacit hermeneutical, ontological pre-understanding of human action differing from the perception of physical objects. It has to be noted, however, that the mentioned three modes of thinking are not necessarily manifested as if in a developmental, normative hierarchical interrelationship. They can also be understood as different cognitive modes to be used in different contexts depending on the ontology of the object or situation at hand. It may be so that single-perspective thinking is preferable in some occasions, like with natural scientific problem solving in line with the Piagetian tasks, while other modes may be suited better to some other settings or the different modes can also be of equal value in some cases. Thus, these modes can be equally useful and appropriate, but used selectively depending on the purpose and domain concerned (see also Figure 2.2).

According to some sources, the first known use of the term "integration" dates back to 1620 (Integrate, 2019). Oxford Lexico tells that the term derives from the "Mid-17th century from Latin integrat- 'made whole', from the verb integrare, from integer 'whole' (see integer) … " (Integration, 2019).

Alexander and Langer (1990, p. 27) define integrative thinking as follows: "Integration (is) … a synthetic form of thinking … that integrates several opposing systems into an abstract whole (and) contains all particulars". In general, integration does not mean simply connecting, uniting, or linking things together. It is about fusing or merging components together, which is more than just assembling things mechanically together.

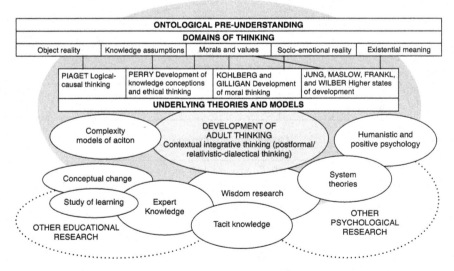

FIGURE 2.2 Main research traditions regarding the development of adult thinking, their connections to other close fields of research, and related ontological pre-assumptions for different domains of thinking.

In the field of cognitive sciences, there are several close concepts to be pondered in comparison to integrative thinking, however. *Integrative complexity* is one possible candidate in this respect. It has been used at least by Suedfeld and Leighton (2002). As a psychometrically validated concept, it was originally introduced both as a personality trait and a cognitive style, but nowadays it is understood rather as a situation-dependent pattern (see also Chapter 6). *Evaluative integrative thinking* seems to refer to the integration of positive and negative self-concepts (Showers, 1992). In both of these concepts, both differentiation (knowledge along different attributes), and then integrating the knowledge to more complex structures are in the core of construct (Showers, 1992).

Also *holistic thinking* is a close term to integrative thinking as opposed to analytical thinking. In holistic thinking the relationships and the wholeness are of primary importance instead of isolated things or objects. Holism implies that no phenomenon can be understood by reducing it to smaller units but only as an integrated whole. Holism vs. analytic cognition refers closely to field independence vs. dependency, i.e., the ability to focus attention either on a larger field or the parts thereof (Choi, Koo, & Choi, 2007). As the mentioned terms (integrative complexity/evaluative integrative/holistic thinking) are set phrases pertaining either to personality- or general cognitive psychology, it is suggested that the use of the term "contextual integrative thinking" should be limited to refer to the domain of adult cognitive development.

Contextual integrative thinking and wisdom research

Wisdom research is currently in the midst of an obvious pluralism as there are already dozens of existing models and new ones are constantly created. In the light of the long historical, cultural, religious, and spiritual traditions tracing back thousands of years, it is evident that wisdom is an elusive concept to define. Here it may be sufficient to define it shortly *as an ideal goal of human development* (Swartwood & Tiberius, 2019, p. 20), and *"value term embedded in cultural context"* (Assmann, 1994, p. 187). Despite or perhaps just because of its elusive nature, wisdom has definitely fascinated people in all cultures at all times and the concept is now living its Renaissance in various scientific disciplines, especially in psychology (Sternberg & Glück, 2019; see also Chapter 10). Wisdom is a phenomenon that has interested researchers in both pre-modern and modern psychology. The concept has a philosophical-theological background related to the cultural wisdom traditions of the East and the West. Wisdom research basically and necessarily calls for connections to various other fields of study besides psychology, such as comparative religion, history of philosophy, cross-cultural studies, and esotericism research (Assmann, 1994; Curnow, 1999, 2015; Helskog, 2019; Walsh, 2015).

Wisdom is intimately linked to adult development, as wisdom is seen as the highest developmental goal and prospect of human progress (Erikson & Erikson, 1998). Significant research into these connections is going on in different domains (see Sternberg & Glück, 2019).

Wisdom research is nowadays highly heterogeneous as diverse models, classifications, and tasks are constantly created. These conceptualisations of psychological wisdom research could perhaps be integrated to constitute a kind of *"Wisdom as an Ideal Goal"* model, linking together various domains of psychological and developmental psychological research, such as those pertaining to neuropsychology, personality, cognitive functions, emotions, morals and values, spirituality, and religious thinking. Such an integrative approach could be most appropriate in analysing the basic psychological mechanisms and processes that underlie wisdom. Drawing on research results from different fields and taking the "ideal goal of human development" as an umbrella term could also be the easiest way to reach a comprehensive definition of wisdom. Each culture seems to have human ideals of this kind, even if the content may vary (e.g., Western vs. Eastern differences between cognitive vs. affective domains of wisdom Assmann, 1994; Takahashi & Bordia, 2000).

In the following I focus on the relationship between wisdom and adult cognitive development. The close connection between postformal or relativistic-dialectical thinking and wisdom has been pointed out by many scholars. In scholarly discussion, postformal and relativistic-dialectical thinking are used interchangeably as a subcomponent of wisdom (Arlin, 1993; Asadi, Khorshidi, & Glück, 2019; Baltes & Staudinger, 2000; Bassett, 2005; Compton & Hoffman, 2013; Gidley, 2016; Grossmann, 2017; Kallio, 2015, 2016b; Kramer, 2003; Kunzmann, 2004; Płóciennik, 2018; Smith, 2019; Staudinger & Glück, 2011; Yang, 2008).

Earlier in this chapter adult cognitive development has been defined in terms of multiperspective and contextual integrative thinking. In multiperspective thinking, a wise person reflects deeply on different viewpoints and weighs them carefully. Multiperspective thinking means the ability to abandon egocentric orientation so as to distance oneself in a problematic situation and consider it from different perspectives. Looking at things from multiple perspectives brings intellectual humility, as one realises that there might be no straightforward, one solution to problems. It also makes it possible to understand the relativity of viewpoints and the context- and situation-dependency of problems, implying also uncertainty of knowledge (e.g., Grossmann, 2017).

As Staudinger and Glück (2011) state, wisdom can be regarded as a skill to integrate necessary factors of existence that contradict with each other. Thus, one is able to understand and connect e.g., moral good and evil, dependency and independency, doubt and certainty, control and chaos, limitedness and infinity, and selfishness and unselfishness. In doing so, one can also integrate motivation, emotion, and thinking. The fusion of rationality and intuition is possible as enabled by flexible logic (Sternberg, 2013). Grossmann (2017, p. 235) and his colleagues have defined wise thinking as "intellectual humility or recognition of limits of own knowledge, appreciation of perspectives broader than the issue at hand, sensitivity to the possibility of change in social relations, and compromise or integration of different opinions".

Figure 2.2 summarises the main views discussed in this chapter. The original key concept of this chapter, adult cognitive development, is rephrased as contextual integrative thinking (i.e., "postformal"/"relativistic-dialectical thinking"). It has direct links to different theoretical traditions, from Piaget's theory to Perry and Kohlberg, and it also has links to more humanistic psychological models (see e.g., Misiak & Sexton, 1973), like those exemplified by Jung and Ken Wilber. All these models have focused on particular psychological domains, like Piaget's theory on the manipulation of physical objects. Also, learning research discussed in this edition is included in the Figure – as, for example, theorisation of tacit and expert knowledge have direct links to wisdom research (Baltes & Staudinger, 2000; Sternberg, 2013; see Chapters 9 and 10). Different ontological preunderstandings and related assumptions are also included in Figure 2.2, indicating adult understanding of qualitative differences in reality.

Conclusions

This chapter has discussed and explicated some philosophical assumptions regarding the basic developmental psychological concepts, like what is change (as assumed both in psychological development and learning theories). Similarly, using hermeneutical pre-understanding as a conceptual tool, it was argued that terms like formal and postformal thinking include different ontological assumptions regarding the object reality humans are acting on. The basic intention has thus been "to dig into the roots" of the concepts used in current discussion. Elaborating on Kramer's (1983) statement that the fundamental difference between formal and postformal theorisations is based on different world-views, it is argued here that perhaps, more specifically, it is a question of different ontological positions within the world-views.

Secondly and along the same lines, a new term is suggested to be used to describe adult cognitive development: contextual integrative thinking. Certain distance is thus taken regarding the current discussion on Piaget's theory and also from the neo-Piagetian models. It is worth noting, however, that as a concept adult cognitive development in terms of contextual integrative thinking is broader than just epistemic or epistemological development (see Chapters 3 and 4), as this kind of integration embraces not only knowledge assumptions but also entirely different domains and fields, like emotions, volition, social processes, existential meanings, and other contexts.

The field of adult cognitive research is in an interesting state; it is simultaneously fragmented but also convergent. We are not dealing with a monolithic common structure here, but a phenomenon that at the moment seems multidimensional and reaches towards many directions. It is fragmented if we think of the number of models and the imaginative power of the scholars working in the field, considering how they have labelled all the various new stages and phenomena of development. This could easily create an impression of conceptual confusion. Although the models are abundant, they all aim at outlining this same phenomenon: in many cases only the conceptual expressions differ from each other.

Adult integrative thinking seems to require an understanding of the multiplicity and plurality of viewpoints, opinions, explanations and domains and also, on the other hand, attempts at reconciling this multiplicity by an integrative approach. It is disputable, however, how justifiable it is to talk about adult integrative thinking as a qualitative category or stage of its own. It is namely possible to argue that integrative thinking develops or progresses from youth to adulthood and up to old age. Thus, it might comprise a continual, gradual progression or a "lifespan learning curve" of integration, with its peak in adulthood and older age – a tempting topic for further research also with respect to wisdom.

This book discusses several interconnected, closely linked domains of adult cognitive development and learning. The book has been edited with a particular observation in mind: scholars from different fields discuss various phenomena which seem to have, at least implicitly, resemblances and features in common across different domains. Hence, we can find analogies or Wittgensteinian "family resemblances" (Wennerberg, 1967) between different traditions pertaining to developmental psychology, learning and wisdom research. For example, discussion about neo-Piagetian concepts like adult integrative thinking, and on the other hand, in research concerning the development of expertise, can feature largely similar arguments (see Chapter 10). Some system theories have obvious links to adult cognitive development theorisation as well (Chapter 12). Furthermore, the study of wisdom seems to have some overlapping features and common elements with both adult development and learning research.

The articles written for this edition are selected with the criterion that they give, at least partly, a multidimensional and thereby a holistic view on the complex phenomena. It is understandable however, that the book concentrates on some major theoretical constructs only, given the limited space and also the fact that all authors of this book share the same national background (Kallio, 2016b), which may be considered a limitation in the global perspective. Further discussion and debate are thus necessary in the future.

Note

1 The article is a modified version of an earlier article by Kallio (2016a).

References

Alexander, C. N., & Langer, E. J. (Eds.). (1990). *Higher stages of human development: Perspectives on adult growth.* New York, NY: Oxford University Press.

Arlin, P. K. (1993). Wisdom and expertise in teaching: An integration of perspectives. *Learning and Individual Differences, 5*(4), 341–349. doi:10.1016/1041-6080(93)90017-M

Asadi, S., Khorshidi, R., & Glück, J. (2019). Iranian children's knowledge about wisdom. *Cognitive Development, 52*, 100814. doi:10.1016/j.cogdev.2019.100814

Assmann, A. (1994). Wholesome knowledge: Concepts of wisdom in a historical and cross-cultural perspective. In D. L. Featherman, R. M. Lerner, & M. Perlmutter (Eds.), *Lifespan development and behavior* (Vol. 12, pp. 187–224). Hillsdale, NJ: Erlbaum.

Baltes, P. B., & Staudinger, U. M. (2000). Wisdom: A metaheuristic (pragmatic) to orchestrate mind and virtue toward excellence. *American Psychologist, 55*(1), 122–136.

Barrouillet, P., & Gauffroy, C. (Eds.). (2013). *The development of thinking and reasoning*. London, England: Psychology Press.

Basseches, M. (1984). *Dialectical thinking and adult development* (Publications for the advancement of theory and history in psychology No. 3). Norwood, NJ: Ablex.

Bassett, C. (2005). Wisdom in three acts: Using transformative learning to teach for wisdom. In D. Vlosak, G. Kielbaso, & J. Radford (Eds.), *Appreciating the best of what is: Envisioning what could be: The proceedings of the sixth international conference on transformative learning* (pp. 29–34). East Lansing, MI: Michigan State University & Grand Rapids Community College.

Becker, K. (2005). Individual and organisational unlearning: Directions for future research. *International Journal of Organisational Behaviour, 9*(7), 659–670.

Beilin, H. (1992). Piaget's enduring contribution to developmental psychology. *Developmental Psychology, 28*(2), 191–204.

Brainerd, C. J. (1978). *Piaget's theory of intelligence*. Englewood Cliff, NJ: Prentice Hall.

Burrow, J. A. (1986). *The ages of man: A study in medieval writing and thought*. Oxford, England: Clarendon Press.

Cavanaugh, J. C., & Blanchard-Fields, F. (2014). *Adult development and aging* (7th ed.). Belmont, CA: Cengage Learning.

Chi, M. T. H., Glaser, R., & Farr, M. J. (Eds.). (2014). *The nature of expertise*. New York, NY: Psychology Press. doi: 10.4324/9781315799681 2014.

Choi, I., Koo, M., & Choi, J. A. (2007). Individual differences in analytic versus holistic thinking. *Personality and Social Psychology Bulletin, 33*(5), 691–705.

Cognition. (2019a). In *Lexico*. Powered by Oxford. Retrieved from www.lexico.com/en/definition/cognition

Cognition. (2019b). In *Online Etymology Dictionary*. Retrieved from www.etymonline.com/word/cognition

Commons, M. L., & Kjorlien, O. A. (2016). The meta-cross-paradigmatic order and stage 16. *Behavioral Development Bulletin, 21*(2), 154–164.

Compton, W. C., & Hoffman, E. (2013). *Positive psychology: The science of happiness and flourishing* (2nd ed.). Belmont, CA: Wadsworth, Cengage Learning.

Curnow, T. (1999). *Wisdom, intuition and ethics* (Avebury series in philosophy). Aldershot, England: Ashgate.

Curnow, T. (2015). *Wisdom: A history*. London, England: Reaktion Books.

Develop. (2019). In *Lexico*. Powered by Oxford. Retrieved from www.lexico.com/en/definition/develop

Dux, G. (2011). *Historico-genetic theory of culture: On the processual logic of cultural change* (N. Solomon, Trans.) (Sociology). Bielefeld, Germany: Transcript.

Edelstein, W., & Noam, G. (1982). Regulatory structures of the self and 'postformal' stages in adulthood. *Human Development, 25*(6), 407–422.

Erikson, E. H. (Ed.). (1978). *Adulthood*. New York, NY: Norton.

Erikson, E. H., & Erikson, J. M. (1998). *The life cycle completed (Extended version)*. New York, NY: WW Norton & Company.

Freud, S. (1989). *The psychopathology of everyday life* (J. Strachey Ed. & Trans.) (Standard edition). New York, NY: Norton.

Gadamer, H.-G. (2008). *Philosophical hermeneutics* (D. E. Linge, Ed. & Trans.) (2nd ed.). Berkeley, CA: University of California Press.

Gidley, J. M. (2016). *Postformal education: A philosophy for complex futures* (Critical studies of education, Vol. 3). Cham, Switzerland: Springer.

Gilligan, C. (1993). *In a different voice: Psychological theory and women's development.* Cambridge, MA: Harvard University Press.

Grossmann, I. (2017). Wisdom in context. *Perspectives on Psychological Science, 12*(2), 233–257.

Gurba, E. (2005). On the specific character of adult thought: Controversies over post-formal operations. *Polish Psychological Bulletin, 36*(3), 175–185.

Helskog, G. H. (2019). *Philosophising the dialogos way towards wisdom in education: Between critical thinking and spiritual contemplation.* London, England: Routledge.

Henderson, G., & Williams, D. C. (Eds.). (2001). *Unending conversations: New writings by and about Kenneth Burke* (Rhetorical philosophy and theory). Carbondale, IL: Southern Illinois University Press.

Hoare, C. (Ed.). (2011). *The Oxford handbook of reciprocal adult development and learning* (2nd ed.). New York, NY: Oxford University Press.

Hussey, T. (2002). Thinking about change. *Nursing Philosophy, 3*(2), 104–113. Modified version 2009, retrieved from https://onlinelibrary.wiley.com/doi/full/10.1046/j.1466-769X.2002.00096.x

Illeris, K. (Ed.). (2009). *Contemporary theories of learning: Learning theorists ... in their own words.* London, England: Routledge.

Inhelder, B., & Piaget, J. (1958). *The growth of logical thinking from childhood to adolescence: An essay on the construction of formal operational structures* (A. Parsons & S. Milgram, Trans.). New York, NY: Basic Books.

Integrate. (2019). In *Lexico.* Powered by Oxford. Retrieved from www.lexico.com/en/definition/integrate

Integration. (2019). In *Merriam-Webster Dictionary.* Retrieved from www.merriam-webster.com/dictionary/integration

Jung, C. G. (1991). *The archetypes and the collective unconscious* (R. F. Hull, Trans.) (The collected works of C. G. Jung, 9:1, 2nd ed.). London, England: Routledge.

Kallio, E. (1998). *Training of students' scientific reasoning skills* (Doctoral dissertation, University of Jyväskylä, Department of Psychology, Jyväskylä, Finland).

Kallio, E. (2001). Reflections on the modern mass university and the question of the autonomy of thinking. In J. Välimaa (Ed.), *Finnish higher education in transition: Perspectives on massification and globalisation* (pp. 73–90). Jyväskylä, Finland: University of Jyväskylä, Finnish Institute for Educational Research.

Kallio, E. (2011). Integrative thinking is the key: An evaluation of current research into the development of adult thinking. *Theory & Psychology, 21*(6), 785–801.

Kallio, E. (2015). From causal thinking to wisdom and spirituality: Some perspectives on a growing research field in adult (cognitive) development. *Approaching Religion, 5*(2), 27–41. doi:10.30664/ar.67572

Kallio, E. (2016a). Aikuisuuden ajattelun kehityksen laaja kenttä: Perusteita ja avoimia kysymyksiä [The broad field of adult cognitive development: Premises and open questions]. In E. Kallio (Ed.), *Ajattelun kehitys aikuisuudessa: Kohti moninäkökulmaisuutta [The development of thinking in adulthood: Towards multiperspective thinking]* (Research in Educational Sciences No. 71, pp. 15–55). Helsinki, Finland: The Finnish Educational Research Association.

Kallio, E. (Ed.). (2016b). *Ajattelun kehitys aikuisuudessa: Kohti moninäkökulmaisuutta* [The Development of thinking in adulthood: Towards multiperspective thinking] (Research in Educational Sciences No. 71). Helsinki, Finland: The Finnish Educational Research Association.

Kallio, E., & Marchand, H. (2012). An overview of the concepts of change and development: From the premodern to modern era. In P. Tynjälä, M.-L. Stenström, & M. Saarnivaara (Eds.), *Transitions and transformations in learning and education* (pp. 21–50). Dordrecht, the Netherlands: Springer.

Kamppinen, M., & Jakonen, J. P. (2015). Systems thinking, spirituality and Ken Wilber: Beyond New Age. *Approaching Religion, 5*(2), 3–14.

Kincheloe, J., & Steinberg, S. (1993). A tentative description of post-formal thinking: The critical confrontation with cognitive theory. *Harvard Educational Review, 63*(3), 296–321.

Kincheloe, J. L., Hayes, K., Steinberg, S. R., & Tobin, K. (2011). *Key works in critical pedagogy* (Bold Visions in Educational Research, Vol. 32). Rotterdam, the Netherlands: Sense.

Kleineberg, M. (2017). Integrative levels. *Knowledge Organization, 44*(5), 349–379. Retrieved from www.isko.org/cyclo/integrative_levels

Kohlberg, L. (1984). *The psychology of moral development: The nature and validity of moral stages* (Essays on moral development, Vol. 2). San Francisco, CA: Harper & Row.

Kohler, A. (2010). To think human out of the machine paradigm. Homo Ex Machina. *Integrative Psychological and Behavioral Science, 44*(1), 39–57.

Kramer, D. A. (1983). Post-formal operations? A need for further conceptualization. *Human Development, 26*(2), 91–105.

Kramer, D. A. (2003). The ontogeny of wisdom in its variations. In J. Demick & C. Andreoletti (Eds.), *Handbook of adult development* (The Plenum series in adult development and aging, pp. 131–151). New York, NY: Kluwer Academic/Plenum.

Kuhn, T. S. (1962). *The structure of scientific revolutions* (International encyclopedia of unified science 2, 2). Chicago, IL: University of Chicago Press.

Kunzmann, U. (2004). Approaches to a good life: The emotional-motivational side to wisdom. In P. A. Linley & S. Joseph (Eds.), *Positive psychology in practice* (pp. 504–517). Hoboken, NJ: Wiley.

Labouvie-Vief, G. (2015). *Integrating emotions and cognition throughout the lifespan*. New York, NY: Springer.

Laslett, P. (1994). The third age, the fourth age and the future. *Ageing & Society, 14*(3), 436–447.

Learning. (2019). In *Online Etymology Dictionary*. Retrieved from www.etymonline.com/word/learning

Lerner, R. M. (2018). *Concepts and theories of human development* (4th ed.). New York, NY: Routledge.

Lerner, R. M., & Overton, W. F. (2008). Exemplifying the integrations of the relational developmental system: Synthesizing theory, research, and application to promote positive development and social justice. *Journal of Adolescent Research, 23*(3), 245–255.

Lourenço, O. M. (2016). Developmental stages, Piagetian stages in particular: A critical review. *New Ideas in Psychology, 40*(Part B), 123–137.

Lovejoy, A. O. (1936). *The great chain of being: A study of the history of an idea*. New York, NY: Harper.

Malott, C. S. (2011) *Critical pedagogy and cognition: An introduction to a postformal educational psychology* (Explorations of Educational Purpose, Vol. 15). Dordrecht, the Netherlands: Springer Netherlands.

Malpas, J. (2018) Hans-Georg Gadamer. In E. N. Zalta (Ed.), *The Stanford encyclopedia of philosophy* (Fall 2018 ed.). Retrieved from https://plato.stanford.edu/archives/fall2018/entries/gadamer/

Marchand, H. (2001). Some reflections on post-formal thought. *The Genetic Epistemologist*, *29*(3), 2–9. Retrieved from www.dareassociation.org/documents/Some%20Reflections%20on%20Postformal%20Thought.html

Mascolo, M. F., & Kallio, E. (2019). Beyond free will: The embodied emergence of conscious agency. *Philosophical Psychology*, *32*(4), 437–462.

Mascolo, M. F., & Kallio, E. (2020). The phenomenology of between: An intersubjective epistemology for psychological science. *Journal of Constructivistic Psychology*, *33*(1), 1–28.

Misiak, H., & Sexton, V. S. (1973). *Phenomenological, existential and humanistic psychologies: A historical survey*. New York, NY: Grune & Stratton.

Mortensen, C. (2016). Change and inconsistency. In E. N. Zalta (Ed.), *The Stanford encyclopedia of philosophy* (Winter 2016 ed.). Retrieved from https://plato.stanford.edu/archives/win2016/entries/change/

Moshman, D. (2013). Epistemic cognition and development. In P. Barrouillet & C. Gauffroy (Eds.), *The development of thinking and reasoning* (pp. 13–33). London, England: Psychology Press.

Ontology. (2019). In *Merriam-Webster Dictionary*. Retrieved from www.merriam-webster.com/dictionary/ontology

Overton, W. F. (2006). Developmental psychology: Philosophy, concepts, methodology. In W. Damon & R.M. Lerner (Eds.), *Handbook of child psychology*. Vol. 1 R. M. Lerner (Ed.), Theoretical models of human development. (6th ed., pp. 18–88). New York, NY: Wiley.

Overton, W. F. (2010). Life-span development: Concepts and issues. In W. F. Overton & R. M. Lerner (Eds.), *The handbook of life-span development: Cognition, biology, and methods* (Vol. 1, pp. 1–29). Hoboken, NJ: Wiley.

Palmer, R. E. (1969). *Hermeneutics: Interpretation theory in Schleiermacher, Dilthey, Heidegger and Gadamer* (Northwestern University studies in phenomenology and existential). Evanston, IL: Northwestern University Press.

Perry, W. G., Jr. (1999). *Forms of intellectual and ethical development in the college years: A scheme* (Jossey-Bass higher and adult education series). San Francisco, CA: Jossey-Bass.

Perttula, J., & Kallio, E. (1996). Postformaali ajattelu ja henkinen tajunnallisina toimintatapoina [Postformal thinking and mental awareness as cognitive practices]. *Psykologia*, *31*(3), 164–173.

Peters, M. A. (2007). Kinds of thinking, styles of reasoning. *Educational Philosophy and Theory*, *39*(4), 350–363.

Piaget, J. (1972). Intellectual evolution from adolescence to adulthood. *Human Development*, *15*(1), 1–12.

Piaget, J., Garcia, R. V., Garcia, R., & Lara, J. (1989). *Psychogenesis and the history of science*. New York, NY: Columbia University Press.

Piaget, J., & Inhelder, B. (1969). *The psychology of the child* (H. Weaver, Trans.). London, England: Routledge.

Płóciennik, E. (2018). Children's creativity as a manifestation and predictor of their wisdom. *Thinking Skills and Creativity*, *28*, 14–20.

Psyche. (2019a). In *Lexico*. Powered by Oxford. Retrieved from www.lexico.com/en/definition/psyche

Psyche. (2019b). In *Online etymology dictionary*. Retrieved from www.etymonline.com/word/psyche

Ptolemy, C. (1940). *Tetrabiblos* (F. E. Robbins, Ed. & Trans.) (Loeb classical library No. 435). Cambridge, MA: Harvard University Press. (Original work published ca. 100–170).

Resnick, L. B. (1991). Shared cognition: Thinking as social practice. In L. B. Resnick, J. M. Levine, & S. D. Teasley (Eds.), *Perspectives on socially shared cognition* (pp. 1–20). Washington, DC: American Psychological Association.

Robinson, O. (2013). *Development through adulthood: An integrative sourcebook*. Basingstoke, England: Palgrave Macmillan.

Schaie, K. W., & Zanjani, F. A. (2006). Intellectual development across adulthood. In C. Hoare (Ed.), *Handbook of adult development and learning* (pp. 99–122). New York, NY: Oxford University Press.

Schraw, G., Dunkle, M. E., & Bendixen, L. D. (1995). Cognitive processes in well-defined and ill-defined problem solving. *Applied Cognitive Psychology, 9*(6), 523–538.

Sears, E. (1986). *The ages of man: Medieval interpretations of the life cycle*. Princeton, NJ: Princeton University Press.

Settersten, R. A. (2003). Age structuring and the rhythm of the life course. In J. T. Mortimer & M. J. Shanahan (Eds.), *Handbook of the life course* (Handbooks of sociology and social research, pp. 81–98). New York, NY: Springer.

Showers, C. (1992). Evaluatively integrative thinking about characteristics of the self. *Personality and Social Psychology Bulletin, 18*(6), 719–729.

Sinnott, J. D. (1998). *The development of logic in adulthood: Postformal thought and its applications* (The Plenum series in adult development age aging). New York, NY: Plenum Press.

Smith, S. (2019). Wisdom as an embodied and embedded process. In G. M. Cseh (Ed.), *5th Annual Applied Positive Psychology Symposium: Proceedings of Presented Papers* (pp. 26–50). Buckinghamshire, England: Bucks New University. Retrieved from https://bucks. repository.guildhe.ac.uk/17819/1/17819_Cseh_G_Smith_M_Sims_C__Worth_P. pdf#page=27

Staudinger, U. M., & Glück, J. (2011). Psychological wisdom research: Commonalities and differences in a growing field. *Annual Review of Psychology, 62*, 215–241.

Sternberg, R. J. (2013). Personal wisdom in the balance. In M. Ferrari & N. M. Weststrate (Eds.), *The scientific study of personal wisdom: From contemplative traditions to neuroscience* (pp. 53–74). Dordrecht, the Netherlands: Springer.

Sternberg, R. J., & Funke, J. (Eds.). (2019). *The psychology of human thought: An introduction.* Retrieved from www.psychologie.uni-heidelberg.de/ae/allg/mitarb/jf/IPHT_Online.pdf

Sternberg, R. J., & Glück, J. (Eds.). (2019). *The Cambridge handbook of wisdom*. New York, NY: Cambridge University Press.

Suedfeld, P., & Leighton, D. C. (2002). Early communications in the war against terrorism: An integrative complexity analysis. *Political Psychology, 23*(3), 585–599.

Swartwood, J., & Tiberius, V. (2019). Philosophical foundations of wisdom. In R. J. Sternberg & J. Glück (Eds.), *The Cambridge handbook of wisdom* (pp. 10–39). New York, NY: Cambridge University Press.

Takahashi, M., & Bordia, P. (2000). The concept of wisdom: A cross-cultural comparison. *International Journal of Psychology, 35*(1), 1–9. doi:10.1080/002075900399475

Teo, T. (2010). Ontology and scientific explanation: Pluralism as an *a priori* condition of psychology. *New Ideas in Psychology, 28*(2), 235–243.

von Wright, G. H. (2004). *Explanation and understanding* (Cornell classics in philosophy). Ithaca, NY: Cornell University Press.

Walsh, R. (2015). What is wisdom? Cross-cultural and cross-disciplinary syntheses. *Review of General Psychology, 19*(3), 278–293.

Wennerberg, H. (1967). The concept of family resemblance in Wittgenstein's later philosophy. *Theoria, 33*(2), 107–132.

Wilber, K. (2001). *A brief history of everything* (2nd ed.). Dublin, Ireland: Gateway.

Wozniak, R. H., & Fischer, K. W. (Eds.). (1993). *Development in context: Acting and thinking in specific environments* (The Jean Piaget symposium series). Hillsdale, NJ: Erlbaum.

Wu, P.-L., & Chiou, W.-B. (2008). *Postformal thinking and creativity among late adolescents: A post-Piagetian approach. Adolescence, 43*(170), 237–251.

Yang, S.-Y. (2008). A process view of wisdom. *Journal of Adult Development, 15*(2), 62–75.

Zerubavel, E. (1989). *The seven day circle: The history and meaning of the week.* Chicago, IL: University of Chicago Press.

3

INTEGRATING EPISTEMIC KNOWLEDGE AND LOGICAL REASONING SKILLS IN ADULT COGNITIVE DEVELOPMENT[1]

Hannele Seppälä, Sari Lindblom-Ylänne, and Eeva K. Kallio

Introduction

The aim of this chapter is to present theories of the development of logical reasoning skills and epistemological beliefs. Both logical reasoning skills and epistemological beliefs are needed in understanding and evaluating knowledge in the different situations of problem solving and decision-making in the everyday life of highly complex societies and also in advanced expertise work. In this chapter the historical basis and the main lines of research traditions of logical reasoning and epistemic knowledge will be presented.

The traditions of developmental psychological models, including logical reasoning and epistemological beliefs, provide a framework for understanding adult cognitive development. Beside the general research tradition of adult cognition these two traditions represent the main lines of research in the area of adult thinking (see Kallio, 2011). Inhelder's and Piaget's (1958) theory on the development of logical thinking is one of the oldest frameworks for studying the development of logical reasoning. The position of Inhelder's and Piaget's theory has been very significant in the history of developmental psychology (e.g., Müller, Ten Eycke, & Baker, 2015; see also Chapter 2) and has also had a strong impact on neo-Piagetian theories (Hoare, 2011). In this article the focus is on causal reasoning at the stage of formal operations, but the aim is to also present later development of the research and give an overview of the research focused on reasoning skills from the 1970s until the present time. This focus is natural, as Piaget and Inhelder originally claimed that formal reasoning is the stage which is available from teenagers to adulthood, and there is no further development in it. During the last decades the most prominent research area has been the research of epistemic knowledge. The most important foundation of this tradition is Perry's (1970) theory of the forms of students' intellectual and ethical development.

Development of reasoning skills

The research tradition of reasoning skills includes three different research approaches that have been developed since the 1950s up till today (see Table 3.1). Reasoning skills have been studied within developmental psychology, educational psychology, and science education (see e.g., Lawson, 2004; Lawson, Banks, & Logvin, 2007). Inhelder's and Piaget's (1958) theory on the development of logical thinking and their attempt to define the key elements in the reasoning process have strongly influenced later research. Inhelder's and Piaget's work formed the first research approach and some scholars, for example Shayer and colleagues (Adey & Shayer, 1994), followed this original theory without formulating or adding new elements to it. The formal operations and hypothetico-deductive causal reasoning processes are the main features of this approach. Later, some scholars extended Inhelder's and Piaget's model and stage of formal operations with additional skills and a broader variation of thinking skills at the stage of formal operations that are not included in the original Piagetian model (see Chapter 2). One example of this approach is the research of metacognitive awareness concerning the thinking processes (e.g., Demetriou & Efklides, 1985).

Also the third approach, which has been developed during the 1980s, 1990s and in the beginning of this millennium, builds more or less on Piaget's theory premises (e.g., Commons & Richards, 1984; Fischer, 1980; King & Kitchener, 2002; Lawson, 2004; Lawson et al., 2007). However, this approach provides logical development models constructed by extending the Piagetian model along the vertical dimension by adding

TABLE 3.1 The research tradition of reasoning skills and the central features of approaches within this tradition (see Seppälä, 2013). Printed with permission. Copyright The Finnish Educational Research Association

	Research tradition of reasoning skills		
	Approaches		
	Causal reasoning at the stage of formal operations (Piaget's theory).	Models extending the Piagetian model with additional skills.	Models of postformal thinking.
Central features of the approach	Hypothetico-deductive causal reasoning process. Ability to test hypothesis experimentally.	Models include a broader variation of thinking skills, including metacognitive awareness of thinking. The level of skills corresponds the stage of formal operations.	Cognitive operations which are logically more complex and challenging than formal operations. Models emphasise contextuality of thinking and acceptance and integration of various truth-claims.

higher cognitive stages. These models are called "postformal operations," or more vaguely just post-Piagetian models. A lot of discussion and also metatheoretical analyses have been conducted in order to show if these cognitive operations described in the new models (e.g., Commons, Gane-McCalla, Barker, & Li, 2014; Commons & Richards, 1984; Fischer, Yan, & Stewart, 2003; Lawson, 2004; Lawson et al., 2007) represent well-developed operations of formal operational thinking. Or is it really possible to speak about a new stage of cognitive development?

Metatheoretical analyses (e.g., Hoare, 2006; Kallio, 2011; Kramer, 1983; Marchand, 2001) have revealed that the use of the concepts and labels describing the higher stages of adult development are not systematic and more conceptual analysis on the characteristics of these postformal models would be needed. In addition, metatheoretical synthesis has indicated that most of the so-called post-formal models share a similar three-phase assumption of development following Perry's model (absolutism, relativism, and dialectical thinking) (Kallio, 2015; Kramer, 1983; Marchand, 2001). Furthermore, Kallio (2015) has suggested that the common feature across the models claimed to be postformal could also be interpreted and replaced with the term of integrative thinking – and the models of postformal thinking can be seen as a combination of the two main research traditions drawing on the ideas of Piaget and Perry.

The Piagetian theory has faced a lot of criticism concerning the possibilities of the theory taking into account various intermediate variables of the social compo-nents and context (see Kallio, 2015). The acceptance and integration of various, and at times incompatible truths, which are highly dependent upon the context, are dis-tinctive characteristics of adult thought according to the theorists of postformal dia-lectical thought (Kramer, 1983; Marchand, 2001). They claim that the development consists of continuous and constant changes in which contradictions are the motor of advances. Thus, the central feature of adult thinking in the models of postformal thinking is the relativistic thought and ability to understand complex relationships with fuzzy logic and ill-defined wicked problems, with no clear-cut objective solu-tion (Kitchener, King, & DeLuca, 2006; Kramer, 1983). Knowledge formation in adulthood emphasizes the integration of subjectivity and objectivity.

Reasoning at the level of formal operations

The stage of formal operational thought provides the individual with the capacity to handle hypothetical and theoretical possibilities and reason in terms of verbally stated hypotheses. To reason hypothetically and to deduce the consequences that the hypotheses necessarily imply is a formal reasoning process. Hypothetico-deductive reasoning, or the whole causal reasoning process, is not possible before the formal operational development stage is reached (Inhelder & Piaget, 1958). Hypothetico-deductive reasoning is a crucial part of many problem-solving situations. Research results have indicated that the problem-solving process, which involves identifying an appropriate question as the object of investigation and the ability to generate one or more hypotheses, is a challenging one, but also contributes significantly to individuals' success (Kuhn, Iordanou, Pease, & Wirkala, 2008). Later in the reasoning process, during the phase of analyzing and establishing conclusions, cognitive abilities are needed to evaluate, compare, and combine different claims and solutions (e.g., such reasoning patterns as probabilistic, proportional, and correlational reasoning) (Lawson, 2004).

Causal reasoning activates relevant sub-processes: 1) exclusion and control of variables, 2) constructing and using formal models, and 3) logical reasoning (Adey & Shayer, 1994). The key element in the causal reasoning is the construction of experiments, which means that one chooses pairs of experiments for further analysis. This reasoning pattern is an important part of advanced "variable-centered reasoning" and it requires the ability to hold several independent variables and one dependent variable in mind, and consider the possible effects of each independent variable on the dependent variable. This schema of "exclusion and control of variables" includes the exclusion of irrelevant variables that requires the identification of variables that do not have any effect. The schema plays an important role in causal reasoning, especially in the natural sciences, but also implicitly or explicitly in all experiments or critical investigations in social sciences as well (Adey & Shayer, 1994). Its importance is in its ability to isolate the factors which may possibly have an effect on an event, to consider each of them in turn and all together, and to make rational assessment of their relative contributions to the effect (Adey & Shayer, 1994). A precondition for the schema which controls the variables is an understanding of combinatorial variables. It is important to be able to make a logical deduction of the role of every variable based on the experiments and to demonstrate if a certain factor is a causal agent, and which other variables have no effect (Inhelder & Piaget, 1958).

An example of a natural-scientific question measuring formal thinking is the Pendulum question (Figure 3.1; see Kallio, 2016). The question demonstrates

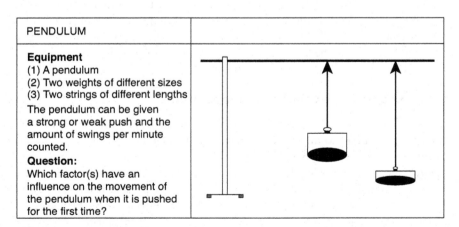

PENDULUM	
Equipment (1) A pendulum (2) Two weights of different sizes (3) Two strings of different lengths The pendulum can be given a strong or weak push and the amount of swings per minute counted. **Question:** Which factor(s) have an influence on the movement of the pendulum when it is pushed for the first time?	

FIGURE 3.1 Pendulum task in formal operational thinking research (Kallio, 2016; see Inhelder & Piaget, 1958; Kallio, 1998; Seppälä, 2013). Printed with permission. Copyright The Finnish Educational Research Association

that, content-wise, the originally used methods are natural-scientific in nature. The research subjects have to assess the influence of three different variables on the fast or slow movement of the pendulum: the length of the string, the size of the weights, and the force of the push given to the weights. The question is which variables have an effect on the pendulum's measured movement within a certain period of time. There is only one correct answer, which means that this type of question is a closed, well-defined problem.

Furthermore, the ability to construct and use formal models is an important element in reasoning. The model that has to be imagined has different parts which move and hold the same relationships to one another. A challenge of the formal model is that their construction requires mental manipulation of many variables together (Adey & Shayer, 1994). Logical reasoning involves the ability to analyze the combinatorial relations present in the information given. The logical operations – implication and the denial of implication – are examples of logical reasoning (Adey & Shayer, 1994).

According to Piaget (1976), a developmental change occurs when contradictory and different experiences that are in contrast to already-formed ways of action are confronted. The process is called reflective abstraction and it occurs when an individual is prompted by contradictory feedback (in the physical environment or in social interaction with other people) and the result is that the individual gains declarative knowledge and becomes more aware and conscious of this knowledge. According to Piaget (1972), the development of thinking and the differences between individuals depend on the social environment, acquired experience, and intellectual stimulation besides the aptitudes, personal interest areas, and professional specializations of the individuals. It is argued that there are great differences between individuals in the skills of formal thought depending on these factors.

Based on current research knowledge, it seems that, unlike Piaget assumed, not everyone can fully master formal thinking in adulthood. For example, not all Finnish adolescents and young adults master it extensively, not even the ones studying at a higher education institute (Hautamäki, 1983; Kallio, 1998; Seppälä, 2013). Research findings from the last decades indicate that even among university students only 60–80% reach the stage of formal operational thinking (see Kallio, 1998; Seppälä, 2013, 2016; Shibley, Milakofsky, Bender, & Patterson, 2003).

According to Dasen (1994), lower-level concrete operational thinking seems to be found across cultures, for example, among Australian aboriginal and Inuit (Eskimo) children. He favors Piaget's claim that the developmental stages are universal. Empirical studies conducted mainly at the end of the 20th century however, indicated that the formal stage is not a universal developmental stage in all cultures (Feldman, 2004). There has not been much research on adults' formal thinking lately, and it has been mostly connected to natural-scientific thinking abilities and academic success (Haider, 2016), and with lower-age subjects (e.g., Thuneberg, Hautamäki, & Hotulainen, 2015). The latest important development is connected to the creation and usage of standardized questionnaires related to formal thinking skills (Adey & Shayer, 1994; Kuhn et al., 2008; Seppälä, 2013).

Development of epistemic knowledge

In order to get a more holistic view on adult thinking and reasoning, we also need to have an understanding of the development of epistemic knowledge: how individuals develop conceptions of knowledge and knowing, and how these are utilized in understanding the reality. The research tradition on epistemological beliefs contributes to these issues and is interested in the definition of knowledge; how knowledge is constructed, how knowledge is evaluated, where it resides, and how knowledge occurs (Hofer, 2002).

Epistemological beliefs are commonly considered to be the lens through which individuals interpret information, set standards, and decide on an appropriate course of action (Hofer & Pintrich, 2002; see also Limón, 2006). Research references include a wide variety of terms, such as epistemic positions (Perry, 1968), epistemic cognition (King & Kitchener, 2002), epistemological reflection (Baxter Magolda, 1992), epistemological understanding (Kuhn, Cheney, & Weinstock, 2000), and epistemological thinking (Kuhn & Weinstock, 2002). Kaartinen-Koutaniemi and Lindblom-Ylänne (2008) and Seppälä (2013) distinguish two different directions for this tradition: 1) the study of epistemological notions, i.e., related to knowledge, beliefs, and 2) the study of epistemological and reflective thinking. There are numerous classifications in the field, and at least three different approaches for epistemological beliefs and how they are studied: developmental, systematic/structural, and resource point of view (Limón, 2006; see also Moshman, 2013, who distinguishes seven different areas for the study of epistemic cognition, cf. Greene, Torney-Purta, & Azevedo, 2010).

In this chapter two approaches under the research tradition of epistemological beliefs are presented: the developmental approach and the epistemological resources approach.

Developmental approach

The developmental approach is widely adopted in epistemological research (Limón, 2006). It focuses on explaining developmental changes in epistemological beliefs and seeks to describe the developmental levels through which an individual progresses. From the historical point of view the most significant name in the field of epistemological development, as well as being a representative of developmental theorists, is William Perry (1968). He was the first to redefine the way cognition develops, by focusing on the development of epistemological assumptions. Perry (1970) examined college students' paths from adolescence to adulthood by interviewing students over their four years at college. Perry was interested in how the students perceived the world around them. He aimed at "mapping development in the forms of seeing, knowing and caring" (Perry, 1970, p. ix).

Perry and his research group conducted interviews at the end of each study year "in as open-ended way as possible" (Perry, 1970, p. 7) to capture the students' experiences. On the basis of the interview data, Perry detected nine positions of development, which are explained in Table 3.2. These nine positions of development cover

TABLE 3.2 Perry's (1970) Developmental Scheme. Printed with permission. Copyright The Finnish Educational Research Association

Position	Description
PART I: THE MODIFYING OF DUALISM	In Part I an absolutistic right-wrong outlook begins to make room to multiplicity, a simple form of pluralism.
1. Basic duality	The student sees the world in polar terms of "we-right-good vs. other-wrong-bad" (p. 9). There are right answers for everything, and these are known to those in authority, whose role is to teach the right answers to the students. The students' role is to learn the right answers.
2. Multiplicity pre-legitimate	The student perceives diversity of opinion and uncertainty, and, and considers them as unnecessary confusion in poorly qualified authorities. Multiplicity of opinion is experienced as annoying, but *some* complexity and uncertainty is allowed as long as it is temporary.
3. Multiplicity subordinate	The student accepts diversity and uncertainty as legitimate, but still considers them as temporary in areas where authority has not yet found the right answers. Trust in authority is not threatened.
PART II: THE REALISING OF RELATIVISM	The student accepts the diversity of opinions and transforms the simple pluralism into contextual relativism. The student needs to follow his or her inner voice, not authority.
4. Multiplicity correlate or relativism subordinate	This position consists of two alternative views, which are developmentally equivalent. In Multiplicity-Correlate path the student feels that anyone has a right to his or her own opinion, even if this view is opposite to that of the authority. The majority of the students follow the second Relativism-Subordinate path to relativism in which multiplicity is not put against authority. This path allows the discovery of relativism by comparing different approaches to a problem and starting to develop one's own opinion.
5. Relativism correlate, competing, or diffuse	Both Relativism Correlate and Relativism Competing contain unresolved elements of transition. Relativism Diffuse describes the completed revolution: the student perceives all knowledge and values as contextual and relativistic. Seeing, thinking, knowing, and valuing take place in a context.
6. Commitment foreseen	The student understands the necessity of orienting him- or herself in a relativistic world through personal commitment. The student apprehends the implications

(Continued)

TABLE 3.2 (Cont.)

Position	Description
	of personal choice in a world (s)he assumes to be relativistic. Commitment is foreseen as the resolution of the problems of relativism, but it has not yet been experienced.
PART III: THE EVOLVING OF COMMITMENTS	Integration of knowledge from authority with own knowledge and experiences through analysis, comparing, and evaluation. The development in Part III is more qualitative than structural.
7. Initial commitment	The student makes an initial commitment in some major areas, such as disciplinary or professional choices.
8. Orientation in implications of commitment	The student experiences the implications of commitment and explores the subjective issues of responsibility.
9. Developing commitments	The student experiences the affirmation of identity among multiple responsibilities and sees commitment as an on-going activity through which (s)he expresses his or her life style.

students' ethical and intellectual development. The development scheme is described in three parts, each comprising three positions.

In any of the nine positions the student may suspend or even reverse the process of development. Thus, also delay, deflection, and regression can occur. Perry (1970) differentiated between three forms of deflection. In temporizing the student may pause his or her development in a position, either by exploring the implications of the position in detail or by hesitating to take the next step. In Retreat the student entrenches him- or herself in the dualistic, absolutistic structures of positions 2 and 3. In Escape the student exploits the opportunity for detachment in positions 4 and 5 to avoid the personal responsibility.

Perry's classification of thinking patterns from absolutism to relativism and to commitment has had a strong impact on the research of adult cognitive development and also, often implicitly, even in wisdom research (Barzilai & Eshet-Alkalai, 2015; Kallio, 2015; see Chapter 2). Examples of the later developmental approaches are Kuhn's (Kuhn et al., 2000; Kuhn & Weinstock, 2002) theory on epistemological thinking, King's and Kitchener's (2002) theory of reflective thinking, and Baxter Magolda's (1992, 2004) model of epistemological reflection. A common element for these developmental models is that the primary task of epistemic development is a progression towards the integration of objectivity and subjectivity. It involves learning to coordinate one's own subjective perceptions and meaning making with the facts about "objective reality" and the knowledge of authorities (Hofer, 2006).

Epistemological resources approach

Beside the developmental approach, the research tradition of epistemological resources underlines that the capacity of thinking is enriched as the individual gains more knowledge and experience with learning (Louca, Elby, Hammer, & Kagey, 2004). Individuals have a mass of epistemological resources available to them, and the context affects what might be evoked (Hofer, 2004a). A distinctive feature of the epistemological resources approach is that belief development will not follow a stage model and ladder path, but rather a web of developmental pathways (Hofer, 2002). The development of personal epistemology is a cyclical process, not linear or stage-like (Hofer, 2005).

The most remarkable theorists within the epistemological resources approach are Barbara Hofer and Paul Pintrich with their theory of personal epistemology (Hofer & Pintrich, 1997). They have argued that the main scopes of epistemic development (personal epistemology) are the nature of knowledge and the process of knowing (Hofer, 2002, 2004b; Hofer & Pintrich, 1997). Their theory also recognizes the multidimensional aspect of beliefs. Epistemic beliefs can be described by four dimensions that can be expressed as a continuum. The dimensions are certainty of knowledge, simplicity of knowledge, source of knowledge, and justification for knowing (Hofer & Pintrich, 1997). Beliefs are organized into "theories," instead of independent beliefs, and they operate at the metacognitive level (Hofer, 2004a; Hofer & Pintrich, 1997). The multidimensional aspect of beliefs has been a significant feature of research for the last 15 years and has been adopted by several researchers (e.g., Buehl & Alexander, 2006; Strømsø, Bråten, & Samuelstuen, 2008).

According to Hofer (2006), individuals hold beliefs about knowledge and knowing that are coherent and congruent across different domains, but also hold beliefs that are affected by and enacted within particular contexts (e.g., variables related to school, such as pedagogical practices, assessment methods, curriculum, teachers' and peers' expectations, and culture). Hofer sees that epistemological beliefs develop from the general to the specific over time and in relation to education and experience (Hofer, 2006).

Connections between the two main approaches to cognitive skills: an example of higher education students

In order to broaden the view on adult thinking, the connections between epistemological beliefs and other cognitive skills have been explored by several researchers. A positive interaction between the development of epistemological beliefs and, for instance, learning strategies, text processing and reading comprehension, mathematical problem solving, and critical thinking has been confirmed (King & Kitchener, 2002; Muis, Bendixen, & Haerle, 2006; Strømsø et al., 2008).

However, research focusing specifically on the connections between epistemic knowledge and the development of logical thinking has been scarce (Seppälä, 2013). One example is Seppälä's (2013) study on higher education students' academic thinking skills, formal operational thinking, and epistemological beliefs.

The research results indicated a connection between the skills of logical thinking and the development of epistemological beliefs. The results showed that the students with higher-level logical thinking skills emphasized more the abilities of knowledge application and logical thinking as key features of academic thinking. Furthermore, it seems that students with good reasoning abilities emphasized more the individual's active role in knowledge construction and in formulating one's own perspectives. These findings suggest that good reasoning abilities reinforce the notion about the individual's own role in knowledge construction, emphasizing the process of justifying knowledge through the use of rules of scientific inquiry. Conversely, sophisticated epistemological beliefs concerning the individual's subjective role may support students' activity in applying their reasoning skills in academic settings.

How to enhance adults' thinking skills?

The aims and expectations of learning in adult and higher education have undergone substantial changes over the last few decades. Especially the mission of higher education which has been diversified along with the changes in society and work life. During their higher education studies, students are expected to develop a wide variety of higher-order skills and competencies to work and to co-operate in the knowledge-intensive society where the role of research and knowledge production as a core element of societal and economic well-being is increased. Also, large international research initiatives have been launched in order to assess and enhance higher education students' thinking skills (e.g., by the OECD[2]).

Expected learning outcomes in today's higher education include research-based expertise and competencies such as understanding the processes of knowledge construction, evaluating the source and validity of information, and applying reasoning skills, i.e., critical thinking skills (e.g., Utriainen, Marttunen, Kallio, & Tynjälä, 2017). In addition, different self-management thinking skills are highlighted in higher-education curricula. The trends of higher education in Europe and also globally indicate that both the scientific higher education tradition and professional higher education tradition have an effect on the current development of higher education degrees. In both of these traditions the growth of professional expertise can be defined in terms of cultural attendance, knowledge acquisition, or producing new knowledge. In both traditions the degree structures and learning pathways are expected to be flexible. Access to adult and higher education as well as opportunities to create individual learning pathways pose a developmental challenge to future education.

One of the most central features of higher education today is its emphasis on student learning, experience, and well-being as a student. Also, in the standards and guidelines for quality assurance in the European higher education area, student-centered learning is pointed out as an important criterion of quality assurance (Standards and guidelines, 2015). According to these criteria, programs should be delivered in a way that encourages students to take an active role in creating the learning process as well as to stimulate students' motivation, self-reflection, and engagement in the learning process (Standards and guidelines, 2015). Understanding higher level thinking as a combination of logical thinking and epistemological beliefs is also in line with the current learning objectives in higher education. While the professions are rapidly changing and working environments are becoming more complex, the nature of knowing is changing as knowledge is increasingly created in a dialogue. Promoting thinking skills is even more important, as it has been noticed that general IQ scores are gradually declining in industrialized countries (Flynn & Shayer, 2018).

In order to promote the development of higher-order thinking in students, special attention should be paid to the learning environment, teaching methods, social inter- action, and the stimulation of cognitive skills (see also Chapter 7). One example of intentional stimulation for epistemological reflection could be, for instance, different dialogical approaches in classroom discussion, such as neo-Socratic dialogue (Helskog, 2019) or Bohmian dialogue (Bohm, 2014). A learning environment that allows stu- dents to discuss, argue, and learn through co-operative methods and project work and to reflect upon their own learning is a significant element in the development of per- sonal epistemology (Hofer, 2006; Kaartinen-Koutaniemi et al., 2008).

In setting the learning objectives, it should also be taken into account that there is a connection between students' logical thinking skills and epistemological beliefs: students with good reasoning abilities tend to put higher emphasis on an individual's active role in knowledge construction (Seppälä, 2013). Attention should also be paid to learning the essence of domain-specific knowledge and how knowledge develops (Hofer, 2006). Therefore, in order to promote the development of advanced thinking skills, the focus should be on the critical evaluation of conflicting knowledge frameworks and on complex problem solving without single solutions, seeking integration, but understanding the limitations of knowledge. The studies should allow learners to doubt and question, and there should be enough time and space for one's own thoughts. Adults should be encouraged to share their views and to develop their thinking in dialogue and co-operation with others.

Notes

1 An earlier and more limited version of this chapter has been presented in Finnish by Seppälä (2016).
2 OECD project: Fostering and assessing students' creative and critical thinking in higher education. www.oecd.org/education/ceri/Fostering-and-assessing-students-cre ative-and-critical-thinking-skills-in-higher-education.pdf

References

Adey, P., & Shayer, M. (1994). *Really raising standards: Cognitive intervention and academic achievement.* London, England: Routledge.

Barzilai, S., & Eshet-Alkalai, Y. (2015). The role of epistemic perspectives in comprehen- sion of multiple author viewpoints. *Learning and Instruction, 36,* 86–103.

Baxter Magolda, M. B. (1992). *Knowing and reasoning in college: Gender-related patterns in stu- dents' intellectual development* (The Jossey-Bass higher and adult education series, The Jossey-Bass social and behavioral science series). San Francisco, CA: Jossey Bass.

Baxter Magolda, M. B. (2004). Evolution of a constructivist conceptualization of epistemological reflection. *Educational Psychologist, 39*(1), 31–42.

Bohm, D. (2014). *On dialogue* (Routledge great minds). London, England: Routledge.

Buehl, M. M., & Alexander, P. A. (2006). Examining the dual nature of epistemological beliefs. *International Journal of Educational Research, 45*(1–2), 28–42.

Commons, M. L., Gane-McCalla, R., Barker, C. D., & Li, E. Y. (2014). The model of hierarchical complexity as a measurement system. *Behavioral Development Bulletin, 19*(3), 9–14.

Commons, M. L., & Richards, F. A. (1984). Applying the general stage model. In M. L. Commons, F. A. Richards, & C. Armon (Eds.), *Beyond formal operations: Late adolescent and adult cognitive development* (pp. 141–157). New York, NY: Praeger.

Dasen, P. R. (1994). Culture and cognitive development from a Piagetian perspective. In W. J. Lonner & R. S. Malpass (Eds.), *Psychology and culture* (pp. 145–149). Boston, MA: Allyn and Bacon.

Demetriou, A., & Efklides, A. (1985). Structure and sequence of formal and postformal thought: General patterns and individual differences. *Child Development, 56*(4), 1062–1091.

Feldman, D. H. (2004). Piaget's stages: The unfinished symphony of cognitive development. *New Ideas in Psychology, 22*(3), 175–231.

Fischer, K., Yan, Z., & Stewart, J. (2003). Adult cognitive development: Dynamics in the developmental web. In J. Valsiner & K. J. Connolly (Eds.), *Handbook of developmental psychology* (pp. 491–516). London, England: SAGE.

Fischer, K. W. (1980). A theory of cognitive development: The control and construction of hierarchies of skills. *Psychological Review, 87*(6), 477–531.

Flynn, J. R., & Shayer, M. (2018). IQ decline and Piaget: Does the rot start at the top? *Intelligence, 66*, 112–121.

Greene, J. A., Torney-Purta, J., & Azevedo, R. (2010). Empirical evidence regarding relations among a model of epistemic and ontological cognition, academic performance, and educational level. *Journal of Educational Psychology, 102*(1), 234–255.

Haider, A. (2016). Students' performance in chemistry in relation to their logical thinking ability. *International Journal of Research, 3*(9), 753–761.

Hautamäki, J. (1983). Aikuisten tieteellisen järkeilyn edellytyksistä [Prerequisities of scientific thinking in adulthood]. *Aikuiskasvatus, 3*(4), 159–161.

Helskog, G. H. (2019). *Philosophising the dialogos way towards wisdom in education: Between critical thinking and spiritual contemplation.* London, England: Routledge.

Hoare, C. (Ed.). (2006). *Handbook of adult development and learning.* New York, NY: Oxford University Press.

Hoare, C. (Ed.). (2011). *The Oxford handbook of reciprocal adult development and learning* (2nd ed.). New York, NY: Oxford University Press.

Hofer, B. K. (2002). Personal epistemology as a psychological and educational construct: An introduction. In B. K. Hofer & P. R. Pintrich (Eds.), *Personal epistemology: The psychology of beliefs about knowledge and knowing* (pp. 3–14). Mahwah, NJ: Erlbaum.

Hofer, B. K. (2004a). Epistemological understanding as a metacognitive process: Thinking aloud during online searching. *Educational Psychologist, 39*(1), 43–55.

Hofer, B. K. (2004b). Introduction: Paradigmatic approaches to personal epistemology. *Educational Psychologist, 39*(1), 1–3.

Hofer, B. K. (2005). The legacy and the challenges: Paul Pintrich's contributions to personal epistemology research. *Educational Psychologist, 40*(2), 95–105.

Hofer, B. K. (2006). Domain specificity of personal epistemology: Resolved questions, persistent issues, new models. *International Journal of Educational Research, 45*(1–2), 85–95.

Hofer, B. K., & Pintrich, P. R. (1997). The development of epistemological theories: Beliefs about knowledge and knowing and their relation to learning. *Review of Educational Research, 67*(1), 88–140.

Hofer, B. K., & Pintrich, P. R. (Eds.). (2002). *Personal epistemology: The psychology of beliefs about knowledge and knowing*. Mahwah, NJ: Erlbaum.

Inhelder, B., & Piaget, J. (1958). *The growth of logical thinking from childhood to adolescence: An essay on the construction of formal operational structures* (A. Parsons & S. Milgram, Trans.). New York, NY: Basic Books.

Kaartinen-Koutaniemi, M., & Lindblom-Ylänne, S. (2008). Personal epistemology of psychology, theology and pharmacy students: A comparative study. *Studies in Higher Education, 33*(2), 179–191.

Kallio, E. (1998). *Training of students' scientific reasoning skills* (Doctoral dissertation, University of Jyväskylä, Department of Psychology, Jyväskylä, Finland).

Kallio, E. (2011). Integrative thinking is the key: An evaluation of current research into the development of adult thinking. *Theory & Psychology, 21*(6), 785–801.

Kallio, E. (2015). From causal thinking to wisdom and spirituality: Some perspectives on a growing research field in adult (cognitive) development. *Approaching Religion, 5*(2), 27–41.

Kallio, E. (2016). Aikuisuuden ajattelun kehityksen laaja kenttä – Perusteita ja avoimia kysymyksiä [The broad field of the development of adult thinking – Premises and open questions]. In E. Kallio (Ed.), *Ajattelun kehitys aikuisuudessa: Kohti moninäkökulmaisuutta* [The development of thinking in adulthood: Towards multiperspective thinking] (Research in Educational Sciences No. 71, pp. 15–55). Helsinki, Finland: The Finnish Educational Research Association.

King, P. M., & Kitchener, K. S. (2002). The reflective judgment model: Twenty years of research on epistemic cognition. In B. K. Hofer & P. R. Pintrich (Eds.), *Personal epistemology: The psychology of beliefs about knowledge and knowing* (pp. 37–61). Mahwah, NJ: Erlbaum.

Kitchener, K. S., King, P. M., & DeLuca, S. (2006). Development of reflective judgment in adulthood. In C. Hoare (Ed.), *Handbook of adult development and learning* (pp. 73–98). New York, NY: Oxford University Press.

Kramer, D. A. (1983). Post-formal operations? A need for further conceptualization. *Human Development, 26*(2), 91–105.

Kuhn, D., Cheney, R., & Weinstock, M. (2000). The development of epistemological understanding. *Cognitive Development, 15*(3), 309–328.

Kuhn, D., Iordanou, K., Pease, M., & Wirkala, C. (2008). Beyond control of variables: What needs to develop to achieve skilled scientific thinking? *Cognitive Development, 23*(4), 435–451.

Kuhn, D., & Weinstock, M. (2002). What is epistemological thinking and why does it matter? In B. K. Hofer & P. R. Pintrich (Eds.), *Personal epistemology: The psychology of beliefs about knowledge and knowing* (pp. 121–144). Mahwah, NJ: Erlbaum.

Lawson, A. E. (2004). The nature and development of scientific reasoning: A synthetic view. *International Journal of Science and Mathematics Education, 2*, 307–338.

Lawson, A. E., Banks, D. L., & Logvin, M. (2007). Self-efficacy, reasoning ability, and achievement in college biology. *Journal of Research in Science Teaching, 44*(5), 706–724.

Limón, M. (2006). The domain generality-specificity of epistemological beliefs: A theoretical problem, a methodological problem or both? *International Journal of Educational Research, 45*(1), 7–27.

Louca, L., Elby, A., Hammer, D., & Kagey, T. (2004). Epistemological resources: Applying a new epistemological framework to science instruction. *Educational Psychologist, 39*(1), 57–68.

Marchand, H. (2001). Some reflections on post-formal thought. *The Genetic Epistemologist*, *29*(3), 2–9. Retrieved from www.dareassociation.org/documents/Some%20Reflections %20on%20Postformal%20Thought.html

Moshman, D. (2013). Epistemic cognition and development. In P. Barrouillet & C. Gauffroy (Eds.), *The development of thinking and reasoning* (pp. 25–45). Hove, England: Psychology Press.

Muis, K. R., Bendixen, L. D., & Haerle, F. C. (2006). Domain-generality and domain-specificity in personal epistemology research: Philosophical and empirical reflections in the development of a theoretical framework. *Educational Psychology Review*, *18*(1), 3–54.

Müller, U., Ten Eycke, K., & Baker, L. (2015). Piaget's theory of intelligence. In S. Goldstein, D. Princiotta, & J. Naglieri (Eds.), *Handbook of intelligence* (pp. 137–151). New York, NY: Springer.

Perry, W. G., Jr. (1968). *Patterns of development in thought and values of students in a liberal arts college: A validation of a scheme.* Cambridge, MA: Harvard University, Bureau of Study Counsel.

Perry, W. G., Jr. (1970). *Forms of intellectual and ethical development in the college years: A scheme.* New York, NY: Holt, Rinehart and Winston.

Piaget, J. (1972). Intellectual evolution from adolescence to adulthood. *Human Development*, *15*(1), 1–12.

Piaget, J. (1976). Piaget's theory. In B. Inhelder, H. H. Chipman, & C. Zwingmann (Eds.), *Piaget and his school: A reader in developmental psychology* (pp. 11–23). New York, NY: Springer-Verlag.

Seppälä, H. (2013). *Students' scientific thinking in higher education: Logical thinking and conceptions of scientific thinking in universities and universities of applied sciences* (Doctoral dissertation, University of Helsinki, Institute of Behavioural Scieces, Helsinki, Finland).

Seppälä, H. (2016). Tieteellisen ajattelun kehittyminen [Development of scientific think-ing]. In E. Kallio (Ed.), *Ajattelun kehitys aikuisuudessa: Kohti moninäkökulmaisuutta* [The development of thinking in adulthood: Towards multiperspective thinking] (Research in Educational Sciences No. 71, pp. 85–107). Helsinki, Finland: The Finnish Educational Research Association.

Shibley, I. A., Jr., Milakofsky, L. M., Bender, D. S., & Patterson, H. O. (2003). College chemistry and Piaget: An analysis of gender difference, cognitive abilities, and achievement measures seventeen years apart. *Journal of Chemical Education*, *80*(5), 569.

Standards and guidelines for quality assurance in the European higher education area (ESG). (2015). Brussels, Belgium: EURASHE. Retrieved from https://enqa.eu/wp-content/uploads/ 2015/11/ESG_2015.pdf

Strømsø, H. I., Bråten, I., & Samuelstuen, M. S. (2008). Dimensions of topic-specific epistemological beliefs as predictors of multiple text understanding. *Learning and Instruc-tion*, *18*(6), 513–527.

Thuneberg, H., Hautamäki, J., & Hotulainen, R. (2015). Scientific reasoning, school achievement and gender: A multilevel study of between and within school effects in Finland. *Scandinavian Journal of Educational Research*, *59*(3), 337–356.

Utriainen, J., Marttunen, M., Kallio, E., & Tynjälä, P. (2017). University applicants' critical thinking skills: The case of the Finnish educational sciences. *Scandinavian Journal of Edu-cational Research*, *61*(6), 629–649.

4

PERSONAL EPISTEMOLOGIES AND SOCIAL REPRESENTATIONS

And how they meet in people's conceptions of the origin of human species[1]

Anna-Maija Pirttilä-Backman, Salla Ahola, and Inari Sakki

Introduction

Whose claims about climate change should one believe? What is the most effective way to defend against economic crises? Which is healthier, butter or margarine? Newspapers and magazines write about these kinds of topics on a regular basis, they are disputed in current affairs and argued in peer groups, homes, workplaces, and more widely on the internet. How do individuals, groups, and societies react and get along amidst contradictory and changing information? Does new research provide adequate grounds for understanding these issues? Or is the information flow a threat under which people feel powerless, become indifferent and withdraw themselves?

What conceptions of knowledge do people have and how do they justify their knowledge claims and how do these change? In this chapter we present one of the better-known developmental models of these issues, namely that of Karen Kitchener (1978) and Patricia King (1977), constructed in the 1970s in their doctoral dissertations. Initially they used the title *Reflective Judgment Model*. They adopted the concept from the century-old texts of John Dewey, in which he deliberated on juridical decision making: the decisions were important, they had important practical consequences for those concerned, and they should not be made arbitrarily. King (1977) and Kitchener (1978) remarked that Dewey did not clarify how the decisions should be made; however, he talked about the selection of the circumstances that should be taken into account and the need to evaluate the validity and applicability of evidence in the situation at hand – about a reflective judgment. In Kitchener's and King's terminology, reflective judgment refers to the most developed way to deal with problems, to which there is no single and unequivocally correct solution. Their developmental model describes a move towards this highest stage.

Since then, the term "personal epistemologies" has been introduced as a distinction to the epistemologies presented by professional philosophies (see, Hofer & Pintrich, 1997; Pintrich, 2002). The term also suits the model of Kitchener and King well, because it describes and explains the development of assumptions of what knowledge is and the ways in which knowledge claims are justified. In this chapter, we first discuss personal epistemologies and their manifestations among adults, as well as their practical significance. After that, we shift the perspective onto groups and communities and their formation of shared everyday knowledge, i.e. social representations. Finally, we make an excursion to people's understanding of the origins of human beings and analyse these conceptions from the perspectives of personal epistemologies and social representations. This example comes from Finnish interviews, from a North European country with highly educated population.

The development of personal epistemologies

The questions raised at the beginning of this chapter were of the type that also concerned Kitchener and King in the 1970s. They wanted to find out how people deal with ill-structured (called also wicked) problems that do not have one obvious solution. For the most part, Kitchener's and King's research was based on the pioneering work of Perry (1970), on what he called the intellectual and ethical development of Harvard students (see Chapter 3).

The key question of Kitchener's and King's dissertations was whether thinking concerning knowledge would actually develop further than what Perry described in his model at stages 1–6 (see Chapter 3). Together they developed a method for studying personal epistemologies. Kitchener's special research question was to find out whether personal epistemologies differ from verbal reasoning and fluency, while King focused on difference from logical reasoning. According to their results, the evolution of personal epistemologies could not be reduced to either logical reasoning or verbal reasoning or fluency, even though some connections between them were found.

Perry's (1970) interview method, starting from questions that were topical to the interviewees, had produced a good description of the personal epistemologies up to a certain point, as the questions related to knowledge were topical to the students at the beginning and intermediate stages of their studies. However, at the end of their studies, questions related to personal life choices were more pressing than issues related to knowing, and Perry's last position reflected this. Kitchener and King specifically asked whether there was epistemic development after the knowing-related positions Perry had described. They ended up presenting their interviewees with dilemmas that were constructed of contradictory claims. They sought their interviewees' standpoints to the dilemmas and how they justified their views. In this way, the researchers were able to concentrate on knowing-related issues. Their final series included dilemmas covering questions in four different areas of life (construction of the Egyptian pyramids, the objectivity of news reporting, the effect of food additives on health, and the origin of the human species). In the dilemmas, both of the contrasting standpoints were presented as having previously been supported, for example, in the discussion of food additives like this:

> There have been frequent reports about the relationship between chemicals that are added to foods and the safety of these foods. Some studies indicate that such chemicals can cause cancer, making these foods unsafe to eat. Other studies, however, show that chemical additives are not harmful, and actually make the foods containing them more safe to eat.
>
> *(King & Kitchener, 1994, p. 260)*

After the presentation of each dilemma, the interviewees were asked for their standpoints, followed by a number of more detailed and deepening questions, such as how they ended up adopting this position and could they ever think differently. If an interviewee said that s/he was unable to take a stand, s/he was asked why this was not possible and whether s/he could ever take a stand on the matter and if so, under what conditions. Further clarifications were requested if an interviewee used words like "theory" or "proof" without further characterisation. The interviewees in King's and Kitchener's PhD dissertations were junior high school students and graduate and postgraduate students in liberal arts.

Kitchener and King presented a seven-stage developmental model of assumptions of knowledge and justifications of knowledge claims (see Table 4.1).

Understandings of knowledge evolve from absolutistic, concrete understanding towards conceiving knowledge as hypothetical constructions. Critical milestones in this development are the gradually deepening understanding of uncertainty and contextuality, as well as the realisation of the possibility to compare different knowledge claims on the basis of negotiable and justified criteria.

Kitchener's and King's work belongs to the group of cognitive-developmental models and theories. Its roots can be found in the theories of Piaget (see Chapters 2, 3), Kohlberg (see Chapters 5, 6) and Perry (see Chapter 3). More specifically, it belongs to the subgroup of complex stage models as defined by Rest (1979). In these models the conceptions and justifications are reorganised during each new stage relative to the previous one. The changes are qualitative transformations in the assumptions and justifications of knowledge, not just linear increases or decreases in some assumptions. Furthermore, it is assumed and also well documented that people's thinking and arguing can have features not only from one stage, but also from several successive stages at the same time.[2] Typically, the developmental models of personal epistemologies have presented a similar line of development as Kitchener's and King's model, though there is variation in the number of stages or levels across models (see, e.g., Hofer, 2016).

A number of Finnish studies that have used Kitchener's and King's method (e.g., Kajanne, 2003; Pirttilä-Backman, 1993; Pirttilä-Backman & Kajanne, 2001) have convincingly demonstrated the connection between educational levels and also educational fields and such factors as diversity of living environments, work experience and role-playing opportunities – and the developmental stages of personal

TABLE 4.1 King and Kitchener's (e.g. 1994) developmental model of personal epistemologies

Stage	Assumptions of knowledge	Justifications
1	Absolute equivalence exists between what is seen and what is: what I see is true.	Because knowing is just seeing, justifications are not needed.
2	There is right and wrong knowledge – and somebody always knows the truth. Uncertainty does not exist.	Facts can be known by one's own observation. If they cannot be directly known, one can appeal to the authorities.
3	Not even authorities always know the truth, but uncertain claims are temporary – the absolute truth can be found.	In uncertain matters beliefs can be justified by what feels right or what one wants to believe.
4	Knowledge per se is uncertain and idiosyncratic. So, uncertainty is a permanent and acceptable condition.	The reasons for uncertainty are concrete. Beliefs and feelings can be used as justifications.
5	Knowledge is always contextual, and beliefs can be justified only in a particular context, as things are interpreted differently in different frameworks.	The justifications of beliefs can be evaluated only within one context. However, the arguments can still be evaluated by looking at the relative merit of their various components.
6	Despite the contextuality of knowledge, some beliefs can be regarded as being better than others. This is based on the ability to make comparisons between reference frames. Research is a process that results in changes in knowledge.	Different beliefs can be compared with each other justifiably.
7	Knowledge is a result of critical combination and evaluation of standpoints and evidence. Some estimates, interpretations, and solutions can therefore be more justified than others. However, the current knowledge will be re-evaluated later. This means that with time, current knowledge will most probably change into newer versions.	Evaluation and comparison are continuing processes in which new viewpoints can come up. Also, new criteria can be brought into consideration.

epistemologies. Pirttilä-Backman (1993) has also demonstrated that the model is not bound to any single theory of truth. Thoughts reflecting critical realism, pragmatism, and relativism can be categorised into the highest stage as long as they are sufficiently well-founded. (For further critical analysis of assumptions in the adult developmental theories, see Chapter 13.)

In the aforementioned Finnish studies (e.g., Pirttilä-Backman, 1993), the interviewees argued in ways that reflected mostly the same stages regardless of the subject matter of the dilemma. This means that the assumptions about knowledge were similar regardless of the substance of the question. Furthermore, the interviewees' own field (i.e., engineering, medicine, or social sciences) did not have a differentiating effect on the argumentation across dilemmas. Also, King's and Kitchener's (2004) respondents argued rather similarly about various dilemmas, although consistency in the US studies has been weaker than in the aforementioned systematically heterogeneous Finnish sample (which consisted of interviewees representing several fields, and both students and those already in working life).

More recently however, researchers have increasingly started to consider that people's conceptions of knowledge could differ depending on the domain, context, academic discipline, school subject, or different areas of life (Greene, Sandoval, & Bråten, 2016; Hofer, 2006; Muis, Bendixen, & Haerle, 2006; Pintrich, 2002). Indeed, the current models are increasingly taking such domain-specific and contextual aspects of knowledge-related thinking into account (Greene et al., 2016).

The significance of personal epistemologies in everyday life

What is the role of personal epistemologies in practice? Several studies have found that they are associated with recognising different views, argumentation, and drawing conclusions. More specifically, they are related, for example, to the ability to recognise contrasting views and to evaluate them (Mason & Boscolo, 2004), skills of argumentation on climate change and genetically modified food (Mason & Scirica, 2006), the ability to recognise reasoning fallacies (Weinstock, Neuman, & Glassner, 2006), as well as views on food additives (Kajanne, 2003) and evolution acceptance (Borgerding, Deniz, & Anderson, 2017). Recently, Staerklé and Green (2014) suggested that personal epistemologies could also contribute to defining intergroup relations.

Other people's personal epistemologies can also have a significant role in making important decisions that concern a particular individual, for example, in contexts such as law (Weinstock, 2016) or medicine (Eastwood et al., 2017). Anyone who ends up on trial or in an equivalent situation, where other people give verdicts or make other important decisions, would probably hope that the decision-makers have personal epistemologies that are as advanced as possible. Less ideal would be that important decisions are made by people who do not want to go to any further effort after finding a solution that seems plausible or who think it is not worthwhile to deliberate and to scrutinise different opinions that seem like knowledge but are not finally backed up by any proper evidence (Weinstock & Cronin, 2003). Similar concerns have been raised recently in discussions about the so-called post-truth age, and unfortunately, there are many recent examples, particularly from public decision-making in which this ideal has not been met.

Social representations: everyday, common-sense theories of groups

When an individual knows something, personal epistemologies provide the framework to it, even though people seldom think about these frames consciously. Knowledge can mean an absolute truth, an opinion, or a well-formulated hypothetical construction to a person. People form their own personal epistemologies and personal standpoints in social interaction, and they also form ideas and build knowledge as groups and communities.

The theory of social representations (SRT) is the most notable approach from which to study groups and communities' shared understandings. The seminal work in the field, Serge Moscovici's (1961/2008) dissertation *La psychanalyse, son image et son public*, is about how psychoanalysis spread to French society – how it was addressed in newspapers representing various ideological trends and how it was rooted in French daily conversations. The liberal, the communist, and the catholic press – the French opinion leaders at that time – presented and discussed psychoanalysis from their own premises, raised and faded out themes according to their own interests, and adjusted concepts and presented them in the light of their own starting points. Moscovici suggested that new things are made familiar and understandable through two processes. In anchoring, something new and unknown is associated with already known phenomena and located in existing conceptual matrixes. For example, a psychoanalytic therapy session is seen as a catholic confession, whereby it becomes understandable. The second process is objectification, in which an abstract case gets almost a concrete manifestation. For example, when God is perceived to be a father, the experience is almost physically touchable.

Émile Durkheim's concept of collective representations provided one theoretical point of reference to the theory of social representations: while Durkheim's collective representations are permanent and unchanging, explanatory and given, social representations are dynamic and something to be explained (Moscovici, 1981). Also, the impact of Piaget on Moscovici's work was profound. Although Moscovici abandoned Piaget's description of human development as being an evolutionary, linear process, he retained the idea of cooperative interaction in the development of knowledge as well as the creative aspect of representation, meaning that in gaining new knowledge, children must reinvent the world since they often have no familiar foundations for those aspects of their environment that they are confronting for the first time (Jovchelovitch, 2007; Sakki, Menard, & Pirttilä-Backman, 2017).

According to Moscovici (1973, p. xiii), social representations are:

> systems of values, ideas and practices with a twofold function; first, to establish an order which will enable individuals to orient themselves in their material and social world and to master it; secondly, to enable communication to take place among the members of a community by providing them with a code for social exchange and a code for naming and

classifying unambiguously the various aspects of their world and their individual and group history.

These representations are the counterparts of our society to myths and belief systems of traditional communities. They are not just about "opinions" or "images of something," or "attitudes towards something" but "theories" or "areas of knowledge" as their own entities and with their own legitimacy. With the formation of common everyday theories, abstract and unknown things become familiar and communicable.

More recently the concept of cognitive polyphasia has gained a lot of interest. The idea of cognitive polyphasia had already been proposed in 1961 by Moscovici when he defined it as "dynamic coexistence – interference and specialization – of distinct modalities of knowledge that correspond to definite relationships of man and his environment" (Moscovici, 2008, p. 190). Thus, the concept helps us understand knowledge as a plurality of parallel and sometimes contradictory forms of thought, meanings, and practices that reside in the same individual, group, or community (Jovchelovitch, 2007; Wagner, Duveen, Verma, & Themel, 2000), and fulfils a variety of functions and responds to different needs of social life (Jovchelovitch, 2008). It means that representations may be heterogeneous and contradictory, and under certain circumstances, they can occur at the same time and in the same situation (Jovchelovitch, 2007; Provencher, 2011).

In this line of thought, in a more recent discussion on cognitive polyphasia, Moscovici (Moscovici & Marková, 2000) emphasises the role of norms, context, and goals in knowledge construction. While norms provide limits to what is considered as rational thinking and knowledge in our societies, the context guides the way people recognise and process information, and goals shape the way people use such knowledge (Provencher, 2011). In other words, cognitive polyphasia is an asset of human cognition, a tool that enables adjustment to different situations and conditions (e.g., Caillaud & Kalampalikis, 2013; Renedo & Jovchelovitch, 2007), the expression of multiple identities (Amer, Howarth, & Sen, 2015; Howarth, Wagner, Magnusson, & Sammut, 2014) as well as the communication between representations in the maintenance or transformation of knowledge (Jovchelovitch, 2008).

A concept tightly related to the cognitive polyphasia is the one of themata (Moscovici & Vignaux, 1994), which refers to the centrality of interdependent antinomies, for example, human/nature or tradition/modern, and thus, to polyphasia in the process of social representation (Marková, 2003). In practice, this means that people draw upon oppositional representations in their construction of knowledge (e.g., Renedo & Jovchelovitch, 2007; Wagner et al., 2000). In line with such a perspective, it also means that social representational processes are linked to power. Through communication and dialogue, some representations gain more success and become self-evident at the expense of other representations of more marginalised groups in society (Howarth, 2006; O'Dwyer, Lyons, & Cohrs, 2016).

Importantly, thus, in comparison with theories based on the cognitive-developmental paradigm presented above, in the social representations theory (SRT) the knowledge about certain objects is not considered as a developmental process that transforms from one representation to another; instead different forms of knowledge co-exist, contradict, and constantly change (Jovchelovitch, 2007, 2008).

How personal epistemologies and social representations help us understand how people make sense of the origin of their species

People have long been fascinated by their own origins, for which various cultures have offered a wide range of explanations during history. Next, we will discuss Finns' understandings of the origin of human beings and what role personal epistemologies and social representations have in these understandings. Evolution theory has a strong position in Finland as an explanation of human origins. It is taught in schools as part of life sciences. Some of its elements are well rooted in people's minds, as manifested in everyday jokes about the cousins in zoos, and in the well-known dialogue in Väinö Linna's (1954/2015) seminal novel *Unknown Soldiers*, in which soldiers chat, reflect, and joke about human prehistory and the place of fish in it. The creation story as an explanation of the origin of human beings has an even longer history than the theory of evolution. Also, it still has a significant place in the worldview of the majority of the population. The creation story of human history, however, can be interpreted in quite different ways. For example, Niiniluoto (1984) has argued that even educated people at the end of the 19th century could literally rely on the creation story as a prehistory of humankind, but today, according to the position prevailing within the Lutheran Church, Finland's majority church, the story of creation must be understood symbolically. However, there is still more variety in the standpoints among the population, as becomes evident below.

At the practical level, science and religion are intertwined in many ways. For example, in Finland, the Lutheran priests receive their education in theological faculties, even though the church ordains the priests. The inauguration programme for the academic year of the largest university in Finland continues to include a worship service. In schools, ethics as an alternative to religion is still an exception to the mainstream. Learning outcomes in religion are rated as in any other school subject. Many Finns get married and buried according to church ceremonies, and relatives and friends not belonging to church customarily participate in these events.

One dilemma Kitchener and King dealt with was the question of human origins. It was presented to Finnish interviewees as a part of a broader project (Pirttilä-Backman, 1993). The dilemma that also covers ontological assumptions says:

Many religions of the world have creation stories. These stories suggest that a divine being created the earth and its people. Scientists claim, however, that people evolved from lower animal forms (some of which were similar to apes) into the human forms we know today.

(King & Kitchener, 1994, p. 260)

In Finland, 142 people responded to all four of Kitchener's and King's dilemmas (Pirttilä-Backman, 1993). The respondents represented different educational levels and fields and included both students halfway through their studies and graduates from the same educational institutions ten years earlier, as well as people with little specialised education.

The interview protocol for each dilemma received three scores according to Kitchener's and King's scoring manual[3], reflecting the development stages manifested in the interviews (see Table 1 for the stage descriptions). For example, if during the interview, views and justifications reflecting only stage 3 were presented, the scorer recorded 333. On the other hand, if the majority of the arguments corresponded to stage 6, but there were also clear indications of stage 5 and some of stage 4, a score of 654 was assigned. Next, an average of each dilemma was calculated for each interviewee, after which a personal stage average was formed by calculating the average of all the dilemmas, except the one concerning human origins. The distribution of these personal averages based on three dilemmas are shown in Table 4.2.

Table 4.2 shows that the most common development stage average was around four, while the next typical averages were five and three. The highest stages were rather exceptional. This has also been the case in studies conducted in the US, with the stage averages varying from 3.6 among high school students to 5.3 among doctoral students (King, Kitchener, & Wood, 1994).[4]

In the dilemma of human pre-history, evolution was chosen by 46% of women, and 65% of men. Creation was selected by 20% of women and 12.5% of men, while 13% of women and 12.5% of men chose both standpoints. For the rest, 21% of women and 10% of men did not take a stand on this dilemma.

TABLE 4.2 The distribution of interviewees' personal stage averages of three dilemmas (N = 142)

Stage mean of three dilemmas	Percentage of respondents
less than 3.49	22.5%
3.5–4.49	41.5%
4.5–5.49	23.9%
5.5–6.49	9.2%
6.5–7	2.8%

Source: Pirttilä-Backman & Hakanen, 1994

Although there was some degree of variation in percentages, the difference between the genders in the basic standpoints was not statistically significant.

The interviewees with the highest stage scores had all chosen the theory of evolution. A considerable proportion of the interviewees who had low stage scores had also come to this solution. Those who had selected evolution had a clearly larger deviation in the mean stage scores than other groups. Looking at group-wise scores, the highest mean stage score (4.7) was in the group that had selected both evolution and creation. The mean score for those who had selected evolution was 4.3 and for those who had selected creation it was 3.8. The differences in group-wise mean stage scores proved statistically significant between those who had selected both standpoints and those who had selected creation only; there were no significant differences between the other groups.

Those who chose evolution justified their view by arguing that there is evidence, knowledge, and proof of evolution. According to the justifications of the statements and their meanings, these interviewees could still be divided into two subgroups. In the first of these, the proof of evolutionary theory was what was known at the moment, while other topics were hardly taken up. This subgroup was categorised as "*There is evidence of evolution, but not about the other option.*" In the second subgroup, "*I'm so realistic that I have never believed in the supernatural,*" evidence and facts were considered to be the sole property of reality and the basis for the solutions, because supernatural reality was regarded as non-existent.

Also, those who chose creation as their only standpoint expressed their choice clearly. They could be divided into the following four subgroups on the basis of their main justifications: 1) *I believe*; 2) *This is what I learnt, and this is how it may be*; 3) *But where did everything begin from?*; 4) *But we are not monkeys.*

Those who chose both standpoints considered that there is no contradiction between evolution and creation. The view was clarified in four different ways that can be summarised as follows: 1) *It is the same thing expressed in different ways*; 2) *Both can be true because neither of them can be said to be wrong*; 3) *Evolution is certain but religion also has its place*; and 4) *Someone created lower forms of animals, which then developed into higher animal forms.*

Those who did not take any stand formed the fourth major class. Each interview had been started by asking for the standpoint. If the interviewee did not choose either of the options presented, later in the interview s/he was asked, inter alia, why the interviewee could not or was not willing to take a stand and whether s/he could at some point and on some premises choose a standpoint. Therefore, in these interviews, the interviewees presented different views on the origin of human beings. Two clear subgroups emerged from this group: 1) *This is unknown*; and 2) *I have not yet solved this for myself.* For more details of the qualitative analysis and results, see Pirttilä-Backman and Hakanen (1994).

Conclusions: social representations and personal epistemologies in making sense of the human origin

In Finland, the evolution theory and the story of creation are both well-known explanations for the origin of human beings. They constitute a largely shared, common knowledge base that people and groups can use when forming and maintaining their own standpoints on the issue. All the interviewees had at least heard about both standpoints, but they used them differently to form their individual standpoints and came to different solutions.

Fish and monkeys were a part of people's talk about the major milestones in the evolution theory. Concrete images of the theory of evolution and objectifications, have thus been formed through them. Animals were also used as anchors for making the scientific theory more familiar. Relevant to the interviewees was also that evolution was a scientific theory; scholarship convinced them, even though the scientific details were not necessarily very clear to them.

The strong position of science in our culture is also reflected in that all the interviewees who had received the highest stage ratings had chosen evolution. The highest developmental stages of personal epistemologies are in line with the scientific worldview. However, the greatest variation in developmental stages was among those who had chosen evolution, which means that some members of this group scored very low in developmental stages. One explanation for this – as well as for those who had chosen creation and had low average stage scores – is these interviewees' difficulty in considering multiple viewpoints simultaneously. An interesting single observation in the study was that those who chose both evolution and creation were also rated with higher average developmental stages. This finding is in line with the hypothesis of cognitive polyphasia discussed above (Moscovici, 1961/2008), indicating that contrasting modes of reasoning can be found co-existing without any tension, even in the same individual. On the contrary, rather than being mutually exclusive, conflicting themes can operate as an asset from which people can draw the resources to deal with in their social life (Renedo & Jovchelovitch, 2007).

Even though evolution as a scientific theory provided assurance for many, it also caused resistance. To some, accepting evolution would have meant betraying their faith. Creation could be seen as part of faith as such, related to the Creator. Religion as such could be seen as bringing safety and feelings of togetherness. However, strictness and rigidity and use of power were also connected to it (Pirttilä-Backman & Hakanen, 1994).

As has been outlined by Moscovici (Moscovici & Marková, 2000), norms provide boundaries for what is considered to be knowledge in certain social groups, thus people may rely on models of explanation that gain broad social acceptance within their social group despite contradictory evidence. Also, in line with the hypothesis of cognitive polyphasia (Moscovici, 1961/2008), knowledge is polymorphic and social subjects may use it in a heuristic manner depending on the context and their needs.

There are several "everyday theories" in Finland about the origin of human beings. It is possible that those who have chosen creation as their only standpoint are more likely than others to form cohesive groups, because they hold a minority standpoint in a society governed by a scientific worldview. These people as a group may also have most clearly formulated an everyday theory of the topic, even though it would not technically correspond the highest stages of personal epistemologies. On average, representatives of the other standpoints do not necessarily have an equally strong need to discuss their choice. Concerning the simultaneous examination of personal epistemologies and social representations, it would be interesting to focus on different communities in which one of the key premises in the group formation is the human origin standpoint.

Even though the connections between personal epistemologies and social representations have not yet been studied extensively, as seen above, personal epistemologies are interestingly linked to the common everyday theories we construct of different types of new, complex, and important issues. On the one hand, we are attached to our groups and communities by these everyday theories. They are an important part of our living environments. We can thus ask whether the everyday theories facilitate or hinder communication with others and facing complex issues. On the other hand, it is equally important to examine if the personal epistemologies of the people support the diverse use of cultural information and different explanation models, or if they constrain the positions that can be formed.

Further attention is also needed to better understand the interplay between cognitive polyphasia, personal epistemologies, and wisdom. In their recent study, Manwaring and colleagues (2018) found that among religious people in the United States, religiosity was positively associated with creationistic views and negatively with acceptance of evolution. However, ability in scientific reasoning did not predict acceptance of evolution among these people. Neither was the acceptance of evolution indicative of high scientific reasoning ability. As a response to the call by Manwaring and colleagues for better understanding the barriers in accepting the evolution theory, the different belief systems could be analysed from the perspective of cognitive polyphasia, which provides a wide framework to analyse the phenomenon simultaneously at both societal and individual levels.

More developed epistemic understanding has already been related to wisdom (for recent reviews of the concept of wisdom, see Grossmann, 2017; Walsh, 2015). The ability to understand the uncertainties related to knowing and the ability to make sound judgements in the face of this uncertainty, have been a part of many definitions of wisdom (Kitchener & Brenner, 1990). These judgements are related to difficult real-life problems to which there are no clear answers. Haste, Markoulis, and Helkama (1998) and Murray (2010) have also suggested that one of the aspects of wisdom would concern understanding the nature and the boundaries of knowledge. Therefore, understanding the development of personal epistemologies can be useful in understanding wisdom – in particular Stages 4 to 7 in Kitchener's and King's model, because they all involve the acknowledgement of the uncertainty of knowing (Kitchener & Brenner, 1990). However, the elements that can be used to characterise wisdom are not present until Stage 7: the ability to integrate opposing views and to make reasoned judgements while recognising the limitations and uncertainties present in all knowing, including one's personal limits (Kitchener & Brenner, 1990).

The analysis presented in this chapter of the relationship between personal epistemologies and social representations has provided new insights to understanding people's thinking about human origins. In a similar way, future research on the relationship between cognitive polyphasia and wisdom may bring new insights to both fields.

Notes

1 An earlier and more limited version of this chapter has been presented in Finnish in Pirttilä-Backman and Ahola (2016). The major difference between these two chapters is in the concept of cognitive polyphasia that is discussed in the current chapter and used in the interpretation of the results.
2 See Pirttilä-Backman (1993) for different types of typical and atypical stage patterns.
3 Neither the interviewers nor the scorers of this study have gone through the certification procedures developed by Karen Kitchener and Patricia King. See Pirttilä-Backman (1993) and Pirttilä-Backman and Kajanne (2001) for the safeguards used to ensure the quality of the interviews and scoring.
4 Detailed information on the mean stages among interviewees representing different fields and levels of education, as well as among current students and those who had graduated ten years ago can be found in Pirttilä-Backman (1993), and longitudinal results can be found in Pirttilä-Backman and Kajanne (2001).

References

Amer, A., Howarth, C., & Sen, R. (2015). Diasporic virginities: Social representations of virginity and identity formation amongst British Arab Muslim women. *Culture and Psychology, 21*(1), 3–19.

Borgerding, L. A., Deniz, H., & Anderson, E. S. (2017). Evolution acceptance and epistemological beliefs of college biology students. *Journal of Research in Science Teaching, 54*(4), 493–519.

Caillaud, S., & Kalampalikis, N. (2013). Focus groups and ecological practices: A psychosocial approach. *Qualitative Research in Psychology, 10*(4), 382–401.

Eastwood, J. L., Koppelman-White, E., Mi, M., Wasserman, J. A., Krug III, E. F., & Joyce, B. (2017). Epistemic cognition in medical education: A literature review. *International Journal of Medical Education, 8*, 1–12.

Greene, J. A., Sandoval, W. A., & Bråten, I. (2016). Reflections and future directions. In J. A. Greene, W. A. Sandoval, & I. Bråten (Eds.), *Handbook of epistemic cognition* (Educational psychology handbook series, pp. 495–510). New York, NY: Routledge.

Grossmann, I. (2017). Wisdom in context. *Perspectives on Psychological Science, 12*(2), 233–257.

Haste, H., Markoulis, D., & Helkama, K. (1998). Morality, wisdom and the life-span. In A. Demetriou, W. Doise, & C. F. M. van Lieshout (Eds.), *Life-span developmental psychology* (pp. 317–350). Chichester, England: Wiley.

Hofer, B. K. (2006). Beliefs about knowledge and knowing: Integrating domain specificity and domain generality: A response to Muis, Bendixen, and Haerle. *Educational Psychology Review, 18*(1), 67–76.

Hofer, B. K. (2016). Epistemic cognition as a psychological construct: Advancements and challenges. In J. A. Greene, W. A. Sandoval, & I. Bråten (Eds.), *Handbook of epistemic cognition* (pp. 19–38). New York, NY: Routledge.

Hofer, B. K., & Pintrich, P. R. (1997). The development of epistemological theories: Beliefs about knowledge and knowing and their relation to learning. *Review of Educational Research, 67*(1), 88–140.

Howarth, C. (2006). A social representation is not a quiet thing: Exploring the critical potential of social representations theory. *British Journal of Social Psychology, 45*(1), 65–86.

Howarth, C., Wagner, W., Magnusson, N., & Sammut, G. (2014). "It's only other people who make me feel black": Acculturation, identity and agency in a multicultural community. *Political Psychology, 35*(1), 81–95.

Jovchelovitch, S. (2007). *Knowledge in context: Representations, community and culture.* London, England: Routledge.

Jovchelovitch, S. (2008). Rehabilitation of common sense: Social representations, science and cognitive polyphasia. *Journal for the Theory of Social Behaviour, 38*(4), 431–449.

Kajanne, A. (2003). Structure and content: The relationship between reflective judgment and laypeople's viewpoints. *Journal of Adult Development, 10*(3), 173–188.

King, P. M. (1977). *The development of reflective judgment and formal operational thinking in adolescents and young adults* (Unpublished doctoral dissertation). University of Minnesota.

King, P. M., & Kitchener, K. S. (1994). *Developing reflective judgment: Understanding and promoting intellectual growth and critical thinking in adolescents and adults* (The Jossey-Bass higher and adult education series, The Jossey-Bass social and behavioral science series). San Francisco, CA: Jossey-Bass.

King, P. M., & Kitchener, K. S. (2004). Reflective judgment: Theory and research on the development of epistemic assumptions through adulthood. *Educational Psychologist, 39*(1), 5–18.

King, P. M., Kitchener, K. S., & Wood, P. K. (1994). Research on the reflective judgment model. In P. M. King & K. S. Kitchener (Eds.), *Developing reflective judgment: Understanding and promoting intellectual growth and critical thinking in adolescents and adults* (The Jossey-Bass higher and adult education series, The Jossey-Bass social and behavioral science series, pp. 124–188). San Francisco, CA: Jossey-Bass.

Kitchener, K. S. (1978). *Intellectual development in late adolescents and young adults: Reflective judgment and verbal reasoning* (Unpublished doctoral dissertation). University of Minnesota.

Kitchener, K. S., & Brenner, H. G. (1990). Wisdom and reflective judgment: Knowing in the face of uncertainty. In R. J. Sternberg (Ed.), *Wisdom: Its nature, origins, and development* (pp. 212–229). Cambridge, England: Cambridge University Press.

Linna, V. (2015). *Unkown soldiers* (L. Yamaguchi, Trans.). London, England: Penguin Classics. (Original work published 1954).

Manwaring, K. F., Jensen, J. L., Gill, R. A., Sudweeks, R. R., Davies, R. S., & Bybee, S. M. (2018). Scientific reasoning ability does not predict scientific views on evolution among religious individuals. *Evolution: Education and Outreach, 11*(2), 1–9.

Marková, I. (2003). *Dialogicality and social representations: The dynamics of mind.* Cambridge, England: Cambridge University Press.

Mason, L., & Boscolo, P. (2004). Role of epistemological understanding and interest in interpreting a controversy and in topic-specific belief change. *Contemporary Educational Psychology, 29*(2), 103–128.

Mason, L., & Scirica, F. (2006). Prediction of students' argumentation skills about controversial topics by epistemological understanding. *Learning and Instruction, 16*(5), 492–509.

Moscovici, S. (1973). Foreword. In C. Herzlich (Ed.) & D. Graham (Trans.), *Health and illness: A social psychological analysis* (European Monographs in Social Psychology No. 5, pp. ix–xiv). London, England: Academic Press.

Moscovici, S. (1981). On social representations. In J. P. Forgas (Ed.), *Social cognition: Perspectives on everyday understanding* (European Monographs in Social Psychology No. 26, pp. 181–209). London, England: Academic Press.

Moscovici, S. (2008). *Psychoanalysis: Its image and its public* (D. Masey, Trans.). Cambridge, England: Polity.

Moscovici, S., & Marková, I. (2000). Ideas and their development: A dialogue between Serge Moscovici and Ivana Marková. In S. Moscovici & G. Duveen (Eds.), *Social representations: Explorations in social psychology* (pp. 224–286). Cambridge, England: Polity.

Moscovici, S., & Vignaux, G. (1994). Le concept de themâta [The concept of themata]. In C. Guimelli (Ed.), *Structures et transformations des représentations sociales* [Structures and transformations of social representations], (pp. 25–72). Neuchâtel, Switzerland: Delachaux et Niestlé.

Muis, K. R., Bendixen, L. D., & Haerle, F. C. (2006). Domain-generality and domain-specificity in personal epistemology research: Philosophical and empirical reflections in the development of a theoretical framework. *Educational Psychology Review, 18*(1), 3–54.

Murray, T. (2010). Exploring epistemic wisdom: Ethical and practical implications of integral studies and methodological pluralism for collaboration and knowledge-building. In S. Esbjörn-Hargens (Ed.), *Integral theory in action: Applied, theoretical, and constructive perspectives on the AQAL model* (pp. 345–367). New York, NY: State University of New York Press.

Niiniluoto, I. (1984). *Tiede, filosofia ja maailmankatsomus: Filosofisia esseitä tiedosta ja sen arvosta* [Science, philosophy and world view: Philosophical essays on knowledge and its value]. Helsinki, Finland: Otava.

O'Dwyer, E., Lyons, E., & Cohrs, J. C. (2016). How Irish citizens negotiate foreign policy: A social representations approach to neutrality. *Political Psychology, 37*(2), 165–181.

Perry, W. G., Jr. (1970). *Forms of intellectual and ethical development in the college years: A scheme.* New York, NY: Holt, Rinehart and Winston.

Pintrich, P. R. (2002). Future challenges and directions for theory and research on personal epistemology. In B. K. Hofer & P. R. Pintrich (Eds.), *Personal epistemology: The psychology of beliefs about knowledge and knowing* (pp. 389–414). Mahwah, NJ: Erlbaum.

Pirttilä-Backman, A.-M. (1993). *The social psychology of knowledge reassessed: Toward a new delineation of the field with empirical substantiation.* (Doctoral dissertation), University of Helsinki, Department of Social Psychology, Helsinki, Finland.

Pirttilä-Backman, A.-M., & Ahola, S. (2016). Henkilökohtaiset tietokäsitykset ja yhteiset arkiteoriat [Personal epistemologies and common everyday theories]. In E. Kallio (Ed.), *Ajattelun kehitys aikuisuudessa: Kohti moninäkökulmaisuutta,* [The development of thinking in adulthood: Towards multiperspective thinking] (Research in Educational Sciences No. 71, pp. 135–153). Helsinki, Finland: The Finnish Educational Research Association.

Pirttilä-Backman, A.-M., & Hakanen, H. (1994). Luomiskertomus ja evoluutio nykysuomalaisen maailmankuvan elementteinä [Creation story and evolution as elements in the worldview of contemporary Finns]. In A.-M. Pirttilä-Backman & K. M. Vesala (Eds.), *Kognitiosta maailmankuvan ulottuvuuksiin* [From cognition to the dimensions of world view]

(University of Helsinki, Department of Social Psychology, Research reports No. 2, pp. 39–83). Helsinki, Finland: University of Helsinki, Department of Social Psychology.

Pirttilä-Backman, A.-M., & Kajanne, A. (2001). The development of implicit epistemologies during early and middle adulthood. *Journal of Adult Development, 8*(2), 81–97.

Provencher, C. (2011). Towards a better understanding of cognitive polyphasia. *Journal for the Theory of Social Behaviour, 41*(4), 377–395.

Renedo, A., & Jovchelovitch, S. (2007). Expert knowledge, cognitive polyphasia and health: A study on social representations of homelessness among professionals working in the voluntary sector in London. *Journal of Health Psychology, 12*(5), 779–790.

Rest, J. R. (1979). *Development in judging moral issues.* Minneapolis, MN: University of Minnesota Press.

Sakki, I., Menard, R., & Pirttilä-Backman, A.-M. (2017). Sosiaaliset representaatiot – Yhteisön ja mielen välinen silta [Social representations – Bridging between mind and society]. In A. Gronow & T. Kaidesoja (Eds.), *Ihmismielen sosiaalisuus* [Human social mind] (pp. 104–129). Helsinki, Finland: Gaudeamus.

Staerklé, C., & Green, E. (2014). Ryhmäkeskeisyydestä moniarvoisuuteen: Ryhmienvälinen reflektiivinen tieto [From group-centrism to pluralism: An intergroup approach to reflexive knowledge]. In L. Myyry, S. Ahola, M. Ahokas, & I. Sakki (Eds.), *Arkiajattelu, tieto ja oikeudenmukaisuus* [Everyday thinking, knowledge and justice] (Publications of the Department of Social Research No. 18, pp. 92–110). Helsinki, Finland: University of Helsinki, Department of Social Research.

Wagner, W., Duveen, G., Verma, J., & Themel, M. (2000). 'I have some faith and at the same time I don't believe' – Cognitive polyphasia and cultural change in India. *Journal of Community & Applied Social Psychology, 10*(4), 301–314.

Walsh, R. (2015). What is wisdom? Cross-cultural and cross-disciplinary syntheses. *Review of General Psychology, 19*(3), 278–293.

Weinstock, M. (2016). Epistemic cognition in legal reasoning. In J. A. Greene, W. A. Sandoval, & I. Bråten (Eds.), *Handbook of epistemic cognition* (Educational psychology handbook series, pp. 215–229). New York, NY: Routledge.

Weinstock, M., & Cronin, M. A. (2003). The everyday production of knowledge: Individual differences in epistemological understanding and juror-reasoning skill. *Applied Cognitive Psychology, 17*(2), 161–181.

Weinstock, M. P., Neuman, Y., & Glassner, A. (2006). Identification of informal reasoning fallacies as a function of epistemological level, grade level, and cognitive ability. *Journal of Educational Psychology, 98*(2), 327–341.

5

DUTIES AND RESPONSIBILITIES IN ADULTHOOD

Integrating care and justice perspectives[1]

Soile Juujärvi and Klaus Helkama

Introduction

Modern democratic societies provide their members with latitude for choice regarding values and moral codes, in interpersonal relations, professional life, as well as political views on a fair society. This chapter examines two research traditions in moral psychology which view adult moral thinking in terms of reflective problem solving aroused by moral conflicts. Pertinent therein are dilemmas, that is, difficult situations in which two or more moral values collide and the individual is unsure about the right thing to do. The Piaget-inspired cognitive-developmental theory founded by Lawrence Kohlberg laid emphasis on the conceptions of justice as a core of moral reasoning and development across lifespans. This view was challenged by Carol Gilligan (1982), who argued that justice does not capture the essence of interpersonal moral conflicts women encounter in their everyday lives and suggested an alternative mode of moral reasoning, the ethic of care, to increase understanding of the essential nature of moral thought.

This chapter describes justice and care as specific modes of moral reasoning that follow developmental trajectories of their own and equip individuals with cognitive tools to solve moral conflicts they encounter in their lives. Despite their differences both of these modes represent the ethic of autonomy, viewing moral agents as free and independent decision-makers, which is a dominant moral discourse in Western countries (see Chapter 6). A great deal of duties and responsibilities assigned to individuals can thus be understood through care and justice reasoning. According to the updated, neo-Kohlbergian view, moral reasoning alone is not enough to constitute moral action: sensitivity to moral issues, motivation to prioritise moral values, ego strength, and implementation skills are needed as well (Rest, Narvaez, Bebeau, & Thoma, 1999). Moral reasoning, also called moral judgment or moral problem solving, or decision-making, still stands for the most important determinant of qualified moral action.

Kohlberg's stages in justice reasoning development

Kohlberg (1976, 1984) was an advocate for the cognitive-developmental paradigm in moral psychology. This paradigm views individuals as active agents constructing moral knowledge in interaction with their social environments. His famous theory of moral development still lays a frame of reference for the contemporary research in moral psychology. While many of his presuppositions have been questioned (e.g., Wark & Krebs, 1996), the emphasis on cognitive processes in moral functioning and viewing moral growth in terms of development, that is, improvements in moral thinking, are still regarded as valid by the neo-Kohlbergian approach. This approach has grown out of the work by Kohlberg's student James Rest and his associates, Bebeau, Narvaez, and Thoma, and it has made the most important contribution to renewing his theory (Rest et al., 1999).

Kohlberg (1984) held the belief that the content of moral judgment (moral belief, opinion, or value) is distinct from the structure of moral judgment. Structure refers to the general organisation of patterns of thoughts. Moral development results from the transformation of those cognitive structures, which takes place across the lifespan. This enables individuals to comprehend rights and duties from increasingly complex perspectives. The developmental stages are thus structural wholes that give the individual the general conceptual framework and a specific sense of certainty when reasoning about moral conflicts. Thus, in order to understand the meaning of an individual's specific moral beliefs, one has to understand the present conceptual framework (stage) within which those beliefs are embedded (see Juujärvi, 2003). The stages are displayed in Table 5.1.

According to Kohlberg, growth in moral development takes place through advances in role-taking that result in increasingly complex social perspectives and an improved understanding of conceptions of fairness and justice. Kohlberg's emphasis on the primacy of justice was inspired by the Nazi era, which raised the question of how civil disobedience against the regime could be justified in moral terms. Like Piaget, Kohlberg saw justice as central to morality, and assumed that a given Piagetian operational stage was a necessary prerequisite of the corresponding justice stage (see Chapters 2 and 3). Moral development beyond adolescence and through to adulthood could be described by using justice-based dilemmas as stimuli in research.

An example of a Kohlbergian dilemma from his Moral Judgment Interview is the euthanasia dilemma. A respondent has to choose whether or not the doctor should illegally give a lethal dose of morphine to a terminally ill cancer patient who is in terrible pain and asks him for a drug that will kill her. While both choices can be justified by arguments that may represent any stage, higher stage arguments are based on more differentiated social perspective taking than lower stage arguments. The choices at Stage 2, the first stage that is found among adults, are simple: it is right to

TABLE 5.1 Kohlberg's stages of justice reasoning: social perspectives and criteria of what is right (adapted from Kohlberg, 1976). Printed with permission. Copyright The Finnish Educational Research Association

---

1 Heteronomous morality

Egocentric perspective. Does not recognize that other people's perspective differs from the actor's; confuses authority's perspective with one's own.
What is right. Avoidance of punishment and obedience of authorities.

2 Instrumental purpose and exchange

Concrete individualistic perspective. Aware that all people have their own interests to pursue and these conflict, so that right is relative.
What is right. Following rules only when it is to someone's immediate interest; acting to meet one's own interests and letting others do the same. Right is also what is fair, what is an equal exchange, a deal, an agreement.

3 Mutual interpersonal expectations, relationships, and interpersonal conformity

Perspective of the individual in relationship with other individuals. Aware of shared feelings, agreements, and expectations which take primacy over individual interests. Relates points of view through the Golden Rule.
What is right. Living up to what is expected of people close to you or what people generally expect of people in your role as son, sister, friend. "Being good" is important and means having good motives.

4 Social system and conscience

Perspective of the system that defines roles and rules. Differentiates societal point of view from interpersonal agreements. Considers individual relations in terms of place in the system.
What is right. Fulfilling the actual duties to which you have agreed. Laws are to be upheld except in extreme cases where they conflict with other fixed duties. Right is also contributing to society, the group, or institution.

5 Postconventional or principled morality

Prior-to-society perspective. Perspective of a rational individual aware of values and rights prior to social attachments and contracts. Integrates perspectives by the formal mechanisms of agreement, contract, objective impartiality, and due process.
What is right. Being aware that people hold a variety of values and opinions that most values and rules are relative to your group. These relative rules should usually be upheld in the interest of impartiality because they are the social contract. Some nonrelative values and rights like life and liberty, however, must be upheld in any society and regardless of majority opinion.

---

give the patient the drug, because she wants it, or it is not right because the doctor might risk going to jail. At Stage 3, it is the motives and interpersonal relations that count. Consequently, euthanasia is right if everybody, including the relatives and medical colleagues agree on that, or it is wrong because good people obey the law. From the Stage 4 social system perspective, the ethics of the medical profession could be interpreted as a duty to show mercy and relieve suffering, or alternatively, as a commitment to preserve life. Finally, from the prior-to-society perspective at Stage 5, mercy killing could be defended by invoking the fundamental right of a person to decide about her life and death, or opposed by invoking long-term consequences of disobeying the law. Kohlberg originally established Stage 6 of universal principled morality as the endpoint of development, but Stage 5 is the highest stage found in empirical studies (Snarey, 1985).

Neo-Kohlbergian view on moral development

The neo-Kohlbergian approach (Rest et al., 1999) originally grew out of the need to devise a less time-consuming and a more user-friendly method to assess moral problem solving. The revised Defining Issues Test (DIT-2) is a multiple-choice test within which respondents are presented with five dilemmas and asked what the protagonist should do. Next, they assess 12 arguments in terms of their importance in solving the dilemma. They represent different Kohlberg's stages, from 2 to postconventional, and after evaluating the items, the respondent is asked to rank in order the four most important ones. The most important index of the DIT is the P score (percentage of postconventional reasoning), which is based on the rankings and indicates the relative weight of the postconventional arguments (Stage 5, see Table 5.1) in the respondents' moral problem solving. There is also a new index, N2 score that is basically a modified P score which measures the preference for the postconventional schema when taking into account rejection of the personal interest schema (Rest et al., 1999).

The DIT is based on the recognition of moral issues instead of verbal expression in the Moral Judgment Interview. It relies on the notion that a tacit understanding of moral concepts is sufficient for adequate moral decision-making, that is, the individual does not need to be able to articulate her moral justifications in order to apply them in practice. Studies have shown that people can comprehend arguments from one stage above their current stage (Walker, deVries, & Bichard, 1984), and furthermore, they also use arguments from lower stages depending on the content of moral conflict they encounter (for a review, see Krebs, Denton, & Wark, 1997). The accumulated empirical evidence has thus led to the theoretical reformulation of Kohlberg's theory. By giving up the radical distinction between structure and content and exclusive reliance on verbally produced data, neo-Kohlbergians have refuted the assumption that moral development would follow a staircase model in which individuals move from stage to stage and using the achieved highest stage reasoning across different moral issues. Instead, moral development means gradually shifting from lower to more complex conceptions of social co-operation, while lower concepts remain available to the individual. Advances in moral reasoning in adolescence and adulthood are best described by three successive schemas, that is, the organised structures of generalised knowledge residing in long-term memory through which people interpret moral issues. They are briefly explained as follows (for further elaboration, see Rest et al., 1999):

The personal interest schema combines Stages 2 and 3 thinking, with a focus on advancing interests of self and significant others in brief exchanges and negotiated co-operation. The individual aims to act according to social role expectations and to fulfil her or his duties as a loyal member of the social group, within the family, or at the workplace. One is able to apply reciprocity in relationships with known others and view strangers as well in terms of advancing personal or group-level interests.

The maintaining norms schema emerges when the individual starts to extend moral questions from interpersonal relations to include strangers in the scope of society. One is troubled with questions such as "how should a fair society be organised?", "what is the role of government?" and "when is it right to use force and who should use it?" The maintaining norms schema matches Stage 4 in Kohlberg's theory and is characterised by the need for generally accepted and uniform norms that are applied to all people in society. The individual understands the hierarchical structure of society as establishing social order and obeys authorities out of respect for "the rule of law" rather than due to their personal qualities.

The postconventional schema transforms the assumption that laws, norms, and practices are moral *per se* and indeed seeks the moral purpose behind them. They could thus be partial and just against some minorities or citizens, and therefore should be subjected to rational critique and can be challenged by novel knowledge and further evidence. Societies should be built on sharable moral ideas that are open to scrutiny and negotiated through means of community life. Consistent with Stage 5, morally valid solutions in society are based on full reciprocity, which means that they must be acceptable or just from the viewpoint of all people (Rest et al., 1999).

Development towards postconventional justice reasoning

The gradual emergence of the maintaining norms schema in adolescence means the discovery of a society that involves hierarchical role structures and chains of command with corresponding duties and responsibilities. In order to grow into a competent citizen, one needs to be able to distinguish public role expectations from personal motivations; know how to act as a responsible spouse, parent, professional, or politician. The maintaining norms schema equips the individual with the capacity to evaluate functioning of organisations and related role behaviours and to recognise moral deficiencies therein, such as discrimination, misuse of power, pursuit of self-interest, or cronyism. As a drawback, because viewing extant laws and norms as a source for morality, the maintaining norms schema can be biased against minorities and the powerless. For instance, abolishing slavery and granting women political rights were once seen as threatening social harmony.

While the maintaining norms schema aids people to behave as decent members in society, the postconventional schema has been regarded as critical for progressive citizenship. It involves four elements: 1) the primacy of moral criteria in formulating and understanding laws and norms, 2) the appeal to the moral ideal of how the society should be ordered, 3) shared moral ideals open to critique with the larger community, and 4) full reciprocity of laws and norms guaranteeing rights across all groups within the society. The postconventional reasoner understands that laws and norms are human constructions, and when biased they need to be changed. In addition to dominant justice-based political philosophies, such as neo-liberalism or welfare state ideology, the individual can pursue any moral philosophy which does not violate anybody's rights. Rest et al. (1999) emphasise that not all current ideologies meet the criterion of full reciprocity and may therefore be biased against some social groups or minorities.

As the neo-Kohlbergian approach sees the shift to postconventional schema as an essential factor in social progress, upbringing and education should support this transition. Education with enhanced cognitive stimulation and role-taking opportunities supports growth in moral reasoning up to the maintaining norms schema, but the attainment of the postconventional schema seems to require qualified higher education or heightened social responsibilities in adult life (Kohlberg, 1984; Rest et al., 1999). Educational institutions should provide supportive learning environments for students to engage in thought provoking debates about moral issues, and ethics should be an explicit content in curricula (Mayhew & King, 2008). With regard to pedagogical interventions, discussions of dilemmas accompanied with reflection (Bebeau, 2002), as well as volunteer and service activities (Lies, Bock, Brandenberger, & Trozzolo, 2012) have been found to be effective in accelerating moral reasoning. In professional education, ethical decision-making should be linked to rehearsing, besides moral reasoning, other components of ethical action as well, including sensitivity to ethical issues in ambiguous situations, prioritising moral values over egoistic values, and implementation skills (Bebeau, 2002).

As mentioned above, the postconventional schema is not supposed to be associated with any specific ideology. Nevertheless, a set of values, called universalism values in Shalom Schwartz's (2016) widely used taxonomy, predict advances in moral judgment (Helkama & Sortheix, 2015; Myyry, Juujärvi, & Pesso, 2013). These values include equality, social justice, world peace, broadmindedness, and wisdom and they aim to promote welfare of all people and nature (Schwartz, 2016) (see Chapter 2). Cultivating these values in institutions and communities would therefore enhance a propensity for advanced moral reasoning. It has furthermore been found that postconventional reasoning varies as a function of the power distance in the culture (Helkama & Sortheix, 2015). In high power distance cultures, people lower in hierarchy think it is natural and desirable that power is distributed unequally (Hofstede, 2001). In egalitarian social systems, value conflicts are legitimate and part of public life, and therefore citizens' autonomous moral problem solving is encouraged, whereas in non-egalitarian systems authorities may dictate not only how to behave but also how to think. In pluralistic democratic societies, there are also religious or political communities built on unequal power and endorsed with partisan or orthodox ideologies, inhibiting moral progress beyond the maintaining norms schema (Rest et al., 1999). Therefore, fostering advanced moral reasoning at the society level is a complex question.

Care and justice as different modes of moral reasoning

While the discussion around the ethic of care has several roots in philosophy, its conceptualisation as a mode of moral thought can be traced to Gilligan's (1982) studies on women's moral conflicts in everyday life. Those conflicts concerned care and responsibilities in relationships, and minimally focused on issues of individuals' rights and duties dominant in Kohlberg's theory. As a consequence, Gilligan claimed that because Kohlberg's theory of moral development was originally derived from a sample comprising of only boys and men, it would be biased against girls and women. As a conclusion, there would be two different moralities, the ethic of justice, more typical of men, and the ethic of care, more typical of women.

Gilligan (1982) specified that the ethics of care and justice represent different modes of moral reasoning that perceive, interpret, and solve moral problems in different ways. The ethic of justice sees a moral conflict as conflicting claims arising from rights and duties between individuals, whereas the ethic of care sees them arising from disturbances and ruptures in relationships. In solving moral conflicts, the ethic of justice seeks to maintain obligation, equity, and fairness through the application of moral principles, rules, and established standards, whereas the ethic of care seeks to sustain and restore good relationships through responding to the needs of others (Gilligan, 1982; Juujärvi, 2006). The ethic of care thus represents *particularistic* moral reasoning and the ethic of justice *universalistic* moral reasoning. Justice reasoning aims to find a generalisable solution that can be applied to similar cases, whereas care reasoning builds on the description of a concrete situation as fully as possible, individuals retaining their particular identities bound by time and place (Blum, 1988; Vreeke, 1991). The two ways of moral judgment have distinctive qualities and therefore cannot be replaced with each other, for instance in helping situations:

> You find yourself in difficulties and someone helps you. Subsequently this person informs you that he would have helped anyone who was in a similar situation. Even though you don't know the person in question, an effect of estrangement would still be produced from such a motivation of action.
>
> *(Vreeke, 1991, p. 39)*

Gilligan viewed care and justice as internal dispositions, women framing moral issues in terms of care and men in terms of justice across different contexts. Lyons (1983), a student of hers, developed a coding scheme for the content analysis of moral dilemmas. It yielded participants' preferences for care and justice considerations, called moral orientations. The substantial body of research since then has supported the idea of distinctive moral frameworks, but their usage has been found to be determined by the content of the moral conflict, rather than gender (Jaffee & Hyde, 2000). Both women and men tend to use care considerations when orienting to prosocial issues, such as helping or responding to others' needs, and justice considerations when orienting to issues of upholding or breaking norms, rules, or law. Complex moral dilemmas involving conflicting claims between different parties tend to invoke both care and justice reasoning among both genders (Juujärvi, 2005; Wark & Krebs, 1996). According to recent neuropsychological research, care and justice issues activate differing processes in the brain. Care reasoning is characterised by balancing empathic response and information processing related to self-knowledge, whereas justice reasoning is driven by activating self-perspective, rule-based learning, and emotional regulation (Cáceda, James, Ely, Snarey, & Kilts, 2011).

While Gilligan's idea of the existence of two distinct modes of moral thought is empirically established, her most famous claim that Kohlberg's theory favours men has been refuted. Extensive meta-analyses have shown that when education and job status are controlled, women perform equally well or even better than men in justice-based moral judgment (Thoma, 1986; Walker, 1991). Kohlberg (1984) nevertheless admitted that his approach did not fully reflect the morality of "special relationships and obligations" and consequently reformulated his theory to describe "a rational reconstruction of the ontogenesis of justice reasoning," leaving it to Gilligan to prove whether there is a care track as well in moral development.

Levels of care reasoning

While research has focused on gender differences, it has obscured Gilligan's (1982) conceptualisation of the ethic of care as a theory of development. She outlined a developmental sequence in care-based reasoning based on a follow-up study of 21 women, diverse in age, social background, and marital status, who were clients on pregnancy counselling services and abortion clinics. These women struggled with a moral crisis whether to continue or abort a pregnancy. Difficult situations raised contemplation of how self and others are affected by a decision and how hurting would be minimised, leaving the ultimate choice for the women themselves. Individual crises differed in character, revealing successive developmental perspectives in women's thought. Gilligan was cautious about calling them stages as Kohlberg did, leaving the validation of her findings to further studies. Below, they are called "levels," following the classification system of care-based reasoning and related studies (see Skoe, 2014).

In Gilligan's (1982) study there were young girls at the first level, concerned selfishly with their own survival; how to manage financially and emotionally without support. At the second level, women have adopted conventional norms of social responsibility of protecting others at one's own expense. They were confronted with the decision-making that would hurt somebody in any case: the unborn baby, the father, and other family members, and they were willing to minimise hurt by sacrificing their own needs and hopes. Finally, there were women who constructed a moral conflict in a totally new way at the third level, recognising and asserting their own needs based on their "inner voice" rather than the expectation of others, and taking responsibility for their judgment and choice. Those women realised that self and others are still interdependent and that life can only be sustained by taking care of both self and others. Between the main levels there were also two transitional points where women's thinking was under change and out of balance (Gilligan, 1982).

Gilligan retreated from studying moral development and moved on to the narrative inquiry of moral voices (Gilligan, Brown, & Rogers, 1990). Skoe (1998, 2014), however, continued her work by devising and validating a developmental measure of care-based reasoning, the Ethic of Care Interview (ECI, hereinafter). The measure distinguishes three main levels (stages) and two transitional levels, reflecting a growingly complex understanding of interdependence of self and others and responsibilities in human relationships (see Table 5.2).

TABLE 5.2 Levels of care development (adapted from Gilligan, 1982; Skoe, 1998, 2014). Printed with permission. Copyright The Finnish Educational Research Association

1. Survival (caring for self)
Moral thinking is characterized by caring for self to ensure survival and personal happiness. The person tends to think about relationships in a self-protecting and pragmatic way. Moral conflicts emerge mainly if one's own needs are in conflict. There is little, if any, evidence of caring for other people and their lives or feelings. Generally, self-interest serves as a basis for moral judgment.

1.5 Transition from survival to responsibility
Moral thinking is characterized by an emerging sense of responsibility towards other people. Concepts of selfishness and responsibility first appear, and the person can criticize one's own judgment and behaviour for being selfish. Although aware of the needs of others, the person still decides to do what she or he wants, what feels good, or what will best protect herself or himself. Self-interest remains the main criterion in moral decision-making, and caring for others occasionally takes place.

2 Caring for others
Moral thinking is characterized by elaborations of responsibility and providing care for other people, especially dependent and weaker ones. Being good is equated with self-sacrificing care for others. The person seeks to follow social norms, and there is a strong need for security. Moral conflicts arise, especially over the issues of hurting, and others are often helped or protected at the expense of self-assertion.

2.5 Transition to reflective care
Moral thinking is characterized by a re-evaluation of the relationship between self and others, as the person questions the moral value of protecting others at one's own expense. Truth and honesty in relationships is emphasized. Compared to the "black-and white" worldview of the previous level, complexities and nuances are expressed. In solving the conflict, one feels partly responsible for other people but is also concerned about oneself and wants to assert one's own views and needs.

3 Caring for self and others
Moral thinking is characterized by balancing needs of both self and others and attempts to minimize hurt or harm of everyone impacted in the situation. The tension between selfishness and responsibility is resolved through a new understanding of the interconnection between others and self. The morality of action is judged on the basis of its actual intention and effects. The criteria for goodness have moved inward. No longer restricted by social convention, the person is able to make complex moral choices, accepts responsibility for decisions, and takes control of one's own life.

The ECI consists of four dilemmas that are administered in a semi-structured interview format. In addition to a real-life conflict generated by the participant, three standard interpersonal dilemmas are presented involving conflicts about unplanned pregnancy, marital fidelity, and care for a parent. These dilemmas are included in the measure to present common interpersonal concerns where the helping of others could be at the expense of hurting oneself (Skoe, 2014). The interviews are audio-recorded and then scored according to the Ethic of Care Interview Manual (Skoe, 1993). In scoring, it is important to discern whose needs and concerns the participant takes into account in the situation and the reasons for the suggested decision, rather than the decision itself. For example, the person should stay married or divorce for the sake of children (Skoe, 1993, 2014).

Studies with the ECI so far have involved over 1500 participants, ranging from 10 to 85 years of age and involving several nationalities from North-America and Scandinavian countries (Skoe, 2014). Cross-sectional studies and three longitudinal studies have unanimously supported the suggested developmental sequence of the levels originally proposed by Gilligan (Juujärvi, 2006; Juujärvi, Myyry, & Pesso, 2012; Pratt, Skoe, & Arnold, 2004). Care reasoning among adults seems to vary across all levels. The construct validity of the levels of care reasoning is supported by findings of positive relations to volunteer helping (Pratt et al., 2004), affective empathy and perspective-taking (Juujärvi, Myyry, & Pesso, 2010), complexity of reasoning, and consultation with others (Skoe, Pratt, Matthews, & Curror, 1996). Furthermore, 51 forensic psychiatric patients who had committed serious violent crimes scored at the lowest ECI levels with two exceptions (Adshead, Brown, Skoe, Glover, & Nicholson, 2008), whereas 25% of social work students had achieved the highest level at the end of their studies (Juujärvi, 2006; Juujärvi et al., 2012).

While gender differences have been non-existent at least among college-educated young adults, levels of care reasoning have been found to be associated with ego identity development, especially for women (Skoe & Diessner, 1994; Skoe & von der Lippe, 2002). This corroborates Gilligan's (1982) classic notion that women's conceptions of self and morality are interwoven and may explain the finding that women face more care based conflicts in their everyday lives than men (Jaffee & Hyde, 2000; Skoe et al., 1996). Which factors do explain advances in care development? Gilligan (1982) proposed that life crises are catalysts for care development, creating an opportunity for moral growth but also for disillusionment and nihilism. In Juujärvi's (2006) longitudinal study the only regressed participant was a male, full of anger and despair, who has recently lost custody of his children. Pratt et al. (2004) found that parents' emphasis on caring and autonomy-encouraging upbringing practices enhanced care development from age 16 to age 20. Juujärvi et al. (2012) observed that affective empathy and preference for values of self-direction predicted care development among nursing and social care students. The examination of specific determinants of care development is still underway, but empirical evidence so far suggests that encouraging children and youth to empathise with other people's emotional states, as well as to explore their own values as a basis for independent decision-making may boost care development.

Care and justice in everyday moral reasoning

The ethic of care deals with issues of micro-morality embedded in the dynamics of close relationships, while the ethic of justice is more focused on issues of macro-morality, including also strangers and impersonal relationships beyond community. Still, they are often intertwined in moral conflicts people encounter in their everyday lives (Juujärvi, 2005; Sherblom, Shipps, & Sherblom, 1993). Personal relationships can be viewed from both perspectives, and care and justice arguments can support as well as contradict each other. To take a usual example, the individual learns that the spouse of a friend has been unfaithful. When considering whether to reveal the affair to the friend, the individual may weigh the consequences of the decision for relationships against the worth of maintaining the moral principles of honesty or marital fidelity. Middle-aged children may wonder whether assisting a parent with dementia to stay at home is within their responsibilities or whether it belongs to the duties of the state.

In addition to peoples' private lives, the ethics of care and justice play an important role in public life through professional ethical decision-making. Especially in Western societies, where the moral discourse of the ethic of autonomy is dominant (see Chapter 6), civil servants have the duty to protect the rights of citizens. In helping professions, care and justice considerations are integrated in high-level ethical decision-making, as the ethic of care enhances relationships with clients, and the ethic of justice guarantees individual rights and the equal treatment of citizens. For example, nurses seek to maintain the ethical principle of self-determination, by respecting patients' autonomous decision-making even when patients take fatal health risks, such as refusing to take medicine, but still sustaining contact and staying attentive to their emerging needs of help (Gremmen, 1999). In increasingly complex healthcare contexts, professionals need to understand various issues of social justice in order to protect the rights of the most vulnerable people, such as the elderly and the disabled (Juujärvi, Ronkainen, & Silvennoinen, 2019).

Although care and justice reasoning represent divergent developmental paths, they have been found to be correlated with each other: the more just one is, the more caring one is, or vice versa, but there is also variation among individuals (Juujärvi, 2006; Juujärvi et al., 2010; Skoe & Diessner, 1994; Skoe et al., 1996; Skoe & von der Lippe, 2002). It is plausible that these two tracks of moral development share the underlying mechanism of perspective-taking and impulse control, because they both describe progress from initial self-oriented concern towards concern for others (Juujärvi et al., 2010). They seem to become integrated in postconventional moral thought which emphasises individuals' rights and responsibilities for their life choices as an ultimate moral criterion (Juujärvi, 2006; Juujärvi, Pesso, & Myyry, 2011). Thus, Kohlberg's (1984) assertion that care and justice are fused in mature moral thought, sharing respect for the human dignity of all people, seems valid in light of the empirical findings. This takes place, especially in mature adulthood, when growth in moral reasoning continues into middle age (Armon & Dawson, 1997; Helkama, 2004; Skoe et al., 1996). The same seems to be true for moral motivation as well. In line with the findings mentioned above, on the increase in the importance of universalism values with age, the relationship between communal (working for others) and agentic (achievement) motives changes to mid-adulthood, so that communal motives become stronger, and agentic ones weaker (Walker & Frimer, 2015), even among ordinary people.

Some people are more than ordinary, however, Colby and Damon (1992) initiated the study of persons who other people admired for their extraordinary moral qualities, sustained commitment to volunteer work, or promoting human rights. A central finding from this study of 22 Americans was that for them, personal and moral concerns had become fused, so that they had overcome the tension between personal interests and prosocial causes. This kind of hierarchical integration of moral concern with personal ambitions has also been observed in the subsequent research programme by Walker and his associates (e.g., Frimer, Walker, Dunlop, Lee, & Riches, 2011). A typical design has been to ask a number of people to nominate others whom they admire, and compare these exemplars with a matched sample of ordinary people. In addition to ordinary adults, speeches and interviews of famous 20th century public persons, some judged by experts as possessing moral character, others less, were studied using a variety of sophisticated techniques, with a view to distinguish instrumental and terminal (ultimate) goals. The message of this research is unambiguous: the moral exemplars, in effect, seem to follow the principle "I use my social status to help others", and not "I help others to improve my social standing". These moral exemplars can be seen as wise people who have transcended their egoistical selves into serving selflessly others through self-development (Ardelt, 2008).

We have described two trajectories related to reflective moral problem-solving, care, and justice, pertaining to thorny issues of right and wrong in everyday lives. The capacity to resolve those issues is called wisdom in everyday language. Wisdom is also one of those values related to self-transcendence whose importance grows across the lifespan. Wisdom has been defined as a combination of cognitive, reflective, and affective qualities with which a person desires to know the truth, is capable of looking at events from different viewpoints and feels compassionate love for others (Ardelt, 2008). These qualities are also characteristics of mature care and justice reasoning which end up in seeking moral truth through balancing the perspectives of all those involved in a situation. Being honest with oneself as well as others signals both moral maturity and wisdom.

Acknowledgements

This article has been supported by the Strategic Research Council at the Academy of Finland (project 303 608).

Note

1 An earlier and more limited version of this chapter has been presented in Finnish by Juujärvi (2016).

References

Adshead, G., Brown, C., Skoe, E., Glover, J., & Nicholson, S. (2008). Studying moral reasoning in forensic psychiatric patients. In G. Widdershoven, J. McMillan, T. Hope, & L. van der Scheer (Eds.), *Empirical ethics in psychiatry* (pp. 211–230). Oxford, England: Oxford University Press.

Ardelt, M. (2008). Self-development through selflessness: The paradoxical process of growing wiser. In H. A. Wayment & J. J. Bauer (Eds.), *Transcending self-interest: Psychological explorations of the quiet ego* (Decade of Behavior, pp. 221–233). Washington, DC: American Psychological Association.

Armon, C., & Dawson, T. L. (1997). Developmental trajectories in moral reasoning across the life span. *Journal of Moral Education, 26*(4), 433–453.

Bebeau, M. J. (2002). The Defining Issues Test and the four component model: Contributions to professional education. *Journal of Moral Education, 31*(3), 271–296.

Blum, L. A. (1988). Gilligan and Kohlberg: Implications for moral theory. *Ethics, 98*(3), 472–491.

Cáceda, R., James, G. A., Ely, T. D., Snarey, J., & Kilts, C. D. (2011). Mode of effective connectivity within a putative neural network differentiates moral cognitions related to care and justice ethics. *PLoS ONE, 6*(2), e14730. doi:10.1371/journal.pone.0014730

Colby, A., & Damon, W. (1992). *Some do care: Contemporary lives of moral commitment.* New York, NY: Free Press.

Frimer, J. A., Walker, L. J., Dunlop, W. L., Lee, B. H., & Riches, A. (2011). The integration of agency and communion in moral personality: Evidence of enlightened self-interest. *Journal of Personality and Social Psychology, 101*(1), 149–163.

Gilligan, C. (1982). *In a different voice: Psychological theory and women's development.* Cambridge, MA: Harvard University Press.

Gilligan, C., Brown, L. M., & Rogers, A. G. (1990). Psyche embedded: A place for body, relationships, and culture in personality theory. In A. I. Rabin, R. A. Zucker, R. A. Emmons, & S. Frank (Eds.), *Studying persons and lives* (pp. 86–147). New York, NY: Springer.

Gremmen, I. (1999). Visiting nurses' situated ethics: Beyond 'care versus justice'. *Nursing Ethics, 6*(6), 515–527.

Helkama, K. (2004). Values, role-taking and empathy in moral development. *New Review of Social Psychology, 3*(1–2), 103–111.

Helkama, K., & Sortheix, F. M. (2015). Moral development, cultural differences. In J. D. Wright (Ed.), *International encyclopedia of the social & behavioral sciences* (2nd ed., Vol. 15, pp. 781–787). Amsterdam, the Netherlands: Elsevier.

Hofstede, G. (2001). *Culture's consequences: Comparing values, behaviors, institutions, and organizations across nations* (2nd ed.). Thousand Oaks, CA: SAGE.

Jaffee, S., & Hyde, J. S. (2000). Gender differences in moral orientations: A meta-analysis. *Psychological Bulletin, 126*(5), 703–726.

Juujärvi, S. (2003). *The ethic of care and its development: A longitudinal study among practical nursing, bachelor-degree social work and law enforcement students.* (Doctoral dissertation, University of Helsinki, Department of Social Psychology, Helsinki, Finland). Retrieved from http://ethesis.helsinki.fi/julkaisut/val/sosps/vk/juujarvi/theethic.pdf

Juujärvi, S. (2005). Care and justice in real-life moral reasoning. *Journal of Adult Development, 12*(4), 199–210.

Juujärvi, S. (2006). The ethic of care development: A longitudinal study of moral reasoning among practical-nursing, social-work and law-enforcement students. *Scandinavian Journal of Psychology, 47*(3), 193–202.

Juujärvi, S. (2016). Oikeudenmukaisuus ja huolenpito aikuisuuden moraaliajattelussa [Justice and care in adult moral thinking]. In E. Kallio (Ed.), *Ajattelun kehitys aikuisuudessa: Kohti moninäkökulmaisuutta [The development of thinking in adulthood: Towards multiperspective thinking]* (Research in Educational Sciences No. 71, pp. 155–181). Helsinki, Finland: The Finnish Educational Research Association.

Juujärvi, S., Myyry, L., & Pesso, K. (2010). Does care reasoning make a difference? Relations between care, justice and dispositional empathy. *Journal of Moral Education, 39*(4), 469–489.

Juujärvi, S., Myyry, L., & Pesso, K. (2012). Empathy and values as predictors of care development. *Scandinavian Journal of Psychology, 53*(5), 413–420.

Juujärvi, S., Pesso, K., & Myyry, L. (2011). Care-based ethical reasoning among first-year nursing and social services students. *Journal of Advanced Nursing, 67*(2), 418–427.

Juujärvi, S., Ronkainen, K., & Silvennoinen, P. (2019). The ethics of care and justice in primary nursing of older patients. *Clinical Ethics, 14*(4), 187–194. doi: 10.1177/ 1477750919876250

Kohlberg, L. (1976). Moral stages and moralization: The cognitive-developmental approach. In T. Lickona (Ed.), *Moral development and behavior: Theory, research, and social issues* (pp. 31–53). New York, NY: Holt, Rinehart and Winston.

Kohlberg, L. (1984). *The psychology of moral development: The nature and validity of moral stages* (Essays on moral development, Vol. 2). San Francisco, CA: Harper & Row.

Krebs, D. L., Denton, K., & Wark, G. (1997). The forms and functions of real-life moral decision-making. *Journal of Moral Education, 26*(2), 131–145.

Lies, J. M., Bock, T., Brandenberger, J., & Trozzolo, T. A. (2012). The effects of off-campus service learning on the moral reasoning of college students. *Journal of Moral Education, 41*(2), 189–199.

Lyons, N. P. (1983). Two perspectives: On self, relationships and morality. *Harvard Educational Review, 53*(2), 125–145.

Mayhew, M. J., & King, P. (2008). How curricular content and pedagogical strategies affect moral reasoning development in college students. *Journal of Moral Education, 37*(1), 17–40.

Myyry, L., Juujärvi, S., & Pesso, K. (2013). Change in values and moral reasoning during higher education. *European Journal of Developmental Psychology, 10*(2), 269–284.

Pratt, M. W., Skoe, E. E., & Arnold, M. L. (2004). Care reasoning development and family socialization patterns in later adolescence: A longitudinal analysis. *International Journal of Behavioural Development, 28*(2), 139–147.

Rest, J., Narvaez, D., Bebeau, M. J., & Thoma, S. J. (1999). *Postconventional moral thinking: A neo-Kohlbergian approach.* Mahwah, NJ: Erlbaum.

Schwartz, S. H. (2016). Basic individual values: Sources and consequences. In T. Brosch & D. Sander (Eds.), *Handbook of value: Perspectives from economics, neuroscience, philosophy, psychology, and sociology* (pp. 63–84). Oxford, England: Oxford University Press.

Sherblom, S., Shipps, T. B., & Sherblom, J. C. (1993). Justice, care, and integrated concerns in the ethical decision making of nurses. *Qualitative Health Research, 3*(4), 442–464.

Skoe, E. E. (1993). *The ethic of care interview manual.* Unpublished manuscript, University of Oslo, Oslo, Norway.

Skoe, E. E., & Diessner, R. (1994). Ethic of care, justice, identity, and gender: An extension and replication. *Merrill-Palmer Quarterly, 40*(2), 272–289.

Skoe, E. E., Pratt, M. W., Matthews, M., & Curror, S. E. (1996). The ethic of care: Stability over time, gender differences and correlates in mid- to late adulthood. *Psychology and Aging, 11*(2), 280–292.

Skoe, E. E., & von der Lippe, A. L. (2002). Ego development and the ethics of care and justice: The relations among them revisited. *Journal of Personality, 70*(4), 485–508.

Skoe, E. E. A. (1998). The ethic of care: Issues in moral development. In E. E. A. Skoe & A. L. von der Lippe (Eds.), *Personality development in adolescence: A cross national and life span perspective* (Adolescence and society, pp. 143–171). London, England: Routledge.

Skoe, E. E. A. (2014). Measuring care-based moral development: The ethic of care interview. *Behavioural Development Bulletin, 19*(3), 95–103.

Snarey, J. R. (1985). Cross-cultural universality of social-moral development: A critical review of Kohlbergian research. *Psychological Bulletin, 97*(2), 202–232.

Thoma, S. J. (1986). Estimating gender differences in the comprehension and preference of moral issues. *Developmental Review, 6*(2), 165–180.

Vreeke, G. J. (1991). Gilligan on justice and care: Two interpretations. *Journal of Moral Education, 20*(1), 33–46.

Walker, L. J. (1991). Sex differences in moral reasoning. In W. M. Kurtines & J. L. Gewirtz (Eds.), *Handbook of moral behavior and development: Volume 2: Research* (pp. 333–364). Hillsdale, NJ: Erlbaum.

Walker, L. J., deVries, B., & Bichard, S. L. (1984). The hierarchical nature of stages of moral development. *Developmental Psychology, 20*(5), 960–966.

Walker, L. J., & Frimer, J. A. (2015). Developmental trajectories of agency and communion in moral motivation. *Merrill-Palmer Quarterly, 61*(3), 412–439.

Wark, G. R., & Krebs, D. L. (1996). Gender and dilemma differences in real-life moral judgment. *Developmental Psychology, 32*(2), 220–230.

6

BROADENING THE VIEW OF MORALITY, AND A STUDY OF MORAL DEVELOPMENT[1]

Jaana-Piia Mäkiniemi and Annukka Vainio

Introduction

The aim of this chapter is to describe how the conceptualisation of what is moral has broadened from Kohlberg's (1984) and Gilligan's (1982) views, presented in Chapter 5, and how that has influenced the study of moral development.

Simply put, moral beliefs are socially shared beliefs about what bad/wrong or good/right is and what one thinks should or should not be done according to a code of conduct put forward in a smaller or larger group (Gert, 2015). Furthermore, it is stated that moral beliefs differ from attitudes and norms, for example, so that they appear to be perceived as more objective and universally true and are treated as morally motivating and obligatory (Skitka, 2010; Turiel, 1983). It is worth noting that it is common to differentiate between ethics and morals, and ethics is often referred to as a philosophical study of morality. However, in moral psychology, the concepts of "ethics" and "morals" tend to be used interchangeably and fairly freely, and typically both of them are used to refer to everyday views of right and wrong (e.g., Rest & Narváez, 1994).

Furthermore, moral psychology has a long tradition of defining morality and moral issues by drawing on philosophy (e.g., Blasi, 1990; Lapsley & Narvaez, 2005). Such research that would have been truly open to respondents' personal views and definitions of morality has been missing. Typically, a researcher selects the issues that she or he considers to be moral questions, and then research participants respond by choosing from preselected options, as on questionnaires (Mäkiniemi, 2016). However, there is disagreement among researchers about what should belong to the moral domain (e.g., Kugler, Jost, & Noorbaloochi, 2014; Suhler & Churchland, 2011). For example, it has been suggested that work-related values, which are not explicitly included in any moral psychology approach, should be defined as moral values (Myyry & Helkama, 2001). It has also been noted that if the definition of morality is too restricted, relevant lay views of morality may be excluded (Blasi, 1990; Vainio, 2005). Therefore, we assume that theories and methods should be broad or open and able to capture possible novel themes and lay definitions associated with the moral domain (cf. Mäkiniemi, 2016; Mäkiniemi, Pirttilä-Backman, & Pieri, 2011, 2013).

Nonetheless, views about the principles that are considered moral ones have broadened in recent decades. In the 1980s, Gilligan's (1982) approach broadened and complemented Kohlberg's (1984) approach of justice-based moral reasoning by focusing on the development of care-based moral reasoning. Evidently, the above-mentioned important debate within moral psychology regarding what belongs to the moral domain has broadened the view of the criteria that characterise morality. Furthermore, a step towards the triadic view of morality was taken in the 1990s with the introduction of the big three of morality: autonomy, community, and divinity (Shweder, Much, Mahapatra, & Park, 1997), and ultimately, the fivefold view of the moral domain was presented in the 2000s by Jonathan Haidt and his colleagues (e.g., Graham, Haidt, & Nosek, 2009). The need to broaden the scope of morality mainly stemmed from cross-cultural and anthropological findings indicating that justice and harm-based morality are not the most relevant aspects of morality outside of Western countries, and therefore, create too narrow a frame of reference for comparative studies (e.g., Haidt & Kesebir, 2010).

Approaches to studying moral issues can be placed along a continuum from moral universalism to moral relativism. Cognitive-developmental approaches (e.g. Kohlberg, see Chapter 5) emphasise the elements that are common across different cultures and social groups and characterise morality as a domain that is perceived as universal and generalisable (e.g., Turiel, 1983). However, in practice, it has been shown that the issues viewed as belonging to the moral domain in one culture or subculture may be perceived as belonging to the personal or social domain in another, supporting the notion of some kind of moral relativism coexisting with the universal aspects of moral reasoning (e.g., Shweder, Mahapatra, & Miller, 1987; Sverdlik, Roccas, & Sagiv, 2012). Within the cognitive-developmental approaches, the universally shared structure of moral reasoning is understood to be distinct from the content, which may vary culturally (e.g., Kohlberg, 1969, 1971; Piaget, 1932), whereas cultural psychological approaches do not make a clear distinction between the structure and content. For example, Richard Shweder and colleagues (1987) suggested that, culturally, there are both universal and variable aspects in what is regarded as structure in the cognitive-developmental approach. In order to capture this variation across different approaches, we use the broad definition proposed by Lind (1992), where structure refers to the relationship of elements of moral reasoning, and content refers to the elements themselves, such as values that people use for justifying their moral views or behaviours and the issues that are discussed.

From two to three moralities

Shweder, a cultural psychologist, used the interviews he had collected in India (Bhubaneswar) and the United States (Chicago) to later develop the big three model of morality in the 1980s and 1990s (Shweder, Haidt, Horton, & Joseph, 2008; Shweder et al., 1987, 1997). According to this approach, there are three different moral codes, or ethics, that conceptualise a moral agent in different ways.

First, the discourse of the ethic of autonomy describes the moral agent as an autonomous individual who is free to make choices only with minor limits. This ethic focuses on an individual's rights and needs: harming oneself or others ought to be avoided, and the rights of other persons ought to be respected. Within the ethic of autonomy, behaviour is assessed from the perspective of harm, rights, fairness, autonomy, and freedom. The second moral discourse, the ethic of community, defines a moral agent in relation to his/her group memberships, such as family, workplace, or society. This kind of moral reasoning is underpinned by role-based duties and obligations. The objectives of moral behaviour are maintaining social order and harmony and avoiding social sanctions. When behaviour is evaluated from this perspective, we often think about duties, role-based commitments, obedience to authorities, loyalty, group reputation, and dependency on other people, as well as including a consideration of what is best for one's community. The third moral discourse, the ethic of divinity, characterises a moral agent as a spiritual being who aspires to follow sacred rules. Moral rules that guide behaviour are based on sacred scriptures or a natural order of things. Moral behaviour in this ethic is defined as the avoidance of moral degradation and striving towards moral purity. When behaviour is assessed from this perspective, we often think about sin, the natural order of things, sanctity, and purity, as well as protecting one's soul and the world from contamination or spiritual desecration (Helkama, 2009; Shweder et al., 1997).

As a whole, research findings support the idea that three moral codes exist in different cultures (for a review, see Jensen, 2008). Between-country differences (e.g., the United States vs. the Philippines, the United Kingdom vs. Brazil) as well as within-country ones (e.g., religious conservatives vs. religious liberals) have been found in the use of these moral codes (Guerra & Giner-Sorolla, 2010; Vainio, 2003, 2015; Vasquez, Keltner, Ebenbach, & Banaszynski, 2001), supporting cultural psychologists' notion of cultural variability in moral reasoning. For example, North Americans seem to prefer the ethic of autonomy more often than Brazilians, Indians, or Filipinos do (Jensen, 2008; Vasquez et al., 2001), and in Finland, liberal religious and non-religious adolescents justified their moral views with autonomy and community equally, whereas conservative religious adolescents used the ethic of divinity most frequently (Vainio, 2011).

Three moralities, culture, and development

The big three model did not describe how the ethics of autonomy, community, and divinity develop as individuals grow older. However, based on the cultural psychological approach to morality and moral socialisation (e.g., Shweder et al., 1987, 1997), Lene Jensen (1997, 2008, 2011) developed a model that integrates the notions of developmental changes occurring throughout the lifespan and the differences between individuals in their cultural understandings of what is considered moral. Within this model, culture is defined as a community that shares key beliefs, values, behaviours, routines, and institutions (Jensen, 2015a). The model is based on the acknowledgement that culture-based models underestimate the role of individual development, while the cognitive-developmental models underestimate the role of culture in trying to understand the development of morality. Therefore, the cultural-developmental template integrates these two lines of research.

The cultural-developmental model describes how the ethics of autonomy, community, and divinity are used throughout the lifespan. In practice, the model describes trends in the use of ethics at different ages along with changes in the kinds of concepts that are typically used at different ages, for example, whether community-based concepts used by children are different from those used by adolescents or adults (Jensen, 2008, 2011). In this model, development is broadly defined as the changes and consistencies in an individual's thinking patterns, looking at either increases or decreases and quantitative or qualitative changes in moral thinking. Moreover, change can be characterised as occurring either gradually or in stages. This definition for development is intentionally broad and flexible and is different from the definition used in cognitive-developmental approaches, which conceptualise development as universal, directional, irreversible, and inevitable (Kallio & Marchand, 2012; Kohlberg & Armon, 1984).

According to this model, the ethic of autonomy is already used in early childhood, and its use continues in more or less the same way throughout adolescence and adulthood in individualistic cultures. However, there are changes in the way autonomy is used. For example, factors related to equality and fairness seem to emerge more frequently in adolescence. In collectivistic cultures such as India, which emphasise the importance of community, the use of autonomy decreases with age, which may reveal the impact of culture (Kapadia & Bhangaokar, 2015).

In adolescence and adulthood, the use of the community ethic increases and becomes conceptually more varied and richer. In addition, the scope of what belongs to one's community broadens with age; it begins with one's own family and friends in childhood and eventually develops through wider consideration to embrace society at large during adolescence and adulthood (cf. Kohlberg's idea of broadening social networks and social perspective).

According to Jensen (2008, 2011), developmental changes occurring in the ethic of divinity are not yet well known. The development of a divinity-based moral discourse appears to be more group-oriented than other moral codes, which typically means something like, for example, belonging to a liberal or conservative religious community shaping the development of divinity-based moral thinking. The ethic of divinity is used rather infrequently in childhood, used increasingly in adolescence, and is used most frequently in adulthood (Jensen, 2008; Jensen & McKenzie, 2016). This may happen because, in some cultures, the concepts around supernatural forces are so abstract that it is not possible to understand them in early childhood (Jensen, 2008, 2011).

The cultural-developmental template assumes that individuals in all cultures share these three ethics or moral codes. However, the model does not assume that age-related development follows the same trajectory in all cultures or communities, as cognitive-developmental models suggest (e.g., Kohlberg, 1984). More specifically, Jensen (2018) identifies two lines of moral development that differ in terms of how moral codes are hierarchically related to each other. These two lines are linked to whether an individual's approach to religion is liberal or conservative (e.g., Bellah, 1987; Jensen, 1998, 2000, 2006). Religious conservatism is associated with the view that a moral code is created by a transcendent authority as well as a concern that contemporary societies are distancing from God. Conversely, religiously liberal individuals are more likely to regard moral issues as being subject to change due to societal developments. Therefore, it is expected that differences between religiously liberal and conservative individuals are such that conservative adults use the concepts of community and divinity in their reasoning more often than autonomy. Religiously conservative individuals emphasise the ethic of divinity as their main moral code, whereas religiously liberal individuals place more emphasis on the ethics of autonomy and community equally (Jensen, 2008, 2011, 2018; Vainio, 2015).

Furthermore, cultural communities may shape an individual's course in life, which in turn, may eventually influence which moral codes the individual regards as most relevant. For example, individualistic cultures such as those in North America emphasise youth and a prolonged phase of concentrating on oneself, which means that the autonomy-based moral code may be used rather than the community-based moral code during adolescence and young adulthood (Jensen, 2008, 2011).

Jensen's (2008, 2011) cultural-developmental and Shweder et al.'s (1997) big three models were empirically tested across five national samples from Brazil, Israel, Japan, New Zealand, and the United Kingdom. A total of 792 emerging adults between the ages of 18 and 23 participated. The novelty value of this study is increased by the fact that there are but few (intercultural) studies of moral thinking among young adults. In practice, it was explored whether, in the course of emerging adulthood, young adults differ in their moral thinking due to a cultural context and age. The key findings indicated that all three ethics were used by young adults in all countries. However, the level of endorsement varied between countries. For example, Japanese young adults endorsed the ethic of divinity significantly less than did young adults from other countries. However, researchers suggested that one explanation for a lower endorsement may be an effect from the type of items included in the method used (CADS divinity subscale; see Jensen, 2015b) which may not necessarily cover some important aspects of Japanese folk and formal religions. Thus, more longitudinal studies focusing on the development of moral codes in different cultural contexts are needed.

From three to five: moral foundations theory

Moral foundations theory (MFT) was developed by Haidt together with Joseph and Graham (Graham et al., 2013; Haidt & Joseph, 2004). The earliest formulation of it was published in 2004, and this first conceptualisation included only four independent modules of morality: suffering, hierarchy, reciprocity, and purity. However, in the footnote of that article, a potential fifth module was already cited as the ingroup/outgroup dimension. MFT was based on the analysis of different studies in social science (Haidt & Joseph, 2004). According to the authors' own words, they wanted to find the common foundation of morality. In practice, the model was based on existing models of morality (in particular, Shweder's three ethics model) and values (Schwartz's Theory of Basic Values). The version of MFT that included five moral foundations was published in 2007, although Haidt and colleagues have considered adding a sixth moral foundation to their model (e.g., Iyer, Koleva, Graham, Ditto, & Haidt, 2012). In addition, the names and contents of the foundations have been slightly modified in that time. For instance, ingroup/loyalty is nowadays also called loyalty/betrayal. So, it seems that MFT is currently more like a developing project than a stable theoretical formulation.

MFT supposes that humans have innate moral intuitions that are instinctive predispositions, or quick gut feelings or "decisions" that come into consciousness within seconds for approval or disapproval (Haidt & Joseph, 2004). According to this theory, these instinctive intuitions cannot be directly observed, but it is possible to study moral reasoning that is based on these intuitions (Haidt & Kesebir, 2010). Even if MFT assumes that moral foundations are intuitive, this theory does not exclusively focus on intuitions but rather on the way moral foundations are expressed in moral discourse or thinking. Despite their intuitive origin, it is assumed that moral foundations occur in moral thinking in general as well as in the moral reasoning that individuals use for resolving moral problems.

MFT also assumes that moral foundations are universal psychological systems enabling people to perceive actions and actors as right or wrong. Therefore, these foundations do not describe only morally right issues but also include more generally morally loaded issues. The fact that cultures and social groups can prioritise them in different ways explains why there are differences in moral norms and practices between and within countries. The five foundations are the following:

1) The *care/harm* foundation describes an individual's capacity to feel compassion towards other people and their willingness to avoid harm. Moral virtues that are based on this foundation are kind-heartedness and compassion. When behaviour is evaluated from this perspective, we ask, for example, whether the behaviour harmed someone.

2) The *fairness/cheating* foundation describes the quality of interaction between individuals, and corresponding moral virtues focus on the unbiased treatment of individuals. When behaviour is assessed from this perspective, it is asked whether someone behaved fairly or unfairly, for example.

3) The *loyalty/betrayal* foundation is based on the idea of favouring one's own ingroup, possibly at the expense of outgroups. Moral virtues include loyalty and trustworthiness, group solidarity, patriotism, and heroism. When behaviour is evaluated from this perspective, it is asked whether someone who was mistreated was a group member or not.

4) The *authority/subversion* foundation describes an individual's willingness and capacity to respect authorities and operate in hierarchical groups. Moral virtues may include showing respect for people with high status or authority, fulfilling duties, and obedience. When behaviour is assessed from this perspective, it is asked whether individuals involved in a situation had the same status or different ones.

5) The *sanctity/degradation* foundation focuses on bodily functions, their purity or impurity, and especially religious activities. From this perspective, carnal desires such as overeating, where animalistic desires control behaviour, are perceived as morally despicable. For example, seeing someone who is overweight would, in this case, raise feelings of disgust. In contrast, controlling one's bodily functions is perceived as morally acceptable. When this moral foundation is used for evaluating behaviour, it is asked whether that behaviour elicited feelings of disgust or not (Haidt & Kesebir, 2010).

Together, the fairness/cheating foundation and the care/harm foundation are called the individualising foundations, whereas loyalty/betrayal, authority/subversion, and sanctity/degradation are named the binding foundations (Haidt & Kesebir, 2010).

According to MFT, these moral intuitions or foundations shape an individual's political orientation (Graham et al., 2013, 2009; van Leeuwen & Park, 2009). Findings suggest that liberals (i.e., typically, supporters of left-wing politics) are likely to consider the individualising foundations more morally relevant than the binding foundations, and conservatives (i.e., typically supporters of right-wing politics) are likely to consider the binding foundations more important from the moral point of view. The existence of the pattern has been demonstrated in different countries, such as in the United States and Finland (Graham et al., 2013, 2009; Mäkiniemi et al., 2013; McAdams et al., 2008; Vainio & Mäkiniemi, 2016; van Leeuwen & Park, 2009). It is worth noting, however, that the liberal/conservative distinction does not match a left-wing/right-wing distinction in all societies, because the political left may in some cases privilege the welfare of the group over the individual liberties (Graham et al., 2009) and therefore, that ideological preferences are often very heterogeneous (Weber & Federico, 2013). For instance, in a Finnish study of moral foundations in food-related moral thinking, there were differences between supporters of left-wing, right-wing, and centrist politics (a common list of political identities in the Finnish context; Mäkiniemi et al., 2013).

Five moralities and development

Although MFT is currently actively utilised in moral psychology studies, there have not been many attempts to relate or integrate MFT with the theories of development. In other words, there have been no serious attempts to describe or conceptualise how moral thinking develops from the perspective of moral foundations, such as whether or not there are common changes in the use of foundations as individuals grow older. This likely stems from the fact that basic assumptions about the nature of morality and moral decision-making differ between the cognitive-developmental approaches (e.g., Kohlberg, 1984) and MFT (cf. Maxwell & Narvaez, 2013). In addition, MFT has a focus on the content of moral thinking and reasoning, whereas cognitive-developmental approaches focus on the structure.

However, there are actually some studies measuring the associations between moral foundations and moral schemas as measured by the Defining Issues Test (DIT). The DIT is a method used in the neo-Kohlbergian approach that corresponds to Kohlberg's stages of moral reasoning (for the description of the stages and their relationships, see Chapter 5). Baril and Wright (2012) found an overlap between the DIT's personal interest schema and Kohlberg's stages 2/3 with the loyalty/betrayal foundation, and another association was found between the maintaining norms schema that corresponds to Kohlberg's stage 4 and to the authority/subversion foundation. In addition, in a study by Glover and colleagues (2014), the binding foundations positively predicted the maintaining norms schema and negatively predicted the postconventional schema, which represents Kohlberg's stages 5 and 6. However, there were no significant associations between the individualising foundations and moral schemas.

The above findings suggest that moral foundations may be more representative of conventional reasoning (Kohlberg's stages 3 and 4) than postconventional reasoning (stages 5 and 6; Glover et al., 2014). Indirectly, these findings may also indicate that a Kohlbergian definition of morality is not as narrow as commonly assumed. This issue also warrants further research because Kohlberg's model of moral development has been accused of favouring Western liberal traditions (e.g., Graham et al., 2013).

Furthermore, at least theoretically, it is possible to assume that developmental changes also appear within moral foundations. As presented in detail below, Jensen (2008, 2011) proposed that there appear to be developmental shifts in the use of Shweder's three ethics that share similarities with moral foundations. It seems that there are developmental changes in the types of concepts used within autonomy, community, and divinity. However, again, the development of the ethic of divinity is still rather unexplored (Jensen, 2008, 2011; Jensen & McKenzie, 2016). The three ethics are conceptually very close to the five moral foundations. More precisely, the care/harm and fairness/cheating foundations share similarities with the ethics of autonomy; the loyalty/betrayal and authority/subversion foundations with the ethics of community; and finally, the sanctity/degradation foundation with the ethics of divinity (Mäkiniemi, 2016; Sverdlik et al., 2012) (see Table 6.1). Consequently, one could assume that moral foundations develop in similar vein given that they have so much in common with the three ethics. However, this assumption should be validated with empirical data. It is worth noting that, with this approach, it is possible to find out only how the content of moral thinking varies and changes across individuals since the three ethics and the foundations refer to the content of moral thinking.

So, are there any potential theoretical approaches for a researcher who is especially interested in a more structural development of moral thinking and wants to take into account the possibility that there are at least five different types of moral issues? As mentioned earlier, the common view is that with Kohlberg's (1984) theory, it is possible to explore justice-based morality, which corresponds quite closely to the fairness/cheating moral foundation. Similarly, Gilligan's (1982) model fits well for measuring the development of care-based morality, which is conceptually close to the care/harm moral foundation (cf. Chapter 5; see Table 6.1).

However, there are three other moral foundations left, and it is likely that the above-mentioned approaches are not able to cover their special aspects.

The first solution could be to develop three new models for describing the development of the remaining foundations. This assumption is in line with the existence of many domain-specific developmental models. These kinds of models imply specific development patterns relative to particular issues; in other words, morality does not necessarily develop in the same way as critical thinking or logical reasoning, for instance. The second – and likely more promising – option could be to apply more general approaches for measuring the development of morality and moral foundations. This assumption can be justified with the notion that cognitive development appears to be quite similar within many domains (Mäkiniemi, 2016). For example, based on the work of Kramer (1983), Kallio (2011) has suggested that, in many models, cognitive development proceeds from youth to adulthood through three phases, which are single perspective, multiperspective, and integrative thinking (see Chapter 2). In practice, thinking develops in these models from the "either-or" type of thinking, which is typical in youth, to the "both-and" type of thinking, which is assumed to be typical in adulthood. Integrative (or relativistic-dialectical) thinking combines these two types of reasoning.

Moreover, Myyry and her colleagues (Myyry & Helkama, 2007; Vartiainen, Siponen, & Myyry, 2011) examined the complexity of moral thinking in moral conflicts utilising the theory of integrative complexity, which can also be seen as a general type of approach. Integrative complexity refers to an individual's cognitive style and ways of information processing. Integrative complexity incorporates the two cognitive structural properties of differentiation and integration. Differentiation refers to the number of characteristics or dimensions of a problem that an individual figures out, and integration refers to the development of complex connections among the characteristics (Suedfeld, Tetlock, & Streufert, 1992). Integrative complexity emphasises the structure of moral thought rather than its content, and therefore, it can be used to analyse the integrative complexity of any issue. From the

TABLE 6.1 Five types of moral issues. Adapted from Sverdlik et al. (2012) *and* Mäkiniemi (2016)

| Author | Key dimension of morality | | | | | Does the model or theory describe the development of moral thinking? |
	Justice	*Care*	*Conformity*	*Social order*	*Divinity*	
Kohlberg (1969, 1984)	Justice (stage 6)					Yes
Gilligan (1982)		Care				Yes
Shweder et al. (1997; Shweder, 2003)	Autonomy	Autonomy	Community	Community	Divinity	No
Haidt et al. (2007)	Fairness/ Cheating	Care/ Harm	Loyalty/ Betrayal	Authority/ Subversion	Sanctity/ Degradation	No
Jensen (2008)	Autonomy	Autonomy	Community	Community	Divinity	Yes

developmental point of view, it is also possible to measure how integrative complexity of moral thinking develops or changes due to aging, or for example, due to ethical training or education. In line with the previous notions, Dawson and Gabrielian (2003) have proposed that one potential approach for investigating the structural development of moral thinking would be a domain-general method called the Hierarchical Complexity Scoring System (for more information, see Commons, 2008; Commons, Gane-McCalla, Barker, & Li, 2014; Fischer, 1980; see also Mäkiniemi, 2016; see Chapter 2).

Conclusions and challenges

To sum up the discussion, we can say that earlier theories in moral psychology clearly distinguished between the structure and the content of moral reasoning and focused mainly on the structure, describing how moral reasoning develops universally. Later theories have, instead, identified different sets of moral codes or ethics that are applied in different ways in different cultures (Graham et al., 2013; Shweder et al., 1997), with recent openings that characterise potentially different developmental pathways for the content of moral reasoning (Jensen, 2011, 2018). In practice, the definition of morality has broadened from one or two key principles to at least five. While the view of morality has expanded, the conventional models used to study the structural development of moral thinking do not necessarily cover all the new dimensions of morality. As a result, there is a need for new empirical and theoretical openings that take the approaches used to measure the structural aspects or changes of moral development and combine them with the approaches used to study the content of moral thinking (Mäkiniemi, 2016). We assume that so-called domain-general models such as the models of integrative complexity and the Hierarchical Complexity Scoring System could be used to study the complexity and development of any kind of moral thinking given that they are not focused on any specific type of moral issues or dilemmas.

As presented in this chapter, the definition of morality has gone through profound changes and become more varied as a constructive response to criticism. How, then, can the definition of morality still be improved in moral psychology? In our view, one issue common to these theories is that they have paid less attention to the context dependence of morality. In all the models, moral reasoning is thought to be a relatively general phenomenon. This careful avoidance of discussing contextual influences is closely related to the lack of discussion about how the concrete issues, behaviours, or topics being discussed shape the criteria or justifications used for evaluating each concrete case. There is some evidence that the characteristics of a concrete moral problem affect the complexity of reasoning used in its evaluation (Myyry & Helkama, 2007). Moreover, it has been shown that different contexts elicit different kinds of criteria, justifications, or principles. For example, moral dilemmas that involve other persons' needs are likely to elicit care-based reasoning, whereas rule violations are likely to elicit justice-based reasoning (Juujärvi, 2005). Furthermore, Jones (1991) suggested that moral decision-making is issue contingent. In other words, issues can be distinguished based on their moral intensity so that some issues are more likely to elicit moral reasoning than others.

We explored the difference between general and issue-specific endorsement of moral foundations in the context of climate change (Vainio & Mäkiniemi, 2016). When the foundations were measured at a general level, individualising foundations were associated with climate-friendly behaviours, and binding foundations were associated with the avoidance of these behaviours. This finding suggests that climate change is likely to be associated with the endorsement of individualising foundations by Finnish young adults. However, the participants also evaluated moral foundations applied to the context of climate change (e.g., sanctity/degradation was measured with a statement as to whether or not climate change causes moral degradation in the world). In this case, both individualising and binding foundations were associated with climate-friendly behaviours. Hence, this result indicates that individualising moral foundations are more likely to be associated with climate change than binding foundations. However, once individuals view climate change as a moral question from any perspective, they are likely to engage in climate change mitigation. These kinds of results can be used to inform the media and politicians on how societal issues should be framed in communications.

The insights of studies applying cognitive-developmental models of moral reasoning have been used extensively for developing school curricula and communities that promote the development of moral reasoning. However, the societal impact of cognitive-developmental models has become less visible (Lapsley & Narvaez, 2005). The extensive body of research using the cultural psychological theories of Shweder, Jensen, and Haidt has focused on describing the multitude of moral discourses and their relationship to sociopolitical problems in society. The broad definition of morality is thought of as being especially useful for studying group-based moral understandings and differences between groups (Haidt & Kesebir, 2010). This line of research carries enormous potential for supporting societal development by trying to solve a wide range of societal challenges, such as the moral roots of prejudice, inter-group conflicts, climate change denial, and populism (see also Lapsley & Carlo, 2014). We assume that analysing everyday situations or even bigger societal challenges from the viewpoints of different moral foundations may enhance perspective taking, and that this kind of capacity to analyse, understand, and integrate divergent moral perspectives can be seen as a type of wisdom (cf. Rakoczy, Wandt, Thomas, Nowak, & Kunzmann, 2018).

Moral psychology carries an enormous potential, but how can it respond to societal needs in ways that can have a real impact? In our view, one of the challenges lies, again, in the definition of morality. For too long, moral psychology has had a close and exclusive relationship with moral philosophy, which may have resulted in increased isolation from multidisciplinary endeavours. Societal challenges are often complex issues that require multidisciplinary, and even transdisciplinary, approaches where non-academic partners play an equally important role together with academic researchers. In such a situation, moral psychology's current philosophical underpinnings can become a burden that hinders productive collaboration with non-academic stakeholders who do not share the philosophical language. This general transformation in science is likely to change research settings in moral psychology as well – moral psychology has to open itself to new methodologies, types of data, and collaborative relationships.

Note

1 This article is a modified longer version of an earlier article in Finnish by Mäkiniemi (2016).

References

Baril, G. L., & Wright, J. C. (2012). Different types of moral cognition: Moral stages versus moral foundations. *Personality and Individual Differences*, *53*(4), 468–473.

Bellah, R. N. (1987). Conclusion: Competing visions of the role of religion in American society. In R. N. Bellah & F. E. Greenspahn (Eds.), *Uncivil religion: Interreligious hostility in America* (pp. 119–232). New York, NY: Crossroad.

Blasi, A. (1990). How should psychologists define morality? Or, the negative side effects of philosophy's influence on psychology. In T. E. Wren (Ed.), *The moral domain: Essays in the ongoing discussion between philosophy and the social sciences* (pp. 38–70). Cambridge, MA: The MIT Press.

Commons, M. L. (2008). Introduction to the model of hierarchical complexity and its relationship to postformal action. *World Futures*, *64*(5–7), 305–320.

Commons, M. L., Gane-McCalla, R., Barker, C. D., & Li, E. Y. (2014). The model of hierarchical complexity as a measurement system. *Behavioral Development Bulletin*, *19*(3), 9–14.

Dawson, T. L., & Gabrielian, S. (2003). Developing conceptions of authority and contract across the lifespan: Two perspectives. *Developmental Review*, *23*(2), 162–218.

Fischer, K. W. (1980). A theory of cognitive development: The control and construction of hierarchies of skills. *Psychological Review*, *87*(6), 477–531.

Gert, B. (2015). The definition of morality. In E. N. Zalta (Ed.), *The Stanford encyclopedia of philosophy*. (Fall 2015 ed.). Retrieved from. https://plato.stanford.edu/entries/morality-definition/

Gilligan, C. (1982). *In a different voice: Psychological theory and women's development*. Cambridge, MA: Harvard University Press.

Glover, R. J., Natesan, P., Wang, J., Rohr, D., McAfee-Etheridge, L., Booker, D. D., ... Wu, M. (2014). Moral rationality and intuition: An exploration of relationships between the defining issues test and the moral foundations questionnaire. *Journal of Moral Education*, *43*(4), 395–412.

Graham, J., Haidt, J., Koleva, S., Motyl, M., Iyer, R., Wojcik, S. P., & Ditto, P. H. (2013). Moral foundations theory: The pragmatic validity of moral pluralism. In P. Devine & A. Plant (Eds.), *Advances in experimental social psychology* (Vol. 47, pp. 55–130). Amsterdam, the Netherlands: Academic Press.

Graham, J., Haidt, J., & Nosek, B. A. (2009). Liberals and conservatives rely on different sets of moral foundations. *Journal of Personality and Social Psychology*, *96*(5), 1029–1046.

Guerra, V. M., & Giner-Sorolla, R. (2010). The community, autonomy, and divinity scale (CADS): A new tool for the cross-cultural study of morality. *Journal of Cross-Cultural Psychology*, *41*(1), 35–50.

Haidt, J., & Joseph, C. (2004). Intuitive ethics: How innately prepared intuitions generate culturally variable virtues. *Dædalus*, *133*(4), 55–66.

Haidt, J., & Joseph, C. (2007). The moral mind: How five sets of innate intuitions guide the development of many culture-specific virtues, and perhaps even modules. In P. Carruthers, S. Laurence, & S. Stich (Eds.), *The innate mind: Foundations and the future* (Evolution and cognition, Vol. 3, pp. 367–391). New York, NY: Oxford University Press.

Haidt, J., & Kesebir, S. (2010). Morality. In S. T. Fiske, D. T. Gilbert, & G. Lindzey (Eds.), *Handbook of social psychology* (5th ed., Vol. 2, pp. 797–832). Hoboken, NJ: Wiley.

Helkama, K. (2009). *Moraalipsykologia: Hyvän ja pahan tällä puolen* [Moral psychology: This side of good and evil]. Helsinki, Finland: Edita.

Iyer, R., Koleva, S., Graham, J., Ditto, P., & Haidt, J. (2012). Understanding libertarian morality: The psychological dispositions of self-identified libertarians. *PloS ONE*, *7*(8), e42366. doi:10.1371/journal/pone.0042366

Jensen, L. A. (1997). Culture wars: American moral divisions across the adult lifespan. *Journal of Adult Development*, *4*(2), 107–121.

Jensen, L. A. (1998). Moral divisions within countries between orthodoxy and progressivism: India and the United States. *Journal for the Scientific Study of Religion*, *37*(1), 90–107.

Jensen, L. A. (2000). Conversions across the culture war divide: Two case studies. In M. E. Miller & A. N. West (Eds.), *Spirituality, ethics, and relationship in adulthood: Clinical and theoretical explorations* (pp. 363–386). Madison, CT: Psychosocial Press.

Jensen, L. A. (2006). Liberal and conservative conceptions of family: A cultural-developmental study. *The International Journal for the Psychology of Religion*, *16*(4), 253–269.

Jensen, L. A. (2008). Through two lenses: A cultural-developmental approach to moral psychology. *Developmental Review*, *28*(3), 289–315.

Jensen, L. A. (2011). The cultural development of three fundamental moral ethics: Autonomy, community, and divinity. *Zygon*, *46*(1), 150–167.

Jensen, L. A. (2015a). Theorizing and researching moral development in a global world. In L. A. Jensen (Ed.), *Moral development in a global world: Research from a cultural-developmental perspective* (pp. 1–19). Cambridge, England: Cambridge University Press.

Jensen, L. A. (2015b). Coding manual: Ethics of autonomy, community, and divinity. In L. A. Jensen (Ed.), *Moral development in a global world: Research from a cultural-developmental perspective* (pp. 221–235). Cambridge, England: Cambridge University Press.

Jensen, L. A. (2018). The cultural-developmental approach to moral psychology: Autonomy, community, and divinity across cultures and ages. In M. J. Gelfand, C. Chiu, & Y. Hong (Eds.), *Handbook of advances in culture and psychology* (Vol. 7, pp. 107–152). New York, NY: Oxford University Press.

Jensen, L. A., & McKenzie, J. (2016). The moral reasoning of U.S. evangelical and mainline protestant children, adolescents, and adults: A cultural-developmental study. *Child Development*, *87*(3), 446–464.

Jones, T. M. (1991). Ethical decision making by individuals in organizations: An issue-contingent model. *The Academy of Management Review*, *16*(2), 366–395.

Juujärvi, S. (2005). Care and justice in real-life moral reasoning. *Journal of Adult Development*, *12*(4), 199–210.

Kallio, E. (2011). Integrative thinking is the key: An evaluation of current research into the development of adult thinking. *Theory & Psychology*, *21*(6), 785–801.

Kallio, E., & Marchand, H. (2012). An overview of the concepts of change and development: From the premodern to modern era. In P. Tynjälä, M.-L. Stenström, & M. Saarnivaara (Eds.), *Transitions and transformations in learning and education* (pp. 21–50). Dordrecht, the Netherlands: Springer.

Kapadia, S., & Bhangaokar, R. (2015). An Indian moral worldview: Developmental patterns in adolescents and adults. In L. A. Jensen (Ed.), *Moral development in a global world: Research from a cultural-developmental perspective* (pp. 69–91). Cambridge, England: Cambridge University Press.

Kohlberg, L. (1969). Stage and sequence. In D. A. Goslin (Ed.), *Handbook of socialization theory* (pp. 347–480). Chicago, IL: Rand McNally.

Kohlberg, L. (1971). *From is to ought: How to commit the naturalistic fallacy and get away with it in the study of moral development.* New York, NY: Academic Press.

Kohlberg, L. (1984). *The psychology of moral development: The nature and validity of moral stages* (Essays on moral development, Vol. 2). San Francisco, CA: Harper & Row.

Kohlberg, L., & Armon, C. (1984). Three types of stage models used in the study of adult development. In M. L. Commons, F. A. Richards, & C. Armon (Eds.), *Beyond formal operations: Late adolescent and adult cognitive development* (pp. 383–394). New York, NY: Praeger.

Kramer, D. A. (1983). Post-formal operations? A need for further conceptualization. *Human Development, 26*(2), 91–105.

Kugler, M., Jost, J. T., & Noorbaloochi, S. (2014). Another look at moral foundations theory: Do authoritarianism and social dominance orientation explain liberal–Conservative differences in "moral" intuitions? *Social Justice Research, 27*(4), 413–431.

Lapsley, D., & Carlo, G. (2014). Moral development at the crossroads: New trends and possible futures. *Developmental Psychology, 50*(1), 1–7.

Lapsley, D., & Narvaez, D. (2005). Moral psychology at the crossroads. In D. K. Lapsley & F. C. Power (Eds.), *Character psychology and character education* (pp. 18–35). Notre Dame, IN: University of Notre Dame Press.

Lind, G. (1992, April). *The measurement of structure: A new approach to assessing affective and cognitive aspects of moral judgment behavior, and findings from research.* Paper presented to the Department of Psychology, Fordham University, Bronx, New York. Retrieved from www.uni-konstanz.de/ag-moral/pdf/Lind-1992_MUT-Fordham.pdf

Mäkiniemi, J. -P. (2016). Moraalin määritelmän laajentuminen ja moraaliajattelun kehitys [Broadening of definition of moral and development of moral thinking]. In E. Kallio (Ed.), *Ajattelun kehitys aikuisuudessa: Kohti moninäkökulmaisuutta,* [The development of thinking in adulthood: Towards multiperspective thinking] (Research in Educational Sciences Vol. 71, pp. 183–202). Helsinki, Finland: The Finnish Educational Research Association.

Mäkiniemi, J.-P., Pirttilä-Backman, A.-M., & Pieri, M. (2011). Ethical and unethical food: Social representations among Finnish, Danish and Italian students. *Appetite, 56*(2), 495–502.

Mäkiniemi, J.-P., Pirttilä-Backman, A.-M., & Pieri, M. (2013). The endorsement of the moral foundations in food-related moral thinking in three European Countries. *Journal of Agricultural and Environmental Ethics, 26*(4), 771–786.

Maxwell, B., & Narvaez, D. (2013). Moral foundations theory and moral development and education. *Journal of Moral Education, 42*(3), 271–280.

McAdams, D. P., Albaugh, M., Farber, E., Daniels, J., Logan, R. L., & Olson, B. (2008). Family metaphors and moral intuitions: How conservatives and liberals narrate their lives. *Journal of Personality and Social Psychology, 95*(4), 978–990.

Myyry, L., & Helkama, K. (2001). University students' value priorities and emotional empathy. *Educational Psychology*, *21*(1), 25–40. doi:10.1080/01443410123128

Myyry, L., & Helkama, K. (2007). Socio-cognitive conflict, emotions and complexity of thought in real-life morality. *Scandinavian Journal of Psychology*, *48*(3), 247–259.

Piaget, J. (1932). *The moral judgment of the child* (M. Gabain, Trans.). London, England: Routledge & Kegan Paul.

Rakoczy, H., Wandt, R., Thomas, S., Nowak, J., & Kunzmann, U. (2018). Theory of mind and wisdom: The development of different forms of perspective-taking in late adulthood. *British Journal of Psychology*, *109*(1), 6–24.

Rest, J. R., & Narváez, D. (1994). *Moral development in the professions: Psychology and applied ethics*. Hillsdale, NJ: Erlbaum.

Shweder, R. A. (2003). *Why do men barbecue? Recipes for cultural psychology*. Cambridge, MA: Harvard University Press.

Shweder, R. A., Haidt, J., Horton, R., & Joseph, C. (2008). The cultural psychology of the emotions: Ancient and renewed. In M. Lewis, J. M. Haviland-Jones, & L. F. Barrett (Eds.), *Handbook of emotions* (3rd ed., pp. 409–427). New York, NY: Guilford Press.

Shweder, R. A., Mahapatra, M., & Miller, J. G. (1987). Culture and moral development. In J. Kagan & S. Lamb (Eds.), *The emergence of morality in young children* (pp. 1–83). Chicago, IL: University of Chicago Press.

Shweder, R. A., Much, N. C., Mahapatra, M., & Park, L. (1997). The "big three" of morality (autonomy, community, divinity) and the "big three" explanations of suffering. In A. M. Brandt & P. Rozin (Eds.), *Morality and health* (pp. 119–169). New York, NY: Routledge.

Skitka, L. J. (2010). The psychology of moral conviction. *Social and Personality Psychology Compass*, *4*(4), 267–281.

Suedfeld, P., Tetlock, P. E., & Streufert, S. (1992). Conceptual/integrative complexity. In C. P. Smith, J. W. Atkinson, D. C. McClelland, & J. Veroff (Eds.), *Motivation and personality: Handbook of thematic content analysis* (pp. 393–400). New York, NY: Cambridge University Press.

Suhler, C. L., & Churchland, P. (2011). Can innate, modular "foundations" explain morality? Challenges for Haidt's moral foundations theory. *Journal of Cognitive Neuroscience*, *23*(9), 2103–2116.

Sverdlik, N., Roccas, S., & Sagiv, L. (2012). Morality across cultures: A value perspective. In M. Mikulincer & P. R. Shaver (Eds.), *The social psychology of morality: Exploring the causes of good and evil* (pp. 219–235). Washington, DC: American Psychological Association.

Turiel, E. (1983). *The development of social knowledge: Morality and convention*. Cambridge, England: Cambridge University Press.

Vainio, A. (2003). *One morality – or multiple moralities? Religious ideology, conceptions of morality and rule systems of Finnish Evangelical Lutheran, Conservative Laestadian and nonreligious adolescents* (Doctoral dissertation, University of Helsinki, Department of Social Psychology, Helsinki, Finland).

Vainio, A. (2005). Moraalipsykologisia näkökulmia moraalin muutokseen ja vaihteluun. [Moral psychology perspectives on morals-related changes and variation]. In A.-M. Pirttilä-Backman, M. Ahokas, L. Myyry, & S. Lähteenoja (Eds.), *Arvot, moraali ja yhteiskunta: Sosiaalipsykologisia näkökulmia yhteiskunnan muutokseen* [Values, morals and society: Social psychology perspectives on social change] (pp. 145–166). Helsinki, Finland: Gaudeamus.

Vainio, A. (2011). Religious conviction, morality and social convention among Finnish adolescents. *Journal of Moral Education*, *40*(1), 73–87.

Vainio, A. (2015). Finnish moral landscapes: A comparison of nonreligious, liberal religious and conservative religious adolescents. In L. A. Jensen (Ed.), *Moral development in a global world: Research from a cultural-developmental perspective* (pp. 46–68). Cambridge, England: Cambridge University Press.

Vainio, A., & Mäkiniemi, J.-P. (2016). How are moral foundations associated with climate-friendly consumption? *Journal of Agricultural and Environmental Ethics, 29*(2), 265–283.

van Leeuwen, F., & Park, J. H. (2009). Perceptions of social dangers, moral foundations, and political orientation. *Personality and Individual Differences, 47*(3), 169–173.

Vartiainen, T., Siponen, M., & Myyry, L. (2011). The effects of teaching the universality thesis on students' integrative complexity of thought. *Journal of Information Systems Education, 22*(3), 261–270.

Vasquez, K., Keltner, D., Ebenbach, D. H., & Banaszynski, T. L. (2001). Cultural variation and similarity in moral rhetorics. Voices from Philippines and the United States. *Journal of Cross-Cultural Psychology, 32*(1), 93–120.

Weber, C. R., & Federico, C. M. (2013). Moral foundations and heterogeneity in ideological preferences. *Political Psychology, 34*(1), 107–126.

PART II

Perspectives of adult learning

7

ADULT LEARNERS AND THEORIES OF LEARNING

Mari Murtonen and Erno Lehtinen

Learning in adulthood: an introduction

It has been argued previously in this book that cognitive development and learning are close concepts. The focus of this chapter is on the concept of learning. Learning is a multifaceted phenomenon that takes place throughout the whole life. When talking about adult learning, we can mean at least four different situations. Firstly, coping in everyday life requires constantly learning new things. Using prior knowledge and learning new things are both prerequisites for, for example, learning how to use a new phone or prepare a new dish. Secondly, an important form of learning in everyday life is *learning at work*. Few work tasks today consist only of repeating some routine procedures. Instead, workers face new, complex problems daily that require innovative solutions and learning, either conscious or unconscious. Thirdly, in the era of lifelong learning we *deliberately educate* ourselves in certain periods of life. The motives for deliberately educating oneself might be related to coping with new demands, for example new challenging problems at work, or a need to educate oneself to something completely new. Fourthly, many of us want to learn new things on *leisure time for a hobby*. These different learning situations often take place in collaboration with other people and sometimes learning is not even possible without the help of others. The social aspect of learning is thus also crucial.

A division between different types of learning processes can be made between *incidental* and *deliberate* learning. In incidental learning, a person unintentionally learns something new that comes up in the situation as a by-product of another activity (Marsick & Watkins, 2015, p. 7). For example, an owner of a new smart phone can learn from a friend how to use a new application by accidentally seeing the friend using it. In this type of learning, the learner did not plan to learn something new; the learning happened unintentionally. In deliberate learning, the learner is aware that her goal is to learn something new and she deliberately pursues learning. In this intentional form of learning, the learner also monitors her learning by assessing whether she has reached the goal or not (Bereiter & Scardamalia, 1989). The basic mechanisms of learning in these different types of learning processes maybe similar, but the factors involved in the processes, such as motivation, goal orientation, and metacognitive regulation, may be very different.

Many researchers have proposed theories of learning that would describe the phenomenon fully and be applicable to a wide range of situations. These "unified" theories have not been successful because learning cannot be dealt with as one specific phenomenon but rather as more like a metaphoric concept that refers to several individual, social, and even organisational processes (Lehtinen, Hakkarainen, & Palonen, 2014). The term "learning" used in everyday discourses and scientific publications refers to a variety of phenomena; including behavioural changes in animals but also the learning of complex conceptual knowledge (Lehtinen, 2012; Säljö, 2009; Sfard, 1998). Recently, several attempts have been made to describe and organise this large variety of theories of learning (Lehtinen, 2012). For example, Sfard (1998) categorised theoretical thinking about learning into two ontologically different categories: the *acquisition* and *participation metaphors of learning*. Paavola, Lipponen, and Hakkarainen (2004) extended Sfard's model by proposing an additional metaphor that they called the *knowledge creation metaphor*. The very idea in this way of thinking is that the different metaphors are not mutually exclusive, but in analysing learning in different situations and contexts, different theoretical approaches are needed (Lehtinen, 2012).

Säljö (2009) has highlighted that relevant understanding of the variety of different theories of learning requires that we pay attention to the differences in the units of analysis used in different theoretical approaches and the suppositions related to them. This leads to an approach in which learning is analysed not as one phenomenon but as a complex system. Learning as an adaptive complex system means that there are processes related to learning taking place on different levels of the system. These levels of the system are mutually interdependent but cannot be reduced to each other (Hurford, 2010; Lehtinen et al., 2014; Ohlsson, 2011). In human learning, there are several levels of the system. They all have unique properties that extend from very basic neural adaptation processes to intentional conceptual learning at the individual level all the way to changes in group processes and larger cultural activity systems. Following the principles of the complex and adaptive system approach we describe in this article the current state of the art as regards knowledge about some of the different systemic levels relevant for understanding adult learning.

This article explores the different types of processes of adult learning from the individual, social, and cultural perspectives. When focusing on the individual level, questions such as the structure and functions of memory, basic mechanisms of formation of concepts and skills, and the development of regulatory processes are crucial. Learners' perceived characteristics in learning situations, such as factors concerning motivation, conceptions, and beliefs, direct the functioning of cognitive processes. Prior knowledge and experiences, as well as regulative skills, set the boundaries for the possibilities of learning in specific situations. On the social level, different forms of collaborative practices and processes that are partly based on the neurological predispositions for cooperation enable learning that would not be possible on the individual level. Cultural factors set a very powerful framework for learning processes. The tools, equipment, language, and signs that we use, as well as their history, have a major impact on what kind of communities of expertise can be formed. Understanding and supporting the types of learning needed in rapidly changing environments requires analysis of the processes related to constructing radically novel concepts and deliberate practice leading to advanced practices. It is also necessary to analyse the functioning of social processes and larger expert networks facilitating the increase of individual and collective intellectual capacity.

Perspectives on philosophical backgrounds of learning theories

The question of learning is inherently intertwined with the question of knowing. Already the earliest philosophers of our Western culture, the ancient Greek philosophers Plato and Aristotle, disagreed on what knowledge is and how it can be acquired. The question is tied to both ontological issues concerning the nature of reality and epistemological issues about how we can acquire knowledge about it. While Plato relied on the power of thought in terms of abstract rational thinking in epistemological questions, Aristotle emphasised the role of empirical observations in our environment. This problem between acquiring knowledge through ideas of our mind or through observations was later explicated by Rene Descartes in the 17th century. He studied the so-called mind-body dichotomy, a schism between the immaterial mind and material body, which later became known as Cartesian dualism.

In the 18th century, Immanuel Kant wanted to pass the traditional epistemological problem and wrote the *Critique of Pure Reason* in 1781. His aim was to show that both our mind and body have an important role in our knowledge formation. While our senses give us information about our environment, our mind works on this information both by affecting how we perceive it and by changing based on the bodily sensations. Thus, our reason is not pure in the sense that it is shaped by our prior experiences and thoughts. Similarly, our sensations are not pure because our mind shapes what we notice and how we interpret our sensations. This was the beginning of a new way of thinking about knowledge and learning, and the current constructivist theories are more or less based on Kant's thoughts. The philosophers of the 21st century have also tried to overcome the old mind-body-problem. For example, Lakoff and Johnson (1999, p. xi), who build on Kant and French existentialists, for example Maurice Merleau-Ponty and Jean-Paul Sartre, state that the whole Cartesian problem has been wrongly formulated. We should have never separated the mind from the body, but instead we should view them as a coherent whole. Our body sets the limits for our cognitive capabilities and correspondingly our mind has an effect on how we interpret our environment and behave in it.

In addition to the philosophers' thoughts and analyses about concepts of the nature of reality and knowledge, the methods of natural sciences have had a tremendous effect on our understanding of human thought and learning. Charles Darwin wrote the *Origin of Species* in 1859 (Darwin, 1979), which had a great impact on the study of human thinking and behaviour. Establishing a link between humans and other animals gave completely new tools and hypotheses to explore behaviour, learning, and individual differences. Psychologists started to make experiments on animals (e.g., Skinner, Watson) hoping that the results would be applicable to human behaviour. Positivists believed that all questions could be solved by empirical observations and inferences from the results of empirical experiments. The strongest effect of positivism on educational theories has been a theory called behaviourism, according to which behaviour can be predicted and controlled if exactly the right operations are applied.

According to Murtonen, Gruber, and Lehtinen (2017), the most profound problem of behaviourism from the viewpoint of learning is the behaviourist epistemology. Since behaviourists considered the mind as a black box that cannot be opened, they were not interested in discussing epistemological questions. Nevertheless, they still made assumptions about the mind. Bereiter and Scardamalia (1998) describe the behaviourist conception of the mind as a mental filing cabinet where separate pieces of knowledge are stored. This type of conception can be seen in various attempts to create taxonomies of learning outcomes where knowledge is seen as memorised pieces of information which then can be applied or evaluated in different ways (for taxonomies, see, Krathwohl, Bloom, & Masia, 1964). These models neglect the important development of the last decades in research on learning and cognition, which highlight the crucial role of knowledge structures and mental models in higher order learning (Murtonen et al., 2017).

One of the most influential theories that have impacted our understanding of learning is Piaget's (1972) theory of cognitive development or genetic epistemology as he called it (see also Chapter 3). The theory shares some of the Kantian ideas but instead of proposing static categories Piaget describes how advanced cognitive structures are gradually constructed from primary reflexes through different stages (Piaget, 1972). The stage theory has been heavily criticised during past decades (e.g., Carey, 1985), but very recent findings of the development of basic cognitive mechanisms (executive functions described later in this chapter) seem to support Piaget's description of general stages of thinking (Carey, Zaitchik, & Bascandziev, 2015). However, later philosophical and empirical research show that humans have much more differentiated innate and embodied predispositions for learning and development than just primary reflexes, which are assumed as starting points for higher cognitive stages in the Piagetian theory. Fodor (1983, 1985) developed a theory of the modularity of mind, according to which "perceptual processes are computationally isolated from much of the background knowledge to which cognitive processes have access" (Fodor, 1985, p. 1). According to Fodor's theory, the human mind has many innate abilities which allow us to cope in different areas of life. Learning is thus based on these basic cognitive functions in the brain, also in adulthood.

Concurrently with the heyday of empirical research and positivism, different types of philosophically inspired ideas, which later became known as sociocultural views, arose elsewhere. Pragmatists Dewey (1938, 1944) and Mead (1934) developed theories about the relationship between a learner and an environment, paying attention to different types of factors than the empiricists in their tests with animals. Dewey explored development and learning in practical situations and also the cultural factors involved. Mead concentrated on social interaction and its' effect on learning. These both are related to the work by Vygotsky, whose sociocultural theory is partly situated within the Marxist philosophical tradition (Vygotsky, 1930/1978). Language is crucial for development in Vygotsky's theory both in individual problem solving situations and in social interaction. One very important concept of Vygotsky's theoretical thinking is the zone of proximal development, which describes a level of development where a learner cannot yet solve problems without the help of the more experienced teacher, adult, or other helper. The sociocultural view has laid the basis for the more recent theories of collaborative learning (Dillenbourg, 1999), such as the knowledge creation (Nonaka & Takeuchi, 1995) and collaborative knowledge building in collaborative networks (Hakkarainen, Palonen, Paavola, & Lehtinen, 2004), which are powerful, especially in explaining learning in adulthood contexts (for analogical conceptualisations in adult cognitive development research, see Part I in this book).

Individual level cognitive theories of adult learning

According to Lehtinen and colleagues (2014), learning can be conceptualised as a complex system where learning processes on different levels interact but are not reducible to each other. One of the difficulties in formulating an exact definition of learning stems from the fact that there is a continuous process of adaptation and learning taking place without any learning intention or awareness. Thus, learning is not a single, well-defined event – it comprises a series of processes. On an individual level, learning refers to a constant developmental process of one's thoughts and actions.

Simple learning processes have already been described in classical theories of conditioning. However, recent studies on brain processes and cell level chemical changes have re-described the elementary mechanisms of this type of learning (Gormezano, Prokasy, & Thompson, 2014). McClelland and his colleagues (McClelland, McNaughton, & O'Reilly, 1995, pp. 427–428) use the term "interleaved learning" to describe learning in which a "particular item is not learned all at once but is acquired only gradually, through a series of presentations interleaved with exposure to other examples from the domain". This unconscious gradual learning is strongly shaping human behaviour and ways to interpret objects and events in the environment. It is a continuous, lifelong process, yet particularly crucial for young children's learning of basic skills (e.g., intonation of mother tongue). This type of gradual formation of neural networks may be one of the key processes leading to tacit knowledge (see Chapter 9) typical of experienced adults. Studies also show that these gradual learning mechanisms based on high frequencies of repeated experiences can result in useful tacit knowledge but often they also lead to unfavourable learning results (Braithwaite, Pyke, & Siegler, 2017). This very basic form of learning is partly an independent process and partly interacts with the other forms of learning as described in the complex system approach.

There has been an important change in recent models explaining early cognitive development and learning. In contrast to the rationalist philosophical ideas developed by the major theories of learning of the 20th century, which claimed that human learning is based on a few general learning mechanisms, the recent models state that all the knowledge and skills an individual has are learned in interaction with the physical, social, and cultural environment. However, there is increasing evidence showing that evolution has equipped human beings with a rich variety of domain-specific innate predispositions called core cognition (Karmiloff-Smith, 2018; Kinzler & Spelke, 2007). These predispositions facilitate the acquisition of understanding in fields such as basic mathematics, geometry, and the physical and biological environment. According to the current viewpoint, innate domain specific dispositions do not directly lead to practical knowledge. For example, natural numbers are not actually "natural" but require a complex construction process based on innate predispositions, culturally mediated knowledge, and practice (Carey, 2009).

It is, however, an open question how domain-specific core cognition affects later learning in adulthood. Recent research on conceptual change (see Chapter 8) has shown that some of the early learning patterns influenced by the innate domain-specific predispositions are in conflict with the more advanced knowledge needed in scientific and complex technology environments. Some very recent evidence shows that early knowledge forms, particularly when related to the core cognition, do not disappear during later learning but co-exist with the more advanced scientific concepts – even in highly educated adults (Brault Foisy, Potvin, Riopel, & Masson, 2015; Obersteiner, Van Dooren, Van Hoof, & Verschaffel, 2013).

Current scientific explanations of conscious learning of conceptual knowledge and complex skills are based on models that describe the basic functioning of human memory. Already in the 1950s, Miller presented the seminal work on the limitations of human information processing in his article "The magical number seven, plus or minus two" (Miller, 1956). These early works marked the beginning of intensive research of the two different memory functions, working (or short-term) memory and long-term memory, and the relations between them in learning and other cognitive processes.

A comprehensive model of working memory has been presented by Baddeley (2007). According to that model, working memory consists of several interacting components such as a central executive, a visuospatial sketchpad, an episodic buffer, and a phonological loop. The central executive is an attention control system and three other components are short-term memory functions specialised for visual, episodic, and language information. The limited capacity of working memory in terms of time and dealing with simultaneous units means that the mechanisms of learning complex knowledge and skills require strategies which help learners adapt and overcome these limitations. The most common of these strategies is chunking or schema building, which means that the well-organised schemas and knowledge structures in long-term memory (prior knowledge, domain expertise) allow the activation of more complex units in working memory and lead to more effective learning and cognitive processing in new situations. These ideas were already developed in early works of cognitive science (e.g., Chase & Simon, 1973) and have later been elaborated further in many research traditions, including text comprehension (Kintsch & Mangalath, 2011), expertise research (Gong, Ericsson, & Moxley, 2015), and cognitive load research (Sweller, van Merrienboer, & Paas, 1998).

The cognitive load research tradition has carefully studied the optimal use of working memory in learning and the features of learning environments that support or hinder learning (Sweller et al., 1998). All learning tasks in intentional conceptual learning mean that the learner has to deal with units and relations between them in working memory. Increasing the elements means increasing the task–intrinsic cognitive load. Extraneous cognitive load refers to the unnecessary load resulting from an inappropriate design or presentation of the learning task. Germane cognitive load refers to the need of cognitive capacity that is related to creation and automatisation of schemas needed in dealing with the complex task. The conclusion for learning strategies and instructional design is to reduce extraneous cognitive load and focus the working memory capacity on intrinsic and germane cognitive load.

Ericsson and Kintsch (1995) have shown that very experienced adults can process tasks of their field of expertise in a way that overcomes the distinction between working and long-term memory. However, these limitations in memory also raise an interesting question of the average adult's ability to handle many thinking systems at once (i.e., multiperspective and integrative thinking), as it is argued in current adult cognitive developmental models (see Part I of this book and Chapter 2). This would mean that adults can compensate the gradually decreasing basic working memory capacity with increasing content knowledge. However, there are other studies which show that working memory capacity and content knowledge both contribute to the learning of new material but the content knowledge does not compensate the age-related decrease of working memory capacity (Hambrick & Engle, 2002).

Recent behavioural and neuroscience studies have focused particularly on the role of executive functions related to working memory, which are considered to be key processes in cognitive activity. Researchers have distinguished different components of executive functions. Of these, the widest interest has focused on updating, shifting, and inhibition. Updating refers to monitoring and the fast addition and deletion of working memory contents; shifting means flexibly changing between tasks; and inhibition means that the cognitive system overrides dominant responses so as to avoid distraction (Miyake & Friedman, 2012). Instead of looking separately at these different components, many researchers have focused on the common core of the functions, executive attention, and defined it as the ability to temporarily maintain goal-relevant information in memory (Schwaighofer, Fischer, & Bühner, 2015).

Executive functions are the basic mechanism for metacognition, self-regulations, and cognitive flexibility, and are thus crucial for the quality and effectiveness of learning. For example, in the research on conceptual change related to scientific concepts, inhibition has a crucial role (Brault Foisy et al., 2015). Executive functions are often related to intelligence, particularly fluid intelligence (Miyake & Friedman, 2012). Some researchers have seen the well-developed executive functions as one of the necessary requirements of more general wisdom, which is also partly linked to the concept of adult development and thus also to learning (see, Carlson et al., 2008; Chapter 2). Research has shown substantial individual differences and stability of the executive functions on the one hand, and malleability of them on the other hand (Miyake & Friedman, 2012; Schwaighofer et al., 2015).

Reviews about the effects of training for working memory and executive functions show that such training can enhance these basic functions but the effects are typically domain-specific and do not easily transfer to other cognitive domains (Schwaighofer et al., 2015). This is in line with the findings of expertise research which show that extensive training of specific skills can dramatically enhance specific cognitive control and attention regulation mechanisms which, according to the brain imaging findings, are related to a reduced activation of general executive functions (Hill & Schneider, 2006). There is a similar relationship between improving expertise and general abilities. Expertise studies show that after extensive deliberate practice leading to domain-specific expertise, the role of intelligence differences gradually fades as a predictor of achievement in that domain (Ericsson, 2014). Deliberate practice is the term proposed by Ericsson and his colleagues (Ericsson, Krampe, & Tesch-Römer, 1993) to describe systematic and intensive training which aims at purposefully developing different aspects of specific expertise. Research findings on deliberate practice are not only important for understanding a few exceptional experts but they also give convincing evidence about the plasticity of human neural and cognitive systems in adulthood (Hill & Schneider, 2006; Merrett, Peretz, & Wilson, 2013).

Mental representations and well-organised knowledge structures, which are developed through extensive deliberate practice, explain the superior achievement of experts (Ericsson & Pool, 2016). Concepts and methods to describe the development of mental representations, schemas, mental models, and knowledge structures are a major contribution of the cognitive research of the last 50 years (Johnson-Laird, 2010; Kintsch, 1998; Kintsch & Mangalath, 2011). Prior knowledge in terms of organised mental models and structures fundamentally affects conscious learning and construction of new knowledge, and the learning of conceptual knowledge can be described as changes in these models and structures. However, besides the conscious construction, human cognition develops also through the unconscious gradual formation of neural networks based on frequencies of features and events, and this can lead to learning which either supports the conscious conceptual construction or causes incorrect behaviour or beliefs that are conflicting with the conscious learning aims (see Braithwaite et al., 2017).

Individual level motivational, metacognitive, and regulation theories of adult learning

While the basic mechanisms of learning set certain frames to our cognitive functions, there is a wide range of other factors that also have a strong impact on our learning, such as motivational issues and different types of conceptions (see e.g., Schneider & Preckel, 2017). In contrast to the "cold cognitive functions", a "warming trend" in educational theories, which underlines the importance of other cognitive processes in learning, has come up every now and then (Sinatra, 2005). Similarly to cognitive functions, these factors can also be involved either consciously or unconsciously. Being aware of and regulating these factors, an adult learner can enhance the learning process.

Motivational processes, such as interest and goal orientation, either guide or inhibit our actions. In the positive case, motivational structures and beliefs both direct and support our learning processes. The classical theory of motivation divides motivation into two types: intrinsic and extrinsic motivation (Deci & Ryan, 2000). Intrinsic motivation refers to a situation where a person performs a task finding it rewarding without some other reward that would be earned as a consequence, whereas an extrinsically motivated person performs a task in order to reach something external to the activity itself (Whang & Hancock, 1994). Intrinsic motivation has been proven to be the most powerful motor in learning, resulting in high-quality deep learning that aims at understanding (Baeten, Kyndt, Struyven, & Dochy, 2010).

Another aspect connected to motivational theories is interest, which can be expressed in terms of deep-seated, long-term interest in the targeted field, or as short-lived situational interest in a specific situation or context (Hidi, 1990). Interest has proven to have a connection to high-quality learning in higher education (Mikkonen, Heikkilä, Ruohoniemi, & Lindblom-Ylänne, 2009).

In addition to the power emerging from intrinsic motivation and interest, the impact of goals for motivation is crucial. Goal orientation refers to what the learner wants to achieve. It can be seen as aiming at mastery, i.e., gaining knowledge and understanding through learning, or as aiming at an achievement, for example reaching a goal by minimum effort (Murphy & Alexander, 2000). In adult learning, strategic use of different motivational patterns and approaches to learning in order to achieve certain goals has proven effective for study success (Heikkilä & Lonka, 2006).

Our motivational factors and conceptions have an effect on our thinking and learning, however, we do not have to be tied with some random motivational features, but instead we can regulate them. Especially with adult learners, the deliberate learning processes require us to monitor our own thinking, reflect it against new information, and adapt it if needed. The process of being aware of and monitoring our own thinking is called metacognition and adjusting the thinking patterns when needed is called regulation. Metacognition – thinking about thinking – is connected to high-quality learning (Iiskala, 2015; Khosa & Volet, 2014). Metacognition is related to critical thinking in university studies (Magno, 2010), conceptual change in learning (Vilppu, Mikkilä-Erdmann, & Ahopelto, 2013), and epistemological beliefs (Ozgelen, 2012). In addition, metacognition is related to knowing what and how we need to adjust in our thinking, i.e., to regulate it. Metacognitive skills are what the person deliberately uses to control and regulate cognition (Efklides, 2006).

Regulatory skills have proven to be central for successful studying. Vermunt and Verloop (1999) point out that the task of an adult education teacher is to guide the learner towards a more self-regulated learning. They describe that learner's low self-regulation is congruent with a situation where a teacher is strictly regulating the learning process for the students. However, such a practice does not activate or encourage the students to develop their own skills to regulate their own learning. Therefore, the teacher should try to push the students towards a more self-regulating behaviour. A competent, self-regulating adult learner thus possesses the agency (e.g., Eteläpelto, Vähäsantanen, Hökkä, & Paloniemi, 2013) of his/her own learning and thinking, i.e., he/she is active and capable of making decisions and guiding his/her own independent thinking processes. Scholars in the field of cognitive adult development (e.g., Edelstein & Noam, 1982; Kallio, 2011) have also underlined the importance of self-regulation and autonomy in adult psychological advancement.

Conceptions and beliefs as fostering or impeding adult learning on an individual level

In addition to cognitive basic mechanisms and motivational factors, different types of conceptions and beliefs that we possess have an impact on learning. These conceptions may affect motivation by acting as if they were factual things even if they are not. For example, having a conception of girls as poor mathematics learners (Bieg, Goetz, Wolter, & Hall, 2015) may cause low motivation for girls in mathematics learning and thereby poor preparation, for example, for further studies, as long as the learner is stuck with the conception. In a learner, conceptions may form conceptual frameworks that include many interconnected conceptions that have an impact on learning. For example, it has been found that university students who thought that they are not mathematically talented, even though they had high grades on math courses, experienced difficulties in the learning of statistics and research skills, and they also thought that they would not need research skills in their future working life (Murtonen, Olkinuora, Tynjälä, & Lehtinen, 2008). Thus, conceptions and beliefs may have powerful consequences in adult learning and development of thinking.

We grouped conceptions and beliefs concerning the learning and teaching situations into five types (see Table 7.1): conceptions about 1) the learner, 2) learning, 3) knowledge, 4) the subject to be learnt, and 5) teaching.

Firstly, the *conceptions about the learner* may concern oneself, fellow learners, or learners generally. These beliefs can be domain-general, such as "I am a good learner", or domain-specific, such as "Oliver is good in drawing". These beliefs can also concern a group of people, for example "Our colleagues are good in learning" or "Our team is not so good in learning of international marketing". The way people see themselves is connected to motivation. The term "self-schema" is used to describe personal knowledge about oneself, such as self-efficacy that is trust in ones' capacity to execute certain tasks (Murphy & Alexander, 2000). According to the classical attribution theory (Weiner, 2010), success in achievement can be attributed as 1) internal or external, 2) stable or unstable, and 3) controllable or uncontrollable. Self-conceptions often tend to be stable, since people seem to rely on unchangeable "self", which, however, has actually been shown to be not so stable after all (e.g., Lakoff & Johnson, 1999).

In addition to the personal conceptions of a learner or learners, which are modified through our personal experiences and interaction with others, we have common cultural conceptions of people, modified and kept alive in our society for some reasons. An example of a harmful but usual common belief is the idea of girls as poor mathematics learners (Bieg et al., 2015). Such conceptions impede individual learning, since these types of conceptions also include the ideas of internality, stability, and uncontrollability, i.e., that these situations cannot be changed. Only by understanding that these are beliefs that we can change if we want to, these types of beliefs and conceptions can be overcome.

The second group of conceptions, *those concerning the learning* itself, have a tremendous impact on thinking and learning in adulthood. If we believe that learning happens by passively receiving facts in a certain place assigned by an authority, it is most unlikely that we are going to form a deep understanding of the subject to be learnt. Instead, if we think that in order to learn we need to participate in knowledge creating processes (Paavola et al., 2004), which may physically take place anywhere, we will probably take part in processes that develop our expertise in a deep manner. The theory of surface and deep learning, i.e., the students' approaches to learning, the SAL tradition (Entwistle & Ramsden, 1983; Marton & Säljö, 1976), has been very powerful in explaining differences among higher education learners. It has been shown that a deep approach, meaning an intention to understand in-depth the subject to be learnt, results in better quality learning than a more superficial learning-by-heart approach (Vermunt, 2005). Students have been

TABLE 7.1 Different types of conceptions affecting learning and teaching processes, presented with examples. (Adapted from Murtonen, 2017)

1. Conceptions of oneself (also a group (or groups) and other people (or groups of people))	2. Conceptions of learning	3. Conceptions of knowledge	4. Conceptions of the subject of learning/teaching	5. Conceptions of teaching
Beliefs of oneself in general. "Usually I'm a good/bad learner/teacher". **Conceptions of things affecting to learning/teaching.** Attributions (external/internal): rush, coincidences, abilities etc. **Beliefs of oneself associated with learning/teaching in a particular field.** "I'm a good/bad – learner/teacher in this field". **Adopted general/cultural beliefs,** such as misconceptions: "women are bad at mathematics".	**What learning is:** Surface approach: remembering/Deep approach: understanding. Misconceptions of learning (e.g. visual, auditory and kinesthetic learning styles). **How learning happens:** Passive: intake of knowledge/Active: developing expertise through participation and knowledge creation. **Where learning happens:** Being in a certain place (e.g. sitting obediently in a lecture hall).	**Certainty of knowledge:** Black-and-white conception/Relativism/Evaluativist commitment to knowledge. **Stability of knowledge:** Stable facts/Changing knowledge. **Origin of knowledge in society:** Eternal facts/Socially produced knowledge (e.g. research done in universities). **Origin of one's own knowledge:** Beliefs of omniscient authority/Own estimation. **How knowledge is acquired:** Innate learning ability/Quick learning/Development process.	**Nature and level of the subject:** Easy/Difficult Abstract/Concrete Theoretical/Pragmatic Simple/Complex Familiar/Unfamiliar Interesting/Not interesting Useful/Not useful. **Competencies needed for a profession:** E.g. do teachers need research skills? **Conceptions related to jobs and professions:** "Do I see myself as a worker on this field?"	**What teaching is:** Content focus: delivering facts/Learning focus: supporting learning as understanding. **How teaching happens:** By lecturing facts/Creating possibilities for learning. **Where teaching happens:** Only in a classroom/By creating a learning environment that supports learning.

found to be very flexible in using different approaches, depending on the subject to be learnt (Vermunt & Vermetten, 2004) and timing of learning (Lindblom-Ylänne, Parpala, & Postareff, 2014). Learning approaches are further connected to other study processes, for example, using a deep approach predicts better persistence in major studies (Lastusaari & Murtonen, 2013).

Learning approaches have been separated from the more general orientations to learning, such as goals and expectations of studying (Vermunt, 1998). According to Vermunt (1998), the term "learning styles" can be used to refer to more generalised collections of cognitive processing strategies, mental models of learning and teaching, learning orientations, and regulation strategies. Although some stability has been discovered among these, they should not be conceived of as unchangeable traits of people. Personality has been found to be very flexible and it changes according to the situation and time (Chamorro-Premuzic & Furnham, 2009), so conceptions of learning or learning styles should not be considered as stable.

However, there is a tendency for people to consider learning processes as stable. This is the case, for example, in an explanation that Howard-Jones (2014) calls a neuromyth. According to this myth, students learn more if they are taught in the learning style they prefer. This myth is based on the simplified idea that because different regions of the cortex have distinct roles (visual, auditory, and kinesthetic/sensory processing), teaching should be designed in a manner that takes into account which part of the student's brain works best. As Howard-Jones argues, the findings of the brain's interconnectivity doesn't support this assumption. In addition, reviews of educational and laboratory studies do not support the idea to modify teaching according to students' learning style.

What was very worrying in a collection of the results of four earlier studies presented by Howard-Jones (2014), 93%–97% of the teachers, as studied in five countries (China, Greece, the Netherlands, Turkey, and United Kingdom), reported agreeing with this neuromyth. In a study by Krätzig and Arbuthnott (2006), it was found out that the learning style preference reported by the learner did not correlate with the objective test performance. Furthermore, they also found out that the preferred learning style was based on memories and beliefs rather than specific experiences of learning when using different modalities. What is most problematic about these false conceptions of learning is that they are often considered as stable and also innate. This may implicate that a learner may think that he or she is receiving the wrong type of teaching and that is why he/she is not learning properly. The learner is viewed as a passive receiver of information who cannot influence his own learning. This type of a misconception of learning harms the learning processes of the learner in a profound way.

The third group, the *conceptions of knowledge* are close to the conceptions of learning, since the views about what knowledge is and how it is received or built is part of the idea of learning, or vice versa. While the conceptions of learning are conceptualised as deep and surface approaches, the conceptions of knowledge are depicted on the axis from dualistic black-and-white truths via relativistic views to personal commitments to knowledge (Perry, 1968; see Part I of this book). Since

Perry's (1968) original theory the domain has been extensively studied. Schommer (1990) studied students' beliefs with respect to simplicity of knowledge, certainty of knowledge, quick learning, and innate abilities. She found out that those students who believed in quick learning had lower study success than others, and the belief in the certainty of knowledge predicted ill-founded absolute conclusions. Hofer and Pintrich (2002) described individual ways to approach knowledge as personal epistemologies, and King and Kitchener (2002) formed a theory of the development of these personal epistemologies. The lowest of the seven levels of the development are called pre-reflective thinking, the intermediate levels are quasi-reflective and the highest two levels depict reflective thinking. Kuhn and Weinstock have also proposed a theoretical model for epistemic development, with a "movement from a dualistic, objectivist view of knowledge to a more subjective, relativistic stance and ultimately to a contextual, constructivist perspective of knowing" (Kuhn & Weinstock, 2002, p. 121).

Fourthly, *conceptions about the subject to be learnt* can be examined either from the perspective of the subject itself or situations where the subject-related skills are needed. Conceptions concerning the subject often focus on the difficulty or easiness of learning. Different factors connected to the level of difficulty have to do with subject matter attributes such as abstract or concrete, theoretical or pragmatical, simple or complex, and familiar or unfamiliar. Factors causing heavy cognitive load (Sweller et al., 1998), e.g., by overburdening one's working memory, increase the experience of difficulty. A target of learning can also be evaluated in terms of how interesting it is to learn. As regards situations where a skill could be needed, the conception of the usefulness of the skill comes in to question. If, for example, a student teacher thinks he/she is not going to need research skills when working as an elementary school teacher, he/she is most probably not interested in learning those skills (Onwuegbuzie, Leech, Murtonen, & Tähtinen, 2010). Mental images of certain careers or practitioners in particular domains may also have an effect on learning motivation. In a study by Hannover and Kessels (2004), some high-school students did not like math and science because they had a conception that the students liking those subjects are not very socially capable, being isolated and less creative. Students thus compared "their self-views to both a prototypical student liking a certain subject and a prototypical student disapproving of it" (Hannover & Kessels, 2004, p. 51).

The fifth group, *the conceptions of teaching* resemble the conceptions of learning, i.e., what teaching is by its' nature, how it happens and where. Similarly to the conceptions of learning, the conceptions of teaching have to do with the question about where the focus of action is. According to Trigwell and Prosser (2004), a teaching approach can be either teacher-focused or student-focused. The former approach means that rather than paying attention to students' learning, the teacher concentrates on the delivery of the content, whereas in the latter approach students' learning is the starting point for the teaching activities. Like having conceptions about learning, students and teachers alike also have conceptions about teaching. A teacher has conceptions about how to teach, and students hold conceptions about how they should be taught. A student may give feedback to a teacher if the teacher's way of teaching is conflicting with the student's own views on how teaching should take place. In addition, this category of conceptions also includes ideas about how and where teaching can take place, i.e., is it only in a traditional setting with a teacher lecturing in a classroom, or can teaching take place in any form in the environment, for example, by creating possibilities for virtual learning.

Social and cultural level mechanisms of adult learning

The individual level learning processes described above never happen in a vacuum but are always situated in physical, social, and cultural contexts. Social support is particularly relevant for the construction of conceptual knowledge and complex skills. Historically, the role of social support by a knowledgeable tutor or teacher has been described in Vygotsky's model of the zone of proximal development (Vygotsky, 1930/1978). Later empirical studies have highlighted the role of knowledgeable support in constructing scientific concepts (Kirschner, Sweller, & Clark, 2006) as well as in the development of expertise (Gruber, Lehtinen, Palonen, & Degner, 2008). Teachers, coaches, and tutors can present learning content, organise learning activities, and scaffold learning so that it supports the above-described individual level learning processes. For example, expert support is often necessary for constructing schemas to reduce the cognitive load caused by increasingly complex tasks, or coaches can guide trainings which lead to the gradual formation of correct physical actions (Ericsson & Pool, 2016). Studies on teaching dialogues and other instructional methods show the variety of ways by which teachers and other knowledgeable people can support the learning of individuals (Schneider & Preckel, 2017).

However, it is not only this expert – novice or teacher – student relation which is important for learning but also the collaboration of peers can fundamentally support learning (Dillenbourg, 1999; Lehtinen, 2003). Recently, studies on socially shared metacognitive regulation have highlighted processes related to individual regulation and executive functions but go beyond the individual learning and regulation (Iiskala, Vauras, Lehtinen, & Salonen, 2011; Iiskala, Volet, Lehtinen, & Vauras, 2015; Malmberg, Järvelä, & Järvenoja, 2017). Research findings on the neural correlates of social interaction have indicated that during evolution the brain has been equipped with functions which support the mutual relationship between humans more deeply than has been assumed before. "These studies have revealed that networks of brain areas support perception of self and others, interpretation of non-verbal and verbal social cues, mutual understanding, and social bonding" (Hari, Sams, & Nummenmaa, 2016, p. 1). Current research approaches for social collaboration and collaborative learning show that these processes are partly unique to the level of social interaction but also connected to the basic mechanisms of the human mind.

The context of learning processes involves not only the immediate social interaction but also the cultural environment in general, which produces and supports activities fundamental for learning (Gutiérrez & Rogoff, 2003; Valsiner, 2012). There is a wide variety of ways to analyse the cultural aspects of learning but for the purposes of this article two approaches can be mentioned: firstly, anthropological studies show that a large part of the cultural skills and knowledge people use in work and societal activities have never been intentionally studied as isolated learning contents. Instead, gradually deepening participation in culturally formatted activities has been identified as a basis for the development of such skills, as described in the seminal book by Lave and Wenger (1991). Within the framework of adaptive complex systems the participation in such cultural activities and communities of practice can be seen as a unique level of learning. However, cultural participation is not independent of the other levels. The individuals approaching as legitimate peripheral participants (the term used by Lave and Wenger), the activities and communities of practice do bring their individual-level cognitive architectures to the situations. Gradual formation of neural networks would be the best candidate for explaining much of the individual-level learning taking place during the deepening participation processes.

Secondly, the cultural aspects of learning mean that culture provides individuals with tools for cognitive functioning. Of course, natural language is the most powerful cultural tool, which has fundamentally shaped human cognition and is involved in practically all learning in adulthood. The alphabet, Arabic numerals, and numerous sign systems have changed learning tasks and processes. Technical tools, such as calculators, can dramatically diminish the intrinsic cognitive load of traditionally demanding tasks (Säljö, 2010). This process opens opportunities to deal with gradually more complex learning tasks because a part of the cognitive load can be outsourced to the tools.

Collaborative learning has been strongly highlighted in the contemporary models of learning for all ages and environments. The research has focused on the basic processes of social interaction (see above) and models which could be applied in formal education and working life contexts. Instead of reviewing different approaches of collaborative learning, we present here a model developed by Hakkarainen and his colleagues (Lehtinen et al., 2014). It focuses on professional learning in an advanced knowledge society and characterises various approaches where the ideas of the adaptive complex system approach are applied to the way learning is conceptualised. Starting from the description of the knowledge acquisition and participation metaphors by Sfard (1998), Hakkarainen and his colleagues constructed a model based on a proposed third metaphor of learning which they call "knowledge-creating metaphor" (Paavola et al., 2004). In this model, learning is connected to a creative knowledge work, which deals with incomplete epistemic objects that are open-ended and generate constantly novel questions (Knorr Cetina, 1999; Lehtinen et al., 2014). The approach builds on three basic ideas: 1) learning is focused on building, extending and sharing knowledge artefacts (ideas, theories, products, etc.), 2) learning takes place in terms of creating collectively shared knowledge practices which aim at creating innovations and novel social practices, and 3) transactive development of expertise, which means the interaction of personal and collaborative knowledge-creating efforts.

The term "knowledge artefacts" has been proposed by Bereiter (2002) to describe the objects knowledge workers have to create, extend, build, and share when working on complex problems. Working on such knowledge artefacts (Bereiter, 2002) or epistemic objects (Knorr Cetina, 1999) is important in knowledge creation because they are incomplete and can be re-interpreted, modified, and connected with other knowledge objects (Bereiter, 2002; Paavola et al., 2004). From the point of view of collaborative professional learning, working with epistemic artefacts is important because they can also work as boundary objects (Akkerman & Bakker, 2011), which facilitate interaction between different epistemic cultures (Knorr Cetina, 1999) leading to knowledge. Wynn, Mosholder, and Larsen (2014) have studied the relationship between collaborative learning and adult cognitive development. Their results indicate that subjects taught with a problem-based learning approach with a learning community reached more often the highest levels of advanced adult thinking, in comparison to the group without such teaching approaches.

Professional creativity and ability for non-monotonic learning do not reside in the human mind only but are embedded in socially shared knowledge practices supported by such knowledge communities (Lehtinen et al., 2014). The process of knowledge creation described in this model is a collective rather than an individual process but it also depends on the individual experts who have a critical role in the pursuit of novelty and innovation. In most working-life contexts, individual and social learning are intertwined. Collaborative processes make use of the expertise of participating experts, and their participation in the collaborative knowledge building process results in individual learning as well (Lehtinen et al., 2014).

Adult learning in context – an example of the learning of broad scientific thinking in higher education

People are confronted today with a very complex life, where skills to search and evaluate knowledge are needed in order to build an understanding of different a phenomena. Adults in general, and higher education graduates in particular, need skills to cope with the complex problems of working life, which require the capability to make evidence-based decisions in collaborative and multidisciplinary contexts. Evidence-based decision-making further requires understanding how knowledge is built in our society. Giere, Bickle, and Mauldin (2006) state that understanding scientific reasoning would be important for anyone because of the current big issues such as the global warming. According to them, understanding scientific reasoning requires many sub-abilities such as understanding and evaluating of theoretical hypotheses, statistical models, probability, correlation, and causation. Especially university graduates need skills such as those listed by Giere and colleagues (2006) above. However, as previous studies have shown, many university students have serious difficulties in learning these skills on research methods courses (e.g., Murtonen, 2015), denoting that these are not easy skills to learn (for more about university students' logical reasoning skills and complex epistemological thinking, see also Chapter 3).

The skills that Giere and colleagues (2006) point out as important in understanding our world are needed in the area of natural sciences but also elsewhere. Hence, many other disciplines also use the same procedures in pursuing an understanding of the phenomena in their respective fields. Developing higher order thinking skills during university education entails understanding how knowledge is built and justified in one's field or discipline. In other words, university students need to learn about the research process via which knowledge is pursued. We call these skills here *broad scientific thinking skills*. These skills are basically common for all disciplines, although their scope and intent may vary.

Previous studies on the development of higher order thinking skills in higher education have shed light on the different aspects of thinking and acting. The topic has been studied, for example, under the concepts of scientific, critical, and epistemological thinking as well as reasoning. In university settings, among the earliest studies concerning students' higher order thinking skills were studies about reasoning. For example, Lehman and Nisbett (1990) studied what kind of effects training in reasoning has. They concluded that these skills can be trained and they also noted that statistical-methodological reasoning skills seem to be especially significant for an ability to think critically. In this context it should be noted that university students usually take many courses on research methodology during their education and these are an essential part of the development of their scientific and critical thinking.

The theories of scientific thinking have been developed originally for the needs of elementary school learning and they aim at giving information about children's ability to control physical objects and reason for it (e.g., Inhelder & Piaget, 1958; Kuhn, 2010; Kuhn, Amsel, & O'Loughlin, 1988). In these studies, the term "scientific" usually refers to natural sciences. Application of these theories to higher education has mainly covered thinking among natural science problems (e.g., Kallio, 1998; Kuhn, Iordanou, Pease, & Wirkala, 2008; Seppälä, 2013).

The traditional theories of scientific thinking have also been criticised. Kuhn and colleagues (2008) propose that the traditional control-of-variables strategy is too narrow a view for studying scientific thinking. They point out three new aspects that are essential for students to master as a foundation for skilled scientific thinking: 1) a strategic aspect that involves the ability to coordinate effects of multiple causal influences on an outcome; 2) a mature understanding of the epistemological foundations of science, recognising scientific knowledge as constructed by humans rather than simply discovered in the world; and 3) an ability to engage in skilled argumentation in the scientific domain (Kuhn et al., 2008, p. 435). Especially the second and the third notions seem to be new and very important aspects in university education across the disciplines (Murtonen, 2015; Seppälä, 2013).

While critical thinking studies do deal with the development of thinking skills at university (e.g., Evens, Verburgh, & Elen, 2014), they are still somewhat limited in their scope in view of describing the whole of higher order thinking skills pursued in higher education. The critical thinking theories (e.g., Behar-Horenstein & Niu, 2011) do not pay attention to students' research training, but instead see critical thinking as an abstract thinking skill of its own. Critical thinking can thus be seen as one factor of broad scientific thinking skills pursued in university education. Research on students' epistemic beliefs (e.g., Hofer & Pintrich, 2002; Perry, 1968, 1970) has focused on students' knowledge beliefs, which have been found important in the development of higher order thinking skills at university. Although proven highly important in explaining the cognitive aspects of university learning, these theories do not point out research methodological training as a central element in university students' knowledge building. Epistemological beliefs have been shown to have a relationship with students' critical thinking (Hyytinen, Holma, Toom, Shavelson, & Lindblom-Ylänne, 2014), indicating a need to explore higher order thinking skills from a wider perspective. Kallio (2011) has emphasised the role of integrative thinking, i.e., adults' ability and need to integrate differing viewpoints based on some connective principles, such as ethical code or scientific argumentation.

Explaining very complex phenomena, such as the development of a broad scientific way of thinking in university studies, requires both understanding the common principles of learning at the individual level and also socio-constructive phenomena in the collaborative practices. Our biology, i.e., the limits of our basic cognitive functions, set also certain restrictions for our learning that we try to overcome with the aid of collaborative actions and training ourselves by deliberate cognitive processes. To demonstrate even further how complex the relationships between many learning and developmental fields are, the role of wisdom is also relevant when looking at higher thinking abilities. Wisdom can refer to different personal and interpersonal competences, such as the ability to listen, evaluate, and give advice. In addition, wisdom means that the person has good intentions to apply these abilities for the well-being of oneself and others (Lehtinen, 2010).

According to Lehtinen (2010), different types of learning environments can focus on very different learning goals, varying from the rapid learning of facts and automatisation of simple skills to environments that are meant for facilitating deep learning of advanced concepts and knowledge structures, promoting also the development of wisdom. When universities educate students, they aim at producing future workers that should express both expertise and wisdom (Sternberg & Frensch, 2014). Universities use vast resources on research education in an attempt to equip students with understanding about how knowledge is produced and how it can be used in evidence-based decision-making. However, studies show that many students have difficulties not only in learning research skills (e.g., Murtonen, 2015) but also generic or working-life-skills (Jääskelä, Nykänen, & Tynjälä, 2018). The problem lies both in the learning of cognitive understanding of research, but also in the understanding of research based scientific actions in wider contexts, such as decision-making in our society. To fully understand the importance of evidence-based decision-making, the students should have possibilities to act as a member of collaborative groups that try to solve the complex problems of our society.

In adult learning, the forms of participation and collaborative knowledge building (e.g., Paavola et al., 2004) seem to be the most crucial ones in order to reach the kind of learning that is important for our society. Adequate conceptions of learning and related phenomena should be taught for all in order to enhance the processes of quality learning. Metacognitive understanding of one's own learning, motivation, and beliefs further support the learning processes. For adult learners, meaningful processes and goals are important in learning. Also, skills in broad scientific thinking are highly important in enabling people to evaluate the information received and to make informed decisions on the basis of it. The study of adult cognitive development together with research on adult learning are thus important in explaining how adults develop their understanding in our society.

References

Akkerman, S. F., & Bakker, A. (2011). Boundary crossing and boundary objects. *Review of Educational Research, 81*(2), 132–169.

Baddeley, A. D. (2007). *Working memory, thought, and action* (Oxford psychology series No. 45). Oxford, England: Oxford University Press.

Baeten, M., Kyndt, E., Struyven, K., & Dochy, F. (2010). Using student-centred learning environments to stimulate deep approaches to learning: Factors encouraging or discouraging their effectiveness. *Educational Research Review, 5*(3), 243–260.

Behar-Horenstein, L. S., & Niu, L. (2011). Teaching critical thinking skills in higher education: A review of the literature. *Journal of College Teaching & Learning, 8*(2), 25–41.

Bereiter, C. (2002). *Education and mind in the knowledge age.* Mahwah, NJ: Erlbaum.

Bereiter, C., & Scardamalia, M. (1989). Intentional learning as a goal of instruction. In L. B. Resnick (Ed.), *Knowing, learning, and instruction: Essays in honor of Robert Glaser* (pp. 361–392). Hillsdale, NJ: Erlbaum.

Bereiter, C., & Scardamalia, M. (1998). Beyond bloom's "taxonomy": Rethinking knowledge for the knowledge age. In A. Hargreaves, A. Lieberman, M. Fullan, & D. W. Hopkins (Eds.), *International handbook of educational change: Part 1–2* (Kluwer international handbooks of education, Vol. 5, pp. 675–692). Dordrecht, the Netherlands: Kluwer Academic Publishers.

Bieg, M., Goetz, T., Wolter, I., & Hall, N. C. (2015). Gender stereotype endorsement differentially predicts girls' and boys' trait-state discrepancy in math anxiety. *Frontiers in Psychology, 6.* Retrieved from www.frontiersin.org/articles/10.3389/fpsyg.2015.01404/full

Braithwaite, D. W., Pyke, A. A., & Siegler, R. S. (2017). A computational model of fraction arithmetic. *Psychological Review, 124*(5), 603–625. doi:10.1037/rev0000072

Brault Foisy, L.-M., Potvin, P., Riopel, M., & Masson, S. (2015). Is inhibition involved in overcoming a common physics misconception in mechanics? *Trends in Neuroscience and Education, 4*(1–2), 26–36.

Carey, S. (1985). *Conceptual change in childhood* (The MIT press series in learning, development, and conceptual change). Cambridge, MA: MIT press.

Carey, S. (2009). *The origin of concepts* (Oxford series in cognitive development). New York, NY: Oxford University Press.

Carey, S., Zaitchik, D., & Bascandziev, I. (2015). Theories of development: In dialog with Jean Piaget. *Developmental Review, 38*, 36–54.

Carlson, M. C., Saczynski, J. S., Rebok, G. W., Seeman, T., Glass, T. A., McGill, S., ... Fried, L. P. (2008). Exploring the effects of an "everyday" activity program on executive function and memory in older adults: Experience corps®. *The Gerontologist, 48*(6), 793–801.

Chamorro-Premuzic, T., & Furnham, A. (2009). Mainly openness: The relationship between the big five personality traits and learning approaches. *Learning and Individual Differences, 19*(4), 524–529.

Chase, W. G., & Simon, H. A. (1973). Perception in chess. *Cognitive Psychology, 4*(1), 55–81.

Darwin, C. (1979). *The origin of species* [P. Horan, Foreword]. New York, NY: Gramercy Books. (Original work published 1859).

Deci, R. M., & Ryan, E. L. (2000). Intrinsic and extrinsic motivations: Classic definitions and new directions. *Contemporary Educational Psychology, 25*(1), 54–67.

Dewey, J. (1938). *Experience and education*. New York, NY: Macmillan Company.

Dewey, J. (1944). *Democracy and education: An introduction to the philosophy of education*. New York, NY: Free Press.

Dillenbourg, P. (1999). What do you mean by "collaborative learning"? In P. Dillenbourg (Ed.), *Collaborative-learning: Cognitive and computational approaches* (Advances in learning and instruction series, pp. 1–19). Amsterdam, the Netherlands: Elsevier Science.

Edelstein, W., & Noam, G. (1982). Regulatory structures of the self and 'postformal' stages in adulthood. *Human Development, 25*(6), 407–422.

Efklides, A. (2006). Metacognition and affect: What can metacognitive experiences tell us about the learning process? *Educational Research Review, 1*(1), 3–14.

Entwistle, N. J., & Ramsden, P. (1983). *Understanding student learning*. London, England: Croom Helm.

Ericsson, K. A. (2014). Why expert performance is special and cannot be extrapolated from studies of performance in the general population: A response to criticisms. *Intelligence, 45*, 81–103.

Ericsson, K. A., & Kintsch, W. (1995). Long-term working memory. *Psychological Review, 102*(2), 211–245.

Ericsson, K. A., Krampe, R. T., & Tesch-Römer, C. (1993). The role of deliberate practice in the acquisition of expert performance. *Psychological Review, 100*(3), 363–406.

Ericsson, K. A., & Pool, R. (2016). *Peak: Secrets from the new science of expertise*. Boston, MA: Houghton Mifflin Harcourt.

Eteläpelto, A., Vähäsantanen, P., Hökkä, P., & Paloniemi, S. (2013). What is agency? Conceptualizing professional agency at work. *Educational Research Review, 10*, 45–65.

Evens, M., Verburgh, A., & Elen, J. (2014). The development of critical thinking in professional and academic bachelor programmes. *Higher Education Studies, 4*(2), 42–51.

Fodor, J. A. (1983). *The modularity of mind: An essay on faculty psychology* (A Bradford book). Cambridge, MA: MIT Press.

Fodor, J. A. (1985). Précis of the modularity of mind. *The Behavioral and Brain Sciences, 8*, 1–42.

Giere, R. N., Bickle, J., & Mauldin, R. F. (2006). *Understanding scientific reasoning* (5th ed.). Belmont, CA: Thomson Wadsworth.

Gong, Y., Ericsson, K. A., & Moxley, J. H. (2015). Recall of briefly presented chess positions and its relation to chess skill. *PLoS ONE, 10*(3), e0118756. doi:10.1371/journal.pone.0118756

Gormezano, I., Prokasy, W. F., & Thompson, R. F. (Eds.). (2014). *Classical conditioning* (3rd ed.). New York, NY: Psychology Press.

Gruber, H., Lehtinen, E., Palonen, T., & Degner, S. (2008). Persons in the shadow: Assessing the social context of high abilities (Research report No. 29). *Psychology Science Quarterly, 50*(2), 237–258.

Gutiérrez, K. D., & Rogoff, B. (2003). Cultural ways of learning: Individual traits or repertoires of practice. *Educational Researcher, 32*(5), 19–25.

Hakkarainen, K., Palonen, T., Paavola, S., & Lehtinen, E. (2004). *Communities of networked expertise: Professional and educational perspectives* (Advances in learning and instruction series, Sitra's publication series No. 257). Amsterdam, the Netherlands: Elsevier.

Hambrick, D. Z., & Engle, R. W. (2002). Effects of domain knowledge, working memory capacity, and age on cognitive performance: An investigation of the knowledge-is-power hypothesis. *Cognitive Psychology, 44*(4), 339–387.

Hannover, B., & Kessels, U. (2004). Self-to-prototype matching as a strategy for making academic choices: Why high school students do not like math and science. *Learning and Instruction, 14*(1), 51–67.

Hari, R., Sams, M., & Nummenmaa, L. (2016). Attending to and neglecting people: Bridging neuroscience, psychology and sociology. *Philosophical Transactions B, The Royal Society Publishing, 371*: 20150365. doi:10.1098/rstb.2015.0365

Heikkilä, A., & Lonka, K. (2006). Studying in higher education: Students' approaches to learning, self-regulation, and cognitive strategies. *Studies in Higher Education, 31*(1), 99–117.

Hidi, S. (1990). Interest and its contribution as a mental resource for learning. *Review of Educational Research, 60*(4), 549–571.

Hill, N. M., & Schneider, W. (2006). Brain changes in the development of expertise: Neuroanatomical and neurophychological evidence about skill-based adaptations. In K. A. Ericsson, N. Charness, P. J. Feltovich, & R. R. Hoffman (Eds.), *The Cambridge handbook of expertise and expert performance* (Cambridge handbooks in psychology, pp. 653–683). Cambridge, UK: Cambridge University Press.

Hofer, B. K., & Pintrich, P. R. (Eds.). (2002). *Personal epistemology: The psychology of beliefs about knowledge and knowing.* Mahwah, NJ: Erlbaum.

Howard-Jones, P. A. (2014). Neuroscience and education: Myths and messages. *Nature Reviews Neuroscience, 15*(12), 817–824.

Hurford, A. (2010). Complexity theories and theories of learning: Literature reviews and syntheses. In B. Sriraman & L. English (Eds.), *Theories of mathematics education: Seeking new frontiers* (Advances in mathematics education, pp. 567–589). New York, NY: Springer.

Hyytinen, H., Holma, K., Toom, A., Shavelson, R. J., & Lindblom-Ylänne, S. (2014). The complex relationship between students' critical thinking and epistemological beliefs in the context of problem solving. *Frontline Learning Research, 2*(5), 1–24.

Iiskala, T. (2015). *Socially shared metacognitive regulation during collaborative learning processes in student dyads and small groups* (Doctoral dissertation, University of Turku, Department of Teacher Education and Centre for Learning Research, Turku, Finland).

Iiskala, T., Vauras, M., Lehtinen, E., & Salonen, P. (2011). Socially shared metacognition of dyads of pupils in collaborative mathematical problem-solving processes. *Learning and Instruction, 21*(3), 379–393.

Iiskala, T., Volet, S., Lehtinen, E., & Vauras, M. (2015). Socially shared metacognitive regulation in asynchronous CSCL in science: Functions, evolution and participation. *Frontline Learning Research, 3*(1), 78–111.

Inhelder, B., & Piaget, J. (1958). *The growth of logical thinking from childhood to adolescence: An essay on the construction of formal operational structures* (A. Parsons & S. Milgram, Trans.). New York, NY: Basic Books.

Jääskelä, P., Nykänen, S., & Tynjälä, P. (2018). Models for the development of generic skills in Finnish higher education. *Journal of Further and Higher Education, 42*(1), 130–142.

Johnson-Laird, P. N. (2010). Mental models and human reasoning. *Proceedings of the National Academy of Sciences of the United States of America, 107*(43), 18243–18250. doi:10.1073/pnas.1012933107

Kallio, E. (1998). *Training of students' scientific reasoning skills* (Doctoral dissertation, University of Jyväskylä, Department of Psychology, Jyväskylä, Finland).

Kallio, E. (2011). Integrative thinking is the key: An evaluation of current research into the development of adult thinking. *Theory & Psychology, 21*(6), 785–801.

Karmiloff-Smith, A. (2018). Précis of beyond modularity: A developmental perspective on cognitive science. In A. Karmiloff-Smith, M. S. C. Thomas, & M. H. Johnson (Eds.), *Thinking developmentally from constructivism to neuroconstructivism: Selected works of Annette Karmiloff-Smith* (pp. 40–63). New York, NY: Routledge. Reprinted from *Behavioral and Brain Sciences, 17*(4), 693–706, 1994.

Khosa, D. K., & Volet, S. E. (2014). Productive group engagement in cognitive activity and metacognitive regulation during collaborative learning: Can it explain differences in students' conceptual understanding? *Metacognition and Learning, 9*(3), 287–307.

King, P., & Kitchener, K. (2002). The reflective judgement model: Twenty years of research on epistemic cognition. In B. K. Hofer, & P. R. Pintrich (Eds.), *Personal epistemology: The psychology of beliefs about knowledge and knowing* (pp. 37–61). Mahwah, NJ: Erlbaum.

Kintsch, W. (1998). *Comprehension: A paradigm for cognition.* Cambridge, England: Cambridge University Press.

Kintsch, W., & Mangalath, P. (2011). The construction of meaning. *Topics in Cognitive Science, 3*(2), 346–370.

Kinzler, K. D., & Spelke, E. S. (2007). Core systems in human cognition. *Progress in Brain Research, 164*, 257–264.

Kirschner, P. A., Sweller, J., & Clark, R. E. (2006). Why minimal guidance during instruction does not work: An analysis of the failure of constructivist, discovery, problem-based, experiential, and inquiry-based teaching. *Educational Psychologist, 41*(2), 75–86.

Knorr Cetina, K. (1999). *Epistemic cultures: How the sciences make knowledge.* Cambridge, MA: Harvard University Press.

Krathwohl, D. R., Bloom, B. S., & Masia, B. B. (1964). *Taxonomy of educational objectives: The classification of educational goals. Handbook II: Affective domain.* New York, NY: McKay.

Krätzig, G. P., & Arbuthnott, K. D. (2006). Perceptual learning style and learning proficiency: A test of the hypothesis. *Journal of Educational Psychology, 98*(1), 238–246.

Kuhn, D. (2010). What is scientific thinking and how does it develop? In U. Goswami (Ed.), *The Wiley-Blackwell handbook of childhood cognitive development* (Blackwell handbooks of developmental psychology 2nd ed., pp. 497–523). Chichester, England: Wiley-Blackwell.

Kuhn, D., Amsel, E., & O'Loughlin, M. (1988). *The development of scientific thinking skills* (Developmental psychology series). San Diego, CA: Academic Press.

Kuhn, D., Iordanou, K., Pease, M., & Wirkala, C. (2008). Beyond control of variables: What needs to develop to achieve skilled scientific thinking? *Cognitive Development, 23*(4), 435–451.

Kuhn, D., & Weinstock, M. (2002). What is epistemological thinking and why does it matter? In B. K. Hofer & P. R. Pintrich (Eds.), *Personal epistemology: The psychology of beliefs about knowledge and knowing* (pp. 121–144). Mahwah, NJ: Erlbaum.

Lakoff, G., & Johnson, M. (1999). *Philosophy in the flesh: The embodied mind and its challenge to western thought.* New York, NY: Basic Books.

Lastusaari, M., & Murtonen, M. (2013). University chemistry students' learning approaches and willingness to change major. *Chemistry Education Research and Practice, 14*(4), 496–506.

Lave, J., & Wenger, E. (1991). *Situated learning: Legitimate peripheral participation.* Cambridge, England: Cambridge University Press.

Lehman, D. R., & Nisbett, R. E. (1990). A longitudinal study of the effects of undergraduate training on reasoning. *Developmental Psychology, 26*(6), 952–960.

Lehtinen, E. (2003). Computer supported collaborative learning: An approach to powerful learning environments. In E. De Corte, L. Verschaffel, N. Entwistle, & J. Van Merriëboer (Eds.), *Powerful learning environments: Unravelling basic components and dimensions* (pp. 35–53). Amsterdam, the Netherlands: Elsevier.

Lehtinen, E. (2010). Potential of teaching and learning supported by ICT for the acquisition of deep conceptual knowledge and the development of wisdom. In E. De Corte & J. E. Fenstad (Eds.), *From information to knowledge, from knowledge to wisdom: Challenges and changes facing higher education in the digital age: Proceedings from a symposium held in Stockholm 5–7 November 2009* (pp. 79–88). London, England: Portland Press. Retrieved from www.portlandpresspublishing.com/sites/default/files/Editorial/Wenner/WG_85/0850079.pdf

Lehtinen, E. (2012). Learning of complex competences: On the need to coordinate multiple theoretical perspectives. In A. Koskensalo, J. Smeds, R. de Cillia, & A. Huguet (Eds.), *Language: Competence – Change – Contact. Sprache: Kompetenz – Kontakt – Wandel* (Dichtung – Wahrheit – Sprache, Vol. 11, pp. 13–27). Berlin, Germany: Lit Verlag.

Lehtinen, E., Hakkarainen, K., & Palonen, T. (2014). Understanding learning for the professions: How theories of learning explain coping with rapid change. In S. Billet, C. Harteis, & H. Gruber (Eds.), *International handbook of research in professional and practice-based learning* (Springer international handbooks of education, pp. 199–224). Dordrecht, the Netherlands: Springer.

Lindblom-Ylänne, S., Parpala, A., & Postareff, L. (2014). Challenges in analysing change in students' approaches to learning. In D. Gijbels, V. Donche, J. T. E. Richardson, & J. D. Vermunt (Eds.), *Learning patterns in higher education: Dimensions and research perspectives* (New perspectives on learning and instruction/EARLI, New perspectives on learning and instruction, pp. 232–248). London, England: Routledge.

Magno, C. (2010). The role of metacognitive skills in developing critical thinking. *Metacognition and Learning, 5*(2), 137–156.

Malmberg, J., Järvelä, S., & Järvenoja, H. (2017). Capturing temporal and sequential patterns of self-, co-, and socially shared regulation in the context of collaborative learning. *Contemporary Educational Psychology, 49*, 160–174.

Marsick, V. J., & Watkins, K. E. (2015). *Informal and incidental learning in the workplace.* Abingdon, England: Routledge Revivals.

Marton, F., & Säljö, R. (1976). On qualitative differences in learning: I. Outcome and process. *British Journal of Educational Psychology, 46*(1), 4–11.

McClelland, J., McNaughton, B., & O'Reilly, R. (1995). Why there are complementary learning systems in the hippocampus and neocortex: Insights from the successes and failures of connectionist models of learning and memory. *Psychological Review, 102*(3), 419–457.

Mead, G. H. 1934. *Mind, self, and society: From the standpoint of a social behaviorist* (C. W. Morris Ed. and with an introduction). Chicago, IL: University of Chicago Press.

Merrett, D. L., Peretz, I., & Wilson, S. J. (2013). Moderating variables of music training-induced neuroplasticity: A review and discussion. *Frontiers in Psychology, 4*. Retrieved from www.ncbi.nlm.nih.gov/pmc/articles/PMC3766835/

Mikkonen, J., Heikkilä, A., Ruohoniemi, M., & Lindblom-Ylänne, S. (2009). "I study because I'm interested": University students' explanations for their disciplinary choices. *Scandinavian Journal of Educational Research, 53*(3), 229–244.

Miller, G. A. (1956). The magical number seven, plus or minus two: Some limits on our capacity for processing information. *Psychological Review, 63*(2), 81–97.

Miyake, A., & Friedman, N. (2012). The nature and organization of individual differences in executive functions: Four general conclusions. *Current Directions in Psychological Science, 21*(1), 8–14.

Murphy, P. K., & Alexander, P. A. (2000). A motivated exploration of motivation terminology. *Contemporary Educational Psychology, 25*, 3–53.

Murtonen, M. (2015). University students' understanding of the concepts empirical, theoretical, qualitative and quantitative research. *Teaching in Higher Education, 20*(7), 684–698.

Murtonen, M. (2017). Käsitykset ja uskomukset oppimisen tukena tai esteenä [Conceptions and beliefs that foster or impede learning]. In M. Murtonen (Ed.), *Opettajana yliopistolla: Korkeakoulupedagogiikan perusteet* [Being a teacher at university: Basics of higher education pedagogy] (pp. 63–82). Tampere, Finland: Vastapaino.

Murtonen, M., Gruber, H., & Lehtinen, E. (2017). The return of behaviourist epistemology: A review of learning outcomes studies. *Educational Research Review, 22*, 114–128.

Murtonen, M., Olkinuora, E., Tynjälä, P., & Lehtinen, E. (2008). "Do I need research skills in working life?" University students' motivation and difficulties in quantitative methods courses. *Higher Education, 56*(5), 599–612.

Nonaka, I., & Takeuchi, H. (1995). *The knowledge-creating company: How Japanese companies create the dynamics of innovation.* New York, NY: Oxford University Press.

Obersteiner, A., Van Dooren, W., Van Hoof, J., & Verschaffel, L. (2013). The natural number bias and magnitude representation in fraction comparison by expert mathematicians. *Learning and Instruction, 28*, 64–72.

Ohlsson, S. (2011). *Deep learning: How the mind overrides experience.* Cambridge, England: Cambridge University Press.

Onwuegbuzie, A. J., Leech, N. L., Murtonen, M., & Tähtinen, J. (2010). Utilizing mixed methods in teaching environments to reduce statistics anxiety. *International Journal of Multiple Research Approaches, 4*(1), 28–39.

Ozgelen, S. (2012). Exploring the relationships among epistemological beliefs, metacognitive awareness and nature of science. *International Journal of Environmental and Science Education, 7*(3), 409–431.

Paavola, S., Lipponen, L., & Hakkarainen, K. (2004). Models of innovative knowledge communities and three metaphors of learning. *Review of Educational Research, 74*(4), 557–576.

Perry, W. G., Jr. (1968). *Patterns of development in thought and values of students in a liberal arts college: A validation of a scheme.* Cambridge, MA: Harvard University, Bureau of Study Counsel.

Perry, W. G., Jr. (1970). *Forms of intellectual and ethical development in the college years: A scheme.* New York, NY: Holt, Rinehart and Winston.

Piaget, J. (1972). *The principles of genetic epistemology* (W. Mays, Trans.). London, England: Routledge & Kegan Paul.

Säljö, R. (2009). Learning, theories of learning, and units of analysis in research. *Educational Psychologist, 44*(3), 202–208.

Säljö, R. (2010). Digital tools and challenges to institutional traditions of learning: Technologies, social memory and the performative nature of learning. *Journal of Computer Assisted Learning, 26*(1), 53–64.

Schneider, M., & Preckel, F. (2017). Variables associated with achievement in higher education: A systematic review of meta-analyses. *Psychological Bulletin, 143*(6), 565–600.

Schommer, M. (1990). Effects of beliefs about the nature of knowledge on comprehension. *Journal of Educational Psychology, 82*(3), 498–504.

Schwaighofer, M., Fischer, F., & Bühner, M. (2015). Does working memory training transfer? A meta-analysis including training conditions as moderators. *Educational Psychologist, 50*(2), 138–166.

Seppälä, H. (2013). *Students' scientific thinking in higher education: Logical thinking and conceptions of scientific thinking in universities and universities of applied sciences* (Doctoral Dissertation, University of Helsinki, Helsinki, Finland).

Sfard, A. (1998). On two metaphors for learning and the dangers of choosing just one. *Educational Researcher, 27*(2), 4–13.

Sinatra, G. M. (2005). The "warming trend" in conceptual change research: The legacy of Paul R. Pintrich. *Educational Psychologist, 40*(2), 107–115.

Sternberg, R. J., & Frensch, P. A. (2014). *Complex problem solving: Principles and mechanisms.* New York, NY: Psychology Press. doi:10.4324/9781315807546

Sweller, J., van Merrienboer, J. J. G., & Paas, F. G. W. C. (1998). Cognitive architecture and instructional design. *Educational Psychology Review, 10*(3), 251–296.

Trigwell, K., & Prosser, M. (2004). Development and use of the approaches to teaching inventory. *Educational Psychology Review, 16*(4), 409–424.

Valsiner, J. (Ed.). (2012). *The Oxford handbook of culture and psychology* (Oxford library of psychology). New York, NY: Oxford University Press.

Vermunt, J. (1998). The regulation of constructive learning processes. *British Journal of Educational Psychology, 68*(2), 149–171.

Vermunt, J. D. (2005). Relations between student learning patterns and personal and contextual factors and academic performance. *Higher Education, 49*(3), 205–234.

Vermunt, J. D., & Verloop, N. (1999). Congruence and friction between learning and teaching. *Learning and Instruction, 9*(3), 257–280.

Vermunt, J. D., & Vermetten, Y. J. (2004). Patterns in student learning: Relationships between learning strategies, conceptions of learning, and learning orientations. *Educational Psychology Review, 16*(4), 359–384.

Vilppu, H., Mikkilä-Erdmann, M., & Ahopelto, I. (2013). The role of regulation and processing strategies in understanding science text among university students. *Scandinavian Journal of Educational Research, 57*(3), 246–262.

Vygotsky, L. S. (1930/1978). *Mind in society: The development of higher psychological processes* (M. Cole, V. John-Steiner, S. Scribner, & E. Souberman, Eds.). Cambridge, MA: Harvard University Press.

Weiner, B. (2010). The development of an attribution-based theory of motivation: A history of ideas. *Educational Psychologist, 45*(1), 28–36.

Whang, P. A., & Hancock, G. R. (1994). Motivation and mathematics achievement: Comparisons between Asian-American and non-Asian students. *Contemporary Educational Psychology, 19*(3), 302–322.

Wynn, C. T., Sr., Mosholder, R. S., & Larsen, C. A. (2014). Measuring the effects of problem-based learning on the development of postformal thinking skills and engagement of first-year learning community students. *Learning Communities Research and Practice, 2*(2). Retrieved from https://washingtoncenter.evergreen.edu/lcrpjournal/vol2/iss2/4

8

DEVELOPING LEARNING AND TEACHING PRACTICES FOR ADULTS

Perspectives from conceptual change and metacognition research[1]

Mirjamaija Mikkilä-Erdmann and Tuike Iiskala

Theoretical issues concerning adult learning – Combining conceptual change and metacognition research to adult development

In adult development and learning research there has been wide discussion concerning how adults develop knowledge and understanding through different phases or levels. Many of the models have already been discussed in this book. We can illuminate adult learning by two theoretical approaches, conceptual change and metacognition, that have widely inspired the research done on learning and instruction during the past 50 years. Our leading question is: how do adults learn and how can their learning processes be facilitated in formal or informal learning environments from the perspective of conceptual change and metacognition? By conceptual change, we mean a specific form of learning in which an individual more or less radically changes their existing knowledge or conceptual structures and perceives the world from a qualitatively different perspective (Sinatra & Mason, 2013; Vosniadou, 1994). Research into conceptual change has been multidisciplinary, stemming from philosophy of science, science education, developmental psychology, and educational psychology.

The metaphor "conceptual change" comes from Thomas Kuhn (1962) who, in his book *The Structure of Scientific Revolution*, describes how changes in paradigms in the scientific community take place. Scientific thinking does not develop logically in a linear way but often seems to be incoherent – requiring researchers to solve cognitive conflicts when counterintuitive evidence is emerging. The changes among paradigms, scientific revolutions, seem to follow a pattern from normal science with a paradigm, to a dedication to solving puzzles, then serious anomalies may come up, leading to crisis and then, finally, resolution by a new paradigm takes place (Kuhn, 1962). The paradigm shift seems not to be a "direct line to the truth, but progress away from inadequate conceptions of, and towards interaction with the world"

(Hacking, 2012). In this process, researchers work hard on problems: they reflect and share their ideas in scientific articles, and become more and more aware of the problems as well as regulating their working towards appropriate theoretical and practical solutions. That is, they work in a metacognitive way.

Metacognition traditionally refers to knowledge of cognition and regulation of cognitive processes (Brown, 1978, 1987; Flavell, 1976, 2000; Flavell, Miller, & Miller, 1993). This means that metacognition consists of two intertwined parts. On the one hand, metacognition refers to knowledge of cognitive matters, e.g., to knowledge of properties of human mind and that a learner is aware that sometimes he or she, some other person or people, in general, understand, do not understand, understand incorrectly, or misunderstand something (Flavell et al., 1993). On the other hand, metacognition consists of a procedural part (e.g., Efklides, 2006; Veenman, 2011; Veenman & Elshout, 1999), which is the executive function for regulating actual cognitive activities (Brown, Bransford, Ferrara, & Campione, 1983; Flavell & Miller, 1998; Veenman & Elshout, 1999), e.g., a learner controls during the learning process: "how I am doing?", "does this make sense?" (see Brown & DeLoache, 1983). In successful learning, both parts are needed. For example, a learner might have knowledge of useful strategies to achieve a learning goal (see Flavell et al., 1993; Veenman & Elshout, 1999). However, this kind of metacognitive knowledge does not necessarily mean that the learner is using that knowledge during the process to achieve the learning goal, for example to understand something (see Veenman, 2011). That is why metacognitive regulation processes are needed while the learner monitors the use of strategies during the process and purposefully changes them if needed.

However, it is important to note that metacognition differs from cognitive strategies as the role of cognitive strategies is to make cognitive progress and to achieve cognitive goals, whereas the role of metacognition is to monitor and regulate them and to make sure that the goal is achieved (see Flavell, 1979, 1987). Thus, metacognition can be seen as a cognitive mechanism which monitors (Flavell, 1979, 1987) and controls (Wertsch, 1977) other cognitive processes. As the prefix "meta" shows, metacognition signifies "cognition about cognition" (Flavell, 2000; Flavell et al., 1993).

As Deanna Kuhn (1989) states, the idea of metacognition can also be seen in many earlier theories of cognition and development (e.g., Piaget, Vygotsky) that view it as a characteristic of human capacity, a person's ability to reflect on his or her own thinking. Also, the conceptual change tradition uses the concept of meta-conceptual awareness which refers to a person's awareness of existing conceptions (Vosniadou, 2013). In this article, in line with Mason and colleagues (2017), awareness is seen at a meta-level, referring to a learner's awareness of his or her own conceptions and scientific conceptions. Thus, the focus of metaconceptual awareness is seen, especially, in the conceptual point of view, whereas the scope of metacognitive knowledge can be seen as broader (e.g., focusing on the nature of knowledge of a person's thinking, tasks and strategies; see Flavell, 2000) and more general (e.g., not so close to actual cognitive processing; see Efklides, 2001) without a specific focus, in particular, on the conceptual point of view.

However, different concepts, such as metacognitive knowledge, regulation, as well as metaconceptual awareness, are regarded as essential in the conceptual change process. In line with these viewpoints, metacognition deals with "reflective abstraction of new or existing cognitive structures. (...) [and] emphasizes learner development over learner-environment interactions" (Dinsmore, Alexander, & Loughlin, 2008, p. 393). Thus, metacognition, as well as strategies, can be seen to have a central role in conceptualising the development of scientific thinking processes and, in this process, thinking about theories and evidence is needed (Kuhn, 1989). This requires learners to inspect and become aware of their thinking processes to gain control over the theories and evidence in their own thinking. If learners are not aware of the nature of theories and their logics and limits, this can cause difficulties to inspect how these theories are or are not made up of evidence (Flavell et al., 1993; Kuhn, 1989, 2000). Hence, metacognition can be seen as a profitable vehicle for inspecting learners' thinking processes and promoting conceptual change. However, the conceptual change and metacognition research traditions have mostly developed separately without close interaction with each other.

Conceptual change: enrichment and radical conceptual change – What does the metacognition research say?

Conceptual change often requires fundamental changes in the concepts and organisations of existing knowledge as well as the development of new learning strategies for deliberate knowledge restructuring and the acquisition of new concepts (Vosniadou, 2013). Conceptual change researchers argue about the type of conceptual changes and on which level the conceptual change takes place (e.g., Chi, 2008; diSessa, 2008; Vosniadou, 1994). There is, however, a general consensus that conceptual change can be seen as a specific form of learning and a process of restructuring domain-specific knowledge.

According to Vosniadou (1994, p. 46), the simplest form of conceptual change is called enrichment. In the process of enrichment, a learner is adding new information to an existing theoretical explanation on the level of specific theories, without changing the framework theory. Framework theory refers to the ontological and epistemological underpinnings of one's knowledge system. Framework theories can be seen as "skeletal structures that ground our deepest ontological commitments concerning how we understand the world" (Vosniadou, 2013, p. 13). Framework theories are not considered to be subject to metaconceptual awareness or they may not be systematically tested for confirmation or falsification (see Vosniadou, 2013).

The enrichment type of conceptual change can be seen as the normal, daily accumulation of information and acquisition of facts and concepts about the topic to be studied, without structural changes in the information-processing system itself (Rumelhart & Norman, 1978, p. 38). The enrichment process can occur at a cognitive level without metacognition in thinking because the enrichment process does not require knowledge or awareness of one's own (or someone else's) thinking or metacognitive regulation of the thinking process.

When reorganisation of the knowledge structure occurs on the level of the framework theory it is called revision, and can be considered the most difficult and significant type of conceptual change, which seems to be an intentional process and often requires systematic instruction (see also Chinn & Brewer, 1993; Hatano & Inagaki, 1997; Sinatra & Mason, 2013). According to Rumelhart and Norman (1978, p. 38), this kind of restructuring of the organisational structures at times seems to be accompanied by a "click of comprehension", a strong feeling for the topic that makes a large body of previously acquired (but ill-structured) knowledge fit into place. A revision process of this kind involves considerable time and effort, and there is still little evidence how the process occurs (Rumelhart & Norman, 1978, pp. 39–40; Mikkilä-Erdmann, 2001; Mikkilä-Erdmann, Penttinen, Anto, & Olkinuora, 2008; Penttinen, Anto, & Mikkilä-Erdmann, 2013).

Recently, some studies using online methodologies, such as eye tracking, have indicated that conceptual change is a gradual and long-lasting process in which learners revise their conceptual structures many times (Mikkilä-Erdmann et al., 2008; Penttinen et al., 2013; Södervik, 2016). Furthermore, studies indicate that learners are often not aware of their prior knowledge and its contradictions with the scientific knowledge (Sinatra & Mason, 2013). Thus, metacognition can be seen as crucial in the revision process: if a learner regulates her/his own thinking process, it supports the learner in becoming aware of her or his own prior knowledge and its contradictions with the scientific knowledge which, in turn, can evoke metacognitive regulation to reorganise the knowledge system facilitating conceptual change. However, from a metacognition point of view, such a revision process requires that metacognition extends as far as the epistemic level, thus, covering Kitchener's (1983) epistemic cognition, in which case metacognition also activates a person's epistemological awareness and understanding (see Hofer, 2004). This points out the connection between conceptual change and developmental adult theories.

Adult learners, just like young learners, bring lots of prior knowledge with them into to formal or informal learning situations. Adults have started to acquire scientific knowledge by constructing a relatively coherent explanatory system and framework theory already at the early ages, based on their observations in everyday interactions (Vosniadou, 2013). When adult students study, for example, biology at university, they bring lots of knowledge with them which can to some extent be in contradiction with the scientific knowledge to be studied in academia. In terms of adult cognitive development, understanding of contradictions or different thought systems around the same phenomenon is regarded as achievement of multiple perspectives. The highest advancement in dealing with multiple perspectives is evaluation (and integration) of different viewpoints (see Chapter 4; Kallio, 2011). Another challenge is that the conceptual change process, revision, often deals with the key concepts of the domain, which are fundamental components of theory and expertise, such as photosynthesis or evolution in biology or the cardiovascular system in medicine. For example, photosynthesis seems to be a key biology concept which opens a new theoretical perspective or horizon for the novice learner. Concepts like photosynthesis are not possible to learn through either enrichment or induction in a situated learning setting (see Ohlsson & Lehtinen, 1997; Roth, Anderson, & Smith, 1987). The student has to become aware of prior knowledge and has to revise the old everyday and human-centred notion of food, so that it includes the critical distinction between energy-containing substances (which can only be made originally by plants through photosynthesis) and other kinds of nutrients that support life but do not provide energy (Mikkilä-Erdmann, 2001). The studies on adult thinking have revealed that humans develop their thinking from concrete to abstract and from one-dimensionality to multiple perspectives and integrative notions. Our thinking in postformal stages seems to be qualitatively different from formal stages (Kallio, 2011). However, postformal thinking seems to be rare, even in adult learners (see Demetriou & Efklides, 1985). We suggest that adults' domain-specific knowledge structures and metacognitive processes differ during conceptual change among adults.

How are personal epistemologies related to metacognition and conceptual change learning?

Inagaki and Hatano (2013) suggest that conceptual change can occur faster in some adults, such as in scientists, than in children because they can be more sensitive to recognise discrepancies in their knowledge system because of fluent metacognition. Thus, metacognition may become more explicit, powerful, and effective during personal development (see Kuhn, 2000). Also, research results have shown that metacognitive skilfulness for a particular task increases with the acquisition of expertise and more advanced learners in a domain are metacognitively more skilled than novices (Veenman & Elshout, 1999). Thus, expertise is seen to involve metacognition, such as monitoring (Sternberg, 1998) and, if adults are advanced in some domain, they may be able to think metacognitively, which, in turn, supports their conceptual change processes in that domain (see Chapter 10). However, adult learners are not always experts in some domains; often they are novices and might not use so much metacognition in their thinking in these domains. Also, they are sometimes unable to transfer their expertise from one domain to another (see Hofer, 2004). Moreover, it is important to note that adult learners are not a homogenous age group from the metacognitive point of view. For example, awareness of and reflection on one's own mental processes have been indicated to vary during adulthood and according to the learning contexts in question (Vukman, 2005). Hence, we cannot axiomatically assume that adults are always more skilful than young learners.

Adult learners are engaged in a dynamic interaction with their environment when learning, for example, biology or physics (Piaget, 1975). They do not only enrich their knowledge structures but also their framework theory, i.e., ontological and epistemological presuppositions behind these conceptual structures. As Kitchener (1983) suggests, adult learners may reflect on epistemic assumptions, such as the limits, certainty, and criteria of knowing, because these kinds of assumptions provide a framework for how they understand the nature of problems and approach them (see also Kuhn, 2000; Chapter 3 and 4). Based on these kinds of epistemic assumptions, adults define and choose different strategies or solutions when they encounter problems and handle conflicting ideas and systems, taking into consideration various issues of logic, ethical choice, and reality. Hence, it is crucial to understand divergence in assumptions in order to understand the different justifications adult learners use when they face unique human issues in everyday life. This requires that we have to go beyond the traditional concept of metacognition and also scrutinise in the epistemic sense how adults acquire knowledge about knowledge and approach ideas and problems (Kitchener, 1983).

Alternatively, knowledge of epistemic assumptions can also be seen as a part of metacognition (see Hofer, 2004; Inagaki & Hatano, 2013; King & Siddiqui, 2011). Either way (i.e., whether metacognition theory itself is seen to cover epistemology or not), it is important that metacognition focuses also on epistemological beliefs when we want a conceptual change process to occur. This means that the conceptual change process is highly metacognitive when prior knowledge is scrutinised in relation to new scientific thinking (Kuhn, 2000) and existing concepts are recognised, evaluated, reviewed, and restructured if needed (Gunstone & Mitchell, 2005; Kuhn, 2000).

The role of personal epistemologies may have an evaluative and even affective nature. A person may have a strong commitment to her/his epistemology, and this can be considered as an essential condition for metacognition and conceptual change. Mason (2002) illustrates how specific beliefs may act as resources or constrain conceptual change. Hence, epistemic cognition seems to be vital to high level conceptual changes. Epistemology seems to develop to some extent parallel to the development of knowledge but can have a different structure. Effective pedagogical interventions in appropriate learning environments and targeting at epistemological beliefs are suggested to be important at two levels: epistemological and conceptual.

Examples of adult learners' conceptual change processes

Next, we take some examples of adult learners in higher education who need to study biological phenomena such as the cardiovascular system or photosynthesis. Medical students and classroom teacher students have to pass an entrance examination (7%–10% acceptance rate) and hence represent highly selected study programmes in Finland. Medical doctors and school teachers are examples of professions that imply theoretical understanding and evidence-based expertise when dealing with patients or with pupils. Both medical and teacher education study programmes are multidisciplinary and aiming at expertise consisting of profound theoretical understanding, metacognition, procedural knowledge, and practical skills (see Chapter 10). Both medical doctors and teachers have to understand the theoretical underpinnings behind the practical problems to be solved in everyday work. Theoretical and practical understanding is important in both professions. Learning medicine requires, for example, an understanding of physics, chemistry, and biology, which is often called biomedical knowledge. Classroom teachers have educational sciences as their major and they study all the subjects to be taught in primary school. Classroom teachers have to be able to teach science contents for the six grades in primary education, which accounts for 60% of all science teaching in the nine-year comprehensive school.

In this context we can ask, for example: how do medical students understand the cardiovascular system? How do student teachers conceive photosynthesis, one of the most important theoretical phenomena in biology? Do adults have a conceptual understanding that differs from scientific notions?

Medical students and the cardiovascular system

Medical students possess large amounts of prior knowledge when entering medical school, consisting of a mixture of formal science knowledge and experimental, informal and even folk knowledge about medical systems and diseases (Boshuizen, Schmidt, Custers, & Van de Wiel, 1995). This is a huge challenge for university teachers who are probably not that well aware of the understandings of their students. Systemic understanding seems to be vital in medical contexts (Södervik, 2016), which requires, for example, understanding of human anatomy and physiology and the functional interactions between both. The basis of systemic understanding is constructed during the first two years in traditional medical study programmes in Europe (pre-clinical phase).

Our studies, capturing the complex phenomenon of developing systemic understanding of the central cardiovascular system (CCVS), were conducted first on longitudinal and cross-sectional levels, and later using online methodology. First, we followed one cohort of medical students (N = 119) during their first study year and another cohort (N = 33) during their third study year. We also investigated internal medicine residents (N = 13) from one university hospital as a control group for the medical students. In our studies, our leading research questions were: "What kind of alternative models do students have; how do the students change their conceptual understanding concerning CCVS during their study years, and how does the quality of conceptual understanding influence the clinical reasoning of the students?" In our longitudinal and cross-sectional study, we used pre- and post-test design and open-ended generative tasks requiring explanations of the cardiovascular system (Ahopelto, Mikkilä-Erdmann, Olkinuora, & Kääpä, 2011; Mikkilä-Erdmann, Södervik, Vilppu, Kääpä, & Olkinuora, 2012; Södervik, Mikkilä-Erdmann, & Vilppu, 2014; Södervik, Vilppu, Österholm, & Mikkilä-Erdmann, 2017).

Our results revealed that highly-selected medical students have many alternative models consisting of misconceptions in the first study year before the introductory course on the central cardiovascular system, revealing that students did not understand the synchronous functioning of the heart and lungs (double loop) (Ahopelto, Mikkilä-Erdmann, Olkinuora, et al., 2011; Mikkilä-Erdmann et al., 2012; Södervik, 2016).

After the introductory course, one-third of the students still had misconceptions. Furthermore, an important finding was that the quality of the biomedical knowledge was connected to the clinical reasoning skills of the students. We also found indicative support in our online study that those students who showed high diagnostic competence in reasoning tasks had also high levels of biomedical understanding (Södervik et al., 2017).

In summary, our results indicate that even high-performing students have misconceptions based on their everyday knowledge and interactions with the world and from school. The cardiovascular system is a typical scientific system that requires understanding two parallel, almost simultaneously functioning systems. It can be suggested that the learning environment also plays a role in conceptual change processes. Medical students studied in a traditional study programme that only partly consisted of a learning environment that promoted active interaction and group work. We assume that medical students need metacognitive, in particular, metaconceptual support in studying complex systems.

Student teachers' challenges in understanding photosynthesis

Classroom teachers play an important role in supporting young students' construction of scientific knowledge and facilitating conceptual change from everyday knowledge to scientific knowledge (Södervik et al., 2014). A classroom teacher is a mediator between the everyday world and scientific knowledge for the children. Photosynthesis is one of the key theoretical concepts in science (i.e., energy comes through plants to the ecosystem), which is dealt with early on during the first school years and so enables students to understand the role of plants in ecosystems and, eventually, how to support sustainable development.

In our first study we used a case study approach in a pre-and post-test laboratory setting. We analysed (through open-ended questions) what kind of conceptions concerning photosynthesis the student teachers had. The results indicated that half of the students (9/18) had severe misconceptions concerning photosynthesis (Ahopelto, Mikkilä-Erdmann, Anto, & Penttinen, 2011; Penttinen et al., 2013; Vilppu, 2016). Most of them thought that a plant takes energy from the soil in the form of water or nutrients. After the pre-test, we let the students read a refutational text, making them aware of their probable misconceptions and then allowing them to revise these. The post-test results showed that adult students changed their conceptions radically and none of them had misconceptions about the nutrient supply of plants; however, five students presented synthetic models which were a mixture of scientific and everyday knowledge (Vosniadou, 1994). Our further study revealed that students' self-regulation, metaconceptual awareness, and learning goals were connected to conceptual change concerning science content. Students who experienced conceptual change had system level learning goals and seemed to have realistic metaconceptual awareness. In summary, self-regulation, metacognition, and metaconceptual awareness seem to play a role in conceptual change (Ahopelto et al., 2011; Penttinen et al., 2013; Vilppu, 2016).

Learning environments and adult learners – How to support conceptual change and metacognitive processes in adult education?

Adult learners seem to have similar kinds of misconceptions to young learners and therefore need to be supported through effective learning environments. We consider a learning environment a system which consists of a student, a teacher, a curriculum, learning materials, instructional activities implying more or less interaction (individual work, group work etc.), and forms of evaluation. The essential question in designing these learning environments was "how do they improve students' metacognition?" – as based on their metaconceptual awareness.

An adult student has acquired much more expertise which often seems to work in everyday practice. To some extent adult students can be more resistant to changing their conceptions, especially if their learning goals do not fit or are incongruent with the goals of teaching (Penttinen et al., 2013). Conceptual change processes are intentional, and students have to first experience dissatisfaction with their existing models to be then replaced with more fruitful and intelligible ones opening new theoretical perspectives or supporting practical problem solving (Posner, Strike, Hewson, & Gertzog, 1982). Moreover, learners can direct their metacognitive monitoring to support their prior personal assumptions which can inhibit their conceptual change processes (see Hofer, 2004).

The role of the teacher in adult education, as in all formal settings, is very important. The teacher has to have effective metacognition, metaconceptual awareness and learning strategies in order to model expert learning. For example, students do not necessarily use metacognition in action, although they are reported to have high levels of metacognitive knowledge and regulation (De Backer, Van Keer, & Valcke, 2012). They may have metacognitive knowledge of strategies, but they are not necessarily able to use this knowledge in learning situations. Thus, learners need to be supported in using metacognition in their learning as well as in socialisation to develop scientific practices in the discipline. This means that learners should learn metacognitive procedures for learning and using information in addition to theoretical knowledge of the subject, to which these procedures are applied (see Sternberg, 1998).

In designing a curriculum, a strict analysis of theoretical core concepts is needed. The amount of knowledge is exponentially increasing and so the selection of theoretically fruitful conceptual contents is needed. Also, the structure of the curriculum should be hierarchically organised and the logic behind the organisation must be visible to the learner.

Meta-teaching (Fisher, 1998), previously conceptualised in interventions for young learners, can also be an important procedure for adults so as to illustrate the learning goals and display how we teach for metacognition, scaffolding and modelling scientific practices in interaction, and through communication. This kind of meta-teaching can also be used in socialising adult learners to academic studies. Metaconceptual teaching that explicitly makes the differences between conceptualisations in science and everyday life visible has particular potential for future interventions (see Wiser & Amin, 2001) on all levels (cognitive, metacognitive, epistemological) according to Kitchener's model (1983). Hence, thinking can be seen to develop as systemic, metasystemic, and epistemic cognition (see Demetriou & Efklides, 1985).

The beginning of the study programme seems to be an important phase for all students, but also for the modelling of the cognitive conflicts and possible solutions of these conflicts. In designing instructional activities, adult students also need scaffolding in higher education studies. It can be suggested that many adults are not autonomous learners, but are a heterogeneous group who can have difficulties studying on their own. Also, in adult education, metacognitive thinking can be seen as a goal, but not a starting point. Yet, the academic learning culture should be in line with the characteristics of the specific discipline to be studied. In the beginning of the studies, the teacher's role is to be a kind of translator and facilitator between everyday language and scientific language. Hence, interaction with the teacher and advanced students would be profitable (see Vygotsky, 1994).

Learning strategies, learning materials, and critical academic reading, alone and in groups

In conceptual change, metacognitive knowledge of the learning strategies and their use in regulation seem to be important since learners who frequently regulate their learning metacognitively seem to have more metaconceptual awareness and vice versa (Saçkes & Trundle, 2017). However, metacognitive regulation alone does not seem to be sufficient for learners to achieve conceptual understanding, although metacognitive regulation does guide cognitive strategies in processing scientific concepts towards a conceptual change (Saçkes & Trundle, 2014). Thus, metacognition as well as cognitive strategies are needed. When learners monitor their thinking processes (e.g., how to approach a text to understand it), they are seen to have better possibilities to regulate their learning (e.g., to choose between different alternatives) and take responsibility for their learning. This kind of metacognitive process, in turn, is suggested to effect students' learning and development, both in formal and informal learning contexts (see King & Siddiqui, 2011).

Pedagogical practice, including textbooks, does not normally take the above-mentioned problems into account. Textbooks often strive for enrichment and assume that what learners already know is compatible with scientific knowledge (see Mikkilä & Olkinuora, 1994; Roth, 1990). Until now there have been few tools to cope with this problem. Presenting a cognitive conflict in the learning situation has been used as a method by science teachers, but it does not seem to be enough for promoting conceptual change in a radical sense as both young learners and older learners can be resistant to change (Limón, 2001; Penttinen et al., 2013). However, learning materials, especially textbooks, play a great role in higher education, and texts can be seen as an important tool for conceptual change.

Recently, the potential of designing texts, especially so-called refutational texts, to facilitate conceptual change has been intensively explored among conceptual change researchers (Broughton, Sinatra, & Reynolds, 2010; Södervik, Virtanen, & Mikkilä-Erdmann, 2015; Tippett, 2010). By refutational texts we refer to texts designed to activate students' prior knowledge by directly addressing their misconceptions, then presenting the scientific explanation as a plausible alternative (Hynd, 2001; Mason et al., 2017; Mikkilä-Erdmann, 2001). For a learner, the process of becoming aware of a possible mismatch between his/her ideas and scientific content to be learned through a text can be an essential factor in promoting metaconceptual awareness. This can therefore be seen as an important prerequisite for conceptual change (see Mason et al., 2017; Vosniadou, 1994, p. 67; Vosniadou & Ioannides, 1998, p. 1224; Mikkilä-Erdmann, 2001). In our studies, the use of refutational texts for adult students seemed to support conceptual change (Ahopelto et al., 2011; Mikkilä-Erdmann et al., 2008; Södervik, 2016). Also, students with lesser prior knowledge seem to benefit from refutational texts (Ahopelto et al., 2011). Furthermore, other instructional activities, such as writing a learning diary consisting of metaconceptual questions, concept mapping, class and group discussions, seem to facilitate students' metaconceptual awareness and thus support conceptual change (Ozturk, 2017).

Interaction, for example in a collaborative learning setting, can help the student to become aware of his or her prior knowledge and possible alternative models (see Chapter 2). For instance, collaborative learning, such as reciprocal peer tutoring, has been indicated to support learners' metacognition (De Backer et al., 2012). In turn, improved metacognitive awareness has been shown to have a relationship, for example, with the development of the conceptions of the nature of science (Abd-El-Khalick & Akerson, 2009). Thus, metacognition can be supported in peer-interaction and this can enhance conceptual understanding.

However, learners' collaboration even at a metacognitive level itself does not necessarily support high-level learning, such as a conceptual change process. Instead, metacognition in collaboration should be focused on high-level knowledge co-construction rather than on low-level task co-production (see Khosa & Volet, 2014). In this setting, it is important that learners make their thinking process visible, also by means of small verbal signs (e.g., "I'm confused", "It can't be so", "It isn't necessarily so because … ", "It doesn't make sense if we think that … ", "Let's think … ") that provide other learners (or teacher) with an opportunity to react to these utterances and help all learners, together, metacognitively regulate the thinking process towards the learning goal (see Iiskala, Vauras, & Lehtinen, 2004; Iiskala, Vauras, Lehtinen, & Salonen, 2011). However, learners can also co-construct misconceptions in a student-led collaboration (see Iiskala, 2015), which can be seen as pedagogically problematic. Hence, a teacher with multiple perspectives (Kallio, 2011), theoretically high-level understanding and pedagogical skills are needed in adult education.

Discussion

In the current article, we have dealt with questions on how adults differ in conceptual change and metacognition processes. We have learned that adults to some extent are similar to younger learners in that their prior knowledge is rich and often a mixture of scientific knowledge and everyday conceptions. Similar challenges can be seen in the metacognition of children and adults, although adults' metacognition and learning strategies can work well. We suggest that also adult students experience many conceptual changes, for example, at the beginning of their studies, on the level of metacognition, theoretical conceptual knowledge, and framework theory. A fallacy in adult education is to presume that all adults are inherently competent learners.

Adult learners need time for systematic studying and also learning environments that support metacognition and conceptual elaboration. Thus, it is important to remember that conceptual change is not necessarily a quick process, rather it may be quite slow and gradual (see Gunstone & Mitchell, 2005; Sinatra & Mason, 2013). In this article, metacognition is seen as an important element in supporting conceptual change processes to occur, because metacognition enables learners to become aware of and to regulate incongruity within their existing knowledge systems, which is needed for the revision process (Inagaki & Hatano, 2013). As previous research has shown, metacognition (e.g., metacognitive regulation such as frequent use of metacognitive strategies) and metaconceptual awareness are in positive relation with each other (see Saçkes & Trundle, 2017). Thus, a conceptual change process seems to require that a learner has metacognitive knowledge of strategies as well as metacognitive regulation when using these strategies in the learning process to gain metaconceptual awareness. Moreover, a revision process seems to demand that metacognition cannot be restricted to knowledge and regulation of strategies and cognition in general but needs to cover epistemological considerations such as a person's awareness of his own epistemic system in relation with other viewpoints (e.g., conflicts between the two).

In this article, we have dealt with conceptual change and metacognition, focusing on cognitive aspects. However, we suggest that another important area for future research is that of motivational and emotional aspects. Conceptual change is a demanding process where a learner needs to give up accustomed conceptual models, including framework theories constructed over many years. The learners feel committed to these previous models and have tested them with everyday observations. In addition, these theories seem to work in practice. Hence, the revision process is not just (meta)cognitive but also, emotionally and motivationally challenging (see Sinatra & Mason, 2013). Conceptual changes can take place on the level of identity. Adult life is not static but requires flexibility. Global problems require the ability to take multiple perspectives and be aware of different perspectives at the same time. Ethical issues become very important and we think that this has something to do with wisdom (see Chapters 2 and 10). It is crucial to consider how to support this kind of identity-level conceptual change in formal and informal education.

Moreover, in this article we have dealt with the conceptual change process and metacognition from an individual point of view. However, adults also work in teams, so it would be interesting to approach conceptual change processes and metacognition from a collaborative point of view. For example, the concept of metacognition has been extended from the traditional individual construct to the construct of socially-shared metacognition, which refers to learners' common goal-directed, consensual, egalitarian, and complementary knowledge and regulation of joint cognitive processes in the collaborative learning context (see Iiskala, 2015; Iiskala et al., 2004, 2011). Thus, we feel it is important to analyse the role of socially-shared metacognition, such as socially-shared metacognitive regulation, in relation to the group's metaconceptual awareness and conceptual change process. Inspired by the socially-shared metacognition research, we raise the question of whether the conceptual change process could also be shared in collaborative learning (socially-shared conceptual change) and what is the role of conceptual change in a group's learning? Also, epistemological beliefs can be socially shared (Mason, 2002) and thus mediate conceptual change in individual and collaborative settings – the simpler and more biased the beliefs are, the more difficult it is to revise them and reach conceptual change.

In the current world, the acquisition of theoretical understanding, metacognition, and strategies is time-consuming and emotionally challenging. This is often problematic from the perspective of an adult. The internet and global media make the situation even more demanding. How do we engage an adult student, who often has family duties and a job, to invest time in systematic deliberate studying? Should we start our teaching in adult education by revising the misconception that you can easily find valid information on the Internet i.e., just Google everything and easily find the right solution? So, as well as the traditional metacognitive strategy interventions, adult students need to revise their conceptions of knowledge and studying in academia, in which case metacognition should cover students' conceptions of knowledge systems. Solving cognitive conflicts is not fun in the beginning but once you find the solution it can be like that. Adults need competent teachers just as younger students do. It is important to create a critical, debating academic learning culture in adult education.

Note

1 This article is inspired by an earlier, more limited version (in Finnish) in Mikkilä-Erdmann (2016) in which only the conceptual change perspective in adult learning is dealt with.

References

Abd-El-Khalick, F., & Akerson, V. L. (2009). The influence of metacognitive training on preservice elementary teachers' conceptions of nature of science. *International Journal of Science Education, 31*(16), 2161–2184.

Ahopelto, I., Mikkilä-Erdmann, M., Anto, E., & Penttinen, M. (2011). Future elementary school teachers' conceptual change concerning photosynthesis. *Scandinavian Journal of Educational Research, 55*(5), 503–515.

Ahopelto, I., Mikkilä-Erdmann, M., Olkinuora, E., & Kääpä, P. (2011). A follow-up study of medical and dental students biomedical understanding and clinical reasoning concerning the cardiovascular system. *Advances in Health Sciences, 16*(5), 655–668.

Boshuizen, H. P. A., Schmidt, H. G., Custers, E. J. F. M., & Van de Wiel, M. W. (1995). Knowledge development and restructuring in the domain of medicine: The role of theory and practice. *Learning and Instruction, 5*(4), 269–289.

Broughton, S. H., Sinatra, G. M., & Reynolds, R. E. (2010). The nature of the refutation text effect: An investigation of attention allocation. *The Journal of Educational Research, 103*(6), 407–423.

Brown, A. L. (1978). Knowing when, where, and how to remember: A problem of meta-cognition. In R. Glaser (Ed.), *Advances in instructional psychology* (Vol. 1, pp. 77–165). Hillsdale, NJ: Erlbaum.

Brown, A. L. (1987). Metacognition, executive control, self-regulation, and other more mysterious mechanisms. In F. E. Weinert & R. H. Kluwe (Eds.), *Metacognition, motivation, and understanding* (pp. 65–116). Hillsdale, NJ: Erlbaum.

Brown, A. L., Bransford, J. D., Ferrara, R. A., & Campione, J. C. (1983). Learning, remembering, and understanding. In P. H. Mussen (Ed.), & J. H. Flavell & E. M. Markman (Vol. Eds.), *Handbook of child psychology: Cognitive development* (4th ed., Vol. 3, pp. 77–166). New York, NY: Wiley.

Brown, A. L., & DeLoache, J. S. (1983). Metacognitive skills. In M. Donaldson, R. Grieve, & C. Pratt (Eds.), *Early childhood development and education: Readings in psychology* (pp. 280–289). New York, NY: Blackwell.

Chi, M. T. H. (2008). Three types of conceptual change: Belief revision, mental model transformation, and categorical shift. In S. Vosniadou (Ed.), *International handbook of research on conceptual change* (Educational psychology handbook series, 2nd ed., pp. 61–82). New York, NY: Routledge.

Chinn, C. A., & Brewer, W. F. (1993). The role of anomalous data in knowledge acquisition: A theoretical framework and implications for science instruction. *Review of Educational Research, 63*(1), 1–49.

De Backer, L., Van Keer, H., & Valcke, M. (2012). Exploring the potential impact of reciprocal peer tutoring on higher education students' metacognitive knowledge and regulation. *Instructional Science, 40*(3), 559–588.

Demetriou, A., & Efklides, A. (1985). Structure and sequence of formal and postformal thought: General patterns and individual differences. *Child Development, 56*(4), 1062–1091.

Dinsmore, D. L., Alexander, P. A., & Loughlin, S. M. (2008). Focusing the conceptual lens on metacognition, self-regulation, and self-regulated learning. *Educational Psychology Review, 20*(4), 391–409.

diSessa, A. A. (2008). A bird's eye-view of the "pieces" vs. "coherence" controversy (from the "pieces" side of the fence). In S. Vosniadou (Ed.), *International handbook of research on conceptual change* (Educational psychology handbook series, 2nd ed., pp. 61–82). New York, NY: Routledge.

Efklides, A. (2001). Metacognitive experiences in problem solving: Metacognition, motivation, and self-regulation. In A. Efklides, J. Kuhl, & R. M. Sorrentino (Eds.), *Trends and prospects in motivation research* (pp. 297–323). Dordrecht, the Netherlands: Kluwer.

Efklides, A. (2006). Metacognition and affect: What can metacognitive experiences tell us about the learning process? *Educational Research Review, 1*(1), 3–14.

Fisher, R. (1998). Thinking about thinking: Developing metacognition in children. *Early Child Development and Care, 141*(1), 1–15.

Flavell, J. H. (1976). Metacognitive aspects of problem solving. In L. B. Resnick (Ed.), *The nature of intelligence* (pp. 231–235). Hillsdale, NJ: Erlbaum.

Flavell, J. H. (1979). Metacognition and cognitive monitoring: A new area of cognitive – Developmental inquiry. *American Psychologist, 34*(10), 906–911.

Flavell, J. H. (1987). Speculations about the nature and development of metacognition. In F. E. Weinert & R. Kluwe (Eds.), *Metacognition, motivation, and understanding* (pp. 21–29). Hillsdale, NJ: Erlbaum.

Flavell, J. H. (2000). Development of children's knowledge about the mental world. *International Journal of Behavioral Development, 24*(1), 15–23.

Flavell, J. H., & Miller, P. H. (1998). Social cognition. In W. Damon (Ed.) & D. Kuhn & R. S. Siegler (Vol. Eds.), *Handbook of child psychology: Cognition, perception, and language* (5th ed., Vol. 2, pp. 851–898). New York: Wiley.

Flavell, J. H., Miller, P. H., & Miller, S. A. (1993). *Cognitive development* (3rd ed.). Englewood Cliffs, NJ: Prentice-Hall.

Gunstone, R., & Mitchell, I. J. (2005). Metacognition and conceptual change. In J. J. Mintzes, J. H. Wandersee, & J. D. Novak (Eds.), *Teaching science for understanding: A human constructivist view* (pp. 133–163). Burlington, MA: Elsevier Academic Press.

Hacking, I. (2012). Introductory essay. In T. S. Kuhn, *The structure of scientific revolutions* (4th ed., pp. vii–xxxviii). Chicago, IL: Chicago University press.

Hatano, G., & Inagaki, K. (1997). Qualitative changes in intuitive biology. *European Journal of Psychology of Education, 12*(2), 111–130.

Hofer, B. K. (2004). Epistemological understanding as a metacognitive process: Thinking aloud during online searching. *Educational Psychologist, 39*(1), 43–55.

Hynd, C. R. (2001). Refutational texts and the change process. *International Journal of Educational Research, 35*(7–8), 699–714.

Iiskala, T. (2015). *Socially shared metacognitive regulation during collaborative learning processes in student dyads and small groups* (Doctoral dissertation, University of Turku, Department of Teacher Education and Centre for Learning Research, Turku, Finland).

Iiskala, T., Vauras, M., & Lehtinen, E. (2004). Socially-shared metacognition in peer learning? *Hellenic Journal of Psychology, 1*(2), 147–178.

Iiskala, T., Vauras, M., Lehtinen, E., & Salonen, P. (2011). Socially shared metacognition of dyads of pupils in collaborative mathematical problem-solving processes. *Learning and Instruction, 21*(3), 379–393.

Inagaki, K., & Hatano, G. (2013). Conceptual change in naïve biology. In S. Vosniadou (Ed.), *International handbook of research on conceptual change* (Educational psychology handbook series, 2nd ed., pp. 195–219). New York, NY: Routledge.

Kallio, E. (2011). Integrative thinking is the key: An evaluation of current research into the development of adult thinking. *Theory & Psychology, 21*(6), 785–801.

Khosa, D. K., & Volet, S. E. (2014). Productive group engagement in cognitive activity and metacognitive regulation during collaborative learning: Can it explain differences in students' conceptual understanding? *Metacognition and Learning, 9*(3), 287–307.

King, P. M., & Siddiqui, R. (2011). Self-authorship and metacognition: Related constructs for understanding college student learning and development. In C. Hoare (Ed.), *The Oxford handbook of reciprocal adult development and learning* (Oxford library of psychology, 2nd ed., pp. 113–131). New York, NY: Oxford University Press.

Kitchener, K. S. (1983). Cognition, metacognition, and epistemic cognition: A three-level model of cognitive processing. *Human Development, 26*(4), 222–232.

Kuhn, D. (1989). Children and adults as intuitive scientists. *Psychological Review, 96*(4), 674–689.

Kuhn, D. (2000). Metacognitive development. *Current Directions in Psychological Science*, *9*(5), 178–181.

Kuhn, T. S. (1962). *The structure of scientific revolutions* (International encyclopedia of united science 2, 2). Chicago, IL: University of Chicago Press.

Limón, M. (2001). On the cognitive conflict as an instructional strategy for conceptual change: A critical appraisal. *Learning & Instruction*, *11*(4–5), 357–380.

Mason, L. (2002). Developing epistemological thinking to foster conceptual change in different domains. In M. Limon & L. Mason (Eds.), *Reconsidering conceptual change: Issues in theory and practice* (pp. 301–335). Dordrecht, the Netherlands: Springer.

Mason, L., Baldi, R., Di Rondo, S., Scrimin, S., Danielson, R. W., & Sinatra, G. M. (2017). Textual and graphical refutations: Effects on conceptual change learning. *Contemporary Educational Psychology*, *49*, 275–288.

Mikkilä, M., & Olkinuora, E. (1994). Problems of current textbooks and workbooks: Do they promote high-quality learning? In F. P. C. M. De Jong & B. H. A. M. van Houtwolters (Eds.), *Process-oriented instruction and learning from text* (pp. 151–164). Amsterdam, the Netherlands: VU University Press.

Mikkilä-Erdmann, M. (2001). Improving conceptual change concerning photosynthesis through text design. *Learning & Instruction*, *11*(3), 241–257.

Mikkilä-Erdmann, M. (2016). Käsitteellinen muutos ja koulutukselliset haasteet aikuisuudessa [Conceptual change and educational challenges in adulthood]. In E. Kallio (Ed.), *Ajattelun kehitys aikuisuudessa: Kohti moninäkökulmaisuutta* [The development of thinking in adulthood: Towards multiperspective thinking] (Research in Educational Sciences No. 71, pp. 205–226). Helsinki, Finland: The Finnish Educational Research Association.

Mikkilä-Erdmann, M., Penttinen, M., Anto, E., & Olkinuora, E. (2008). Constructing mental models during learning from science text: Eye tracking methodology meets conceptual change. In D. Ifenthaler, P. Pirnay-Dummer, & J. M. Spector (Eds.), *Understanding models for learning and instruction: Essays in honor of Norbert M. Seel* (pp. 63–79). New York, NY: Springer.

Mikkilä-Erdmann, M., Södervik, I., Vilppu, H., Kääpä, P., & Olkinuora, E. (2012). First-year medical students' conceptual understanding of and resistance to conceptual change concerning the central cardiovascular system. *Instructional Science*, *40*(5), 745–754.

Ohlsson, S., & Lehtinen, E. (1997). Abstraction and the acquisition of complex ideas. *International Journal of Educational Research*, *27*(1), 37–48.

Ozturk, N. (2017). An analysis of teachers' self-reported competencies for teaching metacognition. *Educational Studies*, *43*(3), 247–264.

Penttinen, M., Anto, E., & Mikkilä-Erdmann, M. (2013). Conceptual change, text comprehension and eye movements during reading. *Research in Science Education*, *43*(4), 1407–1434.

Piaget, J. (1975). *Das Erwachen der Intelligenz beim Kinde* [The Origins of Intelligence in Children engl.] (Gesammelte Werke, Studienausgabe No. 1). Stuttgart, Germany: Klett.

Posner, G. J., Strike, K. A., Hewson, P. W., & Gertzog, W. A. (1982). Accommodation of a scientific conception: Towards a theory of conceptual change. *Science Education*, *66*(2), 211–227.

Roth, K. (1990). Developing meaningful conceptual understanding in science. In B. Jones & L. Idol (Eds.), *Dimensions of thinking and cognitive instruction* (pp. 139–175). Elmhurst, IL: NCREL.

Roth, K., Anderson, C. W., & Smith, E. L. (1987). Curriculum materials, teacher talk and student learning: Case studies in fifth grade science teaching. *Journal of Curriculum Studies*, *19*(6), 527–548.

Rumelhart, D. E., & Norman, D. A. (1978). Accretion, tuning, and restructuring: Three modes of learning. In J. W. Cotton & R. L. Klatzky, *Semantic factors in cognition* (pp. 37–53). Hillsdale, NJ: Erlbaum.

Saçkes, M., & Trundle, K. C. (2014). Preservice early childhood teachers' learning of science in a methods course: Examining the predictive ability of an intentional learning model. *Journal of Science Teacher Education, 25*(4), 413–444.

Saçkes, M., & Trundle, K. C. (2017). Change or durability? The contribution of metaconceptual awareness in preservice early childhood teachers' learning of science concepts. *Research in Science Education, 47*(3), 655–671.

Sinatra, G. M., & Mason, L. (2013). Beyond knowledge: Learner characteristics influencing conceptual change. In S. Vosniadou (Ed.), *International handbook of research on conceptual change* (Educational psychology handbook series, 2nd ed., pp. 377–394). New York, NY: Routledge.

Södervik, I. (2016). *Understanding biological concepts at university: Investigating learning in medical and teacher education* (Doctoral dissertation, University of Turku, Department of Teacher Education, Turku, Finland).

Södervik, I., Mikkilä-Erdmann, M., & Vilppu, H. (2014). Promoting the understanding of photosynthesis among elementary school student teachers through text design. *Journal of Science Teacher Education, 25*(5), 581–600.

Södervik, I., Vilppu, H., Österholm, E., & Mikkilä-Erdmann, M. (2017). Medical students' biomedical and clinical knowledge: Combining longitudinal design, eye tracking and comparison with residents' performance. *Learning and Instruction, 52*(9), 139–147.

Södervik, I., Virtanen, V., & Mikkilä-Erdmann, M. (2015). Challenges in understanding photosynthesis in an introductionary biosciences class. *International Journal of Science and Mathematics Education, 13*(4), 733–750.

Sternberg, R. J. (1998). Metacognition, abilities, and developing expertise: What makes an expert student? *Instructional Science, 26*(1–2), 127–140.

Tippett, C. D. (2010). Refutation text in science education: A review of two decades of research. *International Journal of Science and Mathematics Education, 8*(6), 951–970.

Veenman, M., & Elshout, J. J. (1999). Changes in the relation between cognitive and metacognitive skills during the acquisition of expertise. *European Journal of Psychology of Education, 14*(4), 509–523.

Veenman, M. V. J. (2011). Learning to self-monitor and self-regulate. In R. E. Mayer & P. A. Alexander (Eds.), *Handbook of research on learning and instruction* (Educational psychology handbook series, pp. 197–218). New York, NY: Routledge.

Vilppu, H. (2016). *University students' regulation of learning and text processing: Examples from medical and teacher education* (Doctoral dissertation, University of Turku, Department of Teacher Education, Turku, Finland).

Vosniadou, S. (1994). Capturing and modeling the process of conceptual change. *Learning and Instruction, 4*(1), 45–69.

Vosniadou, S. (2013). Conceptual change in learning and instruction: The framework theory approach. In S. Vosniadou (Ed.), *International handbook of research on conceptual change* (Educational psychology handbook series, pp. 197). New York, NY: Routledge.

Vosniadou, S., & Ioannides, C. (1998). From conceptual development to science education: A psychological point of view. *International Journal of Science Education, 20*(10), 1213–1230.

Vukman, K. B. (2005). Developmental differences in metacognition and their connections with cognitive development in adulthood. *Journal of Adult Development, 12*(4), 211–221.

Vygotsky, L. S. (1994). The development of academic concepts in school aged children. In R. van der Veer & J. Valsiner (Eds.), *The Vygotsky reader* (pp. 355–370). Oxford, England: Blackwell.

Wertsch, J. V. (1977, May). *Metacognition and adult-child interaction.* Paper presented at Northwestern University Annual Conference on Learning Disabilities, Evanston, IL. Abstract retrieved from https://eric.ed.gov/?q=ED180610&id=ED180610

Wiser, M., & Amin, T. (2001). "Is heat hot?" Inducing conceptual change by integrating everyday and scientific perspectives on thermal phenomena. *Learning and Instruction,* *11*(4–5), 331–355.

9

TACIT KNOWLEDGE AND KNOWING AT THE CORE OF INDIVIDUAL AND COLLECTIVE EXPERTISE AND PROFESSIONAL ACTION[1]

Auli Toom and Jukka Husu

Introduction

Tacit knowledge and knowing as manifold, challenging, and fascinating research phenomena has occupied researchers' minds in many disciplines. In this chapter, we review the diversity, essentiality, and significance of tacit knowledge in the construction of expertise as well as in experts' thinking and actions. Expertise and tacit knowledge are often considered together in various fields and professions, because they have several characteristics that are closely intertwined with each other. This chapter examines the relationships between tacit knowledge and expertise, especially taking into account the complexity of tacit knowledge aiming to understand the core of expertise. While professional expertise is often viewed through individual facets, it is equally important to incorporate interactive and object-oriented collaborative aspects to its tacit dimensions (Hakkarainen & Paavola, 2008; Paavola & Hakkarainen, 2005). We elaborate tacit knowledge in relation to skills and competences as well as in relation to the questions of explication and argumentation that are central when thinking about the essence of expertise (cf. Fenstermacher, 1994; Hakkarainen & Paavola, 2008). We elaborate the process and product aspects of tacit knowledge as well as its individual and collective aspects, which are critical when thinking about the core of expertise. We hope to provide a basis upon which dialogue on the issue can progress.

After analysing the aspects of tacit knowledge, we present a model in which the characteristics of tacit knowledge and expertise are intertwined into four different perspectives. First, tacit knowledge can be understood as a gradually accumulated knowledge base which an individual expert can access. Secondly, the tacit expert knowledge base lies in communities, networks, and organisations. Thirdly, tacit knowledge is perceived as individual expert action including accumulated experiences in the form of scripts and agendas of action. Fourth, we conclude by viewing tacit knowledge as active and situationally emerging practices in expert communities' action. Along with these four perspectives, we touch upon current research in which the development of expertise is understood to be a collective process (Sawyer, 2007) that combines individuals, communities, and the objects of their activities (Knorr Cetina, 2001; Paavola & Hakkarainen, 2005; Sfard, 1998). Tacit knowledge is thus understood as being situational and intertwined with a particular social and material context of action. Although it is challenging to explicate tacit knowledge and knowing, they are closely intertwined with cognitive and emotional aspects in experts' thinking and action – and it may be analytically possible to examine them in greater detail.

Characteristics of tacit knowledge

Tacit knowledge and knowing have triggered heated discussions among philosophers (Niiniluoto, 1996; Polanyi, 1966; Rolf, 1995), theologians (Sanders, 1988), social scientists (Gourlay, 2004; Sveiby, 1994), nursing (Nurminen, 2008), as well as among educational scientists (Fenstermacher, 1994; Hager, 2000; Orton, 1993). For example, Fenstermacher (1994), Hager (2000), and Niiniluoto (1996) analyse the complicated characteristics and define tacit knowledge as one form of knowledge. Tacit knowledge has been elaborated from the psychological perspective (Argyris & Schön, 1974; Orton, 1993) as it comes close to routines and automated strategies. Tacit knowledge is analysed in detail in studies investigating apprenticeship settings (Jernström, 2000). Tacit knowledge has also been identified in the business world, and in that context its collective and organisational aspects have been emphasised (Nonaka & Takeuchi, 1995). Even though there is no consensus about the definition of the concept of tacit knowledge, there is general agreement about its complexity among researchers.

Michael Polanyi's (1958, 1966) well-known theory of tacit knowledge is an epistemological theory, in which (tacit) knowledge is understood broadly, and Polanyi uses alternately the concepts of tacit *knowing* and *knowledge*. Polanyi (1966) defines it broadly in a sense that it covers both intellectual knowledge and other aspects, for example skills and abilities. Polanyi's often-cited observation regarding tacit knowledge is: *we know more than we can tell* (Polanyi, 1966, p. 4). The phrase has become a fascinating label, but it is difficult to define what it actually means. Regarding Polanyi, Rolf's (1995) understanding is helpful as he states about tacit knowledge: "As humans orientate themselves to real world, they consider and steer their behaviours by tacitly functioning knowledge in which the conventions and personal aspects are integrated. Integration allows them to orientate towards reality". Polanyi elaborates the "tacit dimension" of knowledge and behaviour, in which cultures and individuals are integrated. There he has identified "tacit knowing" or "knowledge" resource (Rolf, 1995, pp. 20–21).

Despite the multiple perspectives, the majority of discussions and criticisms concerning tacit knowledge seems to date back to the following philosophical-epistemological questions (Toom, 2006, 2012): how is the content of knowledge defined? Does knowledge cover almost all the conscious and unconscious human actions, or does it cover only some of the human actions defined in a certain way? Also, is the demand for explication always linked up with definition and pursuit of knowledge? What about the need for argumentation? Does the focus of interest lie on tacit knowledge substance, or tacit knowledge in action, tacit knowing? In addition, is tacit knowledge situation-specific, and to what extent? We analyse tacit knowledge by leaning on certain key scholars. Our aim is to untangle the shared core questions of tacit knowledge that emerge from different bases, not to juxtapose them (see of expertise, Chapter 10).

Elaborating skills and tacit knowledge

When considering the characteristics of tacit knowledge, it is natural to examine them in relation to the concept of skills. Contrary to Polanyi and Rolf, Niiniluoto (1996) perceives that skills are a pre-stage of knowledge. As a philosopher, Niiniluoto presents a restricted and more traditional understanding of knowledge. According to him, skills are often learnt in the process of trial and error or through imitation or modelling in master-apprentice relationships where learning does not happen according to explicit and rules-governed practices (cf. Rolf, 1995, p. 116). In this sense, a good example of learning skills is learning languages: language, grammar, and vocabulary are learnt in everyday practices in ways that learners are not able to explain how they are actually learning. Here, the learners' knowledge of grammar can be understood as *tacit* because they can act according to its rules but they are not able to formulate and explicate them. In that kind of case tacit knowledge is often non-verbal. This is in contrast with formal and propositional knowledge where things are expressed in declarative sentences.

Argyris and Schön (1974) have been interested in expert action and the concept of skill is central in their analyses. However, instead of using the concept of skill, they describe expert actions through *espoused theories* and *theories-in-use*. Understanding that practice and expertise are embedded in the language, and action of a community is one of their central tenets (Argyris, Putnam, & McLain Smith, 1985). *Theories-in-use* are those that can be inferred from tacit knowledge emerging in expert action, while *espoused theories* are those that experts claim to follow and utilise when describing and justifying their actions. They view skills as dimensions of ability through which it is possible to behave effectively in various situations. Experts learn skills mostly through imitating, e.g., they learn to act in line with new theories of action. They underline that learning does not proceed from espoused theories to theories-in-use. The argument of Argyris, Putnam, and Smith (1985) is that implicit is central in investigations of expert theories of action. Espoused and public reflection is undertaken in the interest of learning and bringing the two theories closer in line for greater effectiveness in practice. We should also remember that experts learn through feedback and critical remarks related to their actions which often do not rely on espoused theories (Argyris & Schön, 1974). Overall, we can conclude that both

Niiniluoto, and Argyris and Schön analyse the concept of skill from different viewpoints but they all claim that action can contribute to skills development without verbalisation.

With his view on skilful expertise, Eraut (1994, pp. 111–112) is in line with the previously mentioned authors and he sees skills as routinized and complex series of actions that experts perform almost automatically. Through routinization the experts become less aware of their actions and experience growing difficulties to explain and explicate their actions after they have been completed. Eraut identifies skills as learnt actions that initially were explicit, but have slowly become routinized. This stance, in line with Niiniluoto (1996) and Argyris and Schön (1974), brings skills to the forefront of experts' professional actions and underlines tacit knowledge as an essential part of expert practice.

Competencies and tacit knowledge

The discussions of tacit expert knowledge and skilful expert action are often bundled with notions of professional *know-how* and competence. This underlies the idea that individual expert competence is always relational and connected to the professional community that they represent. Especially since the 1980s, various professions such as lawyers, physicians, and even teachers have actively claimed expert status and used this status to structure professional competence standards both in the US and Europe (Eraut, 1994; Hager, 1993; Pantić & Wubbels, 2012; Toom, 2017). However, the concept of professional competence dates back to older professions' traditions through which professional excellence and qualifications have been defined (Polanyi, 1958, 1966). Ryle's (1949) well-known classification of two kinds of knowledges – *knowing how* and *knowing that* – can be useful when elaborating the ways in which abilities, skills, and knowledge are connected to expertise. The latter, *knowing that*, states that knowing something can be expressed by mainly propositional claims. Ryle as well as Polanyi and Rolf did not favor this intellectual myth and instead, emphasized that *knowing how* requires some prior and implicit consideration of knowledge or abilities that cannot be stated verbally (cf. Niiniluoto, 1996, pp. 52–53). This viewpoint implies that both knowledges are to some extent dependent: *knowing how* consists of both skills and knowledge disposition (Small, 2017). It is also interesting to note that until recently Ryle's distinction could be straightforwardly deployed in a variety of contexts – but this is no longer true: for example, Stanley and Williamson (2001) started to challenge Ryle's arguments for the distinction and proposed that *knowing how* is (*contra* Ryle) a species of *knowing that* (see Bengson & Moffett, 2011).

The ability to solve challenging situations is also emphasised in competencies, which are often seen as a cognitive capacity to perform professional actions. However, competencies not only call for knowledge and skills, they also require appropriate attitudes, strategic thinking, and awareness of one's own actions (Westera, 2001, p. 80). For example, a teacher's decision-making during classroom ineraction or a researcher's decision-making during an in-depth interview both require immediate action competencies to combine cognitive knowledge with skills and attitudes. Competencies require more than relevant knowledge and skills to provide qualified expert actions. Besides conscious and purposeful decision-making, expert competencies also require a disposition to act, as well as abilities to explain and justify the taken or intended actions (Eraut, 1994, p. 179; Korthagen, 2004, pp. 80–81; Westera, 2001, pp. 75–59). In order to make a clearer distinction between outcome behaviors and competencies, it is important to view competencies, in line with tacit knowledge, as integrated entities comprising knowledge, skills, and attitudes. As such, competencies are potential for behaviour, not just the behaviour itself (Toom, 2017).

Ways to explicate tacit knowledge

Tacit knowledge and its ambiguities have been the subject of critical remarks. Especially explication of tacit knowledge which has been a key theme due to general epistemological demand for anything called knowledge (Rolf, 1995, p. 31). Polanyi's (1966) response that tacit knowledge mainly emerges in immediate action situations, and therefore cannot be accurately explicated, draws the line between the two contesting approaches. Polanyi was well aware of this demand and claimed that not even modern developed ways of communication and articulation could justify the statement that at the moment "we knew more than we could then tell" (Polanyi, 1966, p. 5). When elaborating the explication of experts' tacit knowledge van Manen (1995, p. 45) speaks of active consciousness which experts rely on action, and Molander (1992) emphasises confidence in expert action in specific moments. This particular consciousness is intertwined with expert practical skills that are embedded in practices and, personal ways of doing things, and therefore it is difficult to explicate (van Manen, 1995, pp. 45–46). This kind of practical expertise is also called silent knowledge (Molander, 1992, pp. 11–12) due to its intractiblity when it comes to explication and critical scrutiny.

As noted, explication of tacit knowledge is related to the ways we define knowledge, and to the ways we want, and are able to, elaborate knowledge practices in action. When tacit knowledge is defined as unstated structures and beliefs underlying a person's action, it becomes difficult to explicate. However, defining and understanding tacit knowledge as a process of knowing, similar to competence or know-how opens up new possibilities to search for explications and explanations for it (Toom, 2012).

Perspectives on argumentation of tacit knowledge

In line with explication, argumentation is a key theme as well if tacit knowledge is investigated as knowledge, and it has also confused researchers (Fenstermacher, 1994; Orton, 1993; Rolf, 1995; van Manen, 1995). The demand for argumentation is related to the customary ways of seeing knowledge as a well-argumented and justified true belief to gain certainty (Niiniluoto, 1996, p. 49). This kind of demand for argumentation means that all expert knowledge should be available in verbal statements and shoud be characterised in intellectual terms (Rolf, 1995, pp. 33–34).

This would only limit expert knowledge on occasions where decisions could be based on well-grounded and explicit arguments. Polanyi (1958, 1966), however, defines knowledge from a broader perspective and without the need for such a strict argumentation. In a similar manner, Rosiek (2002, pp. 135–137) claims that knowledge can also be given its status through practical arguments.

Regarding the argumentation and practical knowledge, Fenstermacher (1994) presents a more demanding view and notes that the concept of knowledge is often too tempting and it has often been used too loosely. He points out that knowledge is more than everyday beliefs and opinions, and expert knowledge can involve thoughts and actions which are beyond tacit-bound beliefs or opinions (Fenstermacher, 1994, pp. 33–34). This can be done with the help of practical reasoning where the provision of arguments is intended to support valid and meaningful actions. This provision of reasons, when done well, can make action sensible both for the actor and for the observer. As Fenstermacher (1994) concludes, such reasoning can show that a behaviour is "the reasonable thing to do, the obvious thing to do, or the only thing one could do under the circumstances" (p. 47). The argumentation intends to support the needed epistemic value of practical knowledge claims. However, as Fenstermacher (1994) reminds, caution is required because the argumentation of tacit knowledge is not possible because it is only partially anchored in human consciousness. Therefore, concrete actions are needed for tacit knowledge to emerge and make it available for argumentation.

Contextuality of tacit knowledge

Interestingly, at the moment, Polanyi may be the most modern advocate when it comes to his views of the social and cultural origins of tacit expert knowledge (Rolf, 1995, p. 15). This notion is largely accepted, and it has been explored in many fields e.g., in arts and crafts (Jernström, 2000; Tynjälä, 2008), theology (Sanders, 1988), business (Nonaka & Takeuchi, 1995), the social sciences (Gourlay, 2002, 2004), nursing (Nurminen, 2008), and education (Burbules, 2008; Fenstermacher, 1994; Toom, 2006, 2008, 2012, 2017; van Manen, 1995). In various contexts, tacit knowledge often emerges when immediate actions to demanding situations are needed, and the actions have to be justified in reasonable ways (Toom, 2017; Westera, 2001). Theologians describe various pastoral care situations that call for tacit knowledge. Researchers on nursing refer to demanding caring encounters between patients and nurses, where tacit knowing has played a crucial role in completing them successfully. In teacher research, it has been found that teachers' tacit knowledge is perceived to be especially necessary in surprising pedagogical moments in classroom interactions (van Manen, 1991b, 1995). In these situations, teachers need to act – or not to act – appropriately in relation to their pupils and their learning (Burbules, 2008).

Some situations often require experts to perceive their actions from multiple perspectives: carefully evaluate the situation, know participants, and think about the consequences, also for future actions (see Chapter 2). All the intended and performed actions should be executed in the best interest of all involved. It is certainly impossible to learn this kind of knowledge by simply reading books. Instead, this kind of expertise can only be acquired through action and reflection on action during long periods of time.

Tacit knowledge as individual and collective phenomena

As tacit knowledge contains both skilful, individual, and cumulative expert knowledge and the processes of knowing, some researchers (e.g., Baltes, Staudinger, & Lindenberger, 1999; Krampe & Baltes, 2003) speak about an expert's crystallized intelligence when describing competent expert action. Also, Argyris and Schön (1974), through their theory-in-use views, perceive professional knowledge from an individualistic perspective. They all elaborate on tacit knowledge and expertise from individual sources, through which experts e.g., in master-apprentice relationships build up their skills and knowledge for action (Jernström, 2000; Rolf, 1995). Besides individual sources, tacit knowledge also emerges from co-operation with others, both explicitly and implicitly.

Organizational knowledge creation (Nonaka, 1994; Nonaka & Takeuchi, 1995) makes available and strenghtens knowledge created by individuals together as well as connecting it to an organization's knowledge system. Tacit knowledge is a cornerstone in this shared creation and transforms unarticulated knowledge and skills, senses, and implicit rules of thumb into collective professional practices. Understanding the knowledge conversion between tacit and explicit (Nonaka & von Krogh, 2009) is focal in learning through an organization's knowledge system. This kind of learning process demands social skills, abilities, a willingness to engage in reciprocity, and a sense of belonging to an expert community (Lave & Wenger, 1991; Wenger, 1998). Tacit knowledge in expert communities can be seen as a web of places and a net of people seamlessly working together (Hakkarainen, Lonka, & Lipponen, 2004).

Recent research (Hakkarainen & Paavola, 2008; Lakkala, Toom, Ilomäki, & Muukkonen, 2015) has shown that creative expertise requires well-functioning work groups and networks across various disciplines in order to be able to solve problems and innovate (John-Steiner, 2000; Scardamalia, 2002). Hakkarainen et al. (2004) have put forward a collective intelligence that emerges in joint actions with experts. They argue that the highly complex problems that experts have to resolve in work require greater reliance on socially distributed intelligence and competence. Viewing individual expertise within a social collectivity is crucial to overcoming and exceeding individual resources and capabilities (Sawyer, 2007). Thus, caution is required if we focus only on key experts: tacit knowledge is enrichened by everyone working in an organisation.

Tacit knowledge as a product and process

As we have emphasized, tacit knowledge is closely connected with skilful expert action and it serves both as a knowledge base for action and as continuously shaping the process of knowing. In theory, the two perspectives can be separated. As an accumulated knowledge base, tacit knowledge covers practical experiences and beliefs across many individual and communal contexts and traditions and develops continuously through action and reflection (Hakkarainen & Paavola, 2008). The formation of this kind of expertise happens not only through clarifying skills, beliefs, and attitudes (Rolf, 1995), but also through knowledge conversion between tacit and non-tacit knowledge bases (Collin, Paloniemi, Rasku-Puttonen, & Tynjälä, 2010; Eteläpelto & Tynjälä, 1999). This conversation from intuitive and automatic actions towards more conscious ones, and vice versa, can be seen as an essential condition for becoming an expert (Eraut, 1994; Leinhardt, McCarthy, Young, & Merriman, 1995).

When emphasising the process characteristics of tacit knowledge, tacit *knowing* is often favoured as a concept (Rolf, 1995; Toom, 2012). This shifts the focus to immediate situations where expert practices and decision-making take place in quick and intuitive actualisations of knowledge and skills in various contexts. Experts' capabilities to utilise tacit knowledge emerge in situations when they are able to activate knowledge processes in action. In line with Polanyi (1958, 1966), Rolf (1995) states that experts utilise knowledge like an invisible tool and is thus called tacit. Its broad canvas of competencies is seen as a key to expertise and it relies on the users' understanding and sensitivity of what to do or undo in demanding professional situations.

It is important to note that the product and process aspects of tacit knowledge are not mutually exclusive. Rather, they are complementary as tacit knowledge is developed through practical knowing whenever experts consciously organise, classify, clarifify, and anticipate their practical actions. Thus, it resonates with the current understanding of experts' competence covering the knowledge base, situational observation, and decision-making as well as actual behaviour in order to solve any challenge at hand (Blömeke & Kaiser, 2017; Toom, 2017; Westera, 2001). Next, we will examine the structure and the dimensions of tacit knowing by following Polanyi (1966).

The structure of the process of tacit knowing

Tacit knowing builds upon the two dimensions, the tacit and the focal dimensions (Polanyi, 1966), and the relationships between the two knowing activities. Figure 9.1 presents Rolf's (1995, p. 67) view of the topic and emphasises the tacit dimension as a basis in expert action. As Figure 9.1 shows, tacit knowledge is made of traditional (concepts and theories), material, and situational cues that guide observations and actions. During the process, the experts' perceptions connect their situational cues to concepts familiar through professional tradition, and the integrations are guided by the purposes of professional actions. Together, the elements work like an invisible instrument or tool that purposefully but silently guides experts' process-like knowing and action (Rolf, 1995).

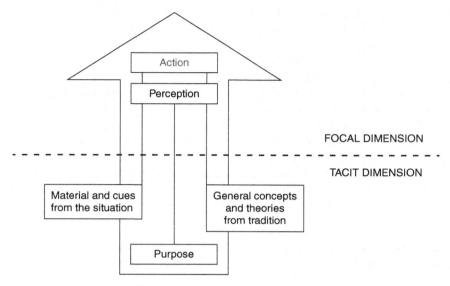

FIGURE 9.1 Structure of tacit knowing according to Polanyi (Rolf, 1995, p. 67; Toom, 2008, p. 49). Printed with permission. Copyright Faculty of Educational Sciences, University of Helsinki, Finland

As Rolf (1995) notes, Polanyi's understanding of the tacit dimensions of knowing and action comes close to the ways experts use information and tools in their professional action. Also, the ways experts choose and justify their knowledge and actions are connected to their value-based decisions in particular situations (Rolf, 1995, p. 70). It is worth noting that Polanyi's strong emphasis on the personal – in the form of norms, habits, and routines – largely arises from professional traditions, through which it is mediated into individual experts' actions. We also highlight the intentional nature of tacit knowing – from perceptions to meanings and understandings – as it moves from situational cues through tradition-laden theories into action.

When Rolf's understanding of the process of tacit pedagogical knowing is brought into the educational context, we can see a strong resemblance to van Manen's (1991b) view on teacher's pedagogical understanding. Pedagogical understanding is a complex skill and underlines a teacher's sensitive listening and observation, and it includes both reflective and interactive elements. Its core characteristic is the ability to see situational cues in students' actions during teaching, and besides immediate demands it also strecthes over momentary reflective needs. Pedagogical understanding is realised through pedagogical tact: a disposition to act in ways that maintain good and workable relations with others. Thus, pedagogical understanding and tact and tacit knowing are different perspectives to the same phenomenon (van Manen, 1991b). Furthermore, excercising this tact (van Manen, 1991a, 1991b, 1995) comes close to tacit knowing. In order to handle interactive situations successfully, an expert needs knowledge and skills to perceive specific situations in detail, understand their meaning from multiple points of view, and know how to act – or not to act – in relation to consequences (see Chapter 3). The process clearly has similar characteristics with Polanyi's tacit knowing and action. Van Manen (1991a, 1991b, 1995) also reminds us that the (reflection and action) phases are closely connected and can be seen as an integrated whole where multiple perspectives and emotions actually build up tactfulness (Kallio, 2011).

The expertise both in Polanyi's tacit knowing and in van Manen's pedagogical understanding share many common features. Their essential core is the purposeful professional action that is guided by both situational cues and more sustained elements of expert knowledge. Tacit pedagogical knowing, in turn, emphasises professional knowledge and skilful action, and can be explicated. Thus, it is comparable to the concept of competence elaborated mentioned earlier in the chapter.

Discussion: the relationship between tacit knowledge and expertise

As we conclude the chapter, we want to pay attention to the core elements of tacit knowledge among experts when tacit knowing is built up by the dimensions of expertise and by the nature of tacit professional knowledge in practice (see Figure 9.2). We have tried to show how expert tacit knowledge has both *individual* and *collective* characteristics that are tighly connected to each other and to expert contexts and cultures. Also, the *product* and the *process* of tacit knowledge can be theoretically and conceptually separated from each other even though these two dimensions work inseparately together in practice.

When we think of experts' tacit knowledge to be *individual* and as *collective* phenomena, we should remind ourselves that collective practices in communities (also) emerge in individuals, much like skilful individual action contributes positively to collective action. Recent research on expertise (Hakkarainen & Paavola, 2008) emphasizes the collective and social characteristics of expertise. It has strong links with socio-cultural theories (Hatano & Oura, 2003; Lave & Wenger, 1991; Wenger, 1998) which underline the fact that intelligent (and skilful) action cannot be executed neither understood without close connections to its social and cultural contexts.

We have emphasised how tacit knowing is a key element in well-functioning expert interactions and work processes. An expert's tacit knowledge closely refers to implicit knowledge elements underlying action, such as personal and collective beliefs, attitudes, and values. While these knowledge processes are conscious makes articulation of tacit knowledge difficult. Expert tacit knowing appears only in competent actions where object-oriented moves, both individual and collective, are realised (Hakkarainen & Paavola, 2008; Paavola & Hakkarainen, 2005). Due to their complexities, it is often possible to articulate the process of knowing only afterwards. As Figure 9.2 shows, the product and process aspects of tacit knowing are reciprocal: while

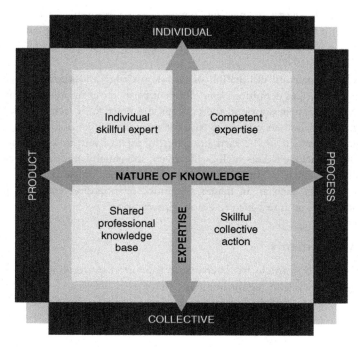

FIGURE 9.2 Elaboration of tacit knowledge in terms of expertise and nature of knowledge (cf. Toom, 2008, p. 54). Printed with permission. Copyright The Finnish Lifelong Learning Foundation, Helsinki, Finland

customary habits and practices are influencing skilful expertise, also new ways of doing and understanding are being developed and constantly adopted in the experts' matrix.

The essential question is then: how are tacit knowledge and knowing intertwined in the construction of expertise? The elaborated aspects of tacit knowledge is closely linked to the research on collective and networked expertise (Sawyer, 2007), where expertise is not only an individual characteristic, but rather it is constructed in interactions between individuals and communities (see also Chapter 7). Expert communities have their unique cultures and practices, on which they rest and function (Lave & Wenger, 1991; Wenger, 1998). Expertise is realised through participation in collective knowledge creation processes and the construction of shared practices (Hakkarainen & Paavola, 2008). In networked expertise, individuals' actions promote the functioning of the whole community and vice versa (Tynjälä, Välimaa, & Sarja, 2003). Thus, the group of experts can survive, or even grow, as they tackle challenges that any individual expert could not solve alone. Within the shared knowledge reserve, experts have their own areas of expertise which they can develop utilising the community's knowledge reserve. In well-functioning expert communities, professionals have shared abilities to solve new and demanding challenges (John-Steiner, 2000; Sawyer, 2007), in which collective tacit knowledge plays a central role as experts can employ networks and thus exceed their individual capabilities. This necessitates well-functioning social relationships between experts, which makes it possible for everybody to explain and understand the functioning of their expert community (Elliot & Pedler, 2018; Tynjälä, Nuutinen, Eteläpelto, Kirjonen, & Remes, 1997).

Finally, our analytical elaboration of tacit knowledge and knowing leads us to bring together various definitions from different perspectives in order to disperse the ambiguity and vagueness around the concept and practice of tacit knowledge and knowing. The analysis encourages us to ask if we are in danger of losing some essential features contained in the tacit knowing of experts, and in expert networks? These features include factors such as affectivity, spontaneity, and interactivity. And if something essential is lost, then can the phenomenon be found again only in authentic contexts such as: in master-apprentice relationships, collective problem solving situations, or in real-life professional interactions?

Acknowledgements

The writing of this article has been partly supported by funding received from the Academy of Finland (Grant number 285806).

Note

1 An earlier and more limited version of this chapter has been presented in Finnish by Toom (2016).

References

Argyris, C., Putnam, R., & McLain Smith, D. (1985). *Action science* (Jossey-Bass management series). San Francisco, CA: Jossey-Bass.

Argyris, C., & Schön, D. A. (1974). *Theory in practice: Increasing professional effectiveness.* San Francisco, CA: Jossey-Bass.

Baltes, P. B., Staudinger, U. M., & Lindenberger, U. (1999). Lifespan psychology: Theory and application to intellectual functioning. *Annual Review of Psychology*, *50*(1), 471–507.

Bengson, J., & Moffett, M. A. (2011). Two conceptions of mind and action: Knowing how and the philosophical theory of intelligence. In J. Bengson & M. A. Moffett (Eds.), *Knowing how: Essays on knowledge, mind, and action* (pp. 3–55). New York, NY: Oxford University Press.

Blömeke, S., & Kaiser, G. (2017). Understanding the development of teachers' professional competencies as personally, situationally and socially determined. In D. J. Clandinin & J. Husu (Eds.), *The SAGE handbook of research on teacher education* (2 volume set, pp. 783–802). London, England: SAGE.

Burbules, N. C. (2008). Tacit teaching. *Educational Philosophy and Theory, 40*(5), 666–677.

Collin, K., Paloniemi, S., Rasku-Puttonen, H., & Tynjälä, P. (Eds.). (2010). *Luovuus, oppiminen ja asiantuntijuus: Koulutuksen ja työelämän näkökulmia* [Creativity, learning and expertise: Perspectives of education and working life]. Helsinki, Finland: WSOYpro.

Elliot, T., & Pedler, M. (2018). Collaborative knowledge and intellectual property: An action learning conundrum. *Action Learning: Research and Pactice, 15*(1), 18–27. doi:10.1080/14767333.2017.1363717

Eraut, M. (1994). *Developing professional knowledge and competence.* London, England: Falmer.

Eteläpelto, A., & Tynjälä, P. (Eds.). (1999). *Oppiminen ja asiantuntijuus: Työelämän ja koulutuksen näkökulmia* [Learning and expertise: Perspectives of working life and education]. Porvoo, Finland: WSOY.

Fenstermacher, G. D. (1994). The knower and the known: The nature of knowledge in research on teaching. *Review of Research in Education, 20*(1), 3–56.

Gourlay, S. (2002, April). *Tacit knowledge, tacit knowing, or behaving?* Paper presented at the 3rd European Organizational Knowledge, Learning and Capabilities Conference, Athens, Greece. Retrieved from http://eprints.kingston.ac.uk/2293/

Gourlay, S. (2004, April). *'Tacit knowledge': The variety of meanings in empirical research.* Paper presented at the 5th European organizational knowledge, learning and capabilities conference, Innsbruck, Austria. Retrieved from https://papers.ssrn.com/sol3/papers.cfm?abstract_id=676466

Hager, P. (2000). Know-how and workplace practical judgement. *Journal of Philosophy of Education, 34*(2), 281–296.

Hager, P. J. (1993). Conceptions of competence. In A. Thompson (Ed.), *Philosophy of education yearbook 1993: Proceedings of the forty-ninth annual meeting of the philosophy of education society.* Urbana, IL: Philosophy of Education Society. Retrieved from web.archive.org/web/20060219222329/www.ed.uiuc.edu/EPS/PES-Yearbook/93_docs/HAGER.HTM

Hakkarainen, K., Lonka, K., & Lipponen, L. (2004). *Tutkiva oppiminen: Järki, tunteet ja kulttuuri oppimisen sytyttäjinä* [Porgessive inquiry: Sense, emotions and culture as triggers for learning] (6th Rev. ed.). Porvoo, Finland: WSOY.

Hakkarainen, K., & Paavola, S. 2008. Asiantuntijuuden kehittyminen, hiljainen tieto ja uutta luovat tietokäytännöt [Development of expertise, tacit knowledge and knowledge creation practices]. In A. Toom, J. Onnismaa, & A. Kajanto (Eds.), *Hiljainen tieto: Tietämistä, toimimista, taitavuutta* [Tacit knowledge: Knowing, acting, skillfulness] (Aikuiskasvatuksen ... vuosikirja.No. 47, pp. 59–82). Helsinki, Finland: Kansanvalistusseura.

Hatano, G., & Oura, Y. (2003). Commentary: Reconceptualizing school learning using insight from expertise research. *Educational Researcher, 32*(8), 26–29. doi:10.3102/0013189X032008026

Jernström, E. (2000). *Lärande under samma hatt: En lärandeteori genererad ur multimetodiska studier av mästare, gesäller och lärlingar* [Learning under the same hat: Learning theory generated from multi-method research on masters and apprentices] (Doctoral dissertation, Luleå University of Technology, Luleå, Sweden).

John-Steiner, V. (2000). *Creative collaboration.* Oxford, England: Oxford University Press.

Kallio, E. (2011). Integrative thinking is the key: An evaluation of current research into the development of adult thinking. *Theory & Psychology, 21*(6), 785–801.

Knorr Cetina, K. (2001). Objectual practice. In T. R. Schatzki, K. Knorr Cetina, & E. von Savigny (Eds.), *The practice turn in contemporary theory* (pp. 175–188). London, England: Routledge.

Korthagen, F. A. J. (2004). In search of the essence of a good teacher: Towards a more holistic approach in teacher education. *Teaching and Teacher Education, 20*(1), 77–97.

Krampe, R. T., & Baltes, P. B. (2003). Intelligence as adaptive resource development and resource allocation: A new look through the lenses of SOC and expertise. In

R. J. Sternberg & E. L. Grigorenko (Eds.), *The psychology of abilities, competencies, and expertise* (pp. 31–69). Cambridge, England: Cambridge University Press.

Lakkala, M., Toom, A., Ilomäki, L., & Muukkonen, H. (2015). Re-designing university courses to support collaborative knowledge creation practices. *Australasian Journal of Educational Technology, 31*(5), 521–536.

Lave, J., & Wenger, E. (1991). *Situated learning: Legitimate peripheral participation.* Cambridge, England: Cambridge University Press.

Leinhardt, G., McCarthy Young, K., & Merriman, J. (1995). Integrating professional knowledge: The theory of practice and the practice of theory. *Learning and Instruction, 5*(4), 401–408.

Molander, B. (1992). Tacit knowledge and silenced knowledge: Fundamental problems and controversies. In B. Göranzon & M. Florin (Eds.), *Skill and education: Reflection and experience* (Artificial intelligence and society pp. 9–31). London, England: Springer-Verlag.

Niiniluoto, I. (1996). *Informaatio, tieto ja yhteiskunta: Filosofinen käsiteanalyysi* [Information, knowledge and society: Philosophical conceptual analysis] (5th Rev. ed.). Helsinki, Finland: Edita.

Nonaka, I. (1994). A dynamic theory of organizational knowledge creation. *Organization Science, 5*(1), 14–37.

Nonaka, I., & Takeuchi, H. (1995). *The knowledge-creating company: How Japanese companies create the dynamics of innovation.* New York, NY: Oxford University Press.

Nonaka, I., & von Krogh, G. (2009). Tacit knowledge and knowledge conversion: Controversy and advancement in organizational knowledge creation theory. *Organization Science, 20*(3), 635–652.

Nurminen, R. (2008). Intuitio ja hiljainen tieto hoitotyössä [Intuition and tacit knowledge in nursing care]. In A. Toom, J. Onnismaa, & A. Kajanto (Eds.), *Hiljainen tieto: Tietämistä, toimimista, taitavuutta* [Tacit knowledge: Knowing, acting, skillfulness] (Aikuiskasvatuksen ... vuosikirja No. 47, 187–200). Helsinki, Finland: Kansanvalistusseura.

Orton, R. E. (1993). Two problems with teacher knowledge. In A. Thompson (Ed.), *Philosophy of education yearbook 1993: Proceedings of the forty-ninth annual meeting of the Philosophy of Education Society.* Urbana, IL: Philosophy of Education Society. Retrieved from web.archive. org/web/20060428202344/www.ed.uiuc.edu/EPS/PES-Yearbook/93_docs/ORTON.HTM

Paavola, S., & Hakkarainen, K. (2005). The knowledge creation metaphor – An emergent epistemological approach to learning. *Science & Education, 14*(6), 535–557.

Pantić, N., & Wubbels, T. (2012). Competence-based teacher education: A change from *Didaktik* to curriculum culture? *Journal of Curriculum Studies, 44*(1), 61–87.

Polanyi, M. (1958). *Personal knowledge: Towards a post-critical philosophy.* London, England: Routledge.

Polanyi, M. (1966). *The tacit dimension.* Garden City, NY: Doubleday.

Rolf, B. (1995). *Profession, tradition och tyst kunskap: En studie i Michael Polanyis teori om den professionella kunskapens tysta dimension* [Profession, tradition and tacit knowledge: A study on Michael Polanyi's theory of the tacit dimension of professional knowledge]. Nora, Sweden: Nya Doxa.

Rosiek, J. (2002). Pragmatism's unfinished project: William James and teacher knowledge researcher. In J. W. Garrison, R. Podeschi, & E. Bredo (Eds.), *William James and education* (pp. 130–150). New York, NY: Teachers College Press.

Ryle, G. (1949). *The concept of mind.* London, England: Hutchinson's University Library.

Sanders, A. F. (1988). *Michael Polanyi's post-critical epistemology: A reconstruction of some aspects of "tacit knowing".* Amsterdam, the Netherlands: Rodopi.

Sawyer, K. (2007). *Group genius: The creative power of collaboration.* New York, NY: Basic Books.

Scardamalia, M. (2002). Collective cognitive responsibility for the advancement of knowledge. In B. Smith (Ed.), *Liberal education in a knowledge society* (pp. 67–98). Chicago, IL: Open Court.

Sfard, A. (1998). On two metaphors for learning and the dangers of choosing just one. *Educational Researcher, 27*(2), 4–13.

Small, W. (2017). Ryle on the explanatory role of knowledge how. *Journal for the History of Analytical Philosophy, 5*(5), 57–76.

Stanley, J., & Williamson, T. (2001). Knowing how. *The Journal of Philosophy, 98*(8), 411–444.

Sveiby, K.-E. (1994). *Towards a knowledge perspective on organisation* (Doctoral dissertation, University of Stockholm, Department of Business Administration, Stockholm, Sweden).

Toom, A. (2006). *Tacit pedagogical knowing: At the core of teacher's professionality* (Doctoral dissertation, University of Helsinki, Department of Applied Sciences of Education, Helsinki, Finland).

Toom, A. (2008). *Hiljainen pedagoginen tietäminen opettajan työssä* [Tacit pedagogical knowing in teachers' work]. In A. Toom, J. Onnismaa, & A. Kajanto (Eds.), *Hiljainen tieto: Tietämistä, toimimista, taitavuutta* [Tacit knowledge: Knowing, acting, skillfulness] (Aikuiskasvatuksen … vuosikirja No. 47, 163–186). Helsinki, Finland: Kansanvalistusseura.

Toom, A. (2012). Considering the artistry and epistemology of tacit knowledge and knowing. *Educational Theory, 62*(6), 621–640.

Toom, A. (2016). Hiljainen tieto ja asiantuntijuus [Tacit knowledge and expertise]. In E. Kallio (Ed.), *Ajattelun kehitys aikuisuudessa: Kohti moninäkökulmaisuutta* [The development of thinking in adulthood: Towards multiperspective thinking] (Research in Educational Sciences No. 71, 245–268). Helsinki, Finland: The Finnish Educational Research Association.

Toom, A. (2017). Teacher's professional and pedagogical competencies: A complex divide between teacher work, teacher knowledge and teacher education. In D. J. Clandinin & J. Husu (Eds.), *The SAGE handbook of research on teacher education* (pp. 803–819). Los Angeles, CA: SAGE.

Tynjälä, P. (2008). Perspectives into learning at the workplace. *Educational Research Review, 3*(2), 130–154.

Tynjälä, P., Nuutinen, A., Eteläpelto, A., Kirjonen, J., & Remes, P. (1997). The acquisition of professional expertise – A challenge for educational research. *Scandinavian Journal of Educational Research, 41*(3–4), 475–494.

Tynjälä, P., Välimaa, J., & Sarja, A. (2003). Pedagogical perspectives on the relationships between higher education and working life. *Higher Education, 46*(2), 147–166.

van Manen, M. (1991a). Reflectivity and the pedagogical moment: The normativity of pedagogical thinking and acting. *Journal of Curriculum Studies, 23*(6), 507–536.

van Manen, M. (1991b). *The tact of teaching: The meaning of pedagogical thoughtfulness.* London, Ontario, Canada: Althouse.

van Manen, M. (1995). On the epistemology of reflective practice. *Teachers and Teaching: Theory and Practice, 1*(1), 33–50.

Wenger, E. (1998). *Communities of practice: Learning, meaning, and identity* (Learning in doing: Social, cognitive, and computational perspectives). Cambridge, England: Cambridge University Press.

Westera, W. (2001). Competences in education: A confusion of tongues. *Journal of Curriculum Studies, 33*(1), 75–88.

10

PROFESSIONAL EXPERTISE, INTEGRATIVE THINKING, WISDOM, AND PHRONĒSIS

Päivi Tynjälä, Eeva K. Kallio, and Hannu L. T. Heikkinen

Introduction

In his novel *Atonement*, Ian McEwan (2001, pp. 276–277) depicts a scene from World War II: a young nurse is facing the problem of a large number of wounded soldiers arriving at the ward. According to normal procedures, arriving patients should be given a bath, changed into hospital pyjamas and be guided to their bed, but these soldiers chose their bed themselves without washing and changing. In this situation, the novice nurse demanded that the soldiers follow the rules, telling them they must get up, as there is a procedure. An expert nurse intervened and solved the situation by being flexible, stating that the men needed to sleep, and the procedures were for later.

The fictional scene above illustrates that *experts think differently from novices*. Research on expertise has identified the following differences between expert performers and beginners (Boshuizen, Bromme, & Gruber, 2004; Chi, Glaser, & Farr, 1988; Ericsson, Charness, Feltovich, & Hoffman, 2006; Feltovich, Prietula, & Ericsson, 2006; Harteis & Billett, 2013; Tynjälä, 2016):

- Experts have larger and more integrative knowledge units, and their representations of information are more functional and abstract than those of novices, whose knowledge base is more fragmentary. For example, a beginning piano player reads sheet music note by note, whereas a concert pianist is able to see the whole row or even several rows of music notation at the same time.
- When solving problems, experts may spend more time on the initial problem evaluation and planning than novices. This enables them to form a holistic and in-depth understanding of the task and usually to reach a solution more swiftly than beginners.
- Basic functions related to tasks or the job are automated in experts, whereas beginners need to pay attention to these functions. For instance, in a driving

school, a young driver focuses his or her attention on controlling devices and pedals, while an experienced driver performs basic strokes automatically. For this reason, an expert driver can observe and anticipate traffic situations better than a beginning driver.

- Experts outperform novices in their metacognitive and reflective thinking. In other words, they make sharp observations of their own ways of thinking, acting, and working, especially in non-routine situations when automated activities are challenged.
- Beginners' knowledge is mainly explicit and they are dependent on learned rules. In addition to explicit knowledge, experts have tacit or implicit knowledge that accumulates with experience. This kind of knowledge makes it possible to make fast decisions on the basis of what is often called *intuition*. To attain the best possible solution to a problem in situations where circumstances radically deviate from the norm, experts may decide to break learned rules, as was the case in the hospital example above.

In situations where something has gone wrong or when experts face totally new problems but are not required to make fast decisions, they critically reflect on their actions. Unlike beginners, experienced professionals focus their thinking not only on details but rather on the totality consisting of the details. Thus, experts' thinking is more holistic than the thinking of novices. It seems that the quality of thinking is associated with the quality and amount of knowledge. With a fragmentary knowledge base, a novice in any field may remain on lower levels of thinking: things are seen as black and white, without any nuances. In contrast, more experienced colleagues with a more organised and holistic knowledge base can access more material for their thinking, and, thus, may begin to explore different perspectives on matters and develop more relativistic views concerning certain problems. At the highest levels of thinking, an individual is able to reconcile different perspectives, either by forming a synthesis or by integrating different approaches or views (e.g., Borawski, 2017; Paletz, Bogue, Miron-Spektor, & Spencer-Rodgers, 2018; Kallio, 2001, 2011, see articles in Part I of this book).

In this chapter, we examine adult thinking from the perspective of professional expertise. Typical of expert work in any domain is solving ill-defined or complex problems, which requires higher-order thinking. In the following sections, we first present three conceptualisations of expertise development that lead us to the notion of the role of multiple perspectives and solving complex problems for the development of higher-order thinking. Furthermore, this examination leads us to the concept of integrative thinking, that is, a form of thinking where an individual integrates ideas and even opposing perspectives, able to form a synthesis based on these different perspectives. Then, we expand the discussion of expertise from traditional cognitive approaches toward more holistic views. In a fast changing world with increasingly complicated problems that are morally and ethically loaded, there is a need to examine professional expertise from more and wider perspectives than before. We suggest that the concept of practical wisdom provides such a broader viewpoint. Integrative thinking has been proven to be an important element of wisdom (Labouvie-Vief, 1990; Kallio, 2015, Chapter 2). In our discussion on wisdom, we rely both on current research on wisdom and, in particular, the Aristotelian notion of *phronēsis*, that is, practical wisdom. Finally, we present a conceptualisation of wisdom in professional expertise needed in the present-day world's problems of unprecedented complexity. At the core of this model are integrative thinking and problem solving, involving ethical judgement and social responsibility.

Development of expertise: the role of complex problems, multiple perspectives, and integrative thinking

Historically, three principal conceptualisations of the development of expertise have been presented. First, Ericsson (2006) has coined the term *deliberate practice* to illustrate the process of expertise development. This concept arose from the observation that extensive experience in a domain does not automatically lead to superior performance, but that an intensive and goal-oriented pursuit of improvement is needed to achieve the highest levels of competence. Characteristic of deliberate practice is an individual's intentional goal setting, continuous monitoring of his or her performance, and recognising errors and correcting them. The aim is to reach goals that are initially outside the individual's achievement but that can be reached with intensive practice. What is of special importance in this is the role of the more experienced colleague, mentor, or coach whose feedback helps to identify the specific components of the task or performance that need improvement. Gradually, the performer acquires mechanisms that help him- or herself to self-evaluate and control his/her own performance. Thus, the acquisition of expertise can be described as a series of states with mechanisms for monitoring and guiding future improvements of specific aspects of performance (Ericsson, 2006).

Secondly, Bereiter and Scardamalia (1993) have described expertise development as a process of *progressive problem solving*. A basic assumption in this model is problem solving at the core of an expert's activities; in their daily work, professionals continuously solve more or less complicated problems. In these activities, knowledge transformations take place: "formal knowledge is converted into informal knowledge by being used to solve problems of understanding; formal knowledge is converted into skill by being used to solve problems of procedure" (Bereiter & Scardamalia, 1993, p. 66). Roughly speaking, professionals can be divided into two groups when it comes to problem solving: first, there are individuals who develop routines that make their work easier and they keep solving familiar problems with familiar ways. At this level, such persons are generally referred to as *routine experts*. Another type of professional, often called *adaptive experts* (Hatano & Oura, 2003), utilise the automatisation and routinising of certain activities so that they can invest their freed mental resources in setting new tasks that are more challenging than the previous ones. In this way, they work on the limits of their competence and rise above their previous achievements while continuously solving more and more demanding problems. In this process of progressive problem solving, their expertise develops further, whereas the routine experts, although skilful, remain fixed at a certain stage in the development of their competence.

In fact, the definition of expertise development as "progressive problem solving" is similar to the concept of "deliberate practice", which Ericsson (2006, p. 694) describes as follows:

> The key challenge for aspiring expert performers is to avoid the arrested development associated with automaticity and to acquire cognitive skills to support their continued learning and improvement. By actively seeking out demanding tasks – often provided by their teachers and coaches – that force the performers to engage in problem solving and to stretch their performance, the expert performers overcome the detrimental effects of automaticity and actively acquire and refine cognitive mechanisms to support continued learning and improvement.

Bereiter and Scardamalia (1993) also pointed out that expertise goes beyond an individual activity. They emphasise the role of team work and workplace culture as a promoter of or barrier to progressive problem solving. Similarly, recent sociocultural theories have stressed that expert problem solving is a social process by nature. For example, Hakkarainen, Palonen, Paavola, and Lehtinen (2004) talk about *networked expertise*, and Engeström (2004) about *negotiated knotworking*. In these views, the development of expertise or progressive problem solving can be characterised as collaborative, expansive, and transformative learning.

The third model of expertise development utilises the concepts of deliberate practice and progressive problem solving, and integrates these with the descriptions of the nature of expert knowledge and adult thinking. According to the model of *integrative pedagogy* (e.g., Tynjälä, 2008; Tynjälä & Gijbels, 2012; Tynjälä, Häkkinen, & Hämäläinen, 2014; Tynjälä, Virtanen, Klemola, Kostiainen, & Rasku-Puttonen, 2016), expertise development can be advanced by supporting learners to integrate and fuse different elements of expert knowledge: conceptual (i.e., theoretical, declarative or statable knowledge), practical (i.e., procedural or experiential knowledge or skill), self-regulatory, and socio-cultural knowledge (e.g., Bereiter, 2002; Bereiter & Scardamalia, 1993; Eraut, 2004; Le Maistre & Paré, 2006; Tynjälä, 2009). Although the different forms of knowledge can be analytically separated, in high-level expertise they are tightly integrated and fused together. For this reason, the Integrative Pedagogy model encourages learners (whether students or professionals) to make connections between these forms of knowledge.

While the first three forms of knowledge are personal, the fourth one, socio-cultural knowledge, is an aspect included in practices and devices of social communities rather than possessed by individuals. For example, every workplace has its own written or unwritten rules on how things are to be taken care of. Therefore, socio-cultural knowledge can only be accessed by participating in communities of practice. The Integrative Pedagogy model is based on the idea that student learning in higher education and vocational education and training should involve participating in authentic practices in the workplace, or, if this cannot be organised, simulations of authentic practices can be utilised. The core processes in learning are problem solving and integrative thinking, which requires combining and fusing the different forms of knowledge.

Cognitive learning theories have suggested that learners benefit from working with various perspectives on a subject and obtaining multiple representations (Kallio, 1998; van Someren, Reimann, Boshuizen, & de Jong, 1998). For example, in a study conducted with students of business administration, the students with multiple perspectives applied their knowledge to complex tasks in a more flexible way than those who tackled the problems only from a single perspective (Stark, Gruber, Hinkofer, & Mandl, 2004, p. 59). Thus, it seems that examining things from different viewpoints is important for the development of thinking. Exposing learners to various perspectives seems to raise the level of complexity in thinking. For instance, Lehtinen (2002), upon examining university students' studying of research methods, concluded that facing complexity from the very beginning helped learners to understand the domain better.

In summary, the conceptualisations of expertise development described above suggest that essential elements in this process are:

* intentional and goal-oriented pursuit of better performance and understanding;
* continuous individual and social problem solving and challenges that go beyond earlier tasks;
* integrative thinking involving connecting and fusing different forms of knowledge and pondering problems from different angles.

In the next section, we examine integrative thinking in more detail.

Integrative thinking

As described above, multiperspective and integrative thinking are important parts of the development of professional expertise. Kallio argues, in Chapter 2, that integration itself is a multi-dimensional concept. Integration presupposes differentiation, that is, separate objects to be integrated (at least two separate objects that are interrelated in one way or another). Etymologically, integration means "rendering something whole". The word integration comes from the Latin *integratus*, the past participle of the verb *integrare* ("to make whole"), which in turn stems from *integer* ("whole" or "complete", figuratively "untainted" or "upright", and literally "untouched"). Literally, the etymological meaning of the word is to "put together parts or elements and combine them into a whole" (Integrate, 2019).

However, whenever we are putting something together from parts, something new emerges that is more than the sum of the parts. According to Kallio (2011), the integration of different objects of thinking goes beyond merely adding or linking things together. Integration, from this perspective, presupposes renewal and something that has not existed before. Thus, in integration, the mental objects are fused together so that the outcome is a synthesis. As the number of related objects increases, the level of complexity increases at the same time. The integration of different viewpoints, angles, perspectives, or objects is not necessarily just cognitive. For example, Labouvie-Vief (1990, 2015) has emphasised the integration of emotions and intellect in adult thinking. Similarly, practical action and theoretical knowledge may be integrated as in the Integrative Pedagogy model described above. These objects of thought may or may not be contradictory, but it is also possible that viewpoints complement each other or at least do not have any contradictory elements. The key outcome in each case is the fusion and synthesis of different elements.

In her review of research on adult thinking, Kallio (2011) has suggested that the integration of different viewpoints or objects of thinking is the key to the development of various forms of higher-order thinking, such as relativistic-dialectical (Marchand, 2002) or postformal (Kallio, 2001) thinking. Typical features of higher-order thinking include understanding the relativistic nature of knowledge, acceptance of contradictions between different viewpoints, and integration of contradictory views (Kramer, 1983).

Based on research findings on expertise, on the one hand, and on adult thinking, on the other hand, we can hypothesise that there is a relationship between the development of thinking and the development of expertise, and that both are related to the quantity and quality of knowledge acquired as well as to the way in which knowledge is processed. In an ideal case, an individual has opportunities to participate in diverse communities of practice (see Wenger, 1998; Wenger-Trayner, Fenton O'Creevy, Hutchinson, Kubiak, & Wenger-Trayner, 2015) where he or she can acquire and utilise different forms of expert knowledge: 1) conceptual or theoretical knowledge that helps him or her understand the topic better, 2) practical or procedural knowledge that develops through experience and improves skills, 3) self-regulative knowledge that develops when an individual reflects on his or her experiences, and 4) socio-cultural knowledge embedded in the social practices of the community. While acting in communities – which may be professional, educational, hobby-related, or personal in nature – an individual encounters what are more or less complicated problems, diverse knowledge, and multiple perspectives, which lead him or her to actively and critically ponder problems from different angles. In this process, an individual realises that knowledge is relative to the angle from which a problem is considered, and thus dualistic thinking is replaced by relativistic thinking. With more experience of ill-defined problems, people come to understand that there are no straightforward solutions for complex problems, and that they need to find solutions with which different, even opposite, approaches can be reconciled. In other words, integrative thinking is needed (Kallio, 2011).

Sometimes, unexpected solutions to complex problems are found when they are considered jointly by different people from various backgrounds. Combinations of experts can be arranged intentionally for this purpose, thereby creating conditions for *emergent systems*. The deliberative collaboration of experts from different backgrounds may generate results that are greater than the sum of the elements involved. These kinds of combinations of experts can constitute conditions for high-performance collaborative processes that nobody has planned and no one can actually plan beforehand or manage alone. This kind of playful and creative collaborative work enabling creative and free combinations of thoughts has also been called *bricolage* (Denzin & Lincoln, 2005). The word "bricolage" comes from the French language and refers to a kind of work in which materials of different types are put together. Bricolage presupposes divergent thinking that allows one to combine and play with things in an unprejudiced way. Breakthroughs in science, technology, and society often involve this kind of *emergent thinking*, which is best achieved by enabling conditions for creative playfulness (Salo & Heikkinen, 2018).

So far in our analysis, we have examined the concepts of expertise and integrative thinking. Both of these concepts seem to have a close connection to the concept of *wisdom*. For example, Kitchener, King and DeLuca (2006, p. 73) define wisdom as expert knowledge involving good judgement and advice in the domain of fundamental pragmatics of life, and emphasise the uncertainty of knowledge. According to Baltes and Staudinger (2000), relativistic-dialectical thinking – which Kallio (2011) redefines as integrative thinking – is an important component of wisdom. Similarly, Kunzmann and Stange (2007) see a close link between wisdom and higher-order thinking, and suggest that the integration of knowledge and character, mind and virtue is at the core of wisdom. In the same vein, Staudinger and Glück (2011, p. 217) see the core of wisdom as consisting of understanding and reconciling contradictory ideas, such as the "dialectic between good and bad, positive and negative, dependence and independence, certainty and doubt, control and lack of control, finiteness and eternity, strength and weakness, and selfishness and altruism". Furthermore, integrative thinking seems to be an essential element of professional expertise, as is wisdom. In the next section, we discuss the concept of wisdom and its relation to expertise.

Wisdom models and their connections to research on professional expertise

The concept of wisdom is multi-dimensional and complex, and it may be analysed according to components with different criteria. The concept of wisdom holds a long-standing status among the ideas of history, philosophy (which means *"love of wisdom"*, literally), science, and all of the world's major religions and cultures (Curnow, 1999, 2010, 2015), and there is not a single discipline that could claim exclusivity for it. In general, wisdom can be defined as the ideal aim of advanced human development and learning, in the study of ontogeny (Swartwood & Tiberius, 2019). There are many definitions of wisdom, and also approaches, methods, and disciplines that focus on it.

Regarding the current scientific wisdom research, there have been many conceptualisation attempts (Bangen, Meeks, & Jeste, 2013). We focus here mainly on those components of wisdom that are in some way linked to the main topics of this chapter: adult integrative cognitive development, Baltes and Staudinger's (2000) and Sternberg's (1998) models of wisdom and their connection to expertise, the role of emotions and practical action, plus the idea of *eudaimonia*, meaning "good life", as a form of wisdom.

First, as already stated, the neo-Piagetian construct of postformal thinking (i.e., integrative thinking) has been commonly defined as a component of wisdom (Baltes & Staudinger, 2000; Grossmann, 2017; Staudinger & Glück, 2011). In this book, some models of adult cognitive development have already been reviewed, such as the Reflective Judgement model (by King & Kitchener, 1994; see also Chapter 4; and for a general review of the field, Chapter 2; and Sinnott's Postformal model in Chapter 12; and for relativistic-dialectical thinking, see Chapter 13).

Secondly, practical life experience in diverse social situations cumulates wisdom. In the Berlin Wisdom Paradigm (Baltes & Staudinger, 2000), wisdom is described as deep understanding and a general expertise in the fundamental pragmatics of life. In the same vein, Swartwood (2013) defines wisdom as an expert skill including intuitive, deliberative, meta-cognitive, self-regulative, and self-cultivation abilities. Here, expertise refers to the kinds of insights that are only available through practical experience during one's life span. According to Baltes and Staudinger (2000), expertise and life knowledge, by definition, include the following aspects: rich declarative or factual knowledge, procedural (strategic) knowledge, contextualism, relativism, acceptance, and management of life's uncertainties. These features are based on experiences that have accumulated during one's life span, and not just in some specialised field as in one's profession or work life. Latent, tacit knowledge can be used to satisfactorily solve problematic, complex, ill-defined questions (regarding tacit knowledge, see Chapter 9).

Sternberg (1998) has created a model of practical wisdom (Balance Wisdom model) in which tacit knowledge is the key component. The model is used to figure out how subjects understand and solve complex, difficult, and contradictory problems in different fields. Wise decision-making implies appropriate procedural and specific knowledge. It also takes into account various perspectives, like intra-, inter-, and extra-personal ones, judged against possible short- and long-term consequences. The goal is always for the common good, aiming at a prosocial, positively ethical result that benefits the larger group. Wisdom, thus, refers to the application of balanced judgement in complex problem situations – and also means that one can change one's judgement according to changes in the circumstances and conditions.

Third, all of these wisdom research models have placed strong emphasis on reflection and cognition. Feelings and emotions are taken into account implicitly, as in tacit knowledge or in adult developmental models integrating emotions and cognition (Labouvie-Vief, 2015). Emotions are also explicitly present in Ardelt's (2003) Three-Dimensional Wisdom model. In this conceptualisation, wisdom is understood as an integrated whole of three elements of personality: the first component, *cognition*, is understood as a deep approach, involving seeking knowledge and truth both in oneself and in social spheres; understanding the contextuality and limits of knowledge are also a part of it. The second component of wisdom in this model is *reflection*: its definition comes close to multiperspective thinking, where one is able to view the relativity of a multitude of viewpoints; at the same time, it incorporates self-understanding regarding one's own behaviour and mind. Finally, the third component, *affect*, refers to emotions like empathy and compassion: a wise person cares for and has positive emotions toward others.

Fourth, Yang (2017) criticises wisdom research for being focused more on thinking and feeling, but not so much on the aspect of *doing*. She uses the term *embodied wisdom* or *process theory of wisdom* to refer to her own three-component wisdom model. She has defined wisdom as an integrative process between thinking, feeling, and acting. Wisdom cannot therefore be just a cognitive capacity. When asking laymen to name a wise person, they tend to nominate persons who have acted out and demonstrated an extraordinary ability. Real-life actions and concrete manifestations of wisdom are thus the major aspects of wisdom, according to Yang (2017).

Similar suggestions regarding the integration of emotion, cognition, and motivation in wisdom have been stated by Staudinger and Glück (2011). "Doing", as an aspect of wisdom, implies a purposeful aim for the benefit of the common social good as a person actualises his or her positive intentions: it includes carefully considering the *ethical prosocial implications of one's actions for the community at large*. Intentions and goals are ethical as it is assumed that the actions are undertaken for the common good and a positive outcome (Staudinger & Glück, 2011).

Law and Staudinger (2016) have analysed wisdom's close connection to *eudaimonia*, which is originally an Aristotelian term referring to leading a "good life". They agree that there are differences between these terms, but add that both constructs refer to high levels of personal growth and human flourishing. Next, we examine the Aristotelian concepts in more detail.

Wisdom as phronēsis: philosophical backgrounds

Wisdom, in professional expertise, can also be approached in terms of the different forms of knowledge, or dispositions to knowledge, and the corresponding forms of action. In this section, we look at the modern classification of expert knowledge through the lens of a synthesis of different forms of knowledge. Our review is based on Stephen Kemmis's interpretation, where Aristotle's forms of reasoning are integrated with the Theory of Knowledge and Human Interests by Jürgen Habermas (Kemmis & Smith, 2008).

Aristotle (384–322 BCE), in his *Book VI of the Ethics* (trans. 2011), discussed three forms of knowledge: one theoretical, called epistēmē, and two practical forms of knowledge: called *technē* and *phronēsis* (Saugstad, 2005; Heikkinen, de Jong, & Vanderlinde, 2016, p. 8). Each of these knowledge forms is actualised through specific activity forms (*epistēmē* ≤ *theoria*; *technē* ≤ *poiesis*; *phronēsis* ≤ *praxis*). These forms of knowledge have had a remarkable influence on Western epistemology. For example, the etymological origins of the words theory and practice as well as technics and technology are rooted in this three-fold categorisation of knowledge (Heikkinen et al., 2016, p. 8).

The ideal form of *epistēmē* is to see the world around us as if seen through the "eyes of the gods on Mount Olympus in Ancient Greece". The form of action associated with *epistēmē* is *theoria*, the original Greek meaning of which was seeing or watching. Literally, *theoria* means "looking at", "gazing at", or "being aware of" (Mahon, Heikkinen, & Huttunen, 2018, p. 4). This form of knowledge is theoretical knowledge, and it was regarded as pure knowledge in the sense that the knowing subject has no aims or aspirations other than just knowing how things are (Mahon et al., 2018). Thus, *epistēmē* is based on the disposition to seek universal and eternal truth for its own sake, regardless of time and place (Aristotle, trans. 2011, 1139a27–8). From that perspective, expert knowledge should be based on objective and universal knowledge, which can be verified through a correspondence between propositions (truth claims) and the state of affairs in the world (Heikkinen et al., 2016, p. 8; Mahon et al., 2018, pp. 3–4).

Another disposition to knowledge is manifested in producing material goods: *technē* (Aristotle, trans. 2011, 1094a5–10). *Technē* is the form of knowledge that is needed in making or producing something; that is, *poiēsis* (making action). In contrast to *epistēmē*, *technē* is not valuable in itself. It is deemed "good" and valid only if it helps to produce usable and appropriate objects or services, or when applied to develop methods that can be used in production. In other words, technical knowledge is instrumental: its aims are external to the knowledge itself. The term *technē* finds expression in the modern concepts of technical knowledge and technology. From this perspective, expert knowledge is understood in terms of technical expertise regarding technology and the production of goods and services (Mahon et al., 2018, pp. 3–4).

The third disposition in Aristotle's classical specification (trans. 2011, 1140b1–6) is *phronēsis*. Often translated as "practical wisdom", *phronēsis* is the disposition to live a meaningful, happy, and worthy life together with others; that is, knowing how to live a "good life", *eudaimonia* (Mahon et al., 2018). The word *eudaimonia* cannot be translated into any language without a remainder, but most often it has been translated by using expressions describing living a "flourishing", "happy", "good", or "worthwhile" life; that is, a life worth living.

The form of action ("doing") associated with *phronēsis* is *praxis*; that is, action oriented toward living a virtuous life through choices based on judgements about what is wise and right to do in everyday human life. *Praxis* is a form of deliberate action in the social (and physical) world, based on reflective thinking about what is the best way to act in order to maximise the common well-being of a social community. In *praxis*, the impacts and consequences of actions are carefully considered (Mahon et al., 2018). As Kemmis and Smith (2008, p. 4) have crystallised, "*praxis* is what people do when they take into account all the circumstances and exigencies that confront them at a particular moment and then, taking the broadest view they can of what is best to do, they act". In *praxis*, unlike *poiēsis*, the goals and means of activity cannot be separated; *praxis* is an end in itself. In terms of professional practice, action as *praxis* is itself rewarding for the expert. An expert enjoys the action itself, which promotes positive social relations achieved through the interaction with other people. From a *praxis* perspective, the ultimate aim and purpose of an expert is to foster understanding about how to live well, and to allow human flourishing and living a meaningful life together with each other, outlining the place of humans in the world (Mahon et al., 2018, pp. 3–6).

In addition to these three forms of disposition toward knowledge, Kemmis and Smith (2008) add a fourth one: a critical-emancipatory disposition to knowledge. The formulation of such interest in knowledge was first introduced in Habermas's (1972) Theory of Knowledge-Constitutive Interests (see Table 10.1). The critical-emancipatory interest in knowledge refers to a disposition to expose belief systems or ideologies that maintain an unreasonable and subordinating power over people. The purpose of critical-emancipatory knowledge is to enable people to critically reflect and to be released from the mechanisms of power that oppress or harm them. From this perspective, the social world is understood as a struggle for power. The *form of action* associated with this disposition is emancipatory action (Habermas, 1972; Kemmis & Smith, 2008), or empowering action (Heikkinen & Huttunen, 2017). This amounts to "collective critical reflection and action to overcome irrationality, injustice, suffering, harm, unproductiveness, or unsustainability" (Kemmis & Smith, 2008, p. 23). It is collective in the sense that it transpires in reflective communication and interaction with others. It is also transformative in that it leads (ideally and simultaneously) to changed circumstances and self-change (Mahon et al., 2018, pp. 3–6).

The dispositions and associated forms of action outlined above are not separate entities. On the contrary, they are interconnected in many ways (Mahon et al., 2018). From this perspective, *expertise is essentially about the integration of these aforementioned forms of or dispositions to knowledge and the ability to act in accordance with them*. In order to achieve expertise in any professional field, we need all of these forms of knowledge; the ability to observe and see, understand and interpret the world *(theoria)*; to utilise techniques, materials and natural resources in our work *(poiēsis)*; as well as to more profoundly understand what is good for humans *(praxis)* and how to overcome injustice, irrationality, and unsustainability in our societies *(emancipatory)* (Mahon et al., 2018). The aforementioned forms of knowledge can be juxtaposed with the concepts used in the contemporary research on professional expertise in the way suggested in Table 10.1.

TABLE 10.1 A Synthesis of the forms of action and dispositions to knowledge of Aristotle (2011) and Jürgen Habermas (1972). (Adapted From Kemmis & Smith, 2008; Heikkinen et al., 2016; Heikkinen, Kiilakoski, Huttunen, Kaukko, & Kemmis, 2018; Mahon et al., 2018)

	Aristotle			
		Habermas		
Knowledge-constitutive interests (Habermas)		Technical	Practical (hermeneutical)	Critical-emancipatory
Dispositions to knowledge (Aristotle)	*Epistēmē*	*Technē*	*Phronēsis*	
Action	*Theoria:* Contemplation, for example, theoretical contemplation about the nature of things; *contemplative action.*	*Poiēsis:* Action aimed at producing known ends; *making action.*	*Praxis:* Action involving practical reasoning about what is wise, right and proper to do in a given situation and in terms of the good life; *doing action.*	*Emancipatory:* Collective critical reflection and action to overcome injustice, irrationality, harm, and unsustainability; *empowering action.*
Realm	*In the realm of ideas*	*In the material realm*	*In the social realm*	
Aim (telos)	Attainment of universal knowledge.	Production of something.	Good life; flourishing; life worth living (*eudaimonia*).	Overcoming irrationality and injustice.
Position of the knowing subject	External observer.	Maker or designer of products.	Agent in the social world.	Questioner, critic (together with others).

Toward a synthesis of expertise, adult cognitive development, and phronēsis

In summary, we suggest two claims. Firstly, as a conclusion based on our analysis of the traditional forms of knowledge (Aristotle), the critical–emancipatory interest in knowledge and the concepts used in contemporary research on expertise, we suggest the following synthesis (Table 10.2). It is evident that declarative knowledge is what we can typically associate with theoretical knowledge or the disposition that can be referred to as *epistēmē* in Aristotelian terms. We may also postulate a direct link between the technical knowledge in contemporary terms, the Aristotelian *technē*, and the Habermasian technical aspect of knowledge. The concepts of practical, procedural, and experiental knowledge, however, cannot be reduced to any of the previously mentioned forms of knowledge. They are, at least to a large extent, associated with technical knowledge, but to some degree also with the *phronēsis* form of knowledge. Self-regulative knowledge, in turn, is clearly an element of *phronēsis*, but also the ability of critical and emancipatory reflection necessitates reflective and metacognitive skills. What is called *socio-cultural knowledge* in the contemporary research literature, in turn, is essentially what can be referred to as the *phronēsis* form of knowledge in the Aristotelian terminology. But likewise, a capacity for socio-cultural understanding is a necessary condition for critical-emancipatory reflection. Therefore, the practical, self-regulative, and socio-cultural forms of knowledge overlap with the *phronēsis* and the critical-emancipatory elements in the columns of Table 10.2.

Secondly, we see resemblances between theoretisations across the three fields of research on professional expertise, adult cognitive development, and wisdom. They have been developed as separate research lines but seem to share certain ideas, or at least exhibit "family resemblances", to apply Ludwig Wittgenstein's well-known concept (Wennerberg, 1967). The integration of practical action and theoretical knowledge is one theme that is common to all these traditions. Thus, wisdom includes theoretical (reflective, contemplative) thinking and understanding, *epistēmē* in Aristotelian terms, but also *technē* ("action aimed at producing known ends"), and *phronēsis*, as one acts for the common good to flourish, and *eudaimonia,* that is, for ethical goals. The practical consequences inform and enable judgement of whether an action has been wise or not. In wise action, positive effects for oneself and others are the natural result.

TABLE 10.2 A synthesis of the forms of action and dispositions to knowledge of Aristotle (2011) and Habermas (1972) and the concepts used in contemporary expert research

	Forms of knowledge			
Aristotle	*Epistēmē*	*Technē*	*Phronēsis*	
Habermas		Technical	Practical (hermeneutical)	Critical-emancipatory
Contemporary research on expertise	*Declarative conceptual* or *theoretical* knowledge	*Technical* knowledge	*Practical, procedural* and *experiential* knowledge *Self-regulative* knowledge (metacognition, reflection) *Socio-cultural* knowledge	

We must also remind readers of the risks of this kind of synthesis, where modern concepts and the concepts of ancient philosophy are merged, and this applies both to our aforementioned synthesis and the one suggested by Kemmis and Smith (2008). As Pierre Hadot (1995), a world-renowned expert on Hellenistic philosophy, has pointed out, the application of ancient Greek and Roman philosophy to present day situations is always risky. According to Hadot, it is not even possible to interpret the ancient philosophies "correctly", because the "lifeworld" of humans today is completely different from that of ancient times. Hadot claims that modern interpretations of ancient philosophy are actually misinterpretations, or even misunderstandings, and calls them "creative misinterpretations". Nonetheless, Hadot does not want to deny anyone the freedom to introduce concepts of ancient philosophy into today's debate; quite the contrary: "In fact, such new meanings correspond to the possibility of a kind of evolution of the original doctrine" (Davidson, 1995, p. 7). However, it is essential to also note that the meanings are construed fundamentally differently than in the ancient days.

Conclusion: integrative model of wisdom in professional practice and expertise

Based on the assumed "family resemblance" of the three fields of research on expertise, adult cognitive development, and wisdom, we suggest an *Integrative Model of Wisdom in Professional Practice and Expertise*, as shown in Figure 10.1.

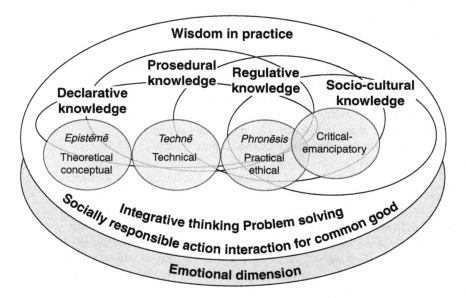

FIGURE10.1 Integrative model of wisdom in professional practice and expertise

Although the components of the model can be analytically discerned from each other, in practice they are tightly integrated so that in an expert's decision-making and action they are fused. In Figure 10.1, this is illustrated by overlapping ovals representing the different forms of knowledge described in previous sections. Our further investigation into the nature of adult thinking and wisdom revealed that typical actions regarded as wise is *integrative thinking*, by which an individual makes connections, reconciliations, and syntheses of different, even opposite, perspectives in order to find solutions to complex problems. For this reason, integrative thinking and *problem solving* are depicted as core processes in wisdom related to professional practice and expertise. The third core process is *socially responsible action and interaction for the common good*, which is required in solving professional problems that typically involve ethical dilemmas. This component of the model reflects our understanding of wisdom not only as an individual phenomenon but also as a highly social one.

Neither the Aristotelian interpretation of knowledge nor modern expertise research have taken the emotional sphere of human life into account. In recent conceptualisations, assumptions of wisdom have been broadened to include emotions and motivation (Ardelt, 2003; Staudinger & Glück, 2011). Similarly, in research on learning (e.g., Pekrun & Linnenbrink-Garcia, 2014), adult development (e.g., Labouvie-Vief, 1990, 2015), and professional development (e.g., Aarto-Pesonen & Tynjälä, 2017), the role of emotions has received significant attention. Thus, *emotions* are included in our model as an essential element.

While the mainstream of research on expertise, as well as on adult thinking and wisdom, has treated these matters as individual phenomena, we argue that – in this world which faces highly complex problems such as climate change, a growing population, economic turbulences, and wars – we need a wider perspective. We need research that goes beyond individual cognitive processes and sees expert thinking as a part of a holistic system of a psychological, social, and physical world. Thus, not only thinking but also *socially responsible action and interaction* are included in our model of Wisdom in Professional Practice and Expertise. We argue that, nowadays, real experts are those individuals who pursue global responsibility and support the well-being of others rather than focusing on pure epistemic, technical, or economic aspects in their work.

An important implication of our analysis is the importance of examining professionals' thinking from the *wisdom* point of view and in relation to action and the social and ecological environment, and as an interaction rather than an isolated individual cognitive activity. For this purpose, we think that a useful framework could be provided by the Practice theory (Heikkinen et al., 2018), where expert thinking is seen as an essential element of practices and – in an ideal case – of *praxis*, contributing positively and meaningfully to society and acting in the interests of humankind; that is, "to live well in a world worth living in" (Kemmis et al., 2014, p. 27).

References

Aarto-Pesonen, L., & Tynjälä, P. (2017). The core of professional growth in work-related teacher education. *The Qualitative Report, 22*(12), 3334–3354.

Ardelt, M. (2003). Empirical assessment of a three-dimensional wisdom scale. *Research on Aging, 25*(3), 275–324.

Aristotle. (2011). *Aristotle's Nicomachean ethics* (R. C. Bartlett & S. D. Collins, Trans.). Chicago, IL: University of Chicago Press. (Original work published ca. 350 BCE).

Baltes, P. B., & Staudinger, U. M. (2000). Wisdom: A metaheuristic (pragmatic) to orchestrate mind and virtue toward excellence. *American Psychologist, 55*(1), 122–136.

Bangen, K. J., Meeks, T. W., & Jeste, D. V. (2013). Defining and assessing wisdom: A review of the literature. *The American Journal of Geriatric Psychiatry, 21*(12), 1254–1266.

Bereiter, C. (2002). *Education and mind in the knowledge age.* Mahwah, NJ: Erlbaum.

Bereiter, C., & Scardamalia, M. (1993). *Surpassing ourselves: An inquiry into the nature and implications of expertise.* Chicago, IL: Open Court.

Borawski, D. (2017). Supporting the development of wisdom: The dialogical perspective. *Roczniki Psychologiczne/Annals of Psychology, 20*(3), 563–578.

Boshuizen, H. P. A., Bromme, R., & Gruber, H. (Eds.). (2004). *Professional learning: Gaps and transitions on the way from novice to expert.* Dordrecht, the Netherlands: Kluwer Academic Publishers.

Chi, M. T. H., Glaser, R., & Farr, M. J. (Eds.). (1988). *The nature of expertise.* Hillsdale, NJ: Erlbaum.

Curnow, T. (1999). *Wisdom, intuition and ethics* (Avebury series in philosophy). Aldershot, England: Ashgate.

Curnow, T. (2010). *Wisdom in the ancient world.* London, England: Duckworth.

Curnow, T. (2015). *Wisdom: A history.* London, England: Reaktion Books.

Davidson, A. I. (1995). Introduction: Pierre Hadot and the spiritual phenomenon of ancient philosophy (M. Chase, Trans.). In P. Hadot (Eds.), *Philosophy as a way of life: Spiritual exercises from Socrates to Foucault* (pp. 1–45). Malden, MA: Blackwell.

Denzin, N. K., & Lincoln, Y. S. (2005). Part II: Paradigms and perspectives in contention. In N. K. Denzin & Y. S. Lincoln (Eds.), *The SAGE handbook of qualitative research* (3rd ed., pp. 183–190). Thousand Oaks, CA: SAGE.

Engeström, Y. (2004). The new generation of expertise. Seven theses. In H. Rainbird, A. Fuller, & A. Munro (Eds.), *Workplace learning in context* (pp. 145–165). London, England: Routledge.

Eraut, M. (2004). Transfer of knowledge between education and workplace settings. In H. Rainbird, A. Fuller, & A. Munro (Eds.), *Workplace learning in context* (pp. 201–221). London, England: Routledge.

Ericsson, K. A. (2006). The influence of experience and deliberate practice on the development of superior expert performance. In K. A. Ericsson, N. Charness, P. J. Feltovich, & R. R. Hoffman (Eds.), *The Cambridge handbook of expertise and expert performance* (pp. 683–703). Cambridge, England: Cambridge University Press.

Ericsson, K. A., Charness, N., Feltovich, P. J., & Hoffman, R. R. (Eds.). (2006). *The Cambridge handbook of expertise and expert performance.* Cambridge, England: Cambridge University Press.

Feltovich, P. J., Prietula, M. J., & Ericsson, K. A. (2006). Studies of expertise from psychological perspectives. In K. A. Ericsson, N. Charness, P. J. Feltovich, & R. R. Hoffman (Eds.), *The Cambridge handbook of expertise and expert performance* (pp. 41–67). Cambridge, England: Cambridge University Press.

Grossmann, I. (2017). Wisdom in context. *Perspectives on Psychological Science*, *12*(2), 233–257.

Habermas, J. (1972). *Knowledge and human interests*. (J. J. Shapiro, Trans.). Boston, MA: Beacon Press.

Hadot, P. (1995). *Philosophy as a way of life: Spiritual exercises from Socrates to Foucault* (A. Davidson, Ed., M. Chase, Trans.). Malden, MA: Blackwell.

Hakkarainen, K., Palonen, T., Paavola, S., & Lehtinen, E. (2004). *Communities of networked expertise: Professional and educational perspectives* (Advances in learning and instruction series, Sitra's publication series No. 257). Amsterdam, the Netherlands: Elsevier.

Harteis, C., & Billett, S. (2013). Intuitive expertise: Theories and empirical evidence. *Educational Research Review*, *9*, 145–157.

Hatano, G., & Oura, Y. (2003). Commentary: Reconceptualizing school learning using insight from expertise research. *Educational Researcher*, *32*(8), 26–29. doi:10.3102/0013189X032008026

Heikkinen, H. L. T., de Jong, F. P., & Vanderlinde, R. (2016). What is (good) practitioner research? *Vocations and Learning*, *9*(1), 1–19.

Heikkinen, H. L. T., & Huttunen, R. (2017). "Mitä järkeä?" Kasvatuksen tietoperusta ja rationaalisuus ["What's the sense?" The knowledge base and rationality of education]. In A. Toom, M. Rautiainen, & J. Tähtinen (Eds.), *Toiveet ja todellisuus: Kasvatus osallisuutta ja oppimista rakentamassa* [Hopes and reality: Education in constructing participation and learning] (Kasvatusalan tutkimuksia No. 75, pp. 31–58). Turku, Finland: Suomen kasvatustieteellinen seura.

Heikkinen, H. L. T., Kiilakoski, T., Huttunen, R., Kaukko, M., & Kemmis, S. (2018). Koulutustutkimuksen arkkitehtuurit [Architectures of educational research]. *Kasvatus*, *49*(5), 368–383.

Integrate. (2019). In *Online Etymological Dictionary*. Retrieved from www.etymonline.com/word/integrate#etymonline_v_9377

Kallio, E. (1998). *Training of students' scientific reasoning skills* (Doctoral dissertation, University of Jyväskylä, Department of Psychology, Jyväskylä, Finland).

Kallio, E. (2001). Reflections on the modern mass university and the question of the autonomy of thinking. In J. Välimaa (Ed.), *Finnish higher education in transition: Perspectives on massification and globalisation* (pp. 73–90). Jyväskylä, Finland: University of Jyväskylä, Finnish Institute for Educational Research.

Kallio, E. (2011). Integrative thinking is the key: An evaluation of current research into the development of adult thinking. *Theory & Psychology*, *21*(6), 785–801.

Kallio, E. (2015). From causal thinking to wisdom and spirituality: Some perspectives on a growing research field in adult (cognitive) development. *Approaching Religions*, *5*(2), 27–41. doi:10.30664/ar.67572

Kemmis, S., & Smith, T. J. (2008). Praxis and praxis development: About this book. In S. Kemmis & T. J. Smith (Eds.), *Enabling praxis: Challenges for education* (Pedagogy, education and praxis No. 1, pp. 3–13). Rotterdam, the Netherlands: Sense Publishers.

Kemmis, S., Wilkinson, J., Edwards-Groves, C., Hardy, I., Grootenboer, P., & Bristol, L. (Eds.). (2014). *Changing practices, changing education*. Singapore, the Republic of Singapore: Springer.

King, P. M., & Kitchener, K. S. (1994). *Developing reflective judgment: Understanding and promoting intellectual growth and critical thinking in adolescents and adults* (The Jossey-Bass higher and adult education series, The Jossey-Bass social and behavioral science series). San Francisco, CA: Jossey-Bass.

Kitchener, K. S., King, P. M., & DeLuca, S. (2006). DDDevelopment of reflective judgment in adulthood. In C. Hoare (Ed.), *Handbook of adult development and learning* (pp. 73–98). New York, NY: Oxford University Press.

Kramer, D. A. (1983). Post-formal operations? A need for further conceptualization. *Human Development, 26*(2), 91–105.

Kunzmann, U., & Stange, A. (2007). Wisdom as a classical human strength: Psychological conceptualizations and empirical inquiry. In A. D. Ong & M. H. M. van Dulmen (Eds.), *Oxford handbook of methods in positive psychology* (Series in positive psychology pp. 306–322). New York, NY: Oxford University Press.

Labouvie-Vief, G. (1990). Wisdom as integrated thought: Historical and developmental perspectives. In R. J. Sternberg (Ed.), *Wisdom: Its nature, origins, and development* (pp. 52–84). Cambridge, England: Cambridge University Press.

Labouvie-Vief, G. (2015). *Integrating emotions and cognition throughout the lifespan.* New York, NY: Springer.

Law, A., & Staudinger, U. M. (2016). Eudaimonia and wisdom. In J. Vittersø (Ed.), *Handbook of eudaimonic well-being* (International handbooks of Quality-of-Life, pp. 135–146). Cham, Switzerland: Springer.

Le Maistre, C., & Paré, A. (2006). A typology of the knowledge demonstrated by beginning professionals. In P. Tynjälä, J. Välimaa, & G. Boulton-Lewis (Eds.), *Higher education and working life: Collaborations, confrontations and challenges* (pp. 103–113). Oxford, England: Elsevier.

Lehtinen, E. (2002). Developing models for distributed problem-based learning: Theoretical and methodological reflection. *Distance Education, 23*(1), 109–117.

Mahon, K., Heikkinen, H. L. T., & Huttunen, R. (2018). Critical educational praxis in university ecosystems: Enablers and constraints. *Pedagogy, Culture & Society, 27*(3), 463–480. doi:10.1080/14681366.2018.1522663

Marchand, H. (2002). Some reflections on postformal stage. *Behavioral Development Bulletin, 11*(1), 39–46.

McEwan, I. (2001). *Atonement.* London, England: Cape.

Paletz, S. B. F., Bogue, K., Miron-Spektor, E., & Spencer-Rodgers, J. (2018). Dialectical thinking and creativity from many perspectives: Contradiction and tension. In J. Spencer-Rodgers & K. Peng (Eds.), *The psychological and cultural foundations of East Asian cognition: Contradiction, change, and holism* (pp. 267–308). New York, NY: Oxford University Press.

Pekrun, R., & Linnenbrink-Garcia, L. (Eds.). (2014). *International handbook of emotions in education* (Educational psychology handbook series). New York, NY: Routledge.

Salo, P., & Heikkinen, H. L. T. (2018). Slow science: Research and teaching for sustainable praxis. *Confero, 6*(1), 87–111. doi:10.3384/confero.2001-4562.181130

Saugstad, T. (2005). Aristotle's contribution to scholastic and non-scholastic learning theories. *Pedagogy, Culture & Society, 13*(3), 347–366.

Stark, R., Gruber, H., Hinkofer, L., & Mandl, H. (2004). Overcoming problems of knowledge application and transfer: Development, implementation and evaluation of an example-based instructional approach in the context of vocational school training in business administration. In H. P. A. Boshuizen, R. Bromme, & H. Gruber (Eds.), *Professional learning: Gaps and transitions on the way from novice to expert* (pp. 49–70). Dordrecht, the Netherlands: Kluwer Academic Publishers.

Staudinger, U. M., & Glück, J. (2011). Psychological wisdom research: Commonalities and differences in a growing field. *Annual Review of Psychology, 62*, 215–241.

Sternberg, R. J. (1998). A balance theory of wisdom. *Review of General Psychology, 2*(4), 347–365.

Swartwood, J., & Tiberius, V. (2019). Philosophical foundations of wisdom. In R. J. Sternberg & J. Glück (Eds.), *The Cambridge handbook of wisdom* (pp. 10–39). New York, NY: Cambridge University Press.

Swartwood, J. D. (2013). Wisdom as an expert skill. *Ethical Theory and Moral Practice, 16*(3), 511–528.

Tynjälä, P. (2008). Perspectives into learning at the workplace. *Educational Research Review, 3*(2), 130–154.

Tynjälä, P. (2009). Connectivity and transformation in work-related learning: Theoretical foundations. In M.-L. Stenström & P. Tynjälä (Eds.), *Towards integration of work and learning: Strategies for connectivity and transformation* (pp. 11–37). Dordrecht, the Netherlands: Springer.

Tynjälä, P. (2016). Asiantuntijan tieto ja ajattelu [Knowledge and thinking of experts]. In E. Kallio (Ed.) *Ajattelun kehitys aikuisuudessa: Kohti moninäkökulmaisuutta* [The development of thinking in adulthood: Towards multiperspective thinking] (Research in Educational Sciences No. 71, pp. 227–244). Helsinki, Finland: The Finnish Educational Research Association.

Tynjälä, P., & Gijbels, D. (2012). Changing world: Changing pedagogy. In P. Tynjälä, M.-L. Stenström, & M. Saarnivaara (Eds.), *Transitions and transformations in learning and education* (pp. 205–222). Dordrecht, the Netherlands: Springer Netherlands.

Tynjälä, P., Häkkinen, P., & Hämäläinen, R. (2014). TEL@work: Toward integration of theory and practice. *British Journal of Educational Technology, 45*(6), 990–1000.

Tynjälä, P., Virtanen, A., Klemola, U., Kostiainen, E., & Rasku-Puttonen, H. (2016). Developing social competence and other generic skills in teacher education: Applying the model of integrative pedagogy. *European Journal of Teacher Education, 39*(3), 368–387. doi:10.1080/02619768.2016.1171314

van Someren, M. W., Reimann, P., Boshuizen, H. P. A., & de Jong, T., (Eds.). (1998). *Learning with multiple representations* (Advances in learning and instruction series). Amsterdam, the Netherlands: Pergamon.

Wenger, E. (1998). *Communities of practice: Learning, meaning, and identity* (Learning in doing: Social, cognitive, and computational perspectives). Cambridge, England: Cambridge University Press.

Wenger-Trayner, E., Fenton O'Creevy, M., Hutchinson, S., Kubiak, C., & Wenger-Trayner, B. (Eds.). (2015). *Learning in landscapes of practice: Boundaries, identity, and knowledgeability in practice-based learning.* London, England: Routledge.

Wennerberg, H. (1967). The concept of family resemblance in Wittgenstein's later philosophy. *Theoria, 33*(2), 107–132.

Yang, S. (2017). The complex relations between wisdom and significant life learning. *Journal of Adult Development, 24*(4), 227–238.

PART III

Open questions and new approaches

11

CHALLENGES IN EXPLORING INDIVIDUAL'S CONCEPTIONS OF KNOWLEDGE AND KNOWING

Examples of research on university students

Heidi Hyytinen, Liisa Postareff, and Sari Lindblom-Ylänne

Introduction

Individuals' conceptions of knowledge and knowing are considered to be a challenging research topic due to their complexity and multidimensional character. As noted in Chapters 3 and 4, these conceptions have been investigated in the context of different disciplines, such as philosophy, psychology, and education. Although previous research in the fields of education and psychology has frequently leant on self-reporting methods, the reliability and adequacy of these methods have recently been questioned, and it has been suggested that they do not capture the complexity of phenomena. The present chapter extends the discussion on epistemological development by introducing and evaluating empirical methods used in investigating individuals' conceptions of knowledge, focusing on the methodological and theoretical challenges related to them. The chapter also presents methodological alternatives for future research, and highlights the need for dialogue between theoretical, methodological, and empirical perspectives to advance research on epistemic conceptions. The chapter particularly focuses on research into university students' conceptions of knowledge from the perspective of developmental and educational psychology.

A Short history of investigating individuals' conceptions of knowledge and knowing

A variety of research methods and materials have been applied when investigating epistemic conceptions within developmental and educational psychology (see Chapter 3). From the 1950s onward, Perry used open-ended interviews, questionnaires, and problem-solving tasks to examine epistemological beliefs – or in

Perry's own words "forms of intellectual and ethical development" (Perry, 1970). However, the next generation of researchers has quite systematically applied different questionnaires, and it was not until the turn of this millennium that qualitative methods became increasingly common.

In his research project, Perry investigated college students at Harvard University and followed their intellectual and ethical development during their four college years by interviewing them at the end of each academic year. The participants were randomly selected white male students who had answered a questionnaire designed by Perry and his colleagues, and entitled "the *Checklist of Educational Views*" (Perry, 1970; Schommer-Aikins, 2004). Interviewing was the main research method because, according to Perry, the use of open-ended interviews enabled the examination of individual development paths during college years. The research group detected a nine-phase development process during which the students' conceptions of the nature of knowledge changed and deepened and their worldviews and self-conceptions changed (Perry, 1970; Schommer-Aikins, 2004).

From interviews to questionnaires and problem-solving tasks

After Perry, research has expanded to include female students (e.g., Belenky, Clinchy, Goldberger, & Tarule, 1986) and the different societal and cultural backgrounds of students (Helsing et al., 2001). Like Perry, Belenky and colleagues also used open-ended interviews in their research project on Women's Ways of Knowing (Belenky et al., 1986). On the basis of the interviews, they described the process of cognitive development comprising of five knowledge positions, from reliance on authorities to constructed knowledge by integrating voices. These five positions follow quite closely Perry's development model, though his model is more detailed at the more developed end.

To conclude, both Perry and Belenky created their development models on the basis of open-ended interview data, focusing on students' experiences, evaluations, and narratives. Both research groups used several raters in analysing the data, and were aware of the limitations of their research methods, in particular the possibility of subjective bias during the analysis process. Furthermore, both groups were aware of the limited generalisability of their findings (Baxter Magolda, 2001; Belenky et al., 1986; Perry, 1970).

Many researchers were concerned about the use of interviews as the main data collection method and began to apply quantitative research methods to explore epistemic conceptions. Interviews were considered slow and expensive, and both data collection and analysis required high expertise compared to questionnaires, which were much faster and cheaper to use, and expertise was not required in scoring students' answers. Moreover, teachers, tutors, and counsellors were all able to use the questionnaires.

Ryan (1984, p. 250) developed a Dualism Scale based on Perry's model. The scale consisted of seven items, with statements such as "*For most questions there is only one right answer once a person is able to get all the facts*" and "*If professors would stick more to the facts and do less theorising, one could get more out of college*". These items were designed to measure the level of students' epistemological development in the "dualism-relativism continuum". A five-point Likert scale was used. An average score lower than 3.0 reflected a relativist conception of knowledge, whereas an average score above 3.0 was judged to reflect a dualist conception of knowledge.

Schommer-Aikins presented a theoretical model (Schommer, 1990) which suggests that epistemological beliefs consist of several more or less independent beliefs which form the individual's epistemological belief system. This broadened view of epistemological beliefs led to a more systematic use of questionnaires in this research field. Schommer-Aikins (2004) has, however, emphasised the difficulties and challenges in measuring epistemological beliefs by using questionnaires. These difficulties were also apparent in her Epistemological Questionnaire (EQ) (Schommer, 1998). Researchers using this questionnaire reported various factor solutions, because in different datasets, the original scales failed to appear. Therefore, Schommer-Aikins shortened the Epistemological Questionnaire from 63 items first to a 34-item and later to a 28-item questionnaire. However, the scale reliabilities remained quite low. Indeed, the key challenge in the use of questionnaires has been to find a way to capture the complex nature of the phenomenon in questionnaire items (e.g., Baxter Magolda, 2001; Schommer-Aikins, 2004).

Besides questionnaires and interviews, additional methods have also been applied in examining individuals' conceptions of knowledge and knowing. Ryan (1984, p. 251) developed a *Comprehension Monitoring Probe*, in which the students were given 15 minutes to answer the following questions:

1) How do you determine (when you have completed a reading assignment or when you are reviewing the material) whether you have understood the material well enough?
2) What specific information do you use to assess the degree to which you have understood the material you have read in a chapter?
3) On what basis would you decide that you need to go over the chapter again or to seek help in figuring it out?

Ryan analysed each student's responses to the comprehension-monitoring probe to determine the specific comprehension criteria employed. An effort was made to score each response for as many different comprehension criteria as possible in order to capture the full range of each student's comprehension monitoring capabilities. The comprehension monitoring criteria (Ryan, 1984) were classified as knowledge criteria or comprehension/application criteria. Ryan showed that it was possible to statistically analyse epistemic conceptions and to demonstrate a correlation between students' conceptions of knowledge and the comprehension criteria they used.

Baxter Magolda and Porterfield developed the *Measure of Epistemological Reflection (MER)* (Baxter Magolda, 2001) on the basis of Perry's model. The

MER contains six short open-ended tasks on the basis of which it is possible to evaluate different areas of epistemological development. These tasks measure students' skills in drawing conclusions, their perceptions of the roles of themselves, teachers and peers in learning, their views of how learning should be evaluated, and how students make decisions about what to believe. The tasks are open-ended to avoid leading or confining the students' responses, and follow-up questions are made to clarify students' perspectives. Because of the use of open-ended tasks, evaluation of students' answers is a demanding process. After the development of MER, Baxter Magolda developed *the MER constructivist interpretation process* on the basis of which it is possible to analyse open-ended interviews on students' epistemological development. The aim of this method is not to evaluate the development phase of individual students, but instead to steer and support the researcher's analysis process.

Based on an extensive review of contemporary research findings and theoretical frameworks, Hofer and Pintrich (1997) proposed that although the number and nature of dimensions of individuals' conceptions of knowledge vary across different theoretical frameworks, they all include some commonalities, such as certainty of knowledge (i.e., an absolutist versus a relativist view), simplicity of knowledge (i.e., simple and concrete versus complex and context-dependent), source of knowledge (from external authorities versus from personal construction), and justification for knowing (criteria for making knowledge claims, use of evidence and reasoning (Hofer & Pintrich, 1997; see also Chapter 3). Around these theoretical findings, Hofer (2000) built the *Discipline-focused Epistemological Belief Questionnaire* (DEBQ), which has become one of the most widely used quantitative measures (Muis, Trevors, Duffy, Ranellucci, & Foy, 2016). Hofer's DEBQ questionnaire is designed to focus on these four commonalities of conceptions of knowledge (Hofer, 2000).

Mixed-method approaches, e.g., combining questionnaire and interview data, have recently become increasingly common in exploring personal epistemology (e.g., Hofer & Sinatra, 2010; Hyytinen, Clancy, Teviotdale, & Postareff, 2016; King & Kitchener, 2004; Muis et al., 2016). For example, King and Kitchener (2004) created the *Reflective Judgment Model* (see Chapter 4). To evaluate the level of students' cognitive development, King and Kitchener used problem-solving tasks. They developed the *Reflective Judgment Interview* in which trained interviewers ask open-ended questions to evaluate the students' cognitive development, the quality of argumentation and their conceptions of knowledge and knowing. The results of the Reflective Judgment Interviews can further be analysed statistically. Kuhn and her colleagues (e.g., Kuhn, Cheney, & Weinstock, 2000; Kuhn, Katz, & Dean, 2004) have also used different problem-solving tasks combined with questionnaires to examine cognitive development from childhood to adulthood. Thus, the methodological approach is similar to that of King and Kitchener (2004).

Addressing concerns about self-report measures

Self-report measures, such as questionnaires and surveys, are often easily implemented to gather a large dataset. Another reason for the preference for self-reports is that they provide a time- and cost-effective way to collect data (DeBacker, Crowson, Beesley, Thoma, & Hestevold, 2008). Therefore, it is not surprising that self-reporting has been a dominant data collection regime in the field of research on individuals' conceptions of knowledge. Although self-report methods are widely used, many researchers nevertheless criticise this method. Among other things, researchers have found that individuals' conceptions of the nature of knowledge and knowing are extremely difficult to measure with self-report assessments (DeBacker et al., 2008; Karabenick et al., 2007; Muis, Duffy, Trevors, Ranellucci, & Foy, 2014; Muis et al., 2016; Schraw, 2013).

One challenge in investigating an individual's conception of knowledge and knowing is that this kind of phenomenon is not directly observable. The interpretations of an individual's conception of knowledge are thus for the most part indirect. Furthermore, epistemic conceptions are characteristically abstract constructs. Therefore, reporting these kinds of conceptions requires considerable self-reflection and abstraction from respondents and it is cognitively, extremely challenging (Karabenick et al., 2007). The most important drawback to self-report assessments is that individuals are to some extent unable to introspectively assess themselves (Bowman, 2010). Previous research has also shown that students' belief in themselves as knowers is not necessarily equivalent to how they perform and assess knowledge in real life (e.g., Hyytinen, Holma, Toom, Shavelson, & Lindblom-Ylänne, 2014). Moreover, individuals are not necessarily aware of their own conceptions and thus they are not competent to describe their perceptions (Bowman, 2010). Therefore, self-report measures may provide incorrect information despite the respondents' best efforts to be honest and accurate in the data collection situation. It has been suggested that self-reports alone cannot adequately assess complex phenomena (Greene & Yu, 2014).

In addition, stronger critiques have questioned the reliability and validity of present self-report assessments (Bowman, 2010; DeBacker et al., 2008; Karabenick et al., 2007; Muis et al., 2014). Previous studies have identified several problematic issues with questionnaires assessing individuals' conceptions of knowledge (e.g., Buehl & Alexander, 2005; DeBacker et al., 2008; Hyytinen et al., 2016; Muis, Bendixen, & Haerle, 2006; Muis et al., 2014). One concern relates to tests and how the phenomenon is operationalised and conceptualised. Students' interpretations of present self-report items have been found to be inconsistent with researchers' assumptions and intended meanings (Greene, Torney-Purta, & Azevedo, 2010; Muis et al., 2014). Previous research has shown that there is clear variation not only between but also within student groups in how students understood, interpreted, and responded to items concerning epistemic conceptions (Muis et al., 2014).

Several reasons for these conceptual shortcomings can be given. Firstly, one reason for inconstancies is that self-report items often include complex concepts (i.e., "truth", "expert", "first-hand knowledge"), which need to be interpreted and combined with relevant contexts and experiences when responding (see Karabenick et al., 2007; Muis et al., 2014). Secondly, some items have been found to include multiple or ambiguous meanings and interpretations (Greene et al., 2010; Hyytinen et al., 2016; Muis et al., 2014) as the following extract from a focus group interview of Finnish students in educational sciences shows:

Hofer's DEBQ questionnaire item *"Truth is unchanging in this subject"*
(see Hofer, 2000, p. 390)

Student 8: For me truth is a matter that is considered correct.
Student 7: Yeah, research tells us what is generally accepted in a specific moment within a particular context.
Student 6: But I considered here that [the meaning of "truth"] was a philosophical view, not a verified fact or something.
Student 7: I thought this [truth] referred to the construction of knowledge.
Student 6: So. What is actually meant [by this item]? This question is really paralysing! For me nothing holds absolute truth but some aspects can be accepted as truthful at a particular moment in a specific context.

Hyytinen and colleagues (2016) found that similar challenges with the questionnaire items in the DEBQ resulted in a high number of missing values. In addition, the problematic items included several "unsure" responses (response alternative 3 on a 5-point Likert scale). Furthermore, related factor analysis resulted in an unclear factor solution, including low commonalities with some items. In a similar vein, DeBacker and colleagues (2008) analysed data from three self-report questionnaires, namely the Epistemological Questionnaire (EQ) (Schommer, 1990), the Epistemic Beliefs Inventory (EBI) (Schraw, Bendixen, & Dunkle, 2002), and the Epistemological Beliefs Survey (EBS) (Wood & Kardash, 2002). Their results indicated psychometric problems with all three. The results demonstrated, among other things, consistent failure of factor analyses (exploratory and confirmatory) to support the hypothesised factor structures. In addition, the reliability of the scales remained rather low, and the scales functioned differently in different contexts. The use of a Likert scale in such measurements has also been debated elsewhere (e.g., Greene et al., 2010; Muis et al., 2006, 2014). Muis and her colleagues (2014) found that students chose option 3 when conflicting items occurred. In contrast, Greene and colleagues (2010) reported that students opt for "3" as a neutral response when they were unfamiliar with the question.

A need for the multiple methods approach

In recent years, the multiple methods approach has been proposed to overcome the above-mentioned challenges of self-report assessments (Hofer, 2004; Muis et al., 2016). Epistemic conceptions literature contains several variants for the term multimethodology, such as triangulation, multi-method, and mixed-method. Sometimes these terms have been used as synonyms, sometimes not. Among researchers there is no all-encompassing agreement about the meanings and definitions of these terms (Teddlie & Tashakkori, 2010). One alternative is to consider the term "multi-method" as referring to research involving multiple qualitative or quantitative methods in data collection and analysis, while "mixed-method" can be used to refer to research in which both quantitative and qualitative methods are combined in the same study or in a series of studies (see also Creswell, 2010; Leech & Onwuegbuzie, 2009). The present discussion pertains to this definition.

As mentioned before, there is a long history of using multiple methods in research on epistemic conceptions (see Hofer, 2004; King & Kitchener, 2004; Kuhn, 2005). In the existing literature, several advantages attributable to the mixed- or multi-method approach have been reported. Firstly, through the use of the mixed- or multi-method approach, it is possible to select and integrate the appropriate methods to gain a more thorough picture of the phenomenon (Ghelbach & Brinkworth, 2011; Karabenick et al., 2007; Muis et al., 2016). Secondly, the use of multiple methods allows a researcher to minimise the weaknesses or complement the strengths of particular methods. Thus, the advantage of combining the different assessment methods by which individuals' conceptions of knowledge are measured is that it offers multiple insights into and thus a more comprehensive view on individuals' conceptions of knowledge and knowing. As Muis and colleagues (2016) have argued, the mixed-method approach (i.e., combining surveys with interviews) provided much deeper nuances of the nature of students' conceptions. This kind of information would have been impossible to gain by means of self-reporting only. Thirdly, through the use of the mixed- and multi-method approach it is also possible to identify and address new and unexplored aspects of students' conceptions and gain a more complete understanding of the phenomenon (see Onwuegbuzie, Johnson, & Collins, 2009). Finally, the mixed- and multi-method approach provides a way to enhance the *cognitive validity* of surveys which focus on abstract constructs, such as conceptions of knowledge and knowing (Ghelbach & Brinkworth, 2011; Karabenick et al., 2007).

It is important to notice that the mixed- and multi-method approach can be employed in data collection, data analysis, and merging interpretations (Creswell, 2010). Epistemic conceptions literature features several variants of multi- and mixed-method research. In essence, these variants can be roughly divided into two main strategies, namely sequential and concurrent strategies (see Figure 11.1). To our knowledge, most mixed- and multi-method research on individuals' conceptions of knowledge have followed a sequential strategy including at least two separate phases or sub-studies. In this approach the

Example 1. Sequential strategy

The study consists of separate phases where each dataset is analysed separately.
The follow-up phase produces answers to the questions which
remain unanswered in Phase 1.

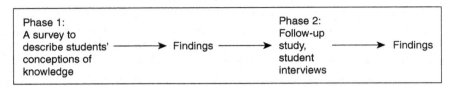

Example 2. Concurrent strategy

A study in which two or more data collection and analytical methods
are used simultaneously. Different stages of study are merged.

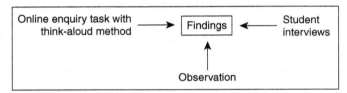

FIGURE 11.1 Examples of sequential and concurrent designs for research on individuals' conceptions of knowledge

researcher typically uses one method to collect and analyse the data. After that, the results that need additional explanations are identified and the researcher accordingly selects a second method. The purpose of the second method, i.e., the follow-up phase, is to provide a better understanding of the research problem than using only the first method. As an example, qualitative analysis of interview data is often used to complement and extend the findings of quantitative analysis of questionnaire data (e.g., Hofer, 2006; Hyytinen et al., 2016; Muis et al., 2014). In these cases, a sequential strategy is used to develop and revise quantitative data collection instruments.

A concurrent strategy, by contrast, is used to confirm and cross-validate findings, to seek information at different levels, and address different questions and perspectives (e.g., Barzilai & Zohar, 2012; Hofer, 2004; Hyytinen et al., 2014; Kienhues, Stadtler, & Bromme, 2011; Strømsø & Bråten, 2014). A concurrent strategy refers to situations in which two or more data collection and analytical methods are simultaneously and interactively applied to understand a phenomenon (Leech & Onwuegbuzie, 2009). In this strategy, the different methods have equal priority. This kind of strategy may help strengthen the validity and reliability of the study. It is worth noting that mixed- and multimethod research is not limited to take either a sequential or concurrent strategy; the same study may employ both these strategies. Figure 11.1 illustrates the main differences between sequential and concurrent strategies.

Measuring the individual's conception of knowledge and knowing in action

To overcome the challenges involved in exploring the conceptions of knowledge, researchers have also pointed out a need for authentic measures (Hofer, 2004; Sandoval, 2009). Here, "authenticity" means that individuals' conceptions of knowledge and knowing are explored in real-world situations, for example in classrooms, and in different problem-solving or information-searching situations. The major advantage of authentic assessment is that it enables capturing such aspects, like students' justification of knowledge, that are too complex and multifaceted to lend themselves to mere self-report methods. Authentic measurement may improve the reliability of the study because the findings do not depend on the respondents' abilities to describe their conceptions. In addition, authentic measurement makes it possible to consider the characteristics of the context in which epistemic thinking is activated (Mason, Ariasi, & Boldrin, 2011; Sandoval, 2009). It provides an opportunity to deepen an understanding of the situated nature of thinking (Barzilai & Zohar, 2012; Hofer, 2004; Kuhn, Iordanou, Pease, & Wirkala, 2008).

Recent studies have found that authentic measurements, such as searching information about a controversial topic and problem-solving tasks with open-ended questions, provide an opportunity for students to reflect spontaneously on their beliefs about knowledge and knowing (Barzilai & Zohar, 2012; Ferguson, Bråten, & Strømsø, 2012; Hyytinen et al., 2014; Mason et al., 2011). These kinds of measurements are found to be rich sources concerning how students analyse, evaluate, integrate, and justify the claims and sources of information and knowledge. They also show the criteria by which students evaluate not only knowledge but also the evidence that supports the knowledge (Hofer, 2004), as well as the way in which students respond to conflicting sources of knowledge.

Literature on these issues displays several facets as to how to explore individuals' conceptions of knowledge and knowing in action. One way is to connect an authentic approach to the concurrent data collection strategy. For example, some researchers have combined online search and knowledge integration with a think-aloud method and video observation (e.g., Barzilai & Zohar, 2012; Hofer, 2004; Strømsø & Bråten, 2014), while others have focused on how students acquire, justify, process, and utilise knowledge from various sources in an open-ended problem-solving situation (e.g., Hyytinen et al., 2014). Furthermore, concept maps together with storylines or detailed written explanations have proved to be valuable tools for exploring students' reflection, justification, and use of knowledge (Koponen & Nousiainen, 2013; Nousiainen, 2013). Such maps have also been found to provide various insights into analysing the development of students' understanding (Schwendimann, 2014).

Although authentic methods bring clear advantages to the exploration of students' conceptions of knowledge and knowing, these methods are not perfect, either. It is very common that data collection situations are video recorded (e.g., Barzilai & Zohar, 2012; Hyytinen et al., 2014; Strømsø &

Bråten, 2014). Analysing video-observation data is time consuming: it takes a lot of time and effort to analyse properly this kind of data. Another challenge is how to combine different kinds of datasets produced in the data collection situation, such as video data on students' think-aloud or written explanations (see Hyytinen et al., 2014; Strømsø & Bråten, 2014). Furthermore, authentic methods can be more demanding for participants than self-reports, because they really need to use higher-order thinking skills in the data collection situation when analysing, justifying, and utilising the various sources of knowledge.

Theoretical challenges

One potential cause of inconsistency and ambiguity in results can be theoretical, that is to say, how researchers have specified and conceptualised the models of epistemic conceptions. In the literature, there is no consensus on what categories and dimensions of multidimensional phenomena are included in the measures (DeBacker et al., 2008; Muis et al., 2014; Schraw, 2013). Schraw (2013, p. 1) sums up the prevailing situation by pointing out that it is unclear whether the measurements used in contemporary research on individuals' conceptions of knowledge really measure the same constructs and phenomena. There is also evidence that researchers define the dimensions of individuals' conceptions of knowledge in conceptually and theoretically different ways (Chinn, Buckland, & Samarapungavan, 2011; Hofer & Pintrich, 2002; Holma & Hyytinen, 2015; Kallio, 2011). For example, the term "relativism" is used to refer to at least three different epistemological positions (Holma & Hyytinen, 2015; for another philosophical critique, see Chapter 13). The theoretical problems with the concept of relativism have also been highlighted elsewhere. Kallio (2011) and Leadbeater (1986), for example, have demonstrated that the definition of relativism is ambiguous.

It is important to understand that theoretical frameworks play a significant role in how the data is analysed and interpreted. A theoretical framework is the researcher's tool for analysing and interpreting data. If the tool is not adequate, then there is a real risk that the analyses will be distorted (Holma & Hyytinen, 2015; Hyytinen, 2015). Therefore, we suggest that theoretical analysis of the current theoretical frameworks of epistemic conceptions would provide a bridge between theory and practice. By applying theoretical analyses it is possible to elucidate theoretical background assumptions as well as contradictory statements and inconsistencies in the theoretical framework by analysing the interconnections between the concepts. In summary, theoretical analyses have great relevance in developing research methods in future research (e.g., Chinn et al., 2011; Holma & Hyytinen, 2015; Kallio, 2011; Leadbeater, 1986).

Conclusions and recommendations for further studies

To conclude, the challenges in exploring conceptions of knowledge are both methodological and theoretical in nature. The methodological challenges include heavy reliance on self-report measures, which have not, however, been able to capture the complexity of the phenomenon in a reliable and valid manner (Buehl & Alexander, 2005; DeBacker et al., 2008; Hyytinen et al., 2016; Muis et al., 2006, 2014). It seems obvious that research on epistemic conceptions benefits from mixed- and multi-method approaches, which enable researchers to identify unexplored aspects of students' conceptions of knowledge and knowing, as well as gain a more complete understanding of the phenomenon at hand. Especially the concurrent strategy, where two or more methods are simultaneously applied, can provide information from different levels and address new perspectives, as well as cross-validate findings obtained through different methods (see Hyytinen et al., 2014; Strømsø & Bråten, 2014). Although the use of multi- and mixed-method approaches has been increasing (e.g., Barzilai & Zohar, 2012; Hofer, 2004; Hyytinen et al., 2014; Kienhues et al., 2011; Muis et al., 2014; Strømsø & Bråten, 2014), it does not solve the underlying challenge related to self-reports, if the combination of methods consists of different self-report measures only. Therefore, there is an urgent need for more authentic measures. Authentic measures seem to capture such aspects, like those related to students' justification of knowledge and the contextual setting in which epistemic thinking is activated, that are too complex and multifaceted to lend themselves to different self-report methods.

The challenges related to using self-report measures in research on epistemic conceptions are also related to the theoretical challenges in the research field (e.g., Chinn et al., 2011; Holma & Hyytinen, 2015; Kallio, 2011). The main challenges concern the inconsistent use and complexity of the concepts commonly used to measure conceptions of knowledge and knowing. This causes inconsistency as to which categories and dimensions should be included in the measures. Furthermore, if research focuses on measuring conceptions of knowledge in a specific context or discipline, it does not necessarily reflect more general conceptions of knowledge. Thus, awareness of what actually is being measured is important.

The use of the concurrent strategy in mixed-method research, as well as authentic measures in exploring individuals' conceptions of knowledge, can serve as a means to further develop the theory of the phenomenon. A more solid theoretical basis, on the other hand, is needed to further develop self-report instruments for measuring conceptions of knowledge. The instruments should be able to capture the elements of this phenomenon and reflect students' conceptions of knowledge clearly and accurately. To ensure valid and reliable research on individuals' conceptions of knowledge, it is essential to enhance the dialogue between theoretical, methodological, and empirical perspectives to extend and enhance previous work in the field. Previous chapters in this book – by Pirttilä-Backman and colleagues and also Seppälä and colleagues – provide innovative examples of how research on epistemic conceptions can be combined with new theoretical insights.

In the following we summarise the main points for enhancing the quality of measurements of individuals' conceptions of knowledge:

- One assessment or analysis method is not enough to evaluate and capture complex and multifaceted phenomena. A mixed- and multi-method approach is needed.
- Authentic methods have been found to be rich sources in exploring how students analyse, evaluate, integrate, and justify knowledge. These methods also provide an opportunity to deepen the understanding of the situated and contextual nature of thinking.
- Instead of a sole focus on empirical, methodological, or theoretical elements, more communication between the theoretical, empirical, and methodological perspectives is required to deepen our understanding of epistemic conceptions (cf. Hyytinen, 2015).

References

Barzilai, S., & Zohar, A. (2012). Epistemic thinking in action: Evaluating and integrating online sources. *Cognition and Instruction, 30*(1), 39–85.

Baxter Magolda, M. B. (2001). A constructivist revision of the measure of epistemological reflection. *Journal of College Student Development, 42*(6), 520–534.

Belenky, M., Clinchy, B., Goldberger, N., & Tarule, J. (1986). *Women's ways of knowing: The development of self, voice, and mind.* New York, NY: Basic Books.

Bowman, N. A. (2010). Can 1st-year college students accurately report their learning and development? *American Educational Research Journal, 47*(2), 466–496.

Buehl, M., & Alexander, P. A. (2005). Motivation and performance differences in students' domain-specific epistemological belief profiles. *American Educational Research Journal, 42*(4), 697–726.

Chinn, C. A., Buckland, L. A., & Samarapungavan, A. (2011). Expanding the dimensions of epistemic cognition: Arguments from philosophy and psychology. *Educational Psychologist, 46*(3), 141–167.

Creswell, J. W. (2010). Mapping the developing landscape of mixed methods research. In A. Tashakkori & C. Teddlie (Eds.), *SAGE handbook of mixed methods in social & behavioral research* (2nd ed., pp. 45–68). Thousand Oaks, CA: SAGE.

DeBacker, T. K., Crowson, H. M., Beesley, A. D., Thoma, S. J., & Hestevold, N. L. (2008). The challenge of measuring epistemological beliefs: An analysis of three self-report instruments. *Journal of Experimental Education, 76*(3), 281–312.

Ferguson, L. E., Bråten, I., & Strømsø, H. (2012). Epistemic cognition when students read multiple documents containing conflicting scientific evidence: A think-aloud study. *Learning and Instruction, 22*(2), 103–120.

Ghelbach, H., & Brinkworth, M. E. (2011). Measure twice, cut down error: A process for enhancing the validity of survey scales. *Review of General Psychology, 15*(4), 380–387.

Greene, J. A., Torney-Purta, J., & Azevedo, R. (2010). Empirical evidence regarding relations among a model of epistemic and ontological cognition, academic performance, and educational level. *Journal of Educational Psychology, 102*(1), 234–255.

Greene, J. A., & Yu, S. B. (2014). Modeling and measuring epistemic cognition: A qualitative re-investigation. *Contemporary Educational Psychology, 39*(1), 12–28.

Helsing, D., Drago-Severson, E., Kegan, R., Portnow, K., Popp, N., & Broderick, M. (2001). Three different types of change. *Focus on Basics, 5*(B), 10–14.

Hofer, B. K. (2000). Dimensionality and disciplinary differences in personal epistemology. *Contemporary Educational Psychology, 25*(4), 378–405.

Hofer, B. K. (2004). Epistemological understanding as a metacognitive process: Thinking aloud during online searching. *Educational Psychologist, 39*(1), 43–55.

Hofer, B. K. (2006). Domain specificity of personal epistemology: Resolved questions, persistent issues, new models. *International Journal of Educational Research, 45*(1–2), 85–95.

Hofer, B. K., & Pintrich, P. R. (1997). The development of epistemological theories: Beliefs about knowledge and knowing and their relation to learning. *Review of Educational Research, 67*(1), 88–140.

Hofer, B. K., & Pintrich, P. R. (2002). *Personal epistemology: The psychology of beliefs about knowledge and knowing.* Mahwah, NJ: Erlbaum.

Hofer, B. K., & Sinatra, G. M. (2010). Epistemology, metacognition, and self-regulation: Musings on an emerging field. *Metacognition and Learning, 5*(1), 113–120.

Holma, K., & Hyytinen, H. (2015). The philosophy of personal epistemology. *Theory and Research in Education, 13*(3), 334–350.

Hyytinen, H. (2015). *Looking beyond the obvious: Theoretical, empirical and methodological insights into critical thinking* (Doctoral dissertation, University of Helsinki, Institute of Behavioural Sciences, Helsinki, Finland). Retrieved from https://helda.helsinki.fi/bitstream/handle/10138/154312/LOOKINGB.pdf?sequence=1

Hyytinen, H., Clancy, D., Teviotdale, W., & Postareff, L. (2016, July). *Problematising the measurement of students' personal epistemologies.* Paper presented at the Higher Education conference, Amsterdam, the Netherlands.

Hyytinen, H., Holma, K., Toom, A., Shavelson, R. J., & Lindblom-Ylänne, S. (2014). The complex relationship between students' critical thinking and epistemological beliefs in the context of problem solving. *Frontline Learning Research, 2*(5), 1–24.

Kallio, E. (2011). Integrative thinking is the key: An evaluation of current research into the development of adult thinking. *Theory & Psychology, 21*(6), 785–801.

Karabenick, S. A., Woolley, M. E., Friedel, J. M., Ammon, B. V., Blazevski, J., Bonney, C. R., ... Kelly, K. L. (2007). Cognitive processing of self-report items in educational research: Do they think what we mean? *Educational Psychologist, 42*(3), 139–151.

Kienhues, D., Stadtler, M., & Bromme, R. (2011). Dealing with conflicting or consistent medical information on the web: When expert information breeds laypersons' doubts about experts. *Learning and Instruction, 21*(2), 193–204.

King, P. M., & Kitchener, K. S. (2004). Reflective judgment: Theory and research on the development of epistemic assumptions through adulthood. *Educational Psychologist, 39*(1), 5–18.

Koponen, I. T., & Nousiainen, M. (2013). Pre-service physics teachers' understanding of the relational structure of physics concepts: Organising subject content for purposes of teaching. *International Journal of Science and Mathematics Education, 11*(2), 325–357.

Kuhn, D. (2005). *Education for thinking.* Cambridge, MA: Harvard University Press.

Kuhn, D., Cheney, R., & Weinstock, M. (2000). The development of epistemological understanding. *Cognitive Development, 15*(3), 309–328.

Kuhn, D., Iordanou, K., Pease, M., & Wirkala, C. (2008). Beyond control of variables: What needs to develop to achieve skilled scientific thinking? *Cognitive Development, 23*(4), 435–451.

Kuhn, D., Katz, J. B., & Dean, D., Jr. (2004). Developing reason. *Thinking & Reasoning, 10*(2), 197–219.

Leadbeater, B. (1986). The resolution of relativism in adult thinking: Subjective, objective, or conceptual? *Human Development, 29*(5), 291–300.

Leech, N. L., & Onwuegbuzie, A. J. (2009). A typology of mixed methods research designs. *Quality & Quantity, 43*(2), 265–275.

Mason, L., Ariasi, N., & Boldrin, A. (2011). Epistemic beliefs in action: Spontaneous reflections about knowledge and knowing during online information searching and their influence on learning. *Learning and Instruction, 21*(1), 137–151.

Muis, K. R., Bendixen, L. D., & Haerle, F. C. (2006). Domain-generality and domain-specificity in personal epistemology research: Philosophical and empirical reflections in the development of a theoretical framework. *Educational Psychology Review, 18*(1), 3–54.

Muis, K. R., Duffy, M. C., Trevors, G., Ranellucci, J., & Foy, M. (2014). What were they thinking? Using cognitive interviewing to examine the validity of self-reported epistemic beliefs. *International Education Research, 2*(1), 17–31.

Muis, K. R., Trevors, G., Duffy, M., Ranellucci, J., & Foy, M. J. (2016). Testing the TIDE: Examining the nature of students' epistemic beliefs using a multiple methods approach. *The Journal of Experimental Education, 84*(2), 264–288.

Nousiainen, M. (2013). Coherence of pre-service physics teachers' views of the relatedness of physics concepts. *Science & Education, 22*(3), 505–525.

Onwuegbuzie, A., Johnson, R. B., & Collins, K. (2009). Call for mixed analysis: A philosophical framework for combining qualitative and quantitative approaches. *International Journal of Multiple Research Approaches, 3*(2), 114–139.

Perry, W. G., Jr. (1970). *Forms of intellectual and ethical development in the college years: A scheme.* New York, NY: Holt, Rinehart and Winston.

Ryan, M. P. (1984). Monitoring text comprehension: Individual differences in epistemological standards. *Journal of Educational Psychology, 76*(2), 248–258.

Sandoval, W. A. (2009). Conceptual and epistemic aspects of students' scientific explanations. *Journal of the Learning Sciences, 12*(1), 5–51.

Schommer, M. (1990). Effects of beliefs about the nature of knowledge on comprehension. *Journal of Educational Psychology, 82*(3), 498–504.

Schommer, M. (1998). The influence of age and education on epistemological beliefs. *The British Journal of Educational Psychology, 68*(4), 551–562.

Schommer-Aikins, M. (2004). Explaining the epistemological belief system: Introducing the embedded systemic model and coordinated research approach. *Educational Psychologist, 39*(1), 19–29.

Schraw, G. (2013). Conceptual integration and measurement of epistemological and ontological beliefs in educational research. *ISRN Education, 2013.* Article ID 327680. doi: 10.1155/2013/327680.

Schraw, G., Bendixen, L. D., & Dunkle, M. E. (2002). Development and validation of the epistemic belief inventory (EBI). In B. K. Hofer & P. R. Pintrich (Eds.), *Personal epistemology: The psychology of beliefs about knowledge and knowing* (pp. 261–275). Mahwah, NJ: Erlbaum.

Schwendimann, B. A. (2014). Making sense of knowledge integration maps. In D. Ifenthaler & R. Hanewald (Eds.), *Digital knowledge maps in education: Technology-enhanced support for teachers and learners* (pp. 17–40). New York, NY: Springer New York.

Strømsø, H. I., & Bråten, I. (2014). Students' sourcing while reading and writing from multiple web documents. *Nordic Journal of Digital Literacy, 9*(2), 92–111.

Teddlie, C., & Tashakkori, A. (2010). Overview of contemporary issues in mixed methods research. In A. Tashakkori & C. Teddlie (Eds.), *SAGE handbook of mixed methods in social & behavioral research* (2nd ed., pp. 1–41). Thousand Oaks, CA: SAGE.

Wood, P., & Kardash, C. (2002). Critical elements in the design and analysis of studies of epistemology. In B. K. Hofer & P. R. Pintrich (Eds.), *Personal epistemology: The psychology of beliefs about knowledge and knowing* (pp. 231–260). Mahwah, NJ: Erlbaum.

12

SYSTEMS THINKING AND ADULT COGNITIVE DEVELOPMENT

Pirjo Ståhle, Laura Mononen, Päivi Tynjälä, and Eeva K. Kallio

Introduction

In today's increasingly complex world, there is an imperative to work constantly to develop one's skills, self-understanding, and other personal resources. This requires human capital – knowledge, creativity, innovativeness, and an ability to solve ill-defined, complex problems – as well as communication skills and a rich social network. All individuals function as part of larger systems, and what they can achieve is largely determined by the opportunities and constraints presented by those systems. The ability to take appropriate action, the ability to solve problems and cognitive development as a whole is dependent on the systems of which we are part. This chapter discusses scientific systems approaches and their links to research on adult thinking. Our aim is to work towards a deeper understanding of the development of adult thinking.

Systems thinking

The purpose of systems sciences is to model and understand different types of systems and the dynamics of the changes, feedback loops, and interactions happening within these systems. Kauffman (1995, p. 24) points out that life is not to be located in its parts, but in the collective emergent properties of the whole they create, that is, the whole is more than the sum of its parts. The concept of system thus refers to a holistic entity composed of and dependent on a series of interconnected and interacting parts. Systems may be physical, biological, abstract, social, or human. Systems thinking is not a uniform, fully integrated field of study, but rather a conceptual frame of reference. Its foundations lie in different systems theories that take a comprehensive and multidisciplinary view on exploring phenomena.

Systems thinking research is basically aimed at understanding phenomena in the systemic context and at applying that understanding to problem solving and learning, but it is more than that. Systems thinking has been described as a framework (Buckle Henning & Chen, 2012), a range of techniques or methods (Ackoff, Addison, & Carey, 2010; Checkland, 1999; Checkland & Poulter, 2006; Jackson, 2003; Stowell & Welch, 2012), and as a way of developing cognitive skills and abilities (Mella, 2012; Senge, 2006, p. 10). Furthermore, systemic understanding may be described in terms of systems intelligence (Hämäläinen, Jones, & Saarinen, 2014). In its broadest sense, systems thinking is seen as a philosophy or worldview (Capra, 2005; Capra & Luisi, 2014), or as an ethical code, identity, and a collective membership of a wider school of thought (Buckle Henning, Wilmshurst, & Yearworth, 2012).

In the systems framework the development of thinking has been described as a double loop learning process in which a narrow, short-sighted, and firmly established worldview evolves into a forward-looking, flexible, and dynamic view that recognises and acknowledges the bigger picture (Sterman, 2000, pp. 3–40). While learning that does not change mental models described as single loop learning, the deeper process of double loop learning has the potential to change the individual's or the community's thought models or actions (Argyris, 1977; Sterman, 2000, pp. 3–40)[1]. This kind of learning that changes mental models is often called conceptual change (Limón & Mason, 2002; see also Chapter 8). In studies of adult learning, these processes have been described by the concept of transformative learning (Mezirow, 1991). Critical reflection and the transformation of thought models are embraced by all major modern theories of learning, which in this sense come quite close to the latest modes of systems theories. Systems thinking is rarely adopted as an explicit starting point in learning research, but learning research shares many basic premises in common with systems thinking. For instance:

- Learning is approached not only as an individual cognitive process, but as a process happening in the complex interaction between individual and environment.
- Learning is seen as an all-embracing phenomenon composed of several systems with interconnected elements.
- Learning is not aimed at reproducing earlier, existing knowledge, but rather at effecting change in thinking or action, at creating or innovating new knowledge.

Systems thinking has addressed learning mainly through its focus on management and organisation research. Senge, known for his concept of the learning organisation, says that the development of systems thinking starts from changing mental models and worldviews by means of awareness and questioning (Goleman & Senge, 2014; Senge, 1990, 2006).

Towards systems theories

The roots of systems thinking lie in physics and the natural sciences. Ludvig von Bertalanffy, commonly acknowledged as the founder of the systems movement, was the first scholar to develop the concept outside the discipline of physics. Talcott Parsons, then, introduced systems thinking into sociology (e.g., Parsons, 1951), using system as an analytical tool for understanding social structures and the way they work. By the end of the 1950s, systemic thought had spread to almost all scientific disciplines. To coordinate the extremely heterogeneous field, the Society for General Systems Research was established in 1954 (Boulding, 1988, p. 33; Von Bertalanffy, 1972, p. 28).

Von Bertalanffy (e.g., 1950, 1968) advanced the concept of open system as a counterpart to the closed systems models that had been developed in the field of physics. Open systems are adaptive to their environment through feedback loops and strive to maintain a steady state. Von Bertalanffy was followed by several other scholars who rejected the former mechanistic view in favour of the organic nature of systems. One of the main trends in the American branch of systems thinking was system dynamics. This concept was developed by Forrester (e.g., 1968), who began to apply the insights of electrical engineering to analysing the behaviour of human and other systems. System dynamics thinking is where people live in a network of feedback structures (economic, political and ecological) whose properties are seen as the determinants of most problems (Bloomfield, 1986, p. viii). Direct or indirect applications of open systems thinking have produced many variations in the field (Ståhle, 1998, pp. 29–54).

In the 1960s a new systems thinking trend began to evolve that was not grounded in the open systems perspective, but which turned the focus to the unpredictable and chaotic behaviour of systems (instead of the steady state) and towards the unpredictable dynamics of systems (instead of feedback processes). This new viewpoint, which later became known as the "science of chaos" and/or "complexity research", evolved from the work of numerous scholars in different fields (Ståhle, 2008).

These trends led to a new research approach known as complexity theory (CT) or complex adaptive systems (CAS) theory (Holland, 1995; Kauffman, 1993; Mitchell, 2009; Poutanen & Ståhle, 2014). Although the two terms have been used interchangeably, CAS is possibly a more coherent strand of study, whereas "complexity theory" refers in general sense to the use of approaches and concepts derived from the study of complex systems. Complexity refers to phenomena like non-linear relationships, systemic interaction, boundary problems, emergence, and adaptation (Cilliers, 2011; Poutanen & Ståhle, 2014). The CT and CAS perspectives have been applied in many studies from organisational and management studies to public policy, health, communication, and engineering research (ibid.). CT originates in the natural sciences, but there is now a growing trend to study social organisations as CAS. Complex systems, such as the human brain, organisations or markets, are capable of adapting and responding to environmental changes and exhibiting self-organising, emergent patterns of behaviour (Poutanen, Soliman, & Ståhle, 2016; Poutanen & Ståhle, 2014; Ståhle & Åberg, 2015). Along with CT research, there has also been growing interest in *innovation ecosystems*, which refer to complexity and to the multifaceted co-creation of innovations and the role of virtual innovation platforms (Karakas, 2009).

Three systems paradigms

Systems have been studied from a variety of different perspectives. Over time the types of systems in focus have also varied, which has led to many different systems theories. Three paradigms can be identified in this development of systems research, as outlined below (for a full elaboration of the paradigms, see Ståhle, 1998, pp. 13–98).

The first presentation of a concrete system with scientifically verified laws was Isaac Newton's model of the solar system as put forward in his Principia (1687/ 1972), which created the foundation for the first systems paradigm. Since then, the Newtonian model has been applied to almost all scientific research. The Newtonian perspective to studying systems is characterised by linear thinking, cause-and-effect thinking, determinism, predictability, universal laws, principles and regularities, as well as preservation and quantification. The research conducted under this paradigm aims to explain and define natural laws and principles and to predict events conforming to the formulated theories. Ultimately, this perspective resulted in a theory that considered systems as machine-like entities following predetermined laws.

The second paradigm started from von Bertalanffy and his understanding of open systems. Systems were now no longer seen as machines but living organisms, and the perspective shifted from closeness to openness. While a closed, mechanistic system had just one optimal way of achieving its goal, an open system has access to multiple avenues. Open systems are flexible, self-regulating, and depend on their environment for survival. They are constantly striving towards equilibrium, as instability is hazardous to the system. Feedback is crucial: the system needs input, throughput, and output in order to maintain its stability (Von Bertalanffy, 1950). This research tradition has gained substantial ground since the 1950s and is still very popular today. Although the open systems view originates in biology, this hypothesis is theoretically grounded in physics: all open systems thinking stems from the second law of thermodynamics, which says that all systems, when left to themselves, are destined for disorder and disintegration. Since the system's survival is thought to require this steady state, maintaining stability is the primary focus of open systems thinking.

The third paradigm concentrates on dynamic, chaotic systems that are capable of self-organisation. While the focus was earlier on systemic order, the research emphasis has now shifted to disorder and to the relationship between chaos and the emergence of order. The starting point for the new emerging paradigm was Edward

Lorenz's chaos research and the famous "butterfly effect" (Lorenz, 1963), but the broadest theoretical contributions have come from two sources. First, Belgian physical chemist Ilya Prigogine published his studies on non-equilibrium statistical mechanics in 1962 and on dissipative systems in 1967. His studies provided systems research with a completely new perspective on how systems reorganise unpredictably and without external control. Prigogine does not contradict the second law of thermodynamics, but instead shows its limitations and argues that most systems are capable of self-organisation (see e.g., Prigogine, 1980). The other revolutionary approach was the autopoiesis theory put forward by Chilean biologists Humberto Maturana and Francisco Varela in the early 1970s. They introduced the term autopoiesis to describe how each living system reproduces its nucleus and struggles for self-renewal (see e.g., Maturana & Varela, 1980, 1992).

The third systems paradigm marked a fundamental break in the understanding of systems. The relationship of individual and system (every individual is always part of a system) and the internal dynamics of systems (self-organisation requires a chaotic state) were now seen in a new way. Theoretically, all these changes profoundly altered the starting point for systems sciences. This radical paradigm shift in the 1970s brought to light the extreme complexity of systems and the significance of chaos for the self-renewal and transformation of systems. This evolution towards quantum physics opened up a broader theoretical perspective with its emphasis on discontinuity, non-determinism, and non-locality.

These three systems paradigms highlight diverse characteristics and dimensions of systems. Although they date back to different eras, all three continue to have relevance today. Nonetheless they do differ in terms of their explanatory power. The third systems paradigm has particular explanatory power in today's volatile world where ecosystems and connectivity are created by the internet and virtual platforms. This does not mean to say it has universal applicability, however. We still have problems that can be well-defined and systems that are controllable and relatively stable. Furthermore, most real-life systems consist of various subsystems that can be closed, open, or dynamic. For instance, business organisations are usually system holograms, that is, simultaneously comprising of mechanistic, organic, and dynamic subsystems (Ståhle & Grönroos, 2000; Ståhle, Ståhle, & Pöyhönen, 2003). Recently, however, the dynamic systems paradigm has gained increasing prominence because of its substantial explanatory power, which at once has demonstrated the limitations of the other system paradigms (see Table 12.1).

Systems paradigms and adult thinking research

Systems paradigms have their roots in the natural sciences, and thus reflect the changes occurring in the academic realm as a whole, including theories of adult thinking. The dominating worldview and connected paradigms can be seen in different sciences, say in psychology and physics, despite the fact

TABLE 12.1 Systems theory paradigms with originators and some key dimensions (Ståhle, 1998, p. 63). Printed with permission. Copyright Faculty of Educational Sciences, University of Helsinki, Finland

Paradigm	Originator	Type of system	Research interest	Operative interest
I Closed systems	NEWTON	Static Deterministic Mechanistic	PRINCIPLES, LAWS	Predicting Controlling
II Open systems	von BERT- ALANFFY	Near Equilibrium Equifinal Living	FEEDBACK PROCESSES	Steering Sustaining
III Dynamic systems	LORENZ PRIGOGINE MATURANA VARELA	Far-from- equilibrium Uncontrollable Emerging	SPONTANEOUS ORGANIZATION	Understanding and cooperating with natural evolvement

that they have no direct interdependence. Scientific advances take place in a different historical period and are influenced by the overall tone and intellectual patterns of that period.

In the field of adult thinking research, Kallio (2015) says that almost all psychological theorisation can be traced to two theorists, Piaget and Perry. The first waves of model creation were based on Piaget's theory of formal thinking, while Perry's model of cognitive development paved the way to various new post-Piagetian models (in this book e.g., Chapters by 2, 3, 4, 11, and for the impact on moral reasoning theorisation, see Chapters 5, 6). For Piaget, formal operations represent the highest level of thinking that cannot be extended, while Perry and other neo-Piagetian scholars claimed that adult development is more complex phenomenon than assumed.

According to Kallio (2015), Perry redefined the study of adult cognition. The new line of research inquiry was first and foremost concerned with conceptual change (changing understandings of concepts and their meaning) as opposed to the Piagetian focus on operational-logical cognition. Perry was concerned with the development of epistemological assumptions in young adulthood, identity formation, and moral development. Neo-Piagetian research called into question the basic assumption of linearity and the endpoint of development, and prioritised logical thinking as the highest level of intellectual operations. This led to the introduction of a new, *postformal stage of thought*[2]: a type of complex logical thinking that develops in adulthood through interaction and co-creation with other people who have contradicting ideas. Other features of postformal thinking include contextualism, value relativism, recognition and management of uncertainty, complex problem solving, tolerance of ambiguity, and dialectics. Several new models of the development of adult thinking emerged, most notably by Mascolo and Fischer (2015), Commons, Gane-McCalla, Barker and Li (2014), Basseches (1984), Labouvie-Vief (2015), Kegan (1982, 1994), Sinnott (2011, 2013), and Kallio (2015).

Kallio (2015) offers some interesting reflections on Piaget's paradigmatic choices. First, she points out that the theory of developmental stages specifically concerns cause-and-effect reasoning regarding physical reality, and thus cannot be a universal theory of all cognitive development. In devising a theory of development for causal thinking, Piaget has used methodology applicable to the natural sciences, which indicates the points of departure of his studies and therefore also has implications for the results. Second, Piaget only uses so-called well-defined problems in his research settings, with no intermediate social or human variables in the testing situation that could enhance confusion in the reasoning process. Third, Piaget has a teleological assumption that the development of causal thinking has a final endpoint, and that this line of development does not allow any exceptions, different developmental routes, or other deterministic changes. One premise of Piaget's theory is that there is a *telos* towards which causal thinking inevitably proceeds. Fourth, Kallio points out that Piaget fails to address many crucial dimensions of adult thinking; for instance, he excludes from consideration problems with foggy premises or complex interdependencies that do not get solved by means of logical reasoning.

Kallio's critique against Piaget's theory clearly rises from the context of the dynamic systems paradigm. Despite the complexity of the phenomena he addressed, Piaget's choices are grounded in the closed mechanistic view of the first systems paradigm, such as the assumption that the development of causal thinking has a final endpoint. Perry's approach, then, incorporates dimensions from both the second systems paradigm with its more self-regulatory and open-ended emphases, and the third paradigm with its focus on complexity, self-transformability, contradictions, meanings, multifaceted reality, and interaction between people. Perry's work represents a clear paradigm shift from Piaget.

The third systems paradigm warrants closer scrutiny here, not only because it can help us understand the functional dynamics of the current world, but also because it is the most complex and chronologically the latest and therefore less well known. Furthermore, this is the most interesting paradigm from the point of view of adult thinking, since the theory of postformal thought, especially as presented by Sinnott (1998), is explicitly grounded in the dynamic systems paradigm. The next section describes the key theories behind the third systems paradigm and then looks at how the paradigm ties in with Sinnott's theory of postformal thought.

Dynamic systems paradigm: self-organising and self-referential systems

The Belgian Nobel laureate Prigogine (1917–2003) is possibly the single most important contributor to the dynamic systems paradigm. Prigogine was awarded the Nobel Prize in 1977 for his theory of dissipative structures. These are physical or chemical systems that appear to develop *order out of chaos*. Prigogine discovered new laws of nature that could connect the natural sciences to the human sciences, and he maintained that these laws were valid and applicable to social systems as well (Prigogine, 1976, pp. 120–126).

Another perspective on systems self-renewal was opened by Chilean biology professors Humberto Maturana (1928–) and Francisco Varela (1946–2001), who introduced the concept of autopoiesis to describe the self-generating, self-maintaining structure of living systems. As early as the 1980s, autopoiesis was recognised as part of the new emerging paradigm that addressed issues of self-organisation and spontaneous phenomena in physical, biological, and social systems (Zeleny, 1980). The main contribution of Maturana's and Varela's research lies in their addressing the question of cognition and knowledge at cell level: they were not just biologists, but also cognition scientists. The most relevant theoretical expansion of autopoiesis in the field of sociology is attributable to Niklas Luhmann (1927–1998) and his theory of self-referential systems. Luhmann is recognised as one of the most important social theorists of the 20th century (Bechmann & Stehr, 2002).

Self-organising systems

Prigogine (1993) maintains that most systems in the world are liable to proceed to the state of far-from-equilibrium, and therefore are inherently capable of re-organising and transforming themselves. These self-organising systems share some features in common with open systems, including feedback loops and dependence on the environment, but they nonetheless function in a radically different way. Open systems are characterised as self-regulating and as having the ability to maintain stability via continuous feedback processes. Chaos is seen as an end and dispersion. In contrast to this view, Prigogine pointed out that rather than an end, chaos marks a new beginning. Indeed, new structures are created out of chaos. Even though this is by no means rare and most systems are self-organising, there are certain preconditions that must be met. Based on Prigogine's publications, Ståhle (1998) lists the following requirements for self-organising systems:

- *State of far from equilibrium*: unstable, chaotic state of a system. In social systems this means tolerance to confusion, discrepancies, and disharmony.
- *Production of entropy*: information that cannot be used by the system. High entropy means greater disorder, wasted resources, lost information, and uncertainty in the system. For a social system this means abundant communication and production of ideas, different angles of information without any certainty as to whether they will prove useful.
- *Iteration*: frequent and sensitive feedback that provides the system with ultimate receptivity. In a social system this means active response to each other's ideas, opinions and reactions.

- *Momentums of bifurcation*: there are certain momentums in the system's life when genuine choices can be made. These choices are irreversible and cannot be predicted in advance. "Bifurcation is a source of innovation and diversification, since it endows a system with a new solution." (Nicolis & Prigogine, 1989, p. 74)

Autopoiesis and self-referential systems

Maturana and Varela take a very different perspective from Prigogine. While Prigogine emphasises the creation of order out of chaos, the dramatic emergence of a new structure, Maturana and Varela highlight the role of continuity, maintenance, and self-reference in the system's renewal.

Autopoiesis is based on the idea of self-reference, which means that "what we see is always a reflection of what we are". In the social realm, this means that whoever prescribes the borders or nature of a system must necessarily be part of the system. Information about a system can only be achieved from within: to understand the system we must be part of it, and being part of the system occurs via interaction and communication. Interaction, in turn, is not possible without self-reference: for instance, a person (or a group, organisation, etc.) who has no reference to it/herself/himself cannot be in authentic interaction with others. Thus, the dynamics of an autopoietic system is described by the system's boundaries (i.e., to become aware of the system), self-reference (becoming aware of oneself), and interaction (restructuring and strengthening both of the previous) (Varela & Johnson, 1976, p. 31).

The autopoietic system has a special relationship with its environment (see Figure 12.1). On the one hand, it needs the environment to keep up its life, but on the other hand, in an operative sense, the system is autonomic. The environment is

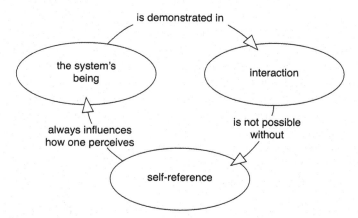

FIGURE 12.1 A system's autopoietic nature (Ståhle, 1998, p. 102). Printed with permission. Copyright Faculty of Educational Sciences, University of Helsinki, Finland

a *point of reference* for an autopoietic system, a kind of a mirror (Maturana & Varela, 1988, p. 75). It might even be described as a negative mirror, telling the system what it is *not*. The creation of a core identity is the main principle and ultimate goal of the system, be it an individual, group, or organisation. All social systems are self-referential, because the system must always define itself in order to be able to exist (Varela & Johnson, 1976, pp. 26–31).

The work of Luhmann represents the most significant application of autopoiesis to a social context. Sociologist Knodt observes that Luhmann's "Social Systems accomplishes in the social realm what Maturana and Varela have done for cognitive biology and Prigogine's work on non-equilibrium thermodynamics for physics" (Luhmann, 1995, p. xxii). Luhmann argues that the theory of autopoietic social systems requires a conceptual revolution within sociology, and also contains an understanding of communication as a particular mode of autopoietic reproduction (Luhmann, 1989, pp. 174, 177–178). Luhmann stresses the immutable identity of the system, that is, the system's capacity to continuously renew its identifiable self, as well as the continuity or the process-like development of a system. Based on Luhmann's work it is possible to identify the following four vital antecedents for a system's self-renewal (Ståhle, 1998, p. 111):

- *Self-reference* means that a system must be in connection with other systems and use them as a point of reference for itself. This is not a process of adaptation, but rather the use of another system as a mirror in order to create self-awareness and strengthen identity: to recognise similarities and differences between others and self, i.e., what it is and what it is not.
- *Double contingency* means positive, mutual interdependence, balance of power, and trust within the system. The people who make up the system are *of equal value* (however, there is no imperative to *have similar values*).
- *Experiential quality of information*. The system's power of renewal lies in the exchange of information. However, it is important to make a distinction between data and information. The latter is closely linked with experience: the information exchanged *influences* the people who make up the system and always changes the state of the system, in one way or another. Luhmann describes information as an event more than a fact.
- *Processing meanings*. Luhmann says that meanings are created collectively within the system through mutually created events. Meanings are the basic structural elements of a self-referential system and guide its functioning.

Next, we proceed to reflect on how all this ties in with the development of adult thinking by exploring Sinnott's theory of postformal thought.

Theory of postformal thought

Sinnott sees the development of thinking as part of the holistic and complex process of human development. It is reflected in wisdom, interpersonal skills, concern for others, spirituality, and an ability to deal with paradoxes. She describes how adult individuals construct their own identities and realities and how this has an impact on their cognitive functions. Meaning and intention form a prominent part of adult life. However, Sinnott points out that we lack studies of higher-level intellectual operations that are required when adults make sense of life and process its meaning. For the holistic challenges of adult life, abstract, formal logics do not work without linkage with emotional, interpersonal, and spiritual aspects. Problems in adult life are most often obscure, and problem-solving is therefore a multidimensional process involving a close interplay of cognitive, emotional, and social processes. Our impact on the evolving systems in which we are involved is permanently transformative for ourselves and other systems. We are neither victims nor outsiders, but instead team members helping design it all. Thus, she says, there is a need not only for new paths of research, but also *for new theoretical paradigms*. She suggests the new physics theory, systems theories, complexity theory, and self-regulating systems theories as prominent frameworks for research into modern adult thinking (Sinnott, 1998, pp. 14–33, 1981, p. 110).

Sinnott says that rather than just the individual's development and connection with the physical world, our research should be concerned with an individual's *interaction* with other developing individuals. This view of social interaction is far more complex than the framework applied in earlier behavioural sciences, she adds, and has implications for understanding social development, emotional growth, and group dynamics, for instance (Sinnott, 1981, p. 301).

Sinnott elaborates the theoretical background of her thinking in great depth, and lays bare the false assumptions of current research. She describes with clarity and precision her new proposed path and argues that the development of adult thinking must be anchored to the elements that guide adult life, that is, meaning, identity, and intention. These can be seen as the determinants of adult development to which cognitive operations are subordinate, and therefore adult thinking *must be studied in this context* rather than seeking to solve predefined problems. Her theorising is surprisingly identical with the three systems paradigms described earlier, and in contrast to most other behavioural scientists she explicitly states her theoretical grounds and anchors her theory to the third systems paradigm.

Sinnott (1998, pp. 23–52) summarises her view on the development of adult thinking and argues that postformal thinking

- is unique to major adult thought and thus exceeds Piaget's theory;
- includes various truth systems, multiple conflicting ideas and uncertainty as a driver;

- is higher-level thinking, although all other levels are also purposefully in use;
- is developed through interaction with other knowers, through social interactions, and co-created by people in those interactions;
- has an impact on one's view of self, the world, other persons, change over time, and our connections with one another over time;
- is complex cognition, a bridge between affect and cognition, between one person and other persons, and a way to make the demands and practical concerns of adult life meaningful;
- refers to knowledge as a subjective component being necessarily incomplete, because any logic we use is self-referential logic (the higher-level postformal system of self-referential truth decisions gives order to lower-level formal truth and logic systems).

The theory of postformal thought has been developed both on the basis of the general systems theory and the theories under the third paradigm, especially chaos and complexity theories and the theory of self-organising systems, and the views on self-renewing systems and postformal thought overlap in significant respects (Table 12.2).

TABLE 12.2 Comparison of the characteristics of self-renewing systems and postformal thought (page references to Sinnott (1998) in parentheses)

Key characteristics of self-organizing and self-referential systems	Requirements of self-renewal of social systems	Assumptions of the theory of postformal thought (Sinnott, 1998)
System's state far from equilibrium	Tolerance to confusion, discrepancies, and disharmony.	Uncertainty is a driver developed through interaction with other knowers. Disorder, potential, unstructuredness are necessary requirements (204).
Production of entropy	Abundant communication and production of ideas, different angles of information without any certainty as to whether they will prove to be useful.	Postformal thinking needs awareness that there are various truth systems, and that contradiction, subjectivity, and choice are inherent in all objective observations and solutions (24).
Iteration	Active and frequent response to each other's ideas, opinions, and reactions.	
Momentums of bifurcation	Momentums in the system's life when genuine choices can be	Chaos theory explains why development of thinking is not

(Continued)

TABLE 12.2 (Cont.)

Key characteristics of self-organizing and self-referential systems	Requirements of self-renewal of social systems	Assumptions of the theory of postformal thought (Sinnott, 1998)
	made. Bifurcation is a source of innovation and diversification, since it endows a system with a new solution.	linear but often happens by leaps (108).
Self-reference	System must interact with other systems and use them as a point of reference for itself: reflection of existence, identity, and boundaries.	The essential notion of self-reference is that we can never be completely free of the built-in limits of our system of knowing (32). Systems construct their own realities, and for this they need to interact with other systems (204).
Double contingency	Mutual interdependence, power balance, and trust within the system. Everyone is of equal value and positively dependent on each other.	
Experiential information	Exchange of information is the system's renewing power. Information must have influence on others and thus it always changes the state of the system.	Complex cognition is a bridge between affect and cognition, and between one person and other persons (52). Cognitive development is dependent on social-cognitive experience; the ideas of others challenge the reality of the knower (27, 28).
Processing meanings	Meanings are created collectively within the system through jointly created events.	Postformal thinking is about making sense of life (26). Making demands and practical concerns of adult life meaningful occurs by co-creation by people in interactions (27).

Conclusions

In this chapter we have briefly discussed some dimensions of systems thinking and the development of systems theories. In addition, we have reflected on the links between systems theories and modern research into adult thinking. As we have seen, both organisational-level research and models of the learning organisation have widely adopted the premises of the open systems paradigm and modified their concept apparatuses for learning. By contrast, it seems that systems theories rarely serve as a generic starting point for learning research, although there are some individual studies that are clearly grounded in systems thinking. However, we have also shown that some models describing adult thinking have a clearly articulated link with systems theories. In particular, Sinnott's theory of postformal thought explicitly leans on the third systems paradigm.

Several interesting research questions that would shed light on the interconnections between thinking and learning still remain unanswered, including whether learning about systems sciences and systems theories can help develop our thinking. Sinnott presents a number of examples and case studies of the development of adult thinking as an empirical basis for her theory. However, the unit of analysis in these studies is always the *individual thinking process*, while the basic unit of analysis in systems research (Luhmann, 1995, p. 123; Ståhle, 1998) is *communication between individuals*. Even though Sinnott's premises and paradigm are clearly systemic, her empirical research still focuses on individuals.

In order to create cross-fertilisation between research on adult thinking and systems science, the next step would be to explore the individual thinking process in conjunction with the collective knowledge creation process. Systems theories would thus not just provide a background for understanding the nature of adult thinking, but thinking could also be studied in the actual social (complex) context, within a system. On the other hand, the individual thinking perspective is completely absent in studies on the self-renewal of systems. A genuine merger of research perspectives might lead to the discovery that systems thinking can only be learned within the system, and not as an isolated piece of knowledge picked up from a textbook or teacher; and furthermore, that self-renewal might not take place in groups that do not have the capacity for formal or postformal thinking. This could surely add to our insight about the required pedagogical methods and collective learning processes or know-how of coping in innovation ecosystems. It seems that postformal or complex adult thought has opened up new understandings, but it still remains for future research to implement them in research settings and methodologies. We hope that this article provides inspiration for such efforts.

Notes

1 Expressed in terms of cognitive development psychology (Piaget, 1950/2002), single loop learning is about assimilation, a process in which new knowledge is added to existing knowledge, whereas double loop learning refers to accommodation, a process in which earlier knowledge structures are adjusted according to new experiences and new knowledge (cf. Chapters 2, 3).
2 Researchers don't agree about the usage of the concept (see e.g., Kallio, 2011).

References

Ackoff, R. L., Addison, H. J., & Carey, A. (2010). *Systems thinking for curious managers: With 40 new management f-Laws.* Axminster, England: Triarchy Press.
Argyris, C. (1977). Double loop learning in organizations. *Harvard Business Review, 55*(5), 115–125.

Basseches, M. (1984). *Dialectical thinking and adult development* (Publications for the advancement of theory and history in psychology No. 3). Norwood, NJ: Ablex.

Bechmann, G., & Stehr, N. (2002). The legacy of Niklas Luhmann. *Society, 39*(2), 67–75.

Bloomfield, B. P. (1986). *Modelling the world: The social constructions of systems analysts.* Oxford, England: Blackwell.

Boulding, K. E. (1988). Systems: Some origins. In W. J. Reckmayer (Ed.), *General systems* (Vol. 31, pp. 31–38). New York, NY: ISSS.

Buckle Henning, P., & Chen, W.-C. (2012). Systems thinking: Common ground or untapped territory? *Systems Research and Behavioral Science, 29*(5), 470–483.

Buckle Henning, P., Wilmshurst, J., & Yearworth, M. (2012). Understanding systems thinking: An agenda for applied research in industry. In *Proceedings of the 56th Annual Meeting of the ISSS – 2012*, San Jose, CA, USA.

Capra, F. (2005). Speaking nature's language: Principles for sustainability. In M. K. Stone & Z. Barlow (Eds.), *Ecological literacy: Educating our children for a sustainable world* (Bioneers series, pp. 18–29). San Francisco, CA: Sierra Club Books.

Capra, F., & Luisi, P. L. (2014). *The systems view of life: A unifying vision.* Cambridge, England: Cambridge University Press.

Checkland, P. (1999). *Systems thinking, systems practice: Includes a 30-year retrospective.* Chichester, England: Wiley.

Checkland, P., & Poulter, J. (2006). *Learning for action: A short definitive account of soft systems methodology and its use for practitioners, teachers and students.* Hoboken, NJ: Wiley.

Cilliers, P. (2011). Complexity, poststructuralism and organization. In P. Allen, S. Maguire, & B. McKelvey (Eds.), *The SAGE handbook of complexity and management* (pp. 142–154). Los Angeles, CA: SAGE.

Commons, M. L., Gane-McCalla, R., Barker, C., & Li, E. Y. (2014). The model of hierarchical complexity as a measurement system. *Behavioral Development Bulletin, 19*(3), 9–14.

Forrester, J. (1968). *Principles of systems: Text and workbook: Chapters 1 through 10* (2nd ed.). Cambridge, MA: Wright-Allen Press.

Goleman, D., & Senge, P. (2014). *The triple focus: A new approach to education.* Florence, MA: More Than Sound.

Hämäläinen, R. P., Jones, R., & Saarinen, E. (2014). *Being better better: Living with systems intelligence* (Aalto University Publications Crossover No. 4/2014). Espoo, Finland: Aalto University.

Holland, J. H. (1995). *Hidden order: How adaptation builds complexity* (Helix books). Reading, MA: Addison-Wesley.

Jackson, M. C. (2003). *Systems thinking: Creative holism for managers.* Chichester, England: Wiley.

Kallio, E. (2011). Integrative thinking is the key: An evaluation of current research into the development of adult thinking. *Theory & Psychology, 21*(6), 785–801.

Kallio, E. (2015). From causal thinking to wisdom and spirituality: Some perspectives on a growing research field in adult (cognitive) development. *Approaching Religion, 5*(2), 27–41.

Karakas, F. (2009). Welcome to world 2.0: The new digital ecosystem. *Journal of Business Strategy, 30*(4), 23–30. doi:10.1108/02756660910972622

Kauffman, S. (1995). *At home in the universe: The search for laws of self-organization and complexity.* New York, NY: Oxford University Press.

Kauffman, S. A. (1993). *The origins of order: Self-organization and selection in evolution.* New York, NY: Oxford University Press.

Kegan, R. (1982). *The evolving self: Problem and process in human development.* Cambridge, MA: Harvard University Press.

Kegan, R. (1994). *In over our heads: The mental demands of modern life.* Cambridge, MA: Harvard University Press.

Labouvie-Vief, G. (2015). *Integrating emotions and cognition throughout the lifespan.* New York, NY: Springer.

Limón, M., & Mason, L. (Eds.). (2002). *Reconsidering conceptual change: Issues in theory and practice.* Dordrecht, the Netherlands: Kluwer Academic.

Lorenz, E. N. (1963). Deterministic nonperiodic flow. *Journal of the Atmospheric Sciences, 20*(2), 130–141.

Luhmann, N. (1989). *Ecological communication* (J. Bednarz Jr., Trans.). Cambridge, England: Polity Press.

Luhmann, N. (1995). *Social systems* (J. Bednarz & D. Baecker, Trans.) (Writing science). Stanford, CA: Stanford University Press.

Mascolo, M. F., & Fischer, K. W. (2015). Dynamic development of thinking, feeling, and acting. In W. F. Overton, P. C. M. Molenaar, & R. M. Lerner (Eds.), *Handbook of child psychology and developmental science: Volume 1: Theory and method* (pp. 113–161). Hoboken, NJ: Wiley.

Maturana, H. R., & Varela, F. J. (1980). *Autopoiesis and cognition: The realization of the living* (Boston Studies in the Philosophy of Science, Vol. 42). Dordrecht, the Netherlands: Reidel.

Maturana, H. R., & Varela, F. J. (1988). *The tree of knowledge: The biological roots of human understanding.* Boston, MA: Shambhala.

Maturana, H. R., & Varela, F. J. (1992). *The tree of knowledge: The biological roots of human understanding.* Boston, MA: Shambhala.

Mella, P. (2012). *Systems thinking: Intelligence in action* (Perspectives in Business Culture, Vol. 2). Milano, Italy: Springer Milan.

Mezirow, J. (1991). *Transformative dimensions of adult learning* (Jossey-Bass higher and adult education series). San Francisco, CA: Jossey-Bass.

Mitchell, M. (2009). *Complexity: A guided tour.* New York, NY: Oxford University Press.

Newton, I. (1972). *Philosophiae naturalis principia mathematica: Vol. 1: The third edition (1726) with variant readings* [Mathematical principles of natural philosophy] (A. Koyré & B. Cohen, Trans.). Cambridge, MA: Cambridge University Press. (Original work published 1687).

Nicolis, G., & Prigogine, I. (1989). *Exploring complexity: An introduction.* New York, NY: W. H. Freeman.

Parsons, T. (1951). *The social system.* Glencoe, IL: Free Press.

Piaget, J. (2002). *The psychology of intelligence* (M. Piercy & D. E. Berlyne, Trans.) (Routledge classics). London, England: Routledge. (Original work published 1947).

Poutanen, P., Soliman, W., & Ståhle, P. (2016). The complexity of innovation: An assessment and review of the complexity perspective. *European Journal of Innovation Management, 19*(2), 189–213.

Poutanen, P. K., & Ståhle, P. (2014). Creativity in short-term self-directed groups: An analysis using a complexity-based framework. *International Journal of Complexity in Leadership and Management, 2*(4), 259–277.

Prigogine, I. (1976). Order through fluctuation: Self-organization and social system. In E. Jantsch & C. H. Waddington (Eds.), *Evolution and consciousness: Human systems in transition* (pp. 93–130). Reading, MA: Addison-Wesley.

Prigogine, I. (1980). *From being to becoming: Time and complexity in the physical sciences.* San Francisco, CA: Freeman.

Prigogine, I. (1993). Time, dynamics and chaos: Integrating poincare's 'non-integrable systems'. In J. Holte (Ed.), *Chaos: The new science* (Nobel Conference No. 26, pp. 55–88). Lanham, MD: University Press of America.

Senge, P. M. (1990). The leader's new work: Building learning organizations. *Sloan Management Review, 32*(1), 7–23.

Senge, P. M. (2006). *The fifth discipline: The art and practice of the learning organization* (Rev ed.). (Currency books). New York, NY: Currency Doubleday.

Sinnott, J. D. (1981). The theory of relativity: A metatheory for development? *Human Development, 24*(5), 293–311.

Sinnott, J. D. (1998). *The development of logic in adulthood: Postformal thought and its applications* (The Plenum series in adult development and aging). New York, NY: Plenum Press.

Sinnott, J. D. (2011). Constructing the self in the face of aging and death: Complex thought and learning. In C. Hoare (Ed.), *The Oxford handbook of reciprocal adult development and learning* (Oxford library of psychology, 2nd ed., pp. 248–264). New York, NY: Oxford University Press.

Sinnott, J. D. (Ed.). (2013). *Positive psychology: Advances in understanding adult motivation.* New York, NY: Springer New York.

Ståhle, P. (1998). *Supporting a system's capacity for self-renewal* (Doctoral dissertation, University of Helsinki, Department of Teacher Education, Helsinki, Finland).

Ståhle, P. (2008). The dynamics of self-renewal: A systems-thinking to understanding organizational challenges in dynamic environments. In A. Bounfour (Ed.), *Organisational capital: Modelling, measuring and contextualising* (Routledge Studies in Innovation, Organizations and Technology, pp. 1–26). London, England: Routledge.

Ståhle, P., & Åberg, L. (2015). Organizations in a non-linear, unpredictable world. *Business and Management Studies, 1*(1), 6–12. doi:10.11114/bms.v1i1.667

Ståhle, P., & Grönroos, M. (2000). *Dynamic intellectual capital – Knowledge management in theory and practice.* Helsinki, Finland: WSOY.

Ståhle, P., Ståhle, S., & Pöyhönen, A. (2003). *Analyzing dynamic intellectual capital: System-based theory and application* (Acta Universitatis Lappeenrantaensis No. 152). Lappeenranta, Finland: Lappeenranta University of Technology.

Sterman, J. D. (2000). *Business dynamics: Systems thinking and modeling for a complex world* (Tmhe Ie Overruns). Boston, MA: McGraw-Hill.

Stowell, F. A., & Welch, C. (2012). *The manager's guide to systems practice: Making sense of complex problems.* Chichester, England: Wiley.

Varela, F. J., & Johnson, D. (1976). On observing natural systems. *CoEvolution Quarterly, 10*, 26–31.

Von Bertalanffy, L. (1950). An outline of general system theory. *The British Journal for the Philosophy of Science, 1*(2), 134–165.

Von Bertalanffy, L. (1968). *General system theory: Foundations, development, applications.* New York, NY: George Braziller.

Von Bertalanffy, L. (1972). The history and status of general systems theory. In G. J. Klir (Ed.), *Trends in general systems theory* (pp. 21–41). New York, NY: Wiley.

Zeleny, M. (1980). Autopoiesis: A paradigm lost? In M. Zeleny (Ed.), *Autopoiesis, dissipative structures, and spontaneous social orders* (AAAS Selected Symposium No. 55, pp. 3–43). Boulder, CO: Westview Press.

13

LOGICAL CONTRADICTION, CONTRARY OPPOSITES, AND EPISTEMOLOGICAL RELATIVISM

Critical philosophical reflections on the psychological models of adult cognitive development[1]

Miira Tuominen and Eeva K. Kallio

Introduction

In recent decades, there has been a dominant tendency within psychological research to explain adult cognitive development by reference to some general notions and distinctions that are also central in philosophy such as epistemological relativism, deontological ethics, determinism and indeterminism, logical contradiction, and two-valued as opposed to many-valued logic. Although developmental models based on a strict division of distinct stages and phases are not unanimously accepted, youthful immature cognition is often distinguished from adult, mature cognition (Hoare, 2011; Kallio, 2001, 2011, 2015). More recently, this tendency has also, to some extent, given way to discussions about wisdom as a mature psychological achievement (Baltes & Staudinger, 2000; Curnow, 1999; Edmondson, 2015; Trowbridge, 2011; Trowbridge & Ferrari, 2011).

In this contribution, we shall first argue that the notions of epistemological relativism and tolerance to logical contradiction, even acceptance of many-valued logic, are not successful in explaining mature adult cognition, as viewed from a philosophical point of view. Rather, mature adult cognition should be characterised as the capacity to *integrate* distinct and diverse elements into one's own cognitive, emotional, and action systems or perspectives (Kallio, 2011, 2016; see also Cavanaugh & Blanchard-Fields, 2014, p. 203 "integrated relativistic-dialectical thinking"). This, as we shall argue, does not mean simple acceptance of everyone's beliefs as true but refers rather to understanding the other person's point of view, emotional state, and the background from which his/her beliefs have been formed. Finally, when such an integrative outlook is cultivated into the capacity of understanding views that are rather different from one's own, with the capacity to form one's own view based on such integration, such an outlook on the world starts to resemble (but is not identical with) what today is described as the cognitive component of wisdom (Grossmann, 2017).

Below we shall first consider the more distinctly cognitive elements in mature adult thinking through a philosophical critique of the central notions of developmental psychology. Then we shall argue that philosophical critique of some core notions of the earlier theories and models leads to a more accurate description of adult cognition as integration.[2]

Our aim is to clarify how the philosophical analysis of logic, knowledge, and beliefs differs from the one of developmental psychology. In a nutshell, while developmental psychology mainly focuses on empirical descriptions of the ways of in which people think and how their thinking develops, philosophical logic pertains to analysing the logical validity of inferences and arguments. If people have contradictory beliefs or make erroneous inferences, this does not have direct consequences for philosophical logic. Similarly, philosophical epistemology in its current standard form[3] focuses on the analysis of the concept of knowledge, its necessary and sufficient conditions, and this is typically quite far from the ways in which the notion of knowledge is used in ordinary language. This means that often the subject matters of philosophical analysis differ from that of developmental psychology: philosophical logic is concerned with logical validity while developmental psychology studies thinking in empirical subjects. However, even when the subject matter is partly the same – philosophers can of course be concerned with thinking as well – the approaches differ. To simplify, for developmental psychologists it is vital to find out how subjects use certain terms and how they think, and thinking is understood very broadly as referring to mental operations on a wide spectrum from sensations and perceptions to emotions, dreaming, and the use of concepts. Philosophers, by contrast, are focused more on the ways in which the notions should be used to preserve clarity and consistency and what kind of different mental operations should be distinguished and on what grounds.

We shall argue that, from the philosophical perspective, two central features of adult mature cognition can be traced: (i) the cognitive ability to see beyond simplified dichotomies,[4] and (ii) an attitude towards one's own beliefs that recognises the evidence and justification for them while allowing that a better, more detailed and accurate view is possible.[5] Such an attitude also recognises that we do not necessarily know how things are without falling into cynical skepticism or "anything goes" sort of relativism. With respect to point (i), youthful cognition can to an extent be characterised by a tendency to see stark oppositions and exhaustive dichotomies, while mature adult cognition means an ability to see that such dichotomies are not necessarily exhaustive. We shall also suggest that often this means a simple distinction, introduced by Aristotle (trans. 1984),[6] between contrary and contradictory opposites, in which contrary opposites (such as good and bad) do not exhaust the logical domain (something can be neutral), while contradictory opposites (good and not good) do so. A youthful attitude towards one's own beliefs or the beliefs taught by some authority (ii) can be described as certainty and dogmatism, whereas mature adults rather understand that it is possible to see matters differently, be mistaken in one's conceptions, or that authorities are not necessarily right or omniscient.

Problems in describing adult cognitive development: philosophical reflections

Adult thinking as development from absolutism to relativistic thinking

The discussion about adult cognitive development in psychology typically refers to Perry's longitudinal study (1970) in which white male university students were interviewed about their conceptions of knowledge and how it is attained. In the study, the researchers monitored the change in students' conceptions of knowledge (and ethics) (Perry, 1970). The central result was that while young students had rather unreserved confidence in the truth of what they learned in class, when they matured they came to think that perhaps all that was taught was not true and started to trust their own abilities to critically evaluate the results, theories and models that they learned. On the basis of the findings, Perry proposed nine distinct levels of knowledge formation, and important notions used to describe them include the following: dualism, multiplicity, and commitment to relativism (see also Chapter 3).

These findings have often been taken to support the claim that when the students learned more and got older, they became epistemological relativists. Another formulation is that first the students believed that there is only one truth and later became relativists about the truth. The mature way of thinking that the students allegedly reached is also often described as being dialectical. The term has various uses in the philosophical tradition, but in the context of developmental psychology it means the students' ability to create a synthesis of contradictory theses and antitheses, which also amounts to the ability to create a stable identity in the midst of multiple perspectives and views. Thus, it is claimed that, in the final phase, contradictions are overcome and mature adults use what is called "dialectical logic" in the context (e.g., Basseches, 1984).

Perry's research is a study within the developmental psychological branch of epistemology which, despite the similarity of its name, is distinct from philosophical epistemology. Other models similar to Perry's have also been proposed, and some general characteristics of them synthesised (e.g., Kramer, 1983) (see Chapter 3 and 4 on different models). Kramer's formulations bear a terminological resemblance to descriptions of relativism in philosophical epistemology and, as mentioned, the term "dialectic" that is often used in the psychological studies has many technical uses in philosophy. Therefore, it is necessary to analyse what exactly is meant by the notions used in the discussion.

In the following, we will first focus on the concept of relativism as it is formulated in Kramer's analysis. It will be argued that a notion of relativism that resembles philosophical epistemological relativism is too vague to capture the core of the studied phenomenon, adult cognitive development. In section 2.3, a similar argument is made about logical contradiction as it appears in the descriptions of dialectical thinking in developmental psychology. In section 2.5, we argue that a philosophically more accurate description with more clearly defined terms can be given in terms of integration. As a whole, section 2 concentrates on arguing why a philosophical analysis of the central notions of psychological studies in the cognitive development of adults is vital for understanding the nature of this debated phenomenon.[7]

Philosophical and psychological epistemology

Epistemology as a branch of philosophy (*PhilEp*) and in its standard form in the latter half of the 20th century involves discussions about the necessary and sufficient conditions of knowledge, its definition, and the reliability of cognitive processes. By contrast, Perry and numerous scholars following him (such as Hofer & Pintrich, 1997; Baxter Magolda, 2004; Schommer-Aikins, 2004; Kuhn & Weinstock, 2002; King & Kitchener, 2004, and others), work in a tradition of psychological epistemology (*PsyEp*) within which, like in philosophical epistemology as well, different views are presented by different scholars. As mentioned, the results of the *PsyEp* studies – especially Perry's (1970) – concern the attitudes of empirically studied groups of students towards their own views about knowledge. From a philosophical point of view, such results do not directly show how knowledge should be analysed and what conditions one should lay out for something to be knowledge. In this section, the basic notions of philosophical epistemology will be elucidated in a standard form that can be found in introductions to 20th-century Western philosophical epistemology. The *Stanford Encyclopedia of Philosophy*, for instance, contains easily accessible articles, references to which are given in the endnotes with respect to the themes discussed in the body text.

In the late 20th century, philosophical epistemology broadly speaking focused on debating a notion of knowledge that is characterised by three conditions:

(KB):   Knowledge is a form of belief.
(TB):   Knowledge is true belief.
(W):   A true belief that counts as knowledge must be *warranted*, i.e., it must be justified either directly by being self-evident or by a non-inferential cognitive process, or through valid inference from other justified beliefs.[8]

Philosophers have different views on how exactly beliefs can be justified (i.e., warranted). One useful distinction is the one mentioned in the formulation of principle (W) above: beliefs can be justified directly through a cognitive process such as perception, or they can be justified through valid inference from other (directly or indirectly) justified beliefs. Typically, some logical principles are also included in the category of justified beliefs. Therefore, if one asks for the justification of my belief that there is a computer screen in front of me, many philosophers agree that the fact that I perceive a computer screen in front of me is sufficient to justify the claim. It is important to note, however, that justification is distinct from truth. Therefore, although my belief that there is a computer in front of me can be justified by reference to my perceiving it, my perception does not make my belief true. We can imagine some optical illusion or mirrors, for example, that create the impression that the screen is there although it in fact is not.

It is also important to note that, in the context of philosophical epistemology, a belief does not mean religious belief or faith but rather that someone takes something to be the case. If person a has a belief that p, a takes p to be true. Here a stands for an individual person and p for a proposition or statement, such as "the earth moves", "it is raining", or "justice is good". Therefore, I have a belief that it is raining (in place x at time t) when I take it to be true that it is raining in place x at time t. A proposition or statement (p) as the object of belief is expressed in natural language as an indicative sentence, as opposed to questions, prayers, exclamations, confessions, and so on.

To see why $PsyEp$'s results do not have direct implications for the analysis of knowledge in the philosophical framework, we need to articulate one more principle.

(BNIT) A believes that p does not imply that p is true.

This principle can, in brief, be articulated as the obvious claim that belief does not imply truth.[9] From the fact that a believes p to be the case, it does not follow that p is the case. For example, if I believe (i.e., take it to be the case) that it is raining in Finland at place x a certain moment of time (t), it does not follow that it is raining in Finland at place x at time t. Whether my belief is true or not, depends on whether it is actually raining in Finland at that place and that moment or not.

This is relevant for the results of $PsyEp$ studies for the following reason. For example, Perry's study concerns how students answer the questions about what they think (i.e., take to be the case) about the truth of what they learn in class. The result is that first students believed (i.e. took it to be the case) that what they learn at the university is true. Based on the principle explicated above (BNIT), this does not imply that what they learn at the university is true. Whether the contents taught are true or not, depends on how things are, not on whether students believe them to be true or not. Similarly, when the students become more critical towards university teaching, this does not make the contents taught change from true to false (or vice versa). If I stop believing that it is raining at place x at time t, my change of belief does not stop the rain.

In addition, it is worth pointing out that truth in the sense that it is used in philosophical epistemology does not come in degrees. Something can be more *like* the truth, *closer* to the truth, or more *likely* (i.e. more probable), but these are degrees of truth-likeness or probability, not of truth as such. Therefore, Perry's study (1970) and the studies of the scholars belonging to the same tradition do *not* show that university teaching would become *less true* as the students' confidence in it diminishes. It shows that the students' confidence in the truth of what is being taught to them diminishes and they start to have greater trust in their own critical ability to distinguish between what is true and what is not.

Dialectical thinking

The notion of dialectical thinking has a long history both in the Eastern and Western cultural traditions (and perhaps in other cultures as well) and in philosophy (Spencer-Rodgers & Peng, 2018). However, there is no one definition of what exactly it is. Although as a philosophical term of art, "dialectical" goes back to Plato (trans. 1997) and Aristotle (trans. 1984)[10], the first person to use the term "dialectical thinking" as a form of adult cognitive development in psychology was Riegel (1973, 1976). His view was a counter-reaction to Piaget's (1976) theory and based on observing limitations to describing cognitive progress in adulthood with a two-valued logical system. Riegel maintains that there are certain dialectical tendencies in Piaget's theory, referring to the role of contradictions and internal play of assimilation and accommodation in knowledge formation (Piaget, 1976). However, Piaget's theory is, according to Riegel, metaphorically a *Homo ex Machina* -type theory.[11]

According to Riegel, "everything is itself and, at the same time, many other things" (Riegel, 1973, p. 6). He continues that while an object is identified as something, it is also something else, something contradictory to it from other viewpoints.[12] Only the totality of these separate, multiple views can yield at least an approximately coherent view of the phenomenon. Riegel assumes that a thing can only be understood in relation to its opposite, as in the famous Laozi's Dao De Jing's claim "Low is understood low only as there is highness". Two valued philosophical logic recognises these kinds of opposites, and in philosophical analysis such opposites are contrary, not contradictory. Contrary opposites are such that they can both be false (something can be in the middle in which case it is false that it is high and false that it is low).

This is important since Piaget (Inhelder & Piaget, 1958) seems to conflate such opposites with contradictory opposites (e.g., high and not high) that cannot be *true or false* at the same time. The problem in Piaget's theory of two-valued thinking is that it requires one to choose between two dichotomous alternatives that do not exhaust the logical domain. Often the problem is precisely that contrary opposites are taken to be contradictory, i.e., that it is assumed that binary thinking operates with contrasts like good and bad and forces one to choose between them, although it is possible that something is neutral (i.e., neither good nor bad). Philosophically speaking, terms like "high" and "low" can be understood in terms of relatives.[13] This means that they refer to something that is defined and can be so only in relation to something else. Therefore, to say that something is high means that it is high in relation to something else (e.g., a branch of a tree is located high in relation to a worm on the ground) but low in relation to something else (e.g., the same branch of a tree is low in relation to the top of a skyscraper next door).

Piaget uses well-defined tasks to determine the cognitive stage of a subject. In well-defined tasks the proper action to solve them is to use what can be called "binary propositional logic" following the law of excluded middle (Inhelder & Piaget, 1958). In well-defined problems, the problem-solver is given choices and it is clear from the beginning what factors must be taken into account to solve the problem, while ill-defined problems are unclear in this respect. From a philosophical point of view, the difference between the tasks thus is whether there is sufficient information and clear instructions for solving the problem. The proponents of a dialectical theory stress that human development as a socially-bound phenomenon naturally includes ill-defined, wicked problems and situations, i.e. problems without clear-cut answers. So the claim that mature thinking is dialectical is based on the impossibility to use what in cognitive psychology is called "formal binary propositional logic" (Inhelder & Piaget, 1958), to solve problems for which there are no clear-cut solutions. In dialectical operations, an individual is able to tolerate contradiction and conflict and understand them as a necessary part for development. Change is thus the core term in dialectical thinking, as a human being is tied in social interaction to constant change (Riegel, 1973, 1976). A limitation in Piaget's theory is that it takes into account only interaction between human beings and physical objects (like in the Pendulum task, Chapter 3), not social life.

It is important to stress that Piaget's binary logic is not the same as two-valued logic in philosophy. While Piaget's binary logic has features of formalism, it is also a model for human problem-solving.[14] Philosophical logic, by contrast, is a theory of valid inference, where inferences are not thought processes. There are of course many different approaches to logic in philosophy today. However, their approach is different from psychological studies of human thinking precisely because they operate on the notion of logical validity constituted by what logically follows from other propositions.[15]

Beside its focus on ill-defined problems, there is certain "systemic-theory" tendency or analogy in the dialectical theory (see Chapter 12): "A dialectical theory of human development focuses on the simultaneous movements along at least the following four dimensions: (1) inner-biological, (2) individual-psychological, (3) cultural-sociological, and (4) outer-physical" (Riegel, 1976, p. 693). In describing human development the dialectal theory takes into consideration these different dimensions, which act like a synchronisation of separate but interdependent systems. These systems are more or less coordinated, and a state of disorganisation leads to conflicts and disruptions, either within a system or between systems. However, in an optimal case such conflicts can fuel further progress and development. Thus, a second argument for the dialectical theory of human development is that the same pattern of binary "logic" cannot be applied to different domains of thinking (mechanical vs. social), as a human being is situated in an intersection of various systems that are not reducible to each other.

A third argument for the dialectical theory of human development comes from the fact that the natural scientific view behind Piaget's theory is outdated. In an article from the early 1970s, Riegel (1973) refers to quantum physics and its claims of the contradictory nature of reality: light can be understood both as waves and particles, and the subject is always tied to the process of observation, i.e. object is influenced by subject (p. 347). This claim has been later used again by Sinnott in her "postformal theory" (see Chapter 12). According to Riegel, Piaget's theory with well-defined problems is based on classical, "old" theory of mechanics and may not express the current state of scientific world-view.

Basseches (1984, 2005), another main scholar of dialectical thinking in psychology, states clearly that he has derived his model from a dialectical philosophical background. He sees that, ontologically and epistemologically, dialectical thinking models share similar features: emphasis on change, on wholeness (as contrasted to atomism and variable-centred approach in classical mechanics), and on relations between objects: nothing exists for itself. Epistemologically, the first point refers to constant construction of knowledge, secondly, knowing is knowing only within some system as concepts and ideas which are tied to each other in the system. Also, concepts are in relationship to the knowers and users of them, and their meaning is related to knowers, and are not stable (Basseches, 2005, p. 50).[16]

Basseches separates formal and dialectical analyses of thinking. Formal analysis is based on closed system thought, and dialectical thinking is based on open system thinking. A closed formal system cannot take into account any other perspective than its own: thus it is powerless to understand different ways of understanding. Analyses of dialectical open-system thinking, by contrast, take into account the limits, contexts and boundaries of thinking and thus offer a more powerful method for development than formal analysis. Formal analysis is not able to take into account multiple, different frames of references, i.e., justifiable coherent ways of interpreting the same facts based on different assumptions: it does not take into account different processes of interpretation and meaning (Basseches, 2005).

Contradictory and contrary opposites in a philosophical analysis of dialectical thinking

One basic difference between philosophical logic and cognitive psychology is that while the latter concerns ways of thinking in the broad sense (including perceptions, emotions, and dreaming) and strives to describe their characteristic features empirically, philosophical logic is a theory of valid inference, in which inference is not a thought process. This means that it is difficult if not impossible to derive conclusions pertaining to philosophical logic from how people, mature or immature, think. In the following, we shall describe this difficulty first from the viewpoint of the notion of contradiction that is also central in the above-described dialectical theories of human cognitive development.

In the psychological descriptions, mature adult ways of thinking are said to be more tolerant towards or even more capable of accepting logical contradictions (Kramer, 1983) than youthful ways of thinking. This might be taken to imply that mature adult thought is not logically two-valued. Two-valued logic acknowledges only two truth-values as possible: true or false. It is important to stress that this question is distinct from the question of whether and how we know which claims are true and which ones false. This means that a claim can have a truth-value even if we do not know what it is. This is because truth depends on how things are, not on whether we know how they are. If I do not know whether it is raining in Finland at place x on 30 June 30, 2017 at 13:45 Greenwich time – let us call this time t – it does not mean that the claim "it is raining in Finland at place x at time t" would lack a truth-value, i.e., that it is not true or false. It simply means that I do not know whether it is true or not.[17]

In the psychological discussion of two-valued *versus* many-valued logic, the cognitive development of adults has been compared to Hegel's "logic" in which the Spirit progresses through thesis, antithesis, and synthesis and this is called "dialectic" (Kramer, 1983, p. 94). It is important to note that Georg W. F. Hegel's "logic" concerns the progress or development of Spirit through history, whereas philosophical logic, as generally understood, is a theory of valid inference.[18] Therefore, we shall use "logic" in quotation marks here because Hegel's dialectic is not a logical theory in the sense of being a theory of valid inference. For developmental psychology and the philosophical analysis of its central notions, the important point is that a mature adult way of thinking will not assume that one must only accept either the thesis or the antithesis but aims at a wider synthesis of the claims made in both. As mentioned, this is sometimes taken to imply that mature adult thought is capable of embracing logical contradictions (Basseches, 1984). Next it will be argued why we should avoid such a description and rather maintain that adult cognition is capable of recognising contradictions that are only apparent and making a difference between contrary and contradictory opposites.

Let us consider the following example to illustrate the claim. Imagine a community in which the notion of orange colour is not known and two members of the community are debating about the colour of oranges (the fruit).[19] One is arguing that oranges are yellow, the other one that they are red. This is a contradiction in the sense that the claim that oranges are yellow and that they are red cannot be true at the same time. However, it is not such a contradiction that exhausts a two-valued logical space (yellow and not yellow) and therefore no third truth-value needs to be introduced in addition to truth and falsity. This is simply because both claims (i.e., the one that oranges are yellow and the one that they are red) are false. Let us then assume that a third person from outside the community enters the scene and says that the colour is orange. This new, enhanced conception of the colour in a sense incorporates the two antithetical views within it because the orange colour is a mixture of yellow and red. However, no many-valued logic is needed to analyse this example because the new claim (oranges are orange) is true, whereas both the antithetical claims (oranges are red, oranges are yellow) are false.

Those views are, in a sense, closer to truth than the claim that oranges are black, for example, but this observation causes no problems for two-valued logic.

Real controversies are of course more complicated than this imagined debate about the colour of oranges. However, a mere increase in complexity does not imply modifications to logic. Rather, it seems that one central feature in adult mature ways of thinking is exactly the capacity to recognise logical space, i.e., the capacity to see that there are possible claims that are perhaps true, in situations of debates analogous to that about the colour of oranges. For instance, the question of whether light should be understood as waves or particles could be a similar case. Although in terms of logic both cannot be true at the same time, they might both be false, analogously, to the claim about oranges as yellow or red. A new perspective might be found that allows one to reconcile between the two interpretations and find a new, more accurate one. In general, recognising the possibility that two opposing views are not necessarily the only alternatives, i.e., that the alternatives in a certain debate can both be false, allows one to form a new, better informed view that is capable of integrating the essential elements from the earlier antithetical views.

The same applies to the concept of change. In the dialectical theories of human development, change is identified as a central feature of reality that dialectical thinking is claimed to reflect. The following simplified example shows why change as such does not require many-valued logic. Consider, for instance, an apple that is first green, then ripens and turns red. In a sense, this entails that the apple is both green and red, which are two conflicting properties that cannot belong to the apple at the same time but come to belong to it at different instances of time. However, recognising this does not influence the way in which we should analyse what logically follows from what. The apparent contradiction is solved simply by recognising that the two conflicting properties belong to the apple at different points of time. It might be a sign of the kind of attitude characteristic of youthful thinking to create a controversy about the colour of the apple on the basis of the evidence, sticking vigorously to the claim that the apple is either red or green. A more mature thinker, by contrast, would be prepared to accept that, at this moment, in this light and under these conditions the apple seems, say, green, but that this does not imply that it should permanently be so. It might change or there might be other lighting conditions in which it appears to be of a different colour.

One additional example can be introduced to illustrate the ways in which mature cognition is able to transcend simplified dichotomies. Sometimes debates are construed in a way that two views are opposed to each other and the impression is created that these views are, as the philosophical terminology puts it, exhaustive. Being exhaustive means that there are no alternatives to the views that are presented. Many classical moral dilemmas are construed in this way. A standard example is the so-called "trolley problem". In the scenario, a trolley is approaching a rail switch between two tracks. On one track there are five people and on the other only one person. The scenario is that one must choose to guide the trolley on either of the two tracks, i.e., to choose between killing one or five people. Moral theories are often tested with respect to their capacity of offering solutions to these kinds of problems.[20] However, some philosophers have criticised these scenarios and suggested that in situations of a moral dilemma one should look for a third alternative.[21]

There is a structural similarity in these dilemmas to the above example about the debate of the colour of oranges. Both assume that two conflicting alternatives (i.e., such that they cannot be true at the same time) exhaust the space of (logical) possibilities. While in principle there could be a pragmatic restriction, the cases are such that there are always other *logical* possibilities. This means that although the orange cannot be yellow and red in the same respect and at the same time, or that one cannot navigate the trolley on two distinct tracks at the same time,[22] the alternatives do not exhaust what is possible from a logical point of view. Orange is a possible answer to the question about the colour of an orange and some moral philosophers argue that we should answer trolley problems in a similar way: look for a third alternative and do everything you can to stop the trolley, for example. There are no logical constraints that would narrow the options down to taking the orange as being either yellow or red or having to choose between running over one person or five people. Unfortunately, logic does not prevent people from sometimes having to face tragic decisions between two or more terrible outcomes. However, such decisions are not a matter of logic, and adding truth-values to logic does not help in saving one from possibly tragic decision-making. It seems, however, that maturity of thought helps one in seeing beyond simplified dichotomies and recognising that there are more options than initially might appear.

Therefore, from the point of view of philosophical logic, there is one central difference between youthful and mature thought: it is the capacity to recognise which oppositions or conflicts are exhaustive and which are not. By contrast, on the basis of the psychological descriptions starting from Piaget's analysis and criticism to it, youthful thought tends to see all conflicts and oppositions as exhaustive. Often this means a tendency to confuse between contrary and contradictory opposites. Confusing between these two might thus lead one to assume that from one pair of contrary opposites the other pair logically follows. This is not the case because contrary opposites can both be false. For example, if one maintains that the world is not good it does not follow that it is bad because both claims can be false at the same time. The world might be in essence neutral with respect to being good or bad. However, not all conflicting notions that youthful thought might assume to exhaust the logical space are contrary opposites. They might be like yellow and red in our example above. Those are conflicting notions in the sense that they cannot be true at the same time. However, they can be false, and thus it would be erroneous to assume that a debate between such notions is exhaustive, i.e., that there are no other alternatives. As we have suggested above, one crucial difference between youthful and mature ways of thinking could be that the latter can recognise which oppositions are which and whether some conflicting notions exhaust the logical space or not, while the former tends to see all conflicts as ones in which it is necessary to choose between two given options.

Epistemological relativism and integration

Should mature adult thinking as a psychological capacity be described as epistemological relativism, then? As mentioned, some descriptions (such as Kramer's, 1983) of mature cognition come rather close to descriptions of epistemological relativism in philosophy, and this is problematic. Relativism as such is a rather weak position. What is relative to what, why, and in what sense? In general, epistemological relativism in philosophy allows there to be contradictory belief systems, i.e., groups of statements, which can, despite being contradictory, be justified or even known.[23] However, in order to merit closer scrutiny, epistemological relativism must recognise that there are some non-relative standards with respect to which it can be assessed whether a belief system (let us call it S_2) is such that it should be accepted alongside another one (let us call it S_1) as true although some beliefs in S_2 contradict one or more belief in S_1.

This general viewpoint can be illustrated by an example. Let us imagine a biologist, who studies rabbits and hares. In her free time, she also writes fables for children with animals such as hares, foxes, and bears as protagonists. The statements that constitute her biological studies about hares contradict some statements in her fables. For instance, although in her studies rabbits flee from foxes, in her fables they might face their fear, talk to the fox and be feisty rather than fearful. A form of epistemological relativism claiming that such an example leads to an alternative belief system, namely that of fables, which competes with the belief system of biological studies, is not a plausible one. A position that poses no restrictions to the standards used to evaluate which belief systems be accepted as true although contradictory, would be absurd. One can imagine, for example, that the status of an alternative true belief would be ascribed to one so that, say, the third word of each sentence of the biologist's studies is written in reverse direction. It is obvious, however, that such a conversion does not have any credentials for truth.

With respect to the original example, it should be noted that one can of course claim that the fables convey some important truths about facing one's fears, for example, but this does not mean that such truths in the fables should be read literally and taken to *replace* or challenge the claims that the biologist makes in her scientific studies. Similarly, famous examples from seemingly contradictory claims between the *Genesis* and the theory of evolution (whether the human being was created on the sixth day of creation or developed from an ancient precedent of apes) is not typically taken to imply two different criteria for evaluating which of these accounts is true. It can rather be suggested that the *Genesis* is a myth or a creation story that as such does not undermine the truth or the epistemic justification or scientific evidence for the evolution theory.

A more important question with respect to epistemological relativism and adult cognition would be what kind of standards are used by mature cognitive agents to *evaluate* which belief systems to accept to have an equal claim to being true and which ones to reject. It is also important to stress that being a relativist about knowledge does not necessarily imply that one is aiming at a more comprehensive overview about things: an unrestricted relativism of an "anything goes" type does not directly support the quest for improving one's own views, attitudes, and conceptions. If all views and collections of them are equally acceptable, why should one strive for any cognitive development? Such a quest for improvement rather requires standards that can be used to critically evaluate which views are sustainable and which ones are not as well as the assumption that one should aim at better and more accurate views in the way of the example of the colour of oranges: to find theories, general views, and notions that allow one to recognise merely apparent contradictions and proceed to form a more unified and complex view that can explain why certain simplified positions seem appealing.

However, it is important to stress that this as such is not epistemological relativism. The kind of respect for different viewpoints that is characteristic of the cognitive component of wisdom (Kallio, 2016; see Chapter 2), as described in today's psychological discussion, does not entail that, for instance, any claim someone holds would have equal status to any other in terms of epistemological justification. An important distinction in this context is the following: a cognitively mature person seems to accept that everyone is entitled to their opinion. However, this is quite different from taking any opinion as having an equal *epistemic* justification as any other. For instance, if someone says, "human beings did not evolve from ape-like creatures because I never saw that happen", this person is merely disregarding the research and the scientific evidence for the theory of evolution and not offering evidence that would genuinely compete with the evidence that backs the theory. Similarly, it would make no sense to say that there are no acceptable epistemic criteria for solving a controversy about whether it is raining or not between two people one of whom is standing outside and perceiving the situation (saying that it is not raining) and another person who is inside with his ears blocked by headphones and eyes blinded by a blindfold (who is saying that it is raining simply because he feels like that). Therefore, although both of these people are entitled to their opinions, only one of them has access to such standards that can be taken as relevant, generally applicable criteria for epistemic justification.

Rather, it can be suggested that a mature adult way of thinking is characterised by integration as the term is used in developmental psychological studies. In order to illustrate what integration means, let us assume a situation in which there are different viewpoints concerning immigration in some groups of people. The types of opinions can be labelled as "highly restrictive", "moderately restrictive", "moderately positive", and "highly positive". These views conflict and offer multiple perspectives to the same phenomenon: one is saying that immigration should be heavily restricted, another one that it should be moderately restricted, a third one that it should be moderately encouraged, and a fourth one that it should be strongly encouraged. Although it is questionable whether there is any absolute truth in such moral or political matters, the example can be used to illustrate a mature adult way of thinking in terms of integration. One of the reasons why it can do so is that the situation is emotionally complex.

According to Kallio (2011), integrative thinking is more than just adding pieces or opinions together. It would hardly make sense, let alone to exemplify mature thinking, to say that one must be everything from highly positive to highly restrictive with respect to immigration. Consequently, integration is not just a sum of things, as in dialectical thinking synthesis is not just a combination or group of former-level thought objects. Integration of these viewpoints might for example mean to take all perspectives and their background emotions into account. For instance, the anger that is driving the highly restrictive view is seen to arise, for instance, from many people losing their jobs and creating the fear that they will not find new ones if more people enter the community. Integration thus understood does not mean that one should accept everyone's views as true – as mentioned, there may not be one true position in these matters. Rather, integrative thinking grants that the person with views that one might reject oneself *is still accepted as a person* whose feelings are recognized and respected. Those views are therefore understood and integrated to the other views of participants of the group, and perhaps an agreement can be reached on something, such as the importance of local values and work, while there is disagreement about other matters. Integration, therefore, can be taken to mean integration of intellect and emotion (see Labouvie-Vief, 1990, has explored this kind of integration process; see also Edmondson & Hülser, 2012).

Moreover, mature integrative thinking can also assume some general ethical standards or principles, such as non-violence and hence maintain that whatever one's view on immigration, for example, it should be peacefully expressed and defended. Therefore, a mature adult way of thinking is far removed from a view that takes all knowledge claims and ethical principles to be merely relative. Respecting others' feelings and other people as persons is central for integration as a mature adult way of thinking, and this does not mean taking all views to be true. Therefore, integration should not be identified with relativism in philosophical epistemology.

Living without certainty

How, then, should one describe mature adult cognition from a point of view of philosophical epistemology? What are the factors that allow one to respect other people's views and emotions even if one takes them to be mistaken or misplaced, and what kind of an attitude best supports the quest for improving one's own views? It is best to begin with identifying what does *not* support such an attitude. It seems that the psychological studies show that overt attachment to the truth of one's own views is not a characteristic of mature thinking. If one simply assumes oneself to be right or dogmatically takes some authority to be right, this of course does not inspire respect for other people's views. However, it is crucial to stress that unrestricted relativism by no means supports the inquiry and research, analysis and curiosity about other people's views that is necessary to mature beyond such a state. The example about the political debate that requires some general principles (such as non-violence) also shows that integration should not be identified with unrestricted relativism.

This suggests that a mature adult attitude to one's own knowledge and cognition should rather be described as one in which one is not so certain about the truth of one's own beliefs and eager to compel others to accept them as well. However, this should be combined with the attitude of striving for reasonable views that incorporate a wealth of information and yet are open to the possibility that new, more accurate views can be found. Such new views might well transcend the conflicts and perhaps apparent contradictions that one might encounter in one's inquiries in a way resembling the example of the debate about the colour of oranges. In this way, one is not trapped by simplified dichotomies ("the orange has to be either yellow or red!") but is free to see the possibility of a more refined cognitive structure that goes beyond them ("oh, it is orange").

Although uncertainty, fallibilism, and probabilism are prominently featured in contemporary epistemological discussion as well, one way to analyse adult mature cognition from the point of view of philosophical epistemology would be to look how it resembles theories in these trends of philosophical epistemology. However, in order to avoid technicalities and to connect the discussion to themes about how one should live and act, as in the examples about integration, a mature adult way of thinking can briefly be compared to ancient Pyrrhonian skepticism, for which Sextus Empiricus (trans. 2000) is the best source.[24] In the following, we shall consider such skepticism to see if we can elicit some similarities to a mature adult way of thinking in developmental psychology.

A general guideline for a Pyrrhonian skeptic is to investigate (Greek *skepsis* means "study", "investigation", "scrutiny") how things seem to be and even to argue about them and compare arguments presented for competing views. However, a Pyrrhonian skeptic claims to live by appearances, which means not being attached to a specific, unchangeable view about how things are. This means that a Pyrrhonian skeptic can very well take something to be the case: if I am a Pyrrhonian skeptic, I can take it to be the case that the soup offered to me now is hot because it seems to me to be so. If I turn the shower on and the warm water has been cut for the day, I can take it to be the case that the water is cold because it seems to me to be so. However, such a skeptic suspends judgment with respect to whether this is the stable nature of things and avoids statements like "the soup is by nature hot", "water is by nature cold". Compared to the temperatures measured on the surface of the sun, my soup is not hot at all, and for a polar bear (or even to a Finn who swims in Finnish lakes in the summer) my shower would be quite warm. However, this is not epistemological relativism: the claims are compatible with it being true that the soup has a certain measured or measurable temperature (say +55°C) and that the water in my shower has one as well (say, +30°C), and that there are some standards of how to measure the temperature and so on that apply to all the cases. Yet, this does not imply claims like "soup is by nature hot and feels hot to all observers in all circumstances" or "water is by nature cold and feels cold to all observers".

Living by appearances, i.e., living on the basis of how things seem to be, Sextus Empiricus (trans. 2000) claims, gives the Pyrrhonian skeptic the space to welcome new appearances – "now things seem different" – without disturbances in the tranquil state of the skeptic's mind. He also claims that such an attitude is necessary to maintain tranquillity through long periods of time.

It is important to stress that even the Pyrrhonian skeptic is committed to searching for the truth. If we suppose that the truth cannot be found, or that there are all kinds of undefinable standards for what knowledge is, such an attitude does not inspire us to cultivate our understanding of the world. Yet the kind of attitude that can be found in a Pyrrhonian skeptic underlines that cognitive maturity is not equivalent to being knowledgeable about particular facts. Although there is nothing wrong with remembering facts, maturity seems to be associated with a comprehensive viewpoint that allows one to see how different things go together. This also constitutes an important difference between cognitive maturity as described in modern cognitive developmental psychology and Pyrrhonian skepticism. Although committed to inquiry (*skepsis*) into how things are, Pyrrhonian skepticism is not especially focused on the quest for understanding comprehensive wholes.

Conclusions

We have argued that philosophical conceptual analysis can be used to clarify the results of empirical research, especially when it pertains to topics such as thinking, contradiction, and knowledge. Unfortunately, conceptual analysis is not often included in the methodological toolbox of the empirical sciences, unless one adds to them studies in philosophy. As our argument shows, a lack of theoretical precision can lead to confusion in the use of terms. At its best, conceptual analysis can give insight into which concepts to use, how they are defined, what kind of limits there are in using them and what kind of boundaries their usages have.[25]

One conceptual tool we have used to clarify how a mature adult way of thinking differs from youthful thinking distinguished in empirical psychological studies is the distinction between contrary and contradictory opposition. Using this distinction, we have shown that rather than a difference between two-valued and many-valued logic, the difference between mature and youthful ways of thinking should be described in terms of a *developing capacity to distinguish between different kinds of conflicts and oppositions*. In Piaget's studies, different conflicts and oppositions are often confused. We have argued that a mature adult way of thinking can be characterised by its capacity to recognise conflicts that allow other alternatives, as is the case between contrary opposites and other conflicts that are not logically exhaustive. For instance, while a youthful way of thinking might take contrary opposites (e.g., between black and white) to be the only alternatives, adult mature thinking recognises that we do not need to choose between black and white (when debating about the colour of an object). The object might be grey or of a different colour altogether. While neo-Piagetians seem to detect the possibility of transcending simplified Piagetian dichoto-mies in what is called "dialectical thinking", they do not use the philosophical con-ceptual tools we have used here to explain what dialectical thinking consists of. More analysis would be needed to articulate how this finding can be used to clarify the theories of adult cognitive development.

We have also argued that it is important to differentiate two approaches to epistem-ology: philosophical (*PhilEp*) and psychological (*PsyEp*) ones. While philosophical epistemology typically contains a normative element and analyses the necessary and sufficient conditions for knowledge (and how the concept of knowledge should be used), psychological epistemology concerns the ways in which subjects describe their own cognition. This means that the results of psychological epistemology are, from the point of view of philosophical epistemology, results about what the studied sub-jects believe, i.e., take to be the case. As has been argued above, this differs from philo-sophical epistemology recognising that belief does not imply truth. In brief, we have pointed out that the notions of philosophical epistemology can be used to clarify what adult mature cognition and way of thinking is like. To avoid confusion, we have moved away from the notions of psychological epistemology and suggested an analysis of mature adult ways of thinking in terms of integration.

As we have seen above, integration differs from epistemological relativism, since it does not require that one assumes different standards of truth for different views. We have illustrated this by the example of conflicting views about immigration. A mature adult way of thinking does not require that one takes all the different views to be true. However, a mature way of approaching such a conflict is one in which the emotions related to the views are recognised and respected and in this sense integrated. Therefore, integration is not a conglomeration of various conflict-ing views but, rather, characterised by recognising that everyone is entitled to their view, the emotions related to them and that they should be respected as persons with views that conflict with one's own. This differs from a youthful approach that would simplify such a complex situation into a debate about who is right and who is wrong and perhaps even assuming that not only the views but also the emotions of the others are misplaced and should be changed.

Finally, we raised the question if we can find an example of an attitude to know-ledge that resembles the one identified as characteristic of a mature adult way of thinking. One example that we have detected is found in Ancient Skepticism and its Pyrrhonian variant. Historical comparisons are common in adult developmental literature (e.g., in the accounts of dialectical thinking referring to Hegel). However, such comparisons are in danger of being misleading if they are made outside the study of the history of philosophy, since the concepts that are used in developmental psychology differ to such a great extent from those of philosophy. We have also suggested that while there are similarities between Ancient Pyrrhonian Skepticism and a mature adult way of thinking, the two differ as well, especially with respect to what extent one strives for a comprehensive view about how things are.

Since adult mature ways of thinking are seen as a part of wisdom in current empirical wisdom studies, we would expect that our analysis could be used to fuel new discussion in wisdom studies as well. What exactly is meant as scholars refer to "relativism" and "relativistic-dialectical thinking" as part of wisdom? We have suggested that we should rather talk about integrative processes to avoid confusion. However, we stay open to any new discussions, with possible counter-arguments to our claims.

Notes

1 An earlier and more limited version of some arguments made in this chapter is found in Tuominen (2016).
2 Other scholars have also called for conceptual clarity; see, e.g., Leadbeater (1986). Leadbeater's analysis, however, remains in the cognitive psychological framework and does not make use of the tools of philosophical conceptual analysis. It is exactly the philosophical analysis that we argue helps to clarify the central issues involved in the discussion. Pillow (1999) moves at the limit of philosophical and psychological analysis but, in the end, uses the central concepts in psychological rather than philosophical sense.
3 In this article, philosophical epistemology refers to the distinct field of philosophy that as such developed in the course of the 20th century and that uses the notions of belief, epistemological justification and truth. There is of course a long history of discussions about knowledge in rather different terms in the history of Western philosophy taking ancient Greek philosophy as its starting point, not to mention the philosophical traditions outside it. We focus on this kind of an epistemology because the relevant cognitive psychological discussion uses its central notions, although in a rather different way as we shall see in the body text.
4 In brief, a dichotomy means a (possibly hierarchical) opposition of two alternatives: male/female, good/bad. Dichotomies often give the false impression that they offer an exhaustive classification of a logical field. For instance, males and females do not exhaust the class of gendered beings, even within the human species, and good or bad do not exhaust the realm of such things, actions, or properties that can be evaluated; also neutral actions are possible.
5 To an extent, Pillow's discussion of postskeptical rationality (1999, p. 421) resembles such an attitude. However, on the whole his analysis is formulated in terms of psychological rather than philosophical epistemology.
6 *On interpretation* 7, 17b16-26; see Aristotle (trans. 1984). Aristotle's original formulation has been revised later because modern logic interprets the relationship between "all" and "some" in a different way. The distinction between contrary and contradictory opposition remains, however.
7 It must be reminded already in this stage of the article that according to other empirical studies it is not so clear that youngsters are incapable to relativistic thinking (Chandler, Boyes, & Ball, 1990; Greene, Azevedo, & Torney-Purta, 2008). It seems merely that youth is an age of epistemic questioning and doubt, not purely absolutism. Thus it may be incorrect to state that relativistic-dialectical thinking is a form of mature adult cognition solely. It might be supposed that cognition under study may involve a life-span development trend, as Riegel (1973) and Basseches (1984) have suggested. Also in the study of wisdom it is currently known that wise thinking and action emerge already in the late youth, not solely in old age as was first assumed (e.g. Bluck & Glück, 2004).
8 The details of these conditions are of course debated. The aim here is not to articulate a specific epistemological theory but to outline the central notions of the discussion. For a general introduction to 20th-century philosophical epistemology, see Steup (2005).

9 See also, e.g., Hendricks and Symons (2015): "belief is not necessarily true". The same principle also applies in epistemic logic where from "*a* believes that *p*", it is not possible to infer the truth of *p*.

10 For Plato, see, e.g., *Republic* 511b, in Plato (trans. 1997); for Aristotle, see *Topics* 100a22, (trans. 1984), vol. 1. In classical Greek *dialagesthai* means simply "to discuss".

11 However, Riegel's claim is possibly limited. Piaget's theory of development of thinking is a constructivist theory, i.e. knowledge-formation is in constant process (Piaget, 1976). There is continuous dynamic movement between mental structures and change. If this is the same what is meant with dialectical thinking in the meaning post-Piagetian scholars use it, it is out of the scope of this article.

12 It seems that Riegel does not discuss the situation where the connection of views is non-contradictory, i.e. there is no disagreement between separate views or statements: The relationship between different things can also be complementary.

13 Plato and Aristotle use the Greek expression *pros ti* with respect to or in relation to something. In the translations of Aristotle's *Categories*, the term is typically translated as "relative" (see, e.g., *Categories* 4, 1b26; tr. Ackrill in Aristotle (trans. 1984), vol. 1. For Plato, see, e.g., *Theaetetus* 160b (trans. 1997).

14 For Piaget's binary logic and its unclarity with respect to whether one is talking about logic as a theory of valid inference or thought processes in individuals, see, e.g., Seltman and Seltman (1985, 220). For a similar conception of logic as problem-solving, see also Chandler et al. (1990).

15 On the question to what extent logical validity should govern human modes of thinking, see, e.g., Steinberger (2017).

16 It is noteworthy that knowledge is a relative for Aristotle as well (*Categories* 7, 6b3); see (trans. 1984), vol. 1.

17 There is a distinct philosophical problem called "vagueness" that is related to the question of whether human notions have clear boundaries or not. Borderline cases such as very light drizzle might be taken to imply raining and not-raining at the same time. However, this is a different question, and it is debated whether vagueness entails more truth-values for logic. On vagueness, see, e.g., Sorensen (2016). In any case, no one assumes that mature cognition implies knowing the boundaries for all notions. Rather, it should be described as recognising that we do not necessarily know where the boundary between raining and not-raining goes. A person with that kind of an attitude can also respect other views that draw the boundary between raining and not-raining in a different way.

18 See Redding (2018), section 3.1.2 *Science of Logic*.

19 In this example, it is assumed, for the sake of simplicity, that oranges are orange. Let us also assume that colour concepts in that community have clear boundaries. This assumption is made to clarify that the example does not concern vagueness also referred to above in note 17, i.e., the question of where the boundaries of qualities such as yellow and red must be drawn and whether they have any.

20 For trolley problems, see Kamm (2016).

21 E.g., Hursthouse (1995).

22 It is also worth noting that, in neither case, the logically contradictory alternative (orange being yellow and red; navigating the trolley on two tracks at the same time) is a solution to the problem. Therefore, enlarging the scope of logic does not really solve the problems involved. Moreover, as the body text shows, there is no need to look for more logical space outside two-valued logic. Quite the contrary, as the body text makes clear, two valued logic contains enough space (i.e., logical possibilities) to solve the problems.

23 For types of philosophical relativism, see Swoyer (2003).

24 See especially his work known with the title *Outlines of Pyrrhonism* (translated into English as *Outlines of Scepticism*, trans. 2000).

25 For a basic collection of philosophical tools, see, e.g., Baggini and Fosl (2010).

References

Aristotle. (1984). *The complete works of Aristotle* (J. Barnes, Ed.) (Bollingen series 71, 2, Vols. 1–2). Princeton, NJ: Princeton University Press. (Original work published between 384–322 BCE/1984).

Baggini, J., & Fosl, P. S. (2010). *The philosopher's toolkit: A compendium of philosophical concepts and methods* (2nd ed.). Malden, MA: Wiley-Blackwell.

Baltes, P. B., & Staudinger, U. M. (2000). Wisdom: A metaheuristic (pragmatic) to orchestrate mind and virtue toward excellence. *American Psychologist, 55*(1), 122–136.

Basseches, M. (1984). *Dialectical thinking and adult development* (Publications for the advancement of theory and history in psychology No. 3). Norwood, NJ: Ablex.

Basseches, M. (2005). The development of dialectical thinking as an approach to integration. *Integral Review, 1*(Jun), 47–63. Retrieved from https://integral-review.org/the-development-of-dialectical-thinking-as-an-approach-to-integration/

Baxter Magolda, M. B. (2004). Evolution of a constructivist conceptualization of epistemological reflection. *Educational Psychologist, 39*(1), 31–42.

Bluck, S., & Glück, J. (2004). Making things better and learning a lesson: Experiencing wisdom across the lifespan. *Journal of Personality, 72*(3), 543–572.

Cavanaugh, J. C., & Blanchard-Fields, F. (2014). *Adult development and aging* (7th ed.). Belmont, CA: Cengage Learning.

Chandler, M., Boyes, M., & Ball, L. (1990). Relativism and stations of epistemic doubt. *Journal of Experimental Child Psychology, 50*(3), 370–395.

Curnow, T. (1999). *Wisdom, intuition and ethics* (Avebury series in philosophy). Aldershot, England: Ashgate.

Edmondson, R. (2015). *Ageing, insight and wisdom: Meaning and practice across the lifecourse.* Bristol, England: Policy Press.

Edmondson, R., & Hülser, K. (2012). Introduction: Integrated practical reasoning. In R. Edmondson & K. Hülser (Eds.), *Politics of practical reasoning: Integrating action, discourse and argument* (pp. 1–14). Lanham, MD: Lexington Books.

Greene, J. A., Azevedo, R., & Torney-Purta, J. (2008). Modeling epistemic and ontological cognition: Philosophical perspectives and methodological directions. *Educational Psychologist, 43*(3), 142–160.

Grossmann, I. (2017). Wisdom in context. *Perspectives on Psychological Science, 12*(2), 233–257.

Hendricks, V., & Symons, J. (2015). Epistemic logic. In E. N. Zalta (Ed.), *The Stanford encyclopedia of philosophy* (Fall 2015 ed.). Retrieved from https://plato.stanford.edu/archives/fall2015/entries/logic-epistemic/

Hoare, C. (Ed.). (2011). *The Oxford handbook of reciprocal adult development and learning.* (Oxford library of psychology, 2nd ed.). New York, NY: Oxford University Press.

Hofer, B. K., & Pintrich, P. R. (1997). The development of epistemological theories: Beliefs about knowledge and knowing and their relation to learning. *Review of Educational Research, 67*(1), 88–140.

Hursthouse, R. (1995). Fallacies and moral dilemmas. *Argumentation, 9*(4), 617–632.

Inhelder, B., & Piaget, J. (1958). *The growth of logical thinking: From childhood to adolescence: An essay on the construction of formal operational structures.* London, England: Routledge & Kegan Paul.

Kallio, E. (2001). Reflections on the modern mass university and the question of the autonomy of thinking. In J. Välimaa (Ed.), *Finnish higher education in transition: Perspectives on massification and globalisation* (pp. 73–90). Jyväskylä, Finland: University of Jyväskylä, Finnish Institute for Educational Research.

Kallio, E. (2011). Integrative thinking is the key: An evaluation of current research into the development of adult thinking. *Theory & Psychology*, *21*(6), 785–801.

Kallio, E. (2015). From causal thinking to wisdom and spirituality: Some perspectives on a growing research field in adult (cognitive) development. *Approaching Religion*, *5*(2), 27–41. doi:10.30664/ar67572

Kallio, E. (2016). *Ajattelun kehitys aikuisuudessa: Kohti moninäkökulmaisuutta* [The development of thinking in adulthood: Towards multiperspective thinking] (Research in Educational Sciences No. 71). Helsinki, Finland: The Finnish Educational Research Association.

Kamm, F. M. (2016). *The trolley problem mysteries* (E. Rakowski (Ed.), Berkeley Tanner lectures). New York, NY: Oxford University Press.

King, P. M., & Kitchener, K. S. (2004). Reflective judgment: Theory and research on the development of epistemic assumptions through adulthood. *Educational Psychologist*, *39*(1), 5–18.

Kramer, D. A. (1983). Post-formal operations? A need for further conceptualization. *Human Development*, *26*(2), 91–105.

Kuhn, D., & Weinstock, M. (2002). What is epistemological thinking and why does it matter? In B. K. Hofer & P. R. Pintrich (Eds.), *Personal epistemology: The psychology of beliefs about knowledge and knowing* (pp. 121–144). Mahwah, NJ: Erlbaum.

Labouvie-Vief, G. (1990). Wisdom as integrated thought: Historical and developmental perspectives. In R. J. Sternberg (Ed.), *Wisdom: Its nature, origins, and development* (pp. 52–84). Cambridge, England: Cambridge University Press.

Leadbeater, B. (1986). The resolution of relativism in adult thinking: Subjective, objective, or conceptual? *Human Development*, *29*(5), 291–300.

Perry, W. G., Jr. (1970). *Forms of intellectual and ethical development in the college years: A scheme*. New York, NY: Holt, Rinehart and Winston.

Piaget, J. (1976). Piaget's theory. In B. Inhelder, H. H. Chipman, & C. Zwingmann (Eds.), *Piaget and his school: A reader in developmental psychology* (pp. 11–23). New York, NY: Springer-Verlag.

Pillow, B. H. (1999). Epistemological development in adolescence and adulthood: A multidimensional framework. *Genetic, Social and General Psychology Monographs*, *125*(4), 413–432.

Plato. (1997). *Plato: Complete works* (J. M. Cooper & D. Hutchinson, Eds.). Indianapolis, IN: Hackett. (Original work published ca. 428/427–348/347 BCE/1997).

Redding, P. (2018). Georg Wilhelm Friedrich Hegel. In E. N. Zalta Ed., *The Stanford encyclopedia of philosophy* (Summer 2018 ed.). Retrieved from https://plato.stanford.edu/archives/sum2018/entries/hegel/

Riegel, K. F. (1973). Dialectic operations: The final period of cognitive development. *Human Development*, *16*(5), 346–370.

Riegel, K. F. (1976). The dialectics of human development. *American Psychologist*, *31*(10), 689–700.

Schommer-Aikins, M. (2004). Explaining the epistemological belief system: Introducing the embedded systemic model and coordinated research approach. *Educational Psychologist*, *39*(1), 19–29.

Seltman, M., & Seltman, P. (1985). *Piaget's logic: A critique of genetic epistemology*. London, England: Allen & Unwin.

Sextus Empiricus. (2000). *Outlines of scepticism* (J. Annas & J. Barnes, Eds.) (Cambridge texts in the history of philosophy). Cambridge, England: Cambridge University Press. (Original work published ca. 2nd century).

Sorensen, R. (2016). Vagueness. In E. N. Zalta (Ed.), *The Stanford encyclopedia of philosophy* (Winter 2016 ed.). Retrieved from https://plato.stanford.edu/archives/win2016/entries/vagueness/

Spencer-Rodgers, J., & Peng, K. (Eds.). (2018). *The psychological and cultural foundations of East Asian cognition: Contradiction, change, and holism.* New York, NY: Oxford University Press.

Steinberger, F. (2017). The normative status of logic. In E. N. Zalta Ed., *The Stanford encyclopedia of philosophy.* (Spring 2017 ed.). Retrieved from https://plato.stanford.edu/archives/spr2017/entries/logic-normative/

Steup, M. (2005). Epistemology. In E. N. Zalta (Ed.), *The Stanford encyclopedia of philosophy* (Summer 2018 ed.). Retrieved from https://plato.stanford.edu/archives/sum2018/entries/epistemology/

Swoyer, C. (2003). Relativism. In E. N. Zalta (Ed.), *The Stanford encyclopedia of philosophy* (Spring 2009 ed.). Retrieved from https://stanford.library.sydney.edu.au/archives/spr2009/entries/relativism/

Trowbridge, R. H. (2011). Waiting for *Sophia*: 30 years of conceptualizing wisdom in empirical psychology. *Research in Human Development, 8*(2), 149–164.

Trowbridge, R. H., & Ferrari, M. (2011). *Sophia* and *Phronesis* in psychology, philosophy, and traditional wisdom. *Research in Human Development, 8*(2), 89–94.

Tuominen, M. (2016). Aikuisen ajattelua koskeva käsitteistö: Filosofista tarkastelua [On concepts concerning adult thinking: Philosophical reflections]. In E. Kallio (Ed.), *Ajattelun kehitys aikuisuudessa: Kohti moninäkökulmaisuutta* [The development of thinking in adulthood: Towards multiperspective thinking] (Research in Educational Sciences No. 71, pp. 355–379). Helsinki, Finland: The Finnish Educational Research Association.

INDEX

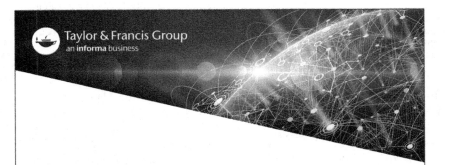